Creating an Enabling Environment

Toward the Millennium Development Goals

*Proceedings of the Berlin Global Forum
of the United Nations ICT Task Force*

Preface by **José Antonio Ocampo**

Edited by
Denis Gilhooly

United Nations

United Nations
Information
and
**Communication
Technologies**
Task Force

Published by
The United Nations Information and Communication Technologies Task Force
One United Nations Plaza
New York, NY 10017
icttaskforce@un.org

Acknowledgements

I would like to thank all the contributors for the painstaking efforts and hope this volume proves of interest and use in our vital and ongoing collaborative work. I also wish to express my gratitude to the many individuals who worked to put together this book. I sincerely appreciate the efforts of the staff of the United Nations ICT Task Force Secretariat, located within the Department of Economic and Social Affairs of the United Nations. Special thanks and gratitude are due to Enrica Murmura, who adeptly coordinated communication between the contributors and myself and skillfully oversaw the publication from its inception, and Robert De Jesus who meticulously compiled the copy and showed dedication and technical skills throughout the process. Additional thanks go to Christiane Bode and Cheryl Stafford who demonstrated acute attention to detail through copy-editing, design, layout and production. Christoffer Häggblom, Matthew Okesola and Farika provided valuable assistance that enabled the book to be delivered by deadline.

CONTENTS

PREFACE

José Antonio Ocampo, Chairman, United Nations Information and Communication Technologies Task Force

On behalf of the members of the United Nations Information and Communication Technologies Task Force, I have the pleasure to present the sixth publication of the ICT Task Force series: *Creating an Enabling Environment: Toward the Millennium Development Goals. Proceedings of the Berlin Global Forum of the United Nations ICT Task Force.*

The Global Forum on "Promoting an Enabling Environment for Digital Development", organized by the United Nations Information and Communication Technologies Task Force, attracted the participation of representatives of all stakeholders, including senior officials of governments of a number of developed and developing countries, executives from the private sector, prominent representatives of civil society and academia, and leading representatives of the ICT-for-Development community.

The United Nations ICT Task Force is working together with governments, the private sector and civil society to identify best practices, which will constitute the road map towards favourable conditions for the development of the Information Society. It is also supporting efforts to benchmark progress in the use of ICT for development, in particular by measuring the impact of ICT on the achievement of the internationally agreed development goals.

The Millennium Declaration, embraced by leaders of all United Nations member states, presented a comprehensive and multi-dimensional development framework, including the Millennium Development Goals, which are aimed at combating poverty and provide the basis for promoting opportunity, prosperity, health, safety and empowerment for all of the world's people, especially the poorest and marginalized groups. In this way the United Nations ICT Task Force and all organizations working to increase access to ICT are contributing to the achievement of the MDGs.

Information and communication technologies are key building blocks for future economic and social development and job creation. ICT can be powerful tools for empowering people to make better choices through improved information flow, making possible broader formal and informal educational opportunities, facilitating human as well as institutional capacity development, and can directly spur economic growth by creating opportunities and addressing barriers and inefficiencies.

However, experience has shown that in order to maximize the social and economic benefits of ICT, a favourable economic, political and regulatory environment is needed. Each of the stakeholders – governments, development agencies, international financing institutions, consumers and business – plays an important part in creating the required conditions. Governments are responsible for eliminating barriers to competition, encouraging investment in communications infrastructure, and establishing an independent regulatory authority. Development agencies could do their part by allocating sufficient resources to support the deployment of ICT in the developing world while respecting fair competition. International financing institutions can assist by giving priority to Information Society development. Industry could contribute by developing more efficient, user-friendly and affordable technologies and solutions, bringing ICT within reach of millions, and also joining various digital bridging and community involvement programs and actions.

Although the leadership demonstrated by the Task Force and its partners is generating discernable results, creating an enabling environment is a task that requires further work. We need to bear this in mind: producing an enabling environment is only the first step down a long road to achieving the universal access and unprecedented human development of which we dream. But it is a destination we must reach.

INTRODUCTION

Denis Gilhooly

Unleashing ICT for Development: the New Enabling Environment

This year the number of people on the planet connected to the Internet will exceed one billion with the majority of users for the first time living in the developing world.[1] Self-sustaining and self-replicating, the Internet has become the fastest-growing medium in the history of computing and communications in less than two decades. This phenomenon has quite simply transformed the way we need to look at science, innovation and technology on the one hand and business, development and governance on the other. In the words of pioneer social scientist Ithiel de Sola Pool, it has become a "technology of freedom"[2], a generic platform technology that defies cost and distance, empowers people and enterprise, enhances lifestyles and learning.

That it has done so in both developed and developing countries, in many cases against the odds of unsuitable enabling environments and dynamic transformations in technological space, is even more remarkable. That innovation and investment involve risk is a given. The trick is establishing an enabling environment to mitigate that risk. In the 1990s, investment in mobile cellular networks in both developed and developing countries was spectacularly rewarded in almost every country that combined a competitive market with a fair and level playing field. Today, the pace of innovation has left the old-style telephone industry licking its wounds and facing billions of dollars of investment write-downs in obsolete fixed networks and inflated spectrum license bids.

A new way forward is needed. It is also now clear that truly innovative nature of the Internet, and the business and development models that can leverage its potential, are still little understood by many of the industry's players and development actors. While some companies and countries have moved to evolve new business models and approaches that can facilitate low-cost access to broadband in developing country contexts,[3] in others backbone infrastructure and affordable interconnection needs remain unmet and costs remain unnecessarily high. Decision-makers, while personally empowered with mobile phones, remain insufficiently aware of the broader implications for and development potential of ICT.

The Information and Communication Technologies (ICT) industry and development in the age of digital technologies are both at a crossroads. The potential for mass-market penetration with wireless and broadband networks is transforming not only its own but all industries and sectors. Yet if this potential is to be realized, the model for the enabling environment put in place for the telecommunications sector in the 1990s is due for a radical overhaul. While the process of liberalization is still incomplete in many countries, it is

---

[1] See Computer Industry Almanac Inc, "Worldwide Internet Users will Top 1 Billion in 2005" (September 2004) at http://www.c-i-a.com/pr0904.htm

[2] Ithiel de Sola Pool, *Technologies of Freedom*, Belknap Press of Harvard University Press, 1983

[3] A consortium of six companies is expected to build a new broadband network in Andhra Pradesh, a state in India, permitting citizens to get Internet connections at very low prices -- about 100 rupees (US$2.2, euro1.7) per month. See http://www.technologyreview.com/articles/05/01/ap/ap_2010305.asp?trk=nl

becoming clear that implementation of this model would be insufficient in and of itself. The main development priority and emerging catalytic model is one of "open access" to all operators and for all of the people all of the time in any place.[4] And that may mean a mix of public and private solutions as well as a role for community networks and other local actors.[5] Meanwhile, the traumatic world events of the past few years have led to a radical re-thinking of the role of networks in the context of national security and just how these concerns can be reconciled with ensuring open and inclusive access for all.

The ICT and development communities have a unique opportunity. The recent report of the United Nations Millennium Project and the United Nations Secretary-General's report "In larger freedom: towards development, security and human rights for all" (A/59/2005) have both highlighted the importance of science, innovation and technology in realizing the MDGs and related national development priorities.[6] ICT have an especially significant role to play here for it is only with the strategic, widespread, intensive and innovative use of ICT in development polices and programmes that the ambitious agenda of the MDGs becomes that much more possible to achieve. But this involves the need not only to unleash the potential of ICT per se but also the need to ensure that an enabling environment and capacities that can facilitate its development uses are in place.

Critical Issues Going Forward

Over the past two decades, thinking about the roles of public and private sectors in providing access and fostering use of ICT have undergone radical transformation. While a level of consensus has been achieved between diverse stakeholders on fostering a supportive enabling environment, in particular earlier for telecommunications and now for the Internet, the issue of how best to address "market failures" and facilitate access to ICT as a "public good" in itself and as a medium to facilitate access to other public goods and services have yet to be adequately addressed.[7]

For the public sector, the mantra of telecommunications privatization – often without liberalization and adequate regulatory oversight – and the concomitant withdrawal of donor financing for public infrastructure projects in developing countries has perhaps the most worrying case in point. It is now clear that the lack – either through choice or lack of resources – of independent regulation in some countries led simply to the establishment of de facto privatized monopolies with little incentive or pressure to build out into underserved areas, which remained forgotten as market forces were seen to take hold. While the private sector has demonstrated that it is capable of dramatic rates of investment and expansion, it

---

[4] e.g. see "Open Access: New Technologies, New Business Models To Enable Access For All" http://www.infodev.org/section/programs/enabling_access/open_access , Open Access 2005 workshop in Mozambique http://www.openaccess.uem.mz/

[5] See case studies and discussion of issues including role of community networks in the Task Force on Financial Mechanisms' report *Financing ICTD: A Review of Trends and an Analysis of Gaps and Promising Practices. The Report of the Task Force on Financial Mechanisms for ICT for Development.* http://www.itu.int/wsis/tffm/final-report.pdf

[6] See http://www.un.org/largerfreedom/ and http://www.unmillenniumproject.org

[7] Results of global ITU Survey point to "overwhelming support for the belief that if the information society is to be one in which all citizens throughout the world can equally access and use information resources for sustainable economic and social development, that cyberspace should be declared a resource to be shared by all for the global public good." http://www.itu.int/newsroom/press_releases/2004/12.html.

alone is not up to the task.[8] And as discussed in a number of papers here, an urgent reassessment of these "market failures" and gaps in delivering public goods is now underway within governments and donors.

There is also now a reassessment of the international donor community's attempts to address these market failures and access gaps through support for pooled public access solutions which in some instances led to unsustainable technology-push projects – for example, "telecenters", which were divorced from a focus on services and support to other development interventions. Thus, there is now an emerging shift in thinking towards technology-pull projects that can maximize public service delivery in health, education and government, as well as foster enterprise and employment. This necessarily implies greater focus on local content and software with stimulation of the grass roots civil society and private sector firms via regulatory incentives for open and affordable access, content and services. That is the role not only for national governments, but also civil society and private sector. Improved donor project coordination is also clearly needed, but a more imaginative step maybe for agreement on "lead role" prioritization of certain sectors by individual donors moving forward. All will depend on the integration of national e-strategies with national economic plans, development strategies and/or MDG-based poverty reduction strategies.

For the private sector, again a reassessment of roles and responsibilities is underway. At the least, the level of investment in corporate social responsibility in developing countries by large firms has been disappointing. Pioneer programmes for digital inclusion have to date either failed to achieve scale, or have been concentrated in the more advanced developing country markets. More positively, new models for public-private partnership to address the needs of the "next billion" show promise when the strengths and weaknesses of each stakeholder are factored in, the emphasis on local relevance is paramount, long term sustainable business models are the lynchpin. What is clear is that the failure of the computing and communications industry so far to develop products and services at price points that will reap the fortune at the bottom of the pyramid may about to be reversed via breakthrough wireless technologies and other low-cost solutions – but critically, and only if, they are deployed in an incentivized and enabled regulatory environment.[9]

So as ICT finally meets development, what are the critical enablers for the scaling up of innovation and investment? A prerequisite will be the early demonstration of evidence of impact. The case for mainstreaming ICT for the achievement of the MDGs has far from been made and new attempts at rigorous and coordinated empirical analysis and indicators described later in the book will be key. At the level of policy development, the new work at monitoring and evaluating national e-strategies and their explicit linkage to national economic plans and poverty reduction strategy plans will be vital – with the special needs of landlocked nations, island states and LDCs becoming increasingly clear via this process. Additional investment and resource mobilization will also clearly be required. Here, ODA may play a role in seed financing for the poorest countries, but its role in ICT should not be

---

[8] See World Bank Study Financing ICT Needs in the Developing World: Public and Private Roles http://lnweb18.worldbank.org/ict/resources.nsf/InfoResources/04C3CE1B933921A585256FB60051B8F5 (draft February 2005)

[9] See http://wdi.umich.edu/ResearchInitiatives/BottomPyramid/Resources/NewsBizPolicy.aspx

over-exaggerated as witnessed by the self-sustaining and self-replicating nature of mobile and Internet networks.

Indeed, it is the grand collaborations of the mobile and Internet phenomena that point the way to meeting the sheer ambition of the MDG challenge, for it demands an unprecedented response at the global as well as at the regional and national levels. Aggregation of knowledge and resources must necessarily be pursued via global coalitions, South-South partnerships and exchanges, and at the grassroots level building on the complementary roles and responsibilities of different stakeholders. The bottom line for ICT and the MDGs moving forward is what, under the conditions of a given and effective enabled environment, will be the development multiplier for every investment dollar made in ICT by government, business and civil society. Answering that question is clearly the next step in efforts to match ICT to the ambitions of the MDGs.

As this book demonstrates the key questions now being asked on scaling innovation and investment in ICT for the achievement of the MDGs are in most cases the same questions being asked by government, business and civil society.

With the coincidence of the five year review of progress toward the MDGs at the Millennium Summit + 5 in New York in September and the second phase of the World Summit on the Information Society in Tunis in November 2005, as discussed in later papers, overarching issues and interests are set to converge. A unique and virtuous opportunity exists both to identify gaps, bottlenecks, pathways and bridges and to strengthen synergies and linkages between the MDGs and ICT. By galvanizing political will and action among government, business and civil society the essential breakthrough criteria can be framed to meet the desired objectives of all stakeholders in moving the network revolution to the inclusive advantage of all.

About this Book

This book is in two parts. The first comprises the proceedings of the Global Forum of the United Nations ICT Task Force on "Promoting an Enabling Environment for Digital Development" held in November 2004. The second part is the result of ongoing work from the Working Groups of the UN ICT Task Force in the context of the MDGs. The MDGs will not happen without both the actions and the collaboration of all stakeholders working in a supportive enabling environment.

The first section of Part I thus focuses on the underpinning issues of policy and regulation. Minister Brito vividly delineates the immense challenges facing a least developed country like Mozambique but demonstrates the potential of unleashing ICT for Development when the national e-strategy can be embedded in the poverty reduction strategy plan (PRSP). Ambassador Gross draws the nexus between competition, private investment, independent regulation, universal access, private sector leadership and maintaining an open and secure global Internet. Thomas Ganswindt makes the link for Siemens between a mix of complementary technologies, open and interoperable standards, independent regulation, profitable business cases for broadband and new public-private partnership models as a precursor to investment. Edvins Karnitis evaluates the lessons learned from Latvia's successful experiment with multi-sector regulation in the context of its applicability to small or emerging countries. Ayesha Hassan of the International Chamber of Commerce gives an exposition of the views and needs of business in establishing an enabling environment. And Heike Jensen of the WSIS Gender Caucus points to the essential importance of equitable gender representation.

The second section of Part I deals with the role of the different stakeholders and actors. Minister Stanca defines a new development paradigm for international donors exemplified by the Italian government's leading role in e-government at home and abroad. Veli Sundbäck of Nokia examines the next wave of mass market penetration for mobile cellular and reports on the results of a survey that discovers that under enabling conditions a latent market of some 700 million developing country users exists. Carlo Ottaviani articulates the importance of human capacity and digital literacy as a key building block of an enabling environment and details a pioneering approach being undertaken by STMicroelectronics and its employees. Danilo Piaggesi and Robert Vitro from the Inter-American Development Bank give their perspective on the shifting role of international organizations in ICT for Development. And Axel Leblois and Peter Orne from the Wireless Internet Institute offer a "primer" for local authorities on the great and latent potential for WiFi and WiMax solutions.[10] In both these sections the common thread is the attempt by different stakeholders to harness rapidly evolving regulatory, business, technology and development models in the service of ICT for development.

The third section of this Part addresses the related topical issue of financing ICT for development. Financing and the enabling environment are both inter-dependent and complementary. Roberto Bissio of the Third World Institute offers a public global goods perspective on financing the information society in the South. Susanne Hesselbarth and Ichiro Tambo of the OECD present trends on official development assistance. Motoo Kusakabe from the European Bank for Reconstruction and Development gives a new analysis of basic and advanced innovation systems in developed and developing countries. Section 4 provides a case study by Gisa Fuatai Purcell of issues facing a small island state from the perspective of the government of Samoa.

Part II presents original work in four areas directly related to the MDGs: unleashing e-strategies, up-scaling of pro-poor ICT policies and practices, MDG indicators, and innovation and investment in ICTs to meet the MDGs. Bruno Lanvin from the World Bank contributes a lucid, practical and comprehensive guide for e-strategy implementation particularly in the context of the MDGs. Richard Gerster and Sonja Zimmerman, in conjunction with the Swiss Agency for Development and Cooperation, concentrate on up-scaling with respect to differences and priorities for low-income African and Asian countries. The UN ICT Task Force Working Party on ICT Indicators and MDG Mapping, led by the government of Canada, details the progress of their work on ICT-MDG indicators to date. And the Innovation and Investment paper authored by myself comprises the report prepared for the UN ICT Task Force in support of the United Nations Millennium Project Task Force on Science, Technology and Innovation, and based on a survey of UN ICT Task Force and United Nations Millennium Project members.

---

[10] Also see "Wireless Internet Institute (2003) "The Wireless Internet Opportunity for Developing Countries" http://www.infodev.org/files/1061_file_The_Wireless_Internet_Opportunity.pdf

All of the papers presented here look toward a constructive analysis of gaps and bottlenecks, challenges and opportunities – for if the MDGs provide a vital roadmap for the way ahead, ICTs offer the pathways and bridges for getting from here to there.

PART I

CREATING AN ENABLING ENVIRONMENT

Section 1

Policy and Regulatory Issues

ENABLING ENVIRONMENT, ICT FOR DEVELOPMENT AND THE MILLENNIUM DEVELOPMENT GOALS

By Lidia Brito, Ministry for Higher Education, Science and Technology, Mozambique

As countries advance and progress, new challenges have to be faced and new goals have to be defined. Today, this is felt in a national, regional and global perspective. There is a moral imperative to reduce the levels of poverty in all countries; to reduce the number of children dying of malnutrition, malaria and HIV/AIDS; to answer the aspirations of all people that want to build a prosperous tomorrow, a future of individual and collective success.

In order to avoid marginalization in the new dynamics of world development, the construction of a knowledge-based information society is a prerequisite. This means investing in the development of science and in the production and appropriation of technology, in an inclusive way so that all are simultaneously agents and beneficiaries of the development process. How can this be accomplished when facing the challenges of a least developing country (LDC) like Mozambique with high levels of illiteracy, low productivity, lack of resources, and even an inability to tap into national resources for development?

The solution lies in adequate and integrated policies and implementation strategies. In Mozambique, a national, multi-stakeholder e-strategy and national policy has been in development since the year 2000 that considers the triad of information, citizenship, and development as fundamental, and their complementary integration with education, science and technology, industrial policy and others as key. By far the most salient lesson of the Mozambique experience has been that the integration of policies and implementation strategies must not only be executed in a multi-stakeholder manner but this must be done from the very beginning of the design process.

In the worldwide debate on ICT for development and the Millennium Development Goals (MDGs), three important questions must be asked. Firstly, to what extent can ICTs contribute to the realization of the MDGs? Secondly, what are achievements of individual countries, and in this case of Mozambique, to date? Thirdly, how can the benefits of ICTs in individual countries, and in this case Mozambique, be maximized and up-scaled?

In addressing the first question it is clear to all that ICTs by themselves cannot resolve the panoply of problems associated with poverty eradication, social inequality and environmental degradation being faced in the developing world. Water cannot by piped through optical fibers and food cannot be served from satellite dishes. However, there is a major role for ICT to play in responding to the challenges developing countries and LDCs are facing.

The most important characteristic of ICT is that it enhances communication. In the context of a resource-poor LDC, the significance of this somewhat obvious point is multiplied considerably when ICTs connect people rather than exclude them, inform people rather than misinform them, save time rather waste it, stimulate thinking rather than induce intellectual laziness, while promoting global citizenship and local empowerment.

Technology is merely an infrastructure. If that infrastructure is not accompanied by the creation of a base in skills and knowledge the adoption of ICT will not help in achieving the MDGs but simply serve the interests of the wealthiest and most powerful nations, enterprises and individuals on the planet. If ICTs are not to become agents of exclusion, time-wasting, and laziness, certain conditions are key in creating an enabling environment in the ICT for development context. For access this means ensuring the availability of all available technologies and equipment, connectivity and affordability. For skills, it means laying the conditions for the ability to acquire and use. And for innovation and investment it means establishing the enabling policy and institutional environment and creating favorable market conditions for the local ICT industry and the development of relevant contents and applications.

In the context of the second question, Mozambique has a number of initiatives underway. In education, Schoolnet is a programme within the Ministry of Education for the delivery of computers to secondary schools across the country to increase computer skills and access to the Internet. CITENET is a network attached to the Ministry of Higher Education, Science and Technology, connecting reflection groups in the provinces. The network has been very important to the formulation of the S&T policy. In distance education, within the Ministry of Higher Education the foundations are being laid for the take-off of distance education through the Internet.

In the area of e-government, most ministries now have their own websites where citizens can find information about their respective activities. Many also have a direct mailing address to the minister. Related to this, certain government agencies such as the Meteorology Service and the Bureau of Statistics already provide Internet services. In rural areas, Multimedia Communication Centers are being promoted where people have access to radio, television, telephones, computers and the Internet. In terms or teledensity, there are currently 400,000 users of cell phones in Mozambique, with a second competitive operator recently beginning operations. In human resources, three out of the nine universities are currently active in Mozambique training computer engineers. Out of the 17,000 students enrolled in the past academic year, over 500 were in computing sciences of which more than 40% were women. In telemedicine, there have been experiments with connecting both national academic hospitals so that real-time technical assistance can be provided.

Overall, the Mozambique e-strategy was approved in December 2000 by the Government with a commission under the leadership of the prime minister and a taskforce for its implementation. This has led to significant investment in ICT for development across government with current activities supportive to education, S&T policy, health and governance. Thus, by default the weaknesses of current activities also become visible: little attention has been paid to the development of content that supports agricultural producers and other economic agents. Moreover, the proportion of the population that through these efforts gains access to ICT is small whereas the skills and knowledge acquired still is insufficient to make Mozambique self-reliant regarding the management of hardware and software, let alone take on its development.

In addressing the third question, how can we raise the benefits of ICT regarding the MDGs? The three important conditions for ICTs being useful are: 1) A population equipped with basic literacy and language skills and with capacity to produce and use knowledge and information; 2) Innovative technology and good connectivity; 3)Technical and financial sustainability. If these conditions are not met, at least as far as the poor are concerned, paying for ICTs is paying the bill for a gate to nowhere. Thus, ICTs have to be introduced in such a way that the efficiency and quality of public and private services increase. Moreover, ICTs need to be a vehicle of empowerment in social and economic relations: between the student and the teacher, the citizen and his government, and between the governments of developing and the developed nations.

Whereas national governments have to lift legal and economic barriers on the flow of information and the acquisition of the necessary infrastructure, such as taxes and levies, at a global level measures have to be taken so that technological wares, either hard or soft, become accessible at a reasonable price and funds earmarked to support the poor do not line the pockets of the wealthy few nor feed the emergence and maintenance of monopolies.

Currently, fair trade in some third world agricultural commodities and handicrafts forms a small fringe to the largely unfavorable conditions that characterize the global commercial system. Fair trade in commodities produced by industries in developed countries such as knowledge and ICT infrastructure is a *sine qua non* if one genuinely wants to avoid that in addition to the agricultural and industrial revolution, the Third World loses the information revolution too.

In the past, the underdevelopment of agriculture and industry of the South has been explained by dependency and unequal terms of trade. In moving forward, different stakeholders from all over the globe can learn the lessons from the past and set the stage for fair conditions that will favor ICT development in the developing countries. In conclusion, a common vision and common commitment will necessarily include five key elements: support integrated approach to development where ICT are one important instrument; development aid for capacity building and skill development in ICTs; increased financial support to allow for scaling-up; more involvement in multi-stakeholders partnerships for development; and, finally, a support frameworks for fair trade in knowledge and commodities.

THE ENABLING ENVIRONMENT: PRO-COMPETITIVE POLICY AND REGULATORY REFORM

By David Gross, Department of State, United States

New technologies may enable economic and social transformation, but only in a conducive policy and regulatory environment. The old model of the state-owned and -managed telecommunications monopoly adopted in the second half of the nineteenth century simply does not accommodate the fast changing, knowledge-based and global information revolution.

Just to survive in the highly competitive world of the global knowledge economy, country after country introduced competition (usually in the form of mobile cellular phone providers); corporatized, if not privatized, the national fixed line provider; and established a more or less independent regulatory agency. Over 70 nations have adopted the World Trade Organization (WTO) Basic Telecommunications Services Agreement of 1998, and many of those also adopted the attached annex on regulatory principles. Over 110 nations since 1990 have established more or less independent regulatory bodies.

Meeting the Challenge

Despite this clearly established trend toward liberalization and privatization, many developing nations still retain telecommunications monopolies, often privatized or, at least, with corporatized management. Indeed, for properly functioning markets, the one thing worse than an inefficient state-owned monopoly, usually responsive to government, is a private monopoly, unfettered to exercise its legal monopoly efficiently. Moreover, the legacy of the old statist monopolistic model still weighs heavy on many countries that are trying to introduce competition.

An independent regulatory body is needed to maintain a level playing field for new entrants, ensure network interconnection and protect consumer interest. The regulator should function in ways that are fair, non-discriminatory, transparent, timely and independent of the operators. However, in the face of a former monopoly, regulators lack the training and experience needed to confront national operators intent on retaining or deepening market dominance and excluding or hobbling competitors. Furthermore, judicial systems do not often provide the necessary reinforcement for regulatory and policy decisions such as requiring the dominant provider to establish interconnection for new competitive entrants.

Universal access programmes may be needed for high-cost, low-income users, often in rural areas. However, these are difficult to implement in countries with a low subscriber base. With appropriate pro-competitive policies in place, private investors will often seek out areas of low return on investment normally shunned by dominant national operators. This competition drives down prices and introduces new services making advanced ICT access newly affordable to large numbers of potential users. Policy and regulatory reform is thus seen as an enabler of expanded and affordable access to and application of ICT for development.

Response

In telecommunications, the U.S. Agency for International Development (USAID) promotes competition, private investment, independent regulation and universal access. In e-commerce, USAID promotes private sector leadership in the conduct of business on the Internet and advocates for an open and secure global Internet. USAID also promotes adherence to international agreements on basic telecommunications services, information technology, intellectual property protection (IPR), tariff moratorium on electronic transmissions and cyber-crime. Among the strategic priorities are:

- **Promoting telecommunications competition and private investment**

  One of the main challenges for developing nations wishing to rapidly expand their ICT infrastructure is to introduce competition and privatization and move to open markets to replace the outmoded state-owned monopoly model. To ensure these ends, USAID provides experts to help draft telecommunications laws and policies that promote adherence and compliance with the Basic Telecommunications Services Agreement (including the Annex on Regulatory Principles), TRIPS (trade-related aspects of intellectual property rights) and other WTO instruments.

- **Strengthening independent regulators**

  Because almost all the telecommunications regulatory bodies in developing nations are less than ten years old, they typically lack the necessary legal, economic and engineering expertise and experience. Drawing on 70 years of U.S. regulatory experience at the federal level and even longer at the state level, USAID can assist independent regulators in building capacity in information management, planning, billing and consumer protection as well as in licensing, interconnection, competition, pricing and spectrum management.

- **Promoting universal access policy**

  In most developing nations, the dominant telecommunications company tends to neglect populations where the return on investment is low in favor of investment in providing new and expanded services in urban areas where profits are higher. USAID support for reaching the neglected populations includes promoting "bottom-up" or community-based universal service policies administered by an independent regulator; encouraging competitively neutral universal access programmes for high-cost and low-income subscribers; and demonstrating new low-cost access technologies and encouraging flexible regulatory procedures to foster their use.

- **Promoting private sector leadership**

  In most developing nations, the private sector, especially small- and medium-sized enterprises (SMEs), is hampered in using the Internet to conduct business by excessive or outmoded policy and regulatory barriers. Hence, they are hampered in participating in global electronic commerce, now measured in trillions of dollars.

USAID has provided country and regional workshops on e-commerce policy and has developed e-commerce policy training tools.

- **Maintaining an open and secure global Internet**

  In keeping with Article 14 of the United Nations Declaration of Human Rights, the U.S. Government strongly supports the free flow of information. USAID assists international policy efforts to maintain an open, affordable Internet by supporting in-country advocacy, training and national/regional Internet exchange points. USAID also seeks to foster international cooperation in combating cyber-crime and other threats against the critical global information infrastructure by conducting regional cyber-security workshops.

Maintaining Leadership

Among the U.S. Government's and USAID's goals and achievements in ICT policy and regulatory reform are:

- Since 1996, the Leland Initiative has helped 22 African countries either to create Internet policies where none existed or to liberalize any existing policies, in particular to lower prices and to introduce competition among Internet Service Providers. In recent years, Leland has also reached out to newly formed telecommunications regulatory bodies to strengthen their ability to monitor and reinforce the competitive "level playing field".

- Through the joint Telecommunications Leadership Programme (TLP), USAID and the State Department have provided expertise from U.S. federal agencies in support of numerous regional workshops, training programmes and international conferences to foster telecommunications and e-commerce policy and regulatory reform. These events have been held in Central America, the Caribbean, West and South Africa, North Africa and the Middle East, and Southeast Asia.

- Recognizing the increased need for protecting the Critical Information Infrastructure, USAID has collaborated with the Department of Justice and the State Department to promote international cooperation in combating cyber-crime and enhancing cyber-security. In little over a year, USAID provided funding for cyber-crime and cyber-security workshops for APEC and aid-recipient Asian nations, for the Middle East, for Southeast Asia, and for East Europe. For distribution at each of these regional workshops, the Department of Justice developed a guide entitled "Legal Frameworks for Combating Cyber-crime". In some cases, follow-on technical assistance has been provided by USAID in order to implement specific cyber-security legislation.

- USAID actively supported the Electronic Commerce Act of the Philippines by providing technical assistance and by supporting the dissemination of information on e-commerce and cyber-crimes. USAID/Philippines helped to establish a Computer Emergency Response Team (CERT) led by Filipino officials. USAID also trained law enforcement agencies and private entities, such as Internet Service Providers, in the investigation of cyber-crimes.

▪ In 1995, the USAID Regional Center for Southern Africa instituted the Regional Telecommunications Restructuring Programme (RTRP) to promote telecommunications policy and regulatory reform in 14 Southern Africa nations. In 1997, with U.S. Government agencies and the ITU, RTRP established the Telecommunications Regulators' Association of Southern Africa (TRASA). The programme now focuses on policy and regulatory activities to support expanded access to information and communications for rural and other populations disadvantaged by income, education, disability or social discrimination.

Future Prospective

There are a growing number of policy issues surrounding the Internet and electronic commerce that will have a profound impact on how ICT will be accessed and used worldwide. USAID is piloting activities in South Africa, Uganda, Namibia and Nigeria to demonstrate how pro-competitive policies and regulation can promote rural access. In addition, USAID is demonstrating new wireless access devices as well as Voice over Internet Protocol (VoIP) that offer new possibilities to provide broadband data and voice services at low costs. Overall, policies that ensure legal certainty, security and consumer protection for online transactions and interactions should be enacted. In order to accomplish this, an appropriate mix of government regulation and private sector solutions should be put in place which considers both consumer and business interests.

PARTNERSHIPS FOR DIGITAL OPPORTUNITY

The recent survey of USAID Mission ICT activities indicates that funds from development partners exceed funds from USAID. Overall, $1 of USAID funds are matched with $1.50 of leveraged funds where USAID is working with other partners to develop the ICT sector. Where ICT are used as a tool, USAID funds are matched dollar for dollar with funds from partnership sources. Samplings of partnerships are included in this section to provide an overall impression of how USAID's way of doing business is evolving.

Partnerships with U.S. Firms

Developing countries look to the United States for ICT know-how, technology, management and business development, and U.S. companies are often anxious to provide that expertise. USAID expects the private sector to lead with investment to stimulate economic growth and job creation to improve the overall economic and social conditions in a country.

U.S. firms have played a significant role in several recent partnerships:

▪ Since 1999, USAID has collaborated with Cisco Systems to expand workforce training for ICT technicians to 89 Cisco Academies in 32 countries with over 5000 students enrolled – 25% are women.

- USAID has joined with IBM and other firms to create IT workforce training centers for youth in poor communities in Brazil. Similar programmes are also being developed in other countries.

- Hewlett-Packard (HP) was a founding partner in developing the Senegal pilot for the Digital Freedom Initiative – a Presidential Initiative established to transfer the benefits of ICT to small businesses and entrepreneurs in the developing world.

Many collaborations with the U.S. private sector are made possible by funds from a new USAID programme, the Global Development Alliance (GDA). GDA facilitates agreements between companies, not-for-profits, and government agencies that maximize the benefit of USAID assistance dollars. In addition, these alliances bring significant new resources, ideas, technologies and partners to bear on ICT problems in countries where USAID works. In the ICT sector, partnerships have been established with private sector companies that leverage private sector to USAID funds at 12:1, 10:1 and 8:1 ratios.

Partnerships with Non-Governmental Organizations

USAID's partnerships with non-governmental institutions are long standing and rooted in the development programmes of every sector. Increasingly, partnerships in the ICT sector are proving successful:

- Throughout the past 20 years, USAID's $10 million investment in USTTI has leveraged more than $45 million from the private sector for policy and regulatory courses and has provided a vital source of funding for over USTTI trainees.

- USAID and the ITAA have established the IT Mentors Alliance (ITMA) to strengthen IT business associations in developing countries. Its goals are to improve IT association management, enhance their advocacy capabilities and improve linkages with member companies.

- Initiated in 2001, the Digital Opportunity through Technology and Communications (DOT-COM) Alliance is a partnership with Academy for Educational Development, Internews, Inc., and Education Development Center involving over 75 affiliated institutions – each with specialized expertise in using ICT for development.

Partnerships with Higher Education Institutions

Partnerships with higher education institutions have played a critical role in building institutional capacity.

Partnerships include:

- NetTel@Africa has developed a comprehensive curriculum for training IT policy and regulatory officials and has developed a growing network of more than 20 higher education institutions in the United States and Africa offering joint degrees in this discipline.

- The WiderNet Project Digital Library, comprised of almost one million documents, has been installed at six African universities to date. The project has made its digital library accessible at no cost to professors and students over local area networks rather than Internet connections.

- In 1999, the Caribbean Institute of Technology was founded in order to train software developers that would support a sustainable software development industry in Jamaica. Established in partnership with Furman University and the University of the West Indies, the institute has trained over 200 students, half of which are women. Over two-thirds of the graduates are employed in the Jamaica IT sector.

Partnerships with other U.S. Agencies

USAID seeks to augment its technical resources and policy expertise by partnering with other U.S. government agencies to deliver development services. Through an interagency agreement, USAID and the State Department have established the Telecommunications Leadership Programme (TLP). This programme provides expertise for ICT policy programmes from the Federal Communications Commission (FCC), the National Telecommunications and Information Administration (NTIA), the Justice and State Departments, and other federal agencies. These experts are not only highly cost-effective and representative of U.S. policy objectives but also often possess knowledge not readily available elsewhere.

USAID ICT activities, in collaboration with other U.S. Government (USG), agencies include:

- FCC and NTIA experts conducted regional and bilateral workshops in telecommunications policy and regulation as well as, in the past year, providing special training in spectrum management for Iraqis and Afghans.

- USAID collaborated with the Departments of Justice and State to promote international and regional cooperation in combating cyber-crime and enhancing cyber-security in APEC and aid-recipient Asian nations, the Middle East, Southeast Asia and Eastern Europe.

- State Department conducted workshops on e-commerce for East Europeans in 2003 and for Mexico in 2002 as well as an International Conference on Implementation of e-Government with the Trade and Development Agency in 2002.

- In collaboration with the Department of Commerce and the State Department, USAID is responsible for implementing the Digital Freedom Initiative. DFI is a White House initiative to help selected countries use ICT to promote small business and to create jobs in the ICT sector. Launched in 2003, DFI is active in Indonesia, Jordan, Peru and Senegal.

Partnerships with International Organizations and Other Bilateral Donors

USAID also seeks to collaborate with international organizations and other donor agencies involved in ICT for development whether through burden sharing on specific activities or through general coordination and knowledge sharing.

USAID ICT activities in partnership with other donors include:

- On telecommunications policy reform, USAID works closely with the Department of State and International Telecommunication Union (ITU). Together, they helped to establish the Arab Telecommunications Regulators Network in 2003 and the West African Telecommunications Regulators Association in 2000. In September 2004 in Almaty, Kazakhstan, the ITU and USAID conducted a workshop on rural access for telecommunications regulators from the Baltic and CIS nations.

- Since September 2000, USAID has been collaborating with the Japanese Ministry of Foreign Affairs (MOFA) and Japanese International Cooperation Agency (JICA) on ICT. Both the U.S. and Japan are active in the Asia region and have conducted joint IT assessments, participated in regional workshops together, and provided a joint planning framework for cooperation.

- USAID collaborated with the Italian government in providing a workshop on e-government strategies for development in March 2004 in Macedonia. The two countries are coordinating their assistance to Macedonia in e-government.

While tremendous progress has been made in providing new digital opportunity to the developing world, billions of people remain out of touch with the benefits of the information revolution, particularly the rural and low-income populations of developing countries. Technological advances in recent years, such as new wireless access devices, have driven down the cost of connectivity and have opened the possibility of affordable access for billions of new users worldwide. The United States Government, through USAID, is taking advantage of these advances and is continuing to pursue the removal of policy and regulatory barriers so that the "last mile" can be bridged in reaching these billions of people.

ENCOURAGING AN ENABLING ENVIRONMENT FOR EFFECTIVE AND SUSTAINABLE USE OF ICT FOR DEVELOPMENT

By Thomas Ganswindt, Siemens AG

The Seventh Meeting of the United Nations Information and Communication Technologies (ICT) Task Force, together with the Global Forum on an Enabling Environment, was held from November 19-20, 2004 in Berlin. Berlin is a good example of how much can change in a few years. Only a little over 15 years ago, this city was divided by the Berlin Wall. The Wall not only divided the city, its people, its culture, but also its telecommunications infrastructure, which developed along different paths during the time of separation. Today, technologically at least, you will hardly notice any difference between the two parts of this city. The ICT infrastructure today is more advanced in the East than it is in the West, due to huge investments made over the past 15 years. This is evidence of what can change, provided the right policies, and wise investments.

Today, another divide is still in evidence, the digital divide between those who do have access to the advanced information and communications technologies and applications, and those who do not have such access. We observe what the different stakeholders can do and must do to bridge the digital divide. Nelson Mandela proffered a vision in 1995: bringing universal access to every village in Africa, and we all here are keenly aware of the fact that we have to go further than that – that we have to bring communications to every village all over the world, a target that was acknowledged and endorsed in the Millennium .

The critical question is: how best can we achieve these goals? Some of the more specific questions are: what are the challenges in building information infrastructure in less-developed areas and in under-served communities? What is the right enabling environment that would promote the use of ICT for development? And how can the various stakeholders collaborate in creating and sustaining such an enabling environment?

Before we can respond to these questions, it may be useful to understand the relationship between the spread and use of information and communication technologies and the level of economic prosperity.

Digital Access Index

If we look at who has digital access in the world today, and who does not, we see a striking correlation between the level of access (Digital Access Index)[1] and economic prosperity (GDP per capita):

---

[1] The Digital Access Index measures the overall ability of citizens to access and use information and communication technologies (ICTs). It is based on eight variables, covering five areas, to provide an overall country score. The areas are availability of infrastructure, affordability of access, educational level, quality of ICT services, and Internet usage. (Source: World Telecommunication Development Report 2003, ITU (2004))

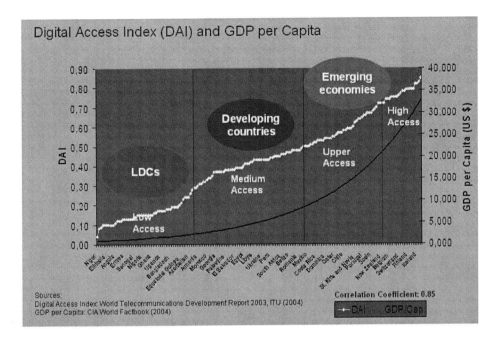

Digital Access Index (DAI) and GDP per Capita

Sources:
Digital Access Index: World Telecommunications Development Report 2003, ITU (2004)
GDP per Capita: CIA World Factbook (2004)

Correlation Coefficient: 0.85

Clearly, poorer countries have low access, and the richer they get, the better their access to ICTs. While there is no causal relationship between these two factors, we can assume that they may positively influence each other in some complex way. To draw up policy recommendations, we need to go deeper than that because other factors are also playing an important role: population density and distribution, geographic topologies, economic and regulatory policies affecting operators and their capabilities. Furthermore, there are digital divides, not just between countries, but between different groups within countries as well.

For example:

- In Chile, 93% of large businesses have Internet access, but only 37% of smaller businesses are connected.

- Mexico's top schools have one computer for every 12 students, but there is only one for every 59 students in the bottom quality of schools.

- And in Peru, while a good 81% of central government agencies have access, only 21% of local government offices have such access.

It is necessary to look at these circumstances from another, more disaggregated, perspective. What is important to look at is not only the digital divide between rich and poor countries, between industrialized and developing countries, or between countries of the north and the south, but we should more closely examine the different factors affecting demand and supply within countries, and the drivers that influence these factors.

Challenges on the Demand Side

What is clear on the demand side within the various countries is a very heterogeneous demand that ranges from basic voice coverage to complex data access, depending on the specific circumstances. This confirms that economic development requires more than just basic voice communication. It also requires access to modern technologies for data communication, or, at least, access to technologies that allow for an evolutionary path to modern communication technologies, because these technologies in turn mean access to knowledge, to know-how, and to business partners. A range of communications services is necessary to facilitate basic and low-cost communications, as well as to ensure a basis for economic development and prosperity via access to broadband data services.

There are some voices in the development community who, faced with the limited financial resources available for development projects, argue that people in developing countries need clean water, and not telecommunications, that they need good schools, and not information technology, basic health services, not broadband access. But, in fact, people in developing countries need both, because health, education, and prosperity go along with and are enhanced by access to and use of information and communication technologies.

To underline the impact of ICTs on basic development goals, the ITU World Telecommunications Development Report 2003 shows a convincing array of data that proves the benefits of ICT. For example, owners of Bangladesh village phones saw a surge in their incomes by 24% over the past 5 years, indicating that ICTs can help reduce extreme poverty. ICTs can also help achieve universal primary education, as the example from Nepal shows, where primary enrolment rose by 5.7% due to teacher training in radio-based distance education. Health has also improved with the use of ICTs as shown by the 10% decrease in infant mortality among low income families with access to telemedicine in the US; 50% decrease in maternal mortality following an ICT-based programme in Uganda; and 143% increase in the use of condoms in St. Lucia after a radio show aired about HIV/AIDS and how to protect oneself from spreading the disease.

Drawing on these examples, a case can be established in favor of advancing information and communication technologies as a supporting technology not in order to compete for scarce resources, but in order to promote basic development goals such as reduction of poverty, improvement of health and provision of education. The main difficulty is in getting them to areas that are currently under-served with these technologies for various reasons.

Therefore, rather than merely viewing the data of the Digital Access Index in terms of differences between countries, we may wish to ask ourselves: How can we help those people in currently underserved, mostly rural, areas to become connected at all? How can we improve access to under-served rural areas? How can we bring the urban low-end users to the networks?

In our experience around the world we have learned that the needs of under-served areas are best met by: a combination of different available technologies that offer the best solution for – or migration path to – broadband access and prevent the digital divide; open and interoperable industry standards; an independent telecommunications regulator; investments by local authorities for broadband access, that will soon pay back (revenues from broadband services, increased productivity, economic growth, etc.); and new business models and public private partnerships that include cost-, risk- as well as revenue- sharing components.

Challenges on the Supply Side

Turning now to the other side of the equation, the constraints and challenges facing operators who are on the supply side must be considered.

To a telecommunication businessperson, it is a tautology that operators need to balance their costs against their revenues, even if their objectives are often set by governments and regulators (such as a universal service obligation or a certain tariff structure). Looking at these two drivers (cost and revenues), it is possible to observe:

- Trends on the revenue side are driven by user demand and are decidedly going down towards $5 per user for mobile voice services. In some countries, such as Korea, you can get 100 MBit broadband access for less than $10 per month on a flat rate basis. Still, for some users on the lower end of the income scale and for those in remote or rural areas, these prices and services may still be out of reach.

- Charges for low-income population groups increase or decrease according to the "Backhauling"[2] and "Aggregation"[3] costs, which is essentially the backbone of the network.

Economic Technology Choices to Bridge the Access Gap

In areas where there is a lot of legacy investment in fixed networks, changing to fast wireless networks may not be the first choice of operators who wish to maximize their profitability using existing infrastructure. For these countries, investing these profits in improving the existing wireless networks, e.g. by enhancing Digital Subscriber Loop (DSL) access, may be the right way.

On the other hand, while fixed or cable-based network solutions may be well-suited for areas with high population-densities and are appropriate for the aggregation at the metro network level, cost drivers, especially those for civil works, make this solution prohibitively expensive for low-density and remote areas.

In this respect, wireless solutions are quickly becoming the most promising technology both in terms of economic efficiency and robustness as well as fast rollout periods. Experience indicates that countries that make a substantial investment in their communications

---

[2] Backhauling costs can make up to 75% of total transportation costs in a network, and therefore are an essential cost driver. What is required is a selection of technologies based on distance, throughput desired, and population densities that can employ satellites for long distances and low densities, optical fibre for medium to long distances with higher population densities, or microwave and wireless IP solutions for the medium range, where high population densities occur.

[3] Aggregation means bringing the different backhauling technologies into the Metro Network. As we move from the current networks divided between fixed line, mobile, between voice and IP-based networks to a Next Generation Network based entirely on IP, we will find that a Carrier-Grade Ethernet will become mandatory for operators if they wish to achieve cost efficiency and scalability.

infrastructure today have a unique opportunity not only to leapfrog technologies but also to avoid the costly mistakes often made by "early-adopter" countries.

Nevertheless, leapfrogging can be a risk because it increases the intervals between investment in available technology, its deployment and end user adoption. The worst-case scenario is operating a network without a sufficient amount of users. User adoption of services is the slowest part of the process. But there are ways to safeguard against these risks. Late-adopter countries should carefully study the following areas in early-adopter countries: technology, government regulation and standardization, and differences in local culture affecting consumer choice. They then have the unique opportunity to benefit from the sometimes hard lessons learned by early-adopter countries. Again, this is the key advantage of leapfrogging, to avoid costly mistakes and learn from best practice made elsewhere, while reaping the benefits of low costs due to mass production according to established industry standards.

Wireless Low-Cost Access

The way to attain low access fees is by focusing on profitability and by bringing more subscribers into the cellular networks without increasing the investment in the networks at the same rate. Cost efficiency can be achieved by increasing network efficiency through enhanced base stations, and by reducing transmission costs through distributed switching systems that bring capacities to where they are needed. To achieve these ends, network integration functions must ascertain that most suitable technology and technological and economic migration paths remain open for future development.

Example Brazil: Fast Rollout of a New Mobile Network

When the Brazilian company Telemar decided to unite Brazil with the mobile world, they concluded that GSM (mobile) technology was the answer. GSM offered Telemar the means to merge service quality with a price that suited the unique social challenges of this country.

Today, Brazil has approximately 54 million mobile subscribers, 61% of whom had no previous telephone service. Boosted by migration to GSM, Brazil is forecast to have 100 million subscribers across all social demographics by the year 2008. This is a true success story.

Example India: More Mobile Users in India than Fixed-Line Subscribers

At the end of October 2004 there were "only" 43.9 million fixed-line users in India while there were 44.9 million mobile subscribers; indicating that there are more mobile subscribers in India than fixed-line users.

Why? Some Indian mobile companies are offering call rates as low as 2 US cents a minute. The result has been that more and more of India's population, millions of whom are economically disadvantaged, can now afford a basic mobile handset and a limited pre-paid tariff. This is a good example of how the above-mentioned cost and revenue dynamics can have a positive impact in real life.

What Does the Near Future of Technology Bring for Underserved Areas?

In the near future, the known mobile telephony networks such as GSM, and those voice networks with added data capability, such as GPRS and UMTS will be complemented by one fairly well-established technology (WiFi) and two rather new technologies (WiMax and Flash OFDM).

While WiFi has already established itself as a *de facto* standard for indoor coverage at home, in the office, and at hot spots in public places such as airports and coffee shops, the other two radio-based technologies (WiMax and Flash OFDM) offer solutions for the backhauling dilemma and thus considerably reduce costs again.

They will also help to provide wireless broadband capability to remote areas, including voice-over-IP solutions. Thus, the future will bring a combination of wireline and wireless access technologies in peaceful coexistence.

Role of Various Stakeholders in Bridging the Digital Divide

With regard to running modern telecommunication networks, the role of government is

- Sometimes overestimated:
    - o When governments try to operate the voice and data networks, which are technical and economic in nature, by using their political instruments;
- Or underestimated:
    - o When governments allow the incumbent operator after privatization to continue to work as the regulator, thus hampering the proper evolution of competitive markets;
    - o Or when unregulated self-interest rules the operation of the networks.

While in the past the economics of wireline networks indicated the need for a regulated monopoly under the direct authority of a ministry or Post, Telephone and Telegraphy Authority, today's market economics show that the market for telecommunications services is of a competitive nature. In making the transition from the old monopoly structures to the new competitive market model, governments are charged with the responsibility of promoting a healthy balance between the interests of incumbent network operators in achieving high penetration rates as fast as possible, and the country's interest in establishing future-proof broadband-enabled telecommunications infrastructure based on a competitive market for operators.

Even if governments are often short on cash, they still have the option to create a business environment that attracts investors, both domestic and foreign. Given the right political, regulatory, and competitive economic environment in a country, investors will seize the opportunities provided and invest considerable amounts of funds in building the necessary networks.

However, to create the suitable environment, a couple of factors require special attention. The making and establishment of strong, agile and independent regulators overseeing regulation that promotes competition is the most powerful instrument any government can wield to achieve the socio-political goal of providing universal access both to rich and poor areas. Competition does ensure that prices will go down to make communications affordable.

Nevertheless, there's plenty of good advice available. Governments can engage experts who can help them in making the right regulatory decisions. The International Telecommunication Union (ITU), the United Nations, the World Bank, the regional development banks and consulting companies – all of these organizations can assist in establishing constructive regulation.

Governments as Market Participants

Governments can do more than this to promote ICTs for economic development. In many countries, government agencies provide essential services to the public and employ large numbers of civil servants; as such they command substantial purchasing power on the demand side of the procurement markets. These factors should be taken into account in the national development plans and strategies for the introduction of ICTs.

Governments at all levels, national, regional, and local, should plan the use of ICTs in their daily operations. This enables more efficient and transparent service provisioning to citizens, fuels the demand for local ICT services, and enables public service employees to become early adopters. In addition, governments should make their learning institutions priority candidates for ICT infrastructure, since education is dramatically improved with the tools and delivery methods made possible by ICTs. This investment will yield "ICT literate" graduates who will in turn set in motion ICT adoption as the standard in the entire national economy. Indeed, because building human capital is a key requirement for the successful adoption of ICTs, equipping the education sector is of great importance.

Unfortunately, sufficient funds to finance these kinds of public projects are often unavailable, undermining national development goals compounded by a lack of ICT-literate young professionals who could otherwise drive ICT development. There are, however, alternatives. Educational funding and similar public ICT projects can, for example, be subsidized by the creation of public-private partnerships and new business models.

Public-Private Partnerships

Public-Private Partnerships (PPPs) can take many different forms, ranging from non-profit-oriented PPPs to those that have a primarily business-oriented perspective. Both can be quite effective in advancing ICT development.

Not-for-profit PPPs that enable wide participation by interested stakeholders help governments in the formulation of national e-strategies. One example of such an non-profit PPP is the "Initiative D21" in Germany, which now has more than 400 individual members, many of whom are on the executive board level of major companies, and who work closely with the under-secretaries of the ministries of finance, health, education, family, and the interior to suggest improvements to the German national ICT action plan. More than 50 joint projects are currently being executed by this non-profit initiative, which has become the largest PPP in Germany. The projects implemented often are pilot projects, or projects with a good value for raising public awareness for the benefits of ICTs.

Such non-profit PPPs are also an excellent venue for civil society to make their concerns heard in a constructive, collaborative way. By working jointly with government officials and with private sector participation, projects benefiting the poor, targeted at minority groups or at specific age or gender groups can be implemented, and the concerns for these population groups can be built into the recommendations for improvement of the national ICT strategy.

New Business Models

Next to the non-profit PPPs there are PPPs formed between government agencies and private industry as a means to raise the necessary financing for large infrastructure projects. These PPPs are more closely understood in terms of what in the United Kingdom is called the Private Finance Initiative (PFI). In these PPPs, private sector participants provide important public services, not under a regular purchase contract with the government, but as partners in a kind of joint venture. Here, a balanced mix of risks and rewards and of the rights and responsibilities of the partners ensures a successful outcome that satisfies both the interests of the private sector and the interests of the public sector, to provide cost-effective services to its citizens.

A good example of such collaboration can be found in Egypt, where private Internet Service Providers (ISPs) work together with the Egypt Telecom in a revenue-sharing model. In this case, the ISPs provide Internet access across Egypt at the price of a local call through special dial-up hosts. Egypt Telecom collects the revenues from the telephone subscribers and shares the proceeds with the ISPs. Thus, an entire country has found a cost-effective way to provide Internet access also in rural areas along the Nile valley where the majority of the population lives.

Summary of Recommendations

In closing, my recommendations would be as follows:

- A mix of complementary (wireline and wireless) technologies that offer the best available solution for broadband access and effectively bridge the digital divide,

- Open and interoperable standards,

- A strong and independent regulator,

- Investments by local authorities in broadband access that yield prompt returns, and

- New business models and public-private partnerships that include cost-, risk- and revenue sharing components.

The prudent combination of these elements can help to advance the implementation of ICT for development purposes, and will contribute to an enabling environment for economic and social advancement. The combination of these elements with a multi-stakeholder approach in devising national strategic development plans will also ensure that local economies, culture and social preferences are accurately taken into account and that no foreign model is rashly adopted without adequate consideration.

OPTIMIZING THE REGULATORY ENVIRONMENT IN EMERGING ECONOMIES

By Edvins Karnitis, Public Utilities Commission, Latvia

In today's interlinked and globalized world, wide and diffuse information flows are a reliable indication of a country's level of development. Electronic communications technologies and their convergence on digital platforms, provide technical opportunities for information transmission. The growing potential of technologies and increasing demand for communications services result in the pre-emptive growth of the electronic communications sector (especially when compared to other sectors of the national economy) leading to increasing density in the gross domestic product.[1] Rapidly and permanently decreasing prices of technologies provide an opportunity to less successful countries to apply advanced communications for knowledge accumulation, sharing and usage.

But the electronic communications sector is not primarily a profitable business sphere or a substantial component of GDP; much more important is the close relationship between the electronic communications sector and general economic growth that can strengthen positive long-term economic feedback. Economic growth means increasing public and private investments in advanced technologies and usage of services, which in turn strongly supports rapid development of all sectors, increased productivity and capacity of businesses and administration, and growing competitiveness of enterprises and regions of the country. Economies obtain knowledge and information on inventions and discoveries as well as advanced technologies and practical experience and enable it to offer its products and knowledge in the global market. This promotes more dynamic development of the country, encourages the creation of new enterprises and jobs, and increases public budgets and social expenditures. The national economy can, thus, take advantage of the development of the electronic communications markets.[2]

In this sense, the development of the electronic communications sector is of national interest. All decisions on the electronic communications sectoral model and support to the sector's evolution have to be in accordance with national development strategy and needs. In general, the needs of any country could be defined quite plainly as general availability of high quality advanced services for affordable prices.

Imperfect rivalry is the basic disincentive of the electronic communications market. Competitive market forces do exist but competition processes are limited. Therefore one of the major components of promotional support should be to strengthen competition processes by state intervention. In order to avoid politicians from meddling in the markets,

---

[1] For example, share of telecommunications revenue in the GDP of OECD countries has increased from 2.0% in 1990 to 3.35% in 2001. The same can be seen in Latvia – increase from 2.8% in 1997 to 4.4% in 2003.

[2] Latvia's regional differences illustrate the significance of advanced electronic communications for development of the country. There are two to three times higher levels of GDP and non-financial investments in Latvian regions where all advanced communications services are fully available in comparison with regions that are underdeveloped in this sense. For more detail on the development of the electronic communications market of Latvia see: A. Dombrovskis, C. Feijoo, E. Karnitis, S. Ramos. "Electronic communications sector and economic development in Latvia: regularities and individualities." *Communications & Strategies*. Special issue: European enlargement and ICTs. Issue 56, 2004 4Q.

the government can create sector-enabling regulatory models and delegate a number of functions at an independent regulatory body.[3]

Utility services (electricity, gas, heat and water supply, postal and passenger transport services, collection of sewage and waste) are also very important for the improvement of living standards. They are an extremely substantial factor for the development of any country since they provide a wide range of goods and advanced services to businesses and citizens.

Increasing the economic efficiency of all utility sectors and improving the economic and socio-political environment associated with utilities services are essential factors for the dynamic, stable and balanced development of any country. The European Union uses the term "services of general economic interest" for this industry to emphasize its social component. General availability (both technological and financial) of quality services is of great importance for equalization of living conditions in the cities and countryside (including remote regions) which is important for nurturing the social and economic cohesion of society.

In order to promote the development of all these sectors, the government should create an enabling, stable and predictable regulatory environment that equally favors both consumers (through the availability and quality of services, choice and affordable prices) and service providers (through adequate profitability, opportunities for innovation, and increasing efficiency).

Sectoral and Multi-Sectoral Regulatory Models

There are two alternatives to the regulatory model that government can create. One could be separate regulation for every utility service sector and the other is a multi-sectoral and unified regulation for all sectors.

The first alternative, which can also be called the sectoral model, is popular among many countries because of its simplicity. However, this model has its limitations. In 1996, a special commission of the United Kingdom, which has the most sophisticated regulatory environment for the utilities sector in Europe, pointed to the lack of coordination among its regulatory institutions and concluded that the UK's regulatory system as a whole was unstable.

In Latvia, until 2001, regulatory functions were performed by sectoral regulatory bodies (energy and telecommunications) as well by divisions of ministries (transport) or local governments (water supply). They were weak and dependent on the government administration. The influence of monopolistic utility companies on them was very high.

---

[3] Thanks to the increasing level of knowledge, a number of traditional processes are changing with development of the economy. In particular, competition is the major force that stimulates companies to act with maximum effectiveness. But in addition to this invisible hand that regulates a traditional free market economy and promotes development, an increasing level of knowledge is characterized by the increasing role of various state regulatory activities in the interests of the whole society. So, terminable exclusive rights on intellectual property (patents, licenses, trade marks, copyright, etc.) are the real support for creative processes. National and international competition authorities control emergence of monopolies and market dominants, hence protecting consumers. Tendencies to regulate capital markets become more and more strong. This also relates to provision of utilities services, too, including electronic communications services.

They also performed very few functions. For example, the Telecommunications Tariffs Council (the telecommunications regulatory body) only set tariffs for services of Lattelekom, the sole company providing fixed telephony in Latvia. The Council's decisions were oftentimes unpredictable and unconnected with interests of the national economy and society. And what could we expect from a regulatory body with a staff of five people, a part-time decision-making board, and with very limited financing?

During 1999–2000, the multi-sectoral regulatory model was introduced in collaboration with World Bank experts. The concept is based on the idea that basic processes in public utilities sectors (and corresponding regulatory activities) are similar and that there can be a unified regulatory process in terms of the development of competition, regulatory balance, social policy, etc.

Today, capital is becoming more mobile, intersectoral convergence has begun, and multi-utility companies are developing (the entry of electricity, railway and postal companies into the electronic communications business). In the next decade they will become significant service providers. Consumers (whether business or residential) are using a number of utility services, and they will require coordinated and predictable regulation. Harmonization of regulation for all sectors' regulation will be favourable for utilities and consumers alike.

With the unified multi-sectoral regulatory model, principles and strategy can be easily implemented thanks to the growing information processing capabilities and introduction of knowledge management principles. Advanced regulation principles and instruments, which are closely inspected in one sector, can be applied to other sectors as well (varieties of services and tariffs, payment systems, soft disconnection schemes, universal service, unbundling, etc.). At the same time, peculiarities of any sector will have to be considered by applying appropriate sector tactics, terms, numerical proportions, etc. In addition, this unified regulation is more competent and cheaper (particularly for small countries). This multi-sectoral model significantly reduces regulatory risks and, consequently, investment risks as well.

Taking into account these considerations, a multi-sectoral regulatory model and the resulting regulatory body – The Public Utilities Commission (PUC) – was established in Latvia in 2001. Latvia, of course, is not the only country that has this multi-sectoral model. In fact, regulation in the US (and the most experienced in this case) uses a multi-sectoral model as well. In the UK, this harmonization of regulatory activities has been considered and the merging of sectoral regulators is now taking place. The UK is now moving towards a unified regulation (unified regulation for electricity and gas sectors was organized some years ago and preparatory activities to form a common regulator for all communications services are taking place). Germany, on the other hand, is developing an energy regulatory body based on existing telecommunications and postal regulations. In Luxembourg, the multi-sectoral model is being established, although without yet the unified regulatory principles for all sectors. Several Latin American, Asian and African countries have also introduced similar multi-sectoral regulation with the support of the World Bank.

Latvia has gained considerable experience in both sectoral and multi-sectoral models after more than three years of the PUC's operation. Consequently, it can get the most out of the fundamental advantages of a multi-sectoral model and develop the optimum regulatory environment (including benefits for the electronic communications sector).

Enabling Regulatory Environment: Compromise between Diverse Interests

There are three parties involved in the provision of services that are of general economic interest. These are the government, the service providers (utilities), and the service users (consumers). All of them favor a normative and regulatory environment that enables the effective provision of services. However, their perception and understanding of the optimum enabling environment may differ.

An enabling regulatory regime can be based only on a favourable normative framework. Building a clear and stable legislative environment and compatibility of general and sectoral legislation should be the priority of the government. This ensures uniformity of principles for all regulated sectors and a more responsible and predictable behavior on the part of the regulator.

The European Union's 1998 telecommunications regulatory framework was based on simple and straightforward principles and methodologies that were elaborated for the first post-market liberalization period. Strict and direct regulations were imposed *ex ante* regardless of the actual situation in the markets and based on several formal criteria (market share above all things).

For the 2002 framework, the main objective of the EU was to bring sectoral regulation closer to the overall principles of competition, making use of general rules for protecting competition. Since new entrants to the market had become quite strong and redivision of the market had continued, legislative changes were deemed necessary to make the regulatory environment more appropriate to the level of market development. The results of analysis of the electronic communications market situation should be applied in one of two ways (the decision depends on existence of effective competition in a given market) accent on monitoring and general anti-trust measures that are applied *ex post* if competition exists, or strong *ex ante* obligations on the operators considered as having dominance in the sector.

The old EU Member States on average had around five years experience of the formal liberalization of the market (typically, in January 1998) for the development of competition before the transition to the 2002 framework. But the new Member States were also asked to adopt the 2002 framework upon their accession on May 1, 2004 really only one to two years had passed since market liberalization. It is indubitable that competition in their markets exists, but it is only in the seed stage. Because of the lack of time for the development of competition, the electronic communications sector is actually not prepared for a new framework.

Consequently the 2002 regulatory package really does not support market development in many new Member States; it precludes an operative regulator's decision-making and thus has created serious barriers for newcomers. Therefore, its full implementation in national laws as of May 1, 2004 can now be seen as premature.

Governments should not intervene in decisions of regulatory bodies. Decisions have to be made perfectly independently; only in this case will regulatory findings be implemented in full. Therefore, all regulatory instruments, which are necessary for monitoring and control, for decision-making and implementation, have to be at the regulators' disposal. Nevertheless, from time to time governments try to retain some regulatory functions in ministries. Such fragmentation of the regulatory environment means an additional burden on business and, of course, is a serious failing for the regulatory system.

Because services are provided to consumers, but at the same time consumers are the most vulnerable party, one of the key principles for all services of general interest is a consumer-oriented manner of regulation. This principle contains *inter alia*:

- general sustained availability of services in the whole territory of the country at affordable prices – the universal service principle is a real instrument for practical realization of availability for low income consumers;

- choice opportunities for consumers – in addition to choice of service provider it contains, for example, availability of several service options including services of diverse quality and volume and the introduction of various tariff and payment systems including a pre-payment option;

- protection of consumers' rights – including the settlement of disputes, compensation procedures for consumers in case they do not receive services or receive substandard services, adaptation of soft disconnection procedures for debtors, and strict protection of personal data and information on services delivered.

Consumers' desire to access to high quality services at low cost is understandable. At the same time regulators have to avoid taking inadequate populistic decisions (excessive decrease of regulated tariffs) under pressure of consumers' associations or in the short term interests of politicians. In the long term they will be disadvantageous for consumers because the given service market will be destroyed.

Service providers (utilities companies), as any business undertaking, are interested in a favourable and predictable business environment, low investment risk and high profitability. In line with these principles, facilitation of effective operation and investment-based growth, reduction of regulatory risks, support to development of competition and assistance to entry of new service providers in the market are the basic tasks for any regulator. Regular market surveys, studies of service providers before and monitoring after licensing, quality of services and its regular increase, monitoring of environment and health protection activities, distribution of scarce resources and common exploitation of bottleneck resources, and other regulatory activities are directed to the improvement of the business environment and services supply.

It is universally recognized that the regulator should not perform activities in line with the direct interests of a historical monopoly or of dominant service provider, a phenomenon known as "capture of the regulator." But on the other hand, support of newcomers does not mean promoting the collapse of the incumbents. Consummation of reasonable profit for service providers should be deemed as a task for the regulator; it should avert utilities' activities directed to achievement of the highest profits (by decrease of system safety and service quality).

Even this short compendium shows how different, even contradictory, is understanding the enabling environment for the provision of services of general interest and how important is the balance between all parties (Fig. 1.). Diverse interests lead to a number of heavy regulatory tasks – resisting pressure to approve inadequate and populistic decisions, balancing interests of the consumers and sustainability of the operation of utilities, using a plain-dealing, yet asymmetric approach to incumbents and newcomers, distributing benefits fairly between service providers and consumers (profit growth for service providers simultaneously with service quality increase and price/tariff decrease), imposing economically well-grounded tariffs on services (reasonable costs for providers and affordable for consumers), and resisting the achievement of goals that are not directly related to service delivery (solving social problems through service tariffs at the expense of other consumers).

In the best case both the normative and regulatory environments will be some compromise between interests of all three parties. Inclination to one of them contains strong risks – business will become unprofitable or services will become unavailable. Both cases are contradictory to general national interests.

Therefore to ensure fair, credible and consistent regulation, and to create an environment that is enabling for all parties, the key issue for any regulatory body is keeping equal distance from all involved parties, and forming and maintaining a continuous, stable and transparent cooperation procedures with them.

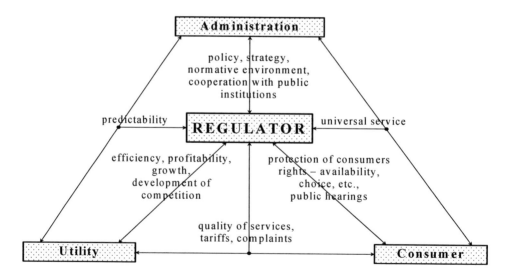

Fig. 1. Actors in services market and the regulator: mutual relations

Optimum Regulation: Several Essential Criteria

In order to be successful in balancing the desires of all parties, the regulators have to comply with several mandatory demands. Let us analyse shortly which regulator – sectoral or multi-sectoral – more completely corresponds to the following criteria.

Strength, high skills, competence

The decision-making body of the regulator (board, council, commissioners) has to have strong political support to make principled decisions that are in the interests of the country and society, to dispute with monopolies and incumbents and to oppose them. The individuals should be nominated by the lawmaking body of the country (Parliament, President) to work full time and hold long terms; no entity should have the possibility to remove them prematurely (including the nominating body).

In addition to sectoral competence (communications, energy, transport) a high legal and economic capacity is necessary for sound performance of the regulatory functions. In the unified regulator both these functions serve all sectors.

The concentration of knowledge and competence in multi-sectoral regulators ensures higher quality of regulation taking into consideration sectoral similarities. It is obvious that staff of a single regulatory body in a country (especially a small country) could be made up of more politically and socially responsible and professionally skilled people than when human resources are dissipated across a number of sectoral regulators. Latvian experience before and after establishment of multi-sectoral regulator corroborates this view.

To further increase the regulator's capacity, it is useful to organize an independent, formal expert body to improve monitoring and control of regulated sectors and to provide expert opinion on drafts of regulatory documents and decisions. For example, leading researchers, lawyers and economists from the Academy of Sciences, University of Latvia and Riga Technical University are members of the PUC's expert council.

Independence

A regulator's independence becomes a particular problem in small countries, where everyone knows everyone. The independence level of the regulator is characterized by several aspects.

High-level nomination of decision makers must not mean politically dependant decisions. A decision-making board in a small country, of course, would be recruited by responsible individuals.

The regulator's decisions have to become valid without any approval. Nobody should have a possibility to change or repeal them; decisions should be appealed only in court within defined time period. In many countries many sectoral regulators are operating as structural divisions of ministries or their decisions become valid only after approval by a minister.

Although formally Latvia's PUC is operating under the supervision of the Ministry of Economy (according to the Constitution of Latvia public institutions should operate within the framework of a ministry), it does not influence independent decisions and activities of the PUC (Fig. 2). Only drafts of normative acts in the Cabinet of Ministers are not submitted directly, but via the ministry. Nevertheless discussions are going on about special adoption of PUC's full legal independence in the Constitution in the future in order to further strengthen its independency level and to also achieve full, formal autonomy of the PUC from the administration.

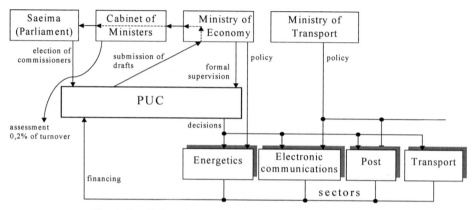

Fig. 2. PUC's interlinkage with administration and utilities

As important is financial independence of the regulator. The chosen financial model should allow constructing an independent regulator's budget, minimizing the possibility of financial pressure on the regulator. This could take place in the case of financing from the public budget or direct payments of utilities for regulatory services.

In order to achieve the highest possible independent financing of the Latvia's PUC, it is determined as fixed percentage (currently 0.2%) of utilities services turnover, assessed by the Cabinet of Ministers and paid by utilities in the special Treasury account. It should be mentioned that regulatory costs for unified regulation are much lower (these costs, of course, are included in tariffs for services).

In total it can be appraised that the independency level of the PUC would be unachievable for any sectoral regulator. The chosen unified regulatory model has helped to achieve a real independency level that is one of the highest for EU national regulators. The risk of regulator capture is far and away less than for a sectoral regulator.

Fairness and transparency

To maintain the equilibrium in the centre of the government-utility-consumer triangle implementation of fair and transparent regulation is a substantial precondition. How is transparency assured by the PUC?

The PUC involves all parties during the decision-making process hearing opinions of all interested parties – citizens and businesses, public and social institutions, experts and interest groups.

Public hearings have been chosen as the advisory procedure in addition to candid, direct discussions with market players. This gives all stakeholders the opportunity to express their attitude and make proposals before approval of decisions. Hearing times and subjects are announced in the official newspaper *Latvijas Vestnesis* (Latvia Herald) and full texts of corresponding draft documents are available. All proposals are examined, but only non-anonymous suggestions are taken into consideration; information on their acceptability is published in the PUC's website.

Sittings of the decision-making board are open for all parties concerned, the agenda and decisions are publicly available on the home page of the PUC, decisions are published in the *Latvijas Vestnesis* also. The PUC is accountable for its activities to the society by publishing a mandatory annual public report.

Implementation Activities of the Multi-Sectoral Regulation

The multi-sectoral regulatory model is a new model for Europe. Therefore development of a regulatory strategy has been the primary task for the PUC in order to ensure coordinated activities and to perform focused regulatory related functions by all involved public institutions.

The basic principles of competition where possible and regulation only where and how much it is necessary have been implemented in the strategy. The PUC directly intervenes in the service provision process only where competition is limited. Sector deregulation is implemented as a transition from direct monopoly regulation to indirect sector regulation simultaneously with the development of competition, not by decreasing PUC's attention to the sectors in which the market is formally liberalized.

The *Strategy and Basic Principles of Operation of the Public Utilities Commission* is the basic strategic document that contains principles and actions related to the competency level of the PUC, including laying out the: goals and principles of the regulatory activities, need for equal distance of the PUC from all involved parties, stable and fair cooperation procedures with both utilities and consumers, promotion of newcomers, long-term national tariff policy and unified tariff calculation principles, protection of consumers' rights and ecological and health protection principles.

A number of secondary documents regulate current tasks and concrete applications; they are devoted to the implementation of principles defined in strategy. It was envisaged that these documents should be as unified as possible for all regulated sectors; they would be updated as experience is accumulated. Many items have been developed: licensing procedures, unified orders for information submission by service providers, procedures for acquaintance with tariff projects, provisions on cooperation and consultation with service providers and consumers (public hearings), regulations on dispute solving, unified methodological principles for determination of tariffs, even practical details such as definition of *force majeure*.

Nevertheless there remains a lot to do in the future. Introduction of a unified universal service model for several sectors (electronic communications, post and electricity first of all), taking into account the sectors' peculiarities, will be the biggest challenge for the PUC. Basic tasks include definition of the set of services (including specification, quality of services, etc.) and client base, principles for determination of universal service providers, principles and criteria for compensation, introduction of matching financing from the national (municipal) budget and conformity with social programmes.

It is necessary to develop a national policy paper containing a clear vision on further development of regulated sectors, general goals and principles of the national regulatory system, socio-economic vision and strategic activities that cannot be performed by the PUC alone. These measures should be taken on governmental level; therefore, this document has to be approved by the Cabinet of Ministers.

Potential Weaknesses of Multi-Sectoral Model: Do they really exist?

In Latvia, proponents of the sectoral regulatory model pose these arguments about potential weak points of the multi-sectoral model.

1. *There are different levels of sectors' liberalization; therefore, intersectoral harmonization problems may be serious.*

Today the objective situation regarding market liberalization in Latvia is very different among the utilities: there are monopolies in electricity and natural gas supply, the fixed telecommunications market was recently liberalized (from January 1, 2003), there is a long-term duopoly in mobile telecommunications market, a high level of competition in Internet service and liquid gas markets, and a composed status in postal services. Of course, regulation regimes should be different, and it is different for monopolies and competitive markets (tariffs setting), but general principles, strategy and instruments are the same (competition support, market surveys, decision-making procedures, licensing principles, etc.).

Problems have not so far arisen for this reason during the operation of the PUC. Rather, a very successful development of the fixed telecommunications market (newcomers took near 6% of the fixed voice services in terms of revenues in the first year, and as an estimated more than 10% market share in 2004; the progress rate of newcomers is much higher than the EU15 average level in the first years after market liberalization) to a great extent is owed to the PUC's experience in operation in open markets. Experience in the electronic communications sector will be very useful to the liberalization of the electricity market in the near future.

2. *There is lower quality of regulation, because a multi-sectoral regulator cannot concentrate on problems of one specified sector.*

The real situation is quite opposite. The aforementioned concentration of economists and lawyers is unified for all sectors divisions of the PUC has shown exceptionally positive results in solving many problems that are common to all sectors (market analysis, tariff methodology, legal substantiation of decisions, representation in legal proceedings, etc.). Such performance would not be achieved by the dissipation of specialists in sectoral regulators.

Collaboration of the PUC's sectoral divisions (electronic communications and post, energy and transport departments) also ensures a synergistic effect. For example, after elaboration of a unified tariff methodology, it was scrutinized, tested and corrected for the electricity sector. Later, the methodology was adapted for all regulated tariffs in gas and telecommunications sectors very quickly and perfectly, thanks to the unified approach and accumulated experience. It could be foreseen that the same will be true for similar activities in the future, such as the introduction of a unified universal service model and the implementation in fixed telephony of visible and transparent principles for distribution of costs among subscription and amount prices that already have been defined for gas supply.

3. *Politically nominated decision makers are not experts in regulated sectors.*

Risks related to the professionalism of politically nominated decision makers really exist, but there is no difference between sectoral and multi-sectoral regulation in this regard. Nevertheless, requirements regarding qualification and knowledge on the regulated sectors for decision makers should be improved; such action would help to avoid the risk of regulators politicization. The next step would be defining skills for all members of decision-making body (economist, lawyer, specialist in telecommunications, energy or transport affairs). Such requirements are useful, particularly when political nomination is taking place.

4. *Regulation expenses are not fully adequate to sectoral payments.*

It is a heavy task to fix accurate expenses for costs of a given sector because economic and legal divisions are working for all sectors. But it is clear that total multi-sectoral regulatory costs for any one sector are lower in comparison with those for sectoral regulators.

In addition some financial maneuverability is very useful. The electronic communications sector is the most labour-intensive for the PUC presently with its recently liberalized fixed voice market, many new secondary normative acts, analysis of all markets (18 markets according EU directives), convergence of technologies (consequently service providers and regulation) and several inexperienced newcomers. Some of these activities are subsidized from other sectors' payments.

But in a short time the situation will change: the electricity market will be liberalized, the amount of regulatory work and costs will increase significantly. It will be possible to concentrate financing for the electricity sector without cradling payments. But application of experience gained during liberalization of fixed telecommunications will reduce regulatory expenses. In total, it means benefit for all parties.

Conclusion

Latvia has made a good start in the creation of a balanced and fair regulatory environment. The results of implementation of the multi-sectoral model demonstrate its efficiency. PUCs three years of operation have corroborated initially anticipated advantages of harmonized regulation for both service providers and consumers. Strengthened level of economic and legal competence and independence of the regulator has increased authority of the PUC in the society and the regulator's strategic influence on policy makers.

Although the creation of the PUC is relatively recent, and comprehensive evaluation of the influence of this regulatory model on Latvian general economic development is still needed, in total the multi-sectoral model can be appreciated as the most advanced and preferable one, especially for a small country (i.e., for the majority of countries). Global tendencies also show that harmonized multi-sectoral regulation is the optimum model for the future if all preconditions have been met.

Each sector (including the electronic communications sector) also wins due to its independent decisions that are not affected by the incumbent or significant market powers, a lack of populism, use of highly skilled economists and lawyers, harmonized regulation for multi-sectoral companies and lower regulatory costs.

Because the influence of the multi-sectoral model on national economies is higher in comparison to the sectoral model, respective fundamental tenets, strategic principles and procedures should be elaborated very carefully. The PUC is using the learning-by-doing principle in many cases nowadays. The World Bank is also actively contributing and an EU White Paper gives some expectations about development of common position. Nonetheless, strategic activities have to be intensified on international scale.

PROMOTING AN ENABLING ENVIRONMENT FOR DIGITAL DEVELOPMENT AND ICT

By Ayesha Hassan, International Chamber of Commerce

The International Chamber of Commerce (ICC) has long recognized the economic and social benefits of information and communication technologies (ICTs) and the Internet. In order for ICTs and the Internet to reach their full potential as engines for economic growth and social development, ICC encourages all governments to develop an enabling environment that promotes competition and private sector investment. In turn, the private sector will continue to play a critical role in building and deploying the necessary infrastructures and services. This contribution provides illustrations of the key enabling environment components.

Executive Summary

This contribution outlines the critical components of an enabling environment for ICTs by elaborating on the following: basic and ICT education; technology neutral laws and regulation; a regulatory framework which promotes competition and fosters entrepreneurship; telecoms and trade liberalization; promoting innovation and creativity (IPR protection); and criteria for a good investment climate, namely, a stable and predictable legal system; a sufficiently comprehensive, transparent and non-discriminatory legal framework; sound macro-economic, fiscal and monetary policies; a dynamic economic base; and rising standards of education, health care and social infrastructure.

To attract investment, promote innovation and foster entrepreneurship in ICTs, governments can provide the needed motivating factors by addressing the legal, policy and regulatory frameworks. Engaging in communication with business and other stakeholders in the development of these frameworks is essential to their success.

Basic and ICT Education[1]

Education is the cornerstone of success in the use of ICTs and in promoting an information society for all. All people must have access to basic education as a first step, and ICT-related skills development as a second step.

An academic approach to education encourages the development of skills that are important in contributing to the society and the economy. It includes working in large organizations or firms even if not necessarily applied in an entrepreneurial career.

The education system must recognize the need for developing the basic skills and attitudes that make up a positive, problem-solving, entrepreneurial mindset such as lateral thinking, questioning, independence and self-reliance. This education should continue through vocational training, business incubation and the start-up phase for young entrepreneurs.

---

[1] "Information and Communication Technology: Gender Issues in Developing Nations", Kimberly Betz Leahy and Ira Yermish, St. Joseph's University, Philadelphia, PA, USA, Informing Science Journal Special Series on Community Informatics, Volume 6, 2003

The curriculum should be relevant to the needs of young people who want to find decent and productive work and serve as productive members of society. Entrepreneurial activities should be encouraged by promoting the concept of entrepreneurship and self-employment as well as training for entrepreneurs of all ages.

Other aspects of education include national, regional and local education and training strategies and programmes that address needs and requirements, and are designed for success. Centrally planned skills training is often not matched to market needs, so young people often gain skills for which there is no market and therefore no jobs.

Job centers should work closely with vocational training organizations to recommend entrepreneurship as an employment option for young people. Business plan training should be easily available either as part of the vocational course or through career planning advice. Also, career advice and counseling at schools, colleges and universities should include self-employment as a viable career option. All students must understand the power and potential of ICT in the workplace.

ICT training should be widely available. Partnerships between governments, employers, schools and college authorities should be developed to provide the necessary training. Practical ways in which new businesses can access the appropriate hardware and communications infrastructure must also be developed. Information about the market (current and expected) should be used to establish what skills and training and required.

There should also be special programmes in developing countries to address societal needs for educating and training women. Women are the heads of 75 percent of the families in the developing world. In addition, women are 70% of the 1.3 billion people living in poverty globally.

Technologically Neutral Laws and Regulations

To increase access and foster diversity of choice, it is important that governments adopt a policy framework that maximizes competition and that allows users of technology to choose the technology that best meets their specific needs based on considerations such as performance, quality, reliability, security and life-cycle cost. Government policies that limit such choice, or that promote one form of technology over another, can deprive users, including governments, of the best solutions and can prevent the realization of the full benefits of available technologies, stifling both competition and innovation, and potentially impairing economic development, productivity and growth.

Users, including government users, benefit from access to competitive markets. Countries benefit from inclusion. Increased market access is the best way to ensure competitiveness in a dynamic global economy. However, in today's global economy, where more than half of the world's trade flows are trade in services, not goods, access to markets is no longer strictly an issue of tariffs. As it relates to investment and services, it is a much broader concept that speaks to the notion of contestability; in other words, the ability to compete effectively once you have invested. As part of this, competition law is needed to ensure that those investing have a fair environment in which to compete, leading to improved market access. Increased market access not only enhances corporate competitiveness but also country competitiveness, increasing the capacity of national governments to improve the standard of living of their citizens.

One of the areas of systemic hindrances to capital formation and investment that needs to be dealt with is that of business environment impediments. These include, for example, cumbersome and multiple steps required to obtain the necessary licenses to do business; complex and time-consuming procedures for customs clearance; and the problems caused by corruption in business relationships.

Telecoms and Trade Liberalization

ICC has formally made recommendations to the WTO regarding trade liberalization of products and services delivered via broadband. Broadband technologies and access are increasingly important in providing users with greater access to information and new applications and in raising productivity. Governments should accept international rules and make full market access and national treatment commitments for products and services that can be delivered via broadband, e.g. software, computer and related services, video-on-demand, etc. Such liberalization would increase innovation, product and service offerings and reduce the cost of such products and services, thereby increasing demand.

Governments should consult with the relevant stakeholders to decide and articulate at the outset what their objectives are. These objectives may differ from country to country and can include: attracting new investment; upgrading national infrastructure; creating jobs; contributing to improving universal access; improving services, pricing and choice for the end-user community; and encouraging innovation.

Benefits and Challenges of Telecoms Liberalization[2]

Economic Growth

Along with road systems, airports and electricity, a modern telecoms system is an essential pre-requisite for economic growth. Indigenous industries and home-grown companies of all sizes need the basic business infrastructure to thrive at home, compete internationally, and contribute to overall economic growth. As liberalization enables the provision of more, better and innovative communication services, it is an essential pre-condition for countries looking to make the most of ICTs.

Good telecoms infrastructure can facilitate overall economic growth where it is needed the most. Studies have shown that developing countries with higher levels of connectivity significantly out-performed others during the 1980s and 1990s.[3] Improvements in telecommunications infrastructure result in better trade and market opportunities, reduced unemployment, improved health care delivery and created higher quality of life.[4]

---

[2] The information in the boxes below are excerpted from ICC's tool for e-Business "Telecoms Liberalization, An international business guide for policymakers"

[3] World Bank- R2002 623-646, 2002. Can Information and communication technologies be pro-poor?

[4] ITU 1998a

The greatest economic benefits are achieved when improved communications are extended throughout the entire country. Achieving universal access should be a vitally important part of any country's economic development strategy.

New Investment

Building a telecoms infrastructure is expensive. Technological barriers to entry to the telecoms sector have been reduced in the last decade, but it remains a capital-intensive industry that relies heavily on private and/or external financing.[5]

Liberalization makes available the private investment necessary to finance the communications infrastructure. Governments have many competing responsibilities and claims on their revenues. The massive and ongoing investment required to upgrade and maintain communications networks and make them available to all citizens may be beyond what is economically and politically feasible for the state. At the same time, both foreign and domestic private investors are eager to invest in upgrading infrastructure and rolling out new networks and services. Liberalizing the telecoms market creates an opportunity to attract that investment.

Success in Attracting Foreign Investment in Communications Infrastructure - Mongolia

Mongolia is a large and land-locked country with a very rural population and one of the lowest population densities in the world. Rolling out fixed line communications to its scattered population was proving time-consuming and expensive. In 1992, Mongolia took the first steps to liberalize its communications infrastructure which was then in the hands of a fully state-owned monopoly. In 1996, new service providers (mobile, fixed and ISPs) numbered fourteen. After that, significant changes to the regulatory framework were made.

In 1999, Mongolia awarded a second mobile licence to a private operator, Skytel, which was funded by two Korean communications providers. In the following two years, the number of mobile phone subscribers increased by 400%. Although mobile coverage by Skytel and the incumbent's mobile operator, Mobicom, is still concentrated around urban areas,[6] coverage is rapidly increasing. By 2002, the number of communications service providers overall was over 130.

Mongolia today is leap-frogging straight into mobile phone and wireless services. The number of mobile phone subscribers per capita is almost double that of fixed lines[7] and the country is now considering using innovative new technologies such as wireless local loop (WLL) and power line technology to extend broadband deployment across the country. Opening up its telecoms market allowed Mongolia to attract domestic and foreign investment that can now adapt to the country's unique circumstances.

Between 1990 and 2001, the telecom industry drew more investment in developing countries than any other sector, totalling 331 billion dollars. Half of this investment went to Latin America and the Caribbean, who led the charge towards liberalization in the 1990s. But Sub-Saharan Africa, which had no private telecoms investment at all in 1993, managed to account for 5% of the global total in the sector by 2001. The ability to attract private investment in telecoms is not confined to any one part of the globe. When investment figures are adjusted to reflect investment per head of population, countries as far flung as Panama and Estonia are included in the top five countries worldwide.

---

[5] Economic impact of trade and investment liberalization in the telecoms sector, a survey of issues and arguments; Daniel Roseman, The Journal of World Investment, December 2002

[6] http://www.cellular-news.com/coverage/mongolia.shtml

[7] The World Bank Fact Book 2002

Where Does the Investment Money Go?

Telefonica's[8] operations in Latin America spend at least 75% of their purchasing budgets through local suppliers. The benefits of foreign direct investment in telecoms are enjoyed by many local firms, as well as the direct users of new and improved telecoms services.

Country	Distribution of purchases per country (%)	Number of suppliers	% of local suppliers per country	% of purchases made from local suppliers
Spain	59.10%	4,457	93%	90%
Argentina	3.80%	1,174	96%	95%
Brazil	21.50%	3,684	99%	98%
Chile	3.90%	1,590	98%	85%
Peru	4.50%	1,412	89%	77%

Foreign direct investment in telecoms infrastructure brings more than hard currency. Companies investing in national telecoms bring with them new technologies, business processes, methods, and valuable global brands. By far the greatest rewards to countries that have liberalized their telecoms sectors are the indirect revenues; the benefits that are spread throughout the economy and society as a whole as more and better communications services benefit the entire population.

Liberalization commitments taken in the context of the GATS negotiations on basic services or value-added services have been a significant factor in attracting foreign direct investment in telecoms. They signal to private investors that governments are serious about opening their telecoms sectors to competition, and that the returns on investment in more and better services are secure.

To promote full implementation of existing commitments made under the WTO framework and further liberalization of all basic telecoms, value-added, computer and related services, governments should ensure: market access and national treatment commitments for all service sectors without restrictions; earlier implementation dates; reduction or elimination of foreign ownership restrictions; adherence to the "Reference Paper" commitments for basic telecoms services only; and compliance with the GATS Annex on Telecoms for access to and use of public telecoms networks for the provision of value-added services, including Internet services, and other sectors to which countries have made commitments.

Foreign investment contributes directly or indirectly to a country's economic prosperity in many different ways: as a source of additional capital, as a means to increase competitiveness and productivity, as a source of employment creation, as an incentive to rationalize production, as a vehicle for the transfer of technology, and as a source of managerial know-how.

The basic policies and conditions which are most conducive to attracting foreign investment are by and large the same as those which encourage domestic private investment (Note: Policies that prohibit foreign investment are clearly not conducive to attracting external investment!).

---

[8] Corporate Responsibility Annual Report 2002, Telefonica SA, http://www.telefonica.es/memoria/ingles/memoria2002/responsabilidadcorp/pdfs/todo.pdf

Determinants of foreign investment comprise a variety of public and private factors, including:

- A **stable political system** supported by a professional and accountable public service; an open and constructive attitude towards the private sector and other stakeholders, both local and foreign; a predictable and transparent regulatory framework; and a respect for the rule of law and due process.

- A **sufficiently comprehensive, transparent and non-discriminatory legal framework** to operate modern commercial operations (including company law, bankruptcy law, competition law, protection of property rights including intellectual property), and free access to an impartial judicial system to redress wrongs and settle disputes.

- **Sound macro-economic, fiscal and monetary policies** (including currency stability and convertibility) sufficiently flexible to adapt to market signals, and moderate levels of personal and corporate taxation.

- A **dynamic economic base** supported by an expanding domestic market, growing demand and purchasing power, a healthy local private sector of suppliers, distributors and competitors, and efficient capital markets and financial services.

- **Rising standards of education, health care and social infrastructure** to encourage human resource development, an adequately educated and trained work force, and an efficient system of physical infrastructure, especially in the key areas of transportation and communications.

Further Elements of an Attractive Local Investment Climate

The local investment climate in any given country can be significantly improved by the removal of most common obstacles faced by companies seeking to establish and maintain market access through investment. Policy initiatives that encourage foreign investment include:

- the **removal of conditions** on foreign investment in the form of various performance requirements, such as: minimum investment levels, a commitment to manufacturing, transfer of specific technology, establishment of research and development (R&D) facilities, mandatory partnering, mandatory export requirements, and local content requirements;

- the **elimination of licensing or screening of investment** to limit or prevent access to certain sectors or industries;

- the implementation of transparent, open and non-discriminatory rules and practices in the buying, selling and regulatory activities of state-sanctioned private or public monopolies and concessions;

- the removal of any and all policy and regulatory initiatives that discriminate against foreign companies. Foreign investors are increasingly looking to measurements of the **contestability of a local market** particularly as it relates to investment in the services sector.

- the **reform of various private practices** that exclude new market entrants or restrict access to distribution networks and other necessary business infrastructure, as well as corporate governance practices that limit or prevent participation by foreign firms.

The key policy issues related to mobilizing private sector resources and attracting both foreign and domestic investment are the 'enabling environment' criteria in general which include:

- transparency

- rule of law ("predictability" is critical)

- liberalization

- competitive frameworks

- fighting corruption

All of the issues above help attract investment because decisions are more objective and based on facts and results can be anticipated and planned for appropriately.

Supply of Broadband Infrastructure

A specific aspect of integration and the enabling environment includes broadband deployment. This section addresses key components of the broadband "enabling environment".

1. Ensuring a Competitive Marketplace

   Governments should ensure a pro-competitive and market-driven policy framework that promotes investment in and deployment of broadband for business users as well as consumers. Actions necessary to promote such a policy framework include:

   - Telecommunications liberalization:

     Liberalization of the telecommunications market has been a powerful economic driver in many countries. Business users need innovation and choice in broadband services. This can best be achieved through open and competitive markets which also create incentives for continued investment. Therefore, it is critically important that governments make meaningful market opening commitments for basic and value-added telecommunication services and effectively enforce existing telecommunication commitments in the WTO and other trade agreements. WTO members that have not yet made telecommunications market-opening commitments should do so. WTO members that have made commitments should implement them in a timely fashion.

- Pro-competitive regulation for basic telecommunications:

  Ensuring effective application of the pro-competitive policy principles enshrined in the WTO Reference Paper is essential. ICC supports the migration away from the application of *ex ante* regulation to general competition law after a truly competitive marketplace for basic telecommunications exists. Broadband services can be delivered with a variety of technologies, and business users will benefit from competition at all levels; infrastructure, technologies and services.

- Limiting regulation of emerging technologies and services:

  Allowing emerging technologies and services offered in a competitive marketplace to flourish through innovation requires regulatory restraint. New technologies and services offered in a competitive marketplace should only be subject to general competition law to address specific market failures, not *ex ante* regulation.

2. Requirements with which the host country receiving foreign investment must Comply

Essentially the country must generate confidence. Investors must be confident in the durability and potential of their investment in the host country. They will not invest if they do not feel confident in the good management of a country in its resources (natural and/or human), in its potential economic growth and in its market (domestic and/or regional). The resources at stake can be significant for investing companies and these companies need to be assured that their return on investment will materialize, that they will be able to generate the expected/project cash-flows with a reasonable probability. The country needs to comply with a subtle and pervasive set of factors which one could define as "confidence raising" elements. Perceived risks for the investor have to be minimized or else a risk premium is charged by foreign investors in the form of a more expensive equity or financing.

Promoting Innovation and Creativity (IPR Protection)

This section outlines key ICC recommendations to promote innovation and creativity through the protection of intellectual property rights (IPR).

- Governments should adopt policies to foster innovation and creativity on the Internet that include the effective protection of intellectual property rights. For innovators and creative people to offer their work products to others and to release them for public consumption, they must have assurances that their creative processes are sustainable and protected. Otherwise, the societal benefits of their creativity, including local creativity, could be very limited. To promote sustainable innovation and creativity, governments should update copyright protection both in substance (by implementation of WIPO Internet Treaties) and in terms of enforcement mechanisms (by, at a minimum, implementing the terms of the TRIPS Agreement). The goal must be the establishment of a balanced and realistic framework of accountability that respects international norms, provides incentives for increased inter-industry cooperation to deter and respond to infringements, promotes responsible business practices, does not impose unreasonable burdens on intermediaries, and preserves an appropriate role for courts. Any legislation that deals with the applicability of copyright infringement liability rules should examine carefully how these rules apply to all stakeholders in the digital networked environment.

- While intellectual property norms are still largely national or regional, ICT are inherently global. Thus, more than ever, the chain of national intellectual property laws will only be as strong as its weakest link, and the ability to meaningfully enforce rights will be crucial. This will accentuate the need for increased international cooperation. Voluntary codes of conduct, guidelines and contracts may well present a way to supplement national legislation in this endeavour.

- Governments should promptly and faithfully implement the 1996 WIPO Internet Treaties, including appropriate legal frameworks for effective technological protection measures and against circumvention-related activities and devices. Governments should refrain from intervening with the use and deployment of technical protection measures except in the case of market failure or to ensure compliance with industry-agreed standards. They should also permit industry agreements to be implemented.

- Governments should support, and if appropriate, participate in private-public partnerships that permit legal access to content on the Internet, such as the development and deployment of baseline standards for content protection.

- Another measure that would be practical and highly effective is to ensure that differential pricing mechanisms do not hurt or backfire on rights holders seeking to make content legally accessible to markets that are less well developed or with a lower level of demand for high-end content.

- Governments should adopt a flexible and responsive approach to the protection of personal data, including the acceptance of self-regulatory solutions and technological innovations that empower the user, and balance those interests with other public policy objectives, such as the fight against cyber-crime and counterfeiting and piracy. Governments should work to ensure that data protection policy does not impede the legitimate protection of intellectual property rights. This should be achieved through a balanced approach that protects both the rights of content providers and the interests of other stakeholders in the digital-networked environment.

Relevant ICC materials and resources

Telecoms Liberalization – An international business guide for policymakers
http://www.iccwbo.org/home/statements_rules/statements/2004/LIBERAL-final.pdf

ICC statement on Information and Commission Technologies and the Internet for Economic Growth and Social Development signed at ICC 35th World Congress, Marrakech 6-9 June 2004,
http://www.iccwbo.org/home/e_business/ICC%20Statement%20on%20ICTs%20and%20the%20Internet.pdf

Current and emerging intellectual property issues for business - a roadmap for business and policy makers http://www.iccwbo.org/IP_RoadMap/index.asp

Appendix B, D, F and I of Summary report since last report to United Nations Financing for Development (FfD) meeting in April 2003
http://www.iccwbo.org/home/ebitt/FfD%20business%20Initiatives.pdf

Additional relevant materials are available on the ICC website at: http://www.iccwbo.org/

ENABLING COOPERATIVE AND GENDER-EQUITABLE INFORMATION SOCIETIES

By Heike Jensen, WSIS Gender Caucus[1]

The manifold challenges being faced with respect to the current global upheavals and restructuring can only be met in a productive and concerted effort if we commit ourselves to collaboration on the basis of shared norms and values, as expressed by United Nations Secretary-General, Kofi A. Annan in the Millennium Report and as affirmed in the Declaration of Principles of the World Summit on the Information Society (WSIS) in Geneva. Many of the norms and values we uphold presently are not all that new, but are, for instance, already enshrined in the Charter of the United Nations of 1945[2] and the Universal Declaration of Human Rights (UDHR) of 1948[3].

What has developed over time, however, is a threefold gain in knowledge with respect to these norms and values. Firstly, they have been rearticulated to better address the lived realities of people and constituencies who used to be *de facto* excluded from benefiting from them. Secondly and concurrently, these norms and values have been reconceptualized in view of new global developments such as the dawn of information societies and the opportunities and challenges provided by the new information and communication technologies (ICTs) for fulfilling and safeguarding central human rights provisions such as equality, self-expression, privacy, security and development. Thirdly, it has become glaringly obvious that the nuanced and timely rearticulation of these norms and values will not lead to substantial change in the direction of gender equality, non-discrimination and sustainable development if the stakeholder groups only utilize this rearticulation to the limited extent that until now has been visible to guide their concrete actions.

To truly build sustainable information societies that merit the name, it is necessary to profit from this threefold increase in knowledge and let it guide our actions. This paper attempts to explain in more detail the knowledge gained with respect to gender in these respects. And I will point out important ramifications of this knowledge for the different stakeholders and their roles and responsibilities in encouraging effective and sustainable use of ICTs for promoting development. The focus is not on providing a long list of tasks that each stakeholder group needs to carry out[4], but on clarifying the root norms, values, concepts and strategies to empower all stakeholder groups to identify crucial areas of intervention.

---

[1] The author wishes to thank Charlie Boyd and Savitri Bisnath for their valuable comments on draft versions of this paper.

[2] UNX.122(73) C613.

[3] A/RES/217 A (III).

[4] For a comprehensive list of tasks for each stakeholder group with respect to gender-equitable media and ICT development, see the Report of the Expert Group Meeting on Participation and Access of Women to the Media, and the Impact of Media on and its Use as an Instrument for the Advancement and Empowerment of Women, held in Beirut, Lebanon, 12-15 November 2002 (Division for the Advancement of Women EGM/MEDIA/2002 REPORT). See also the Agreed Conclusions of the Forty-seventh Session of the Commission on the Status of Women (CSW) on Participation and Access of Women to the Media, and Information and Communication Technologies and their Impact on and Use as an Instrument for the Advancement and Empowerment of Women, held 3-14 March 2003. Available at http://www.un.org/womenwatch/daw/csw/csw47/AC-medialCT-auv.PDF.

Bringing Norms to Life: Mapping the Human Rights of Girls and Women

The articulation of the human rights of girls and women constitutes one of the most successful examples of how abstract norms and values can and need to be brought to life.[5] When the principle of equality between the sexes and the prohibition of discrimination on the basis of sex were enshrined in the United Nations Charter and the UDHR[6], a traditional liberal framework for interpreting human rights was in place that used to tacitly understand human rights violations as actions by state agents in the public realm against politically active men. Violations of human rights of women consequently were hardly registered as such and were rather defined as private matters or as cultural or religious traditions. In contrast, taking the lived realities of girls and women as the starting point, and exploring how and by whom girls and women are hindered from exercising their fundamental rights and freedoms, has decisively shifted and broadened the prevalent understanding of human rights violations.

As codified in the Convention on the Elimination of all Forms of Discrimination against Women, (CEDAW)[7] which constitutes the most comprehensive human rights instrument for girls and women we have to date and to which more than 90 percent of the states of the world are parties[8], human rights violations against women are all forms of discrimination that prevent women's equality with men in all spheres of society, irrespective of whether the discrimination is intentional or unintentional. Following CEDAW, governments have to protect, promote and fulfill girls' and women's human rights in all spheres of society. For one thing, this requires pursuing and punishing any discrimination. For another, this encompasses bringing about their *de facto* equality by any appropriate means, from influencing social norms and countering sexual stereotypes to establishing concrete actions to promote women. To give an example, it is no longer seen as sufficient to legally allow women to study computer science, when in fact only a tiny percentage of women avail themselves of this opportunity. What needs to be countered in such an instance is the informal power networks and gender stereotypes that keep women from studying computer science. Consequently, special initiatives and incentives for women might be required to facilitate their taking up such a field of study.

Building on CEDAW and articulating its provisions to the realities of the 1990s is the Beijing Declaration and Platform for Action (BPfA)[9], adopted at the Fourth World Conference on Women in Beijing in 1995. The BPfA delineates a comprehensive catalog of priorities for bringing about women's equality with men, including the issues of media and ICTs. And it spells out the twofold strategy to bring about gender equality that has since been adopted by many countries of the world and by the United Nations: gender mainstreaming coupled with targeted intervention. Gender mainstreaming requires an exploration of how a given issue, policy or programme (potentially) impacts on women and men[10], or rather on different

---

[5] A good introduction is provided by the International Women's Tribune Centre, Rights of Women: A Guide to the Most Important United Nations Treaties on Women's Human Rights. New York: International Women's Tribune Centre, 1998.

[6] In the preamble and article 1.3 of the UN Charter as well as in the preamble and Article 2 of the UDHR.

[7] A/RES/2263(XXII), adopted by the General Assembly in 1979 and entered into force in 1981.

[8] For an overview of the state parties, see www.un.org/womenwatch/daw/cedaw/states.htm. Note that the USA is the only OECD country among the less than 10 percent of countries of the world that are not parties to CEDAW.

[9] A/CONF.177/20/Rev.1 (96.IV.13).

[10] See, for example, the definition of gender mainstreaming provided in ECOSOC Agreed Conclusions 1997/2.

groups of women and men insofar as other forms of social stratification such as race, ethnicity, class, and age intersect with the one of gender. In other words, gender mainstreaming is a strategy to take into account the lived realities of specific groups of women and men, girls and boys, to move from issues in the abstract to an understanding of how these issues relate to people and their specific places and hierarchies in society. For instance, decisions about the provision of e-health services with regard to sexual education need to take into account who provides formal and informal sexual education and health care, which providers or target groups experience, what kinds of shortcomings or difficulties, and what kinds of services would best be suited to address their needs and problems.

Targeted intervention is the strategy to bring about women's empowerment and gender equality. It builds on the knowledge gleaned through gender mainstreaming, and seeks to impact gender arrangements in the direction of non-discrimination and equality. Thus, targeted intervention in the above example of e-health services concerning sexual education might require different kinds of training for men and women. Yet more often than not, targeted intervention has only taken the form of affirmative action on behalf of girls and women. This has also constituted one of its serious limitations, because gender is a relational construct, and one gender cannot change without the necessary accommodations made by the other gender, which have to be just as carefully enabled. Thus it is insufficient to teach girls and women about their right to sexual self-determination when the corresponding message and values are not simultaneously transmitted to boys and men and when the autonomy of some women is curtailed by economic plight and threats of violence from men.

The Limited Realization of Women's Human Rights and its Negative Impact on Development

From the years of assessment by the Commission for the Elimination of all Forms of Discrimination against Women of the CEDAW state reports, and from the five-year review of Beijing in the year 2000[11] to the current Beijing+10 review process, the limited success and nonlinear development of gender equality undertakings has become obvious. It appears that there is a lack of commitment on the part of great sections of each stakeholder group – from international organizations to ministries to the private sector to civil society groups – to seriously promote and achieve gender equality.[12] Gender mainstreaming, just as any other strategy, is only as effective in preparing the ground for such changes as the commitment, understanding, intellectual rigor and resources of those involved allows it to be. Without a true interest in the mapping of the lived realities of people, their social structures of hierarchies and interdependences, and the proper frameworks and indicators to trace these, gender mainstreaming remains an empty exercise.

Without a true commitment to gender equality, targeted interventions on behalf of girls and women most likely constitute a marginal concern. Consequently, they run the risk of being

---

[11] See the Report of the Secretary-General, Beijing to Beijing+5: Review and Appraisal of the Implementation of the Beijing Platform for Action. New York: United Nations, 2001.

[12] As Joanne Sandler, Deputy Executive Director of UNIFEM, pointed out, gender equality as a norm has become more widespread, but implementation and accountability have lagged behind, so that "action and commitment beyond current levels" are needed for this norm to translate into real changes. See the paper she presented at the UN Economic Commission for Europe (ECE) Regional Preparatory Meeting for the 10-year Review of Implementation of the Beijing Platform for Action, entitled "Beyond Beijing: Partnerships for Gender Equality and Women's Empowerment" (Geneva, 14 December 2004).

short-lived and may involve a loss of investments and resources. They may also be met with resentment and hegemonic resistance. Yet this also means that development itself is endangered, because it is very doubtful that sustainable development can occur as long as the female half of the population by default remains in a politically, economically and socially inferior position and is, hence, more dependent and less able to contribute creativity, visions, values and energy to this formidable task. Development can only be sustainable if individual freedom and human rights, a sufficient material quality of life, social cohesion, stability and cooperation are promoted for all. This is impossible without attention to gender equality and non-discrimination, because gender hierarchies and discrimination constitute rifts which breed exploitation, dependencies, resentment, violence and fear.

Moreover, the prevalent view that gender issues can be addressed on a minor level after the truly major issues have been dealt with[13] is a false premise: gender mainstreaming shows that issues invariably affect men and women of various groups in different ways, and that conceptualizing issues "as such" more often than not constitutes a generalization from men's lives that is inevitably insufficient. This is the case because girls and women make up at least half of world's inhabitants and because gender is a form of social stratification that is practiced the world over and that results in differences between women's and men's lived realities everywhere.

Similarly, the notion that benefits that are first enjoyed by men will inevitably "trickle down" and will eventually benefit women cannot be substantiated historically. Just as with respect to other forms of social stratification that intersect with gender, there is no automatic diffusion of benefits to those at the low end of the hierarchy. This is why development has to be planned and engineered and why gender equality and non-discrimination have to be promoted as integral and central parts, and not merely minor parts of that development. Therefore all stakeholder groups need to achieve in order to create an enabling environment for the effective use of ICTs for promoting development is a deep understanding of the intrinsic connections between gender equality, non-discrimination and sustainable development.

Applying the Principle of Gender Equality to Bring about Development and Sustainable Information Societies

Gender equality needs to be at the center, not at the margins of any development project, including the realization of information societies. Such a goal, moreover, can only be reached in a spirit of solidarity and cooperation, which in fact is the key to bridging all digital divides and to achieving sustainable development in all parts of the world. Hence, an individualist human rights approach constitutes a strong normative starting point, but requires a global worldview and commitment in addition. The WSIS Declaration of Principles attempted to articulate such a worldview and commitment, and the task is now to translate its norms and values into concrete guidelines for action. For finding the way toward enabling "women's empowerment and their full participation on the basis on [sic.] Equality in all spheres of society and in all decision-making processes" with the help of a "gender equality

---

[13] A faulty concept that has quite memorably expressed this view is the Marxist concept of Nebenwiderspruch or "side contradiction" to the class issues accorded central status and mistakenly seen as non-gendered in the classic version of this theory.

perspective" and "ICTs as a tool to that end"[14], we are in the fortunate position to be able to draw on the broad gender-sensitive knowledge base and recommendations that have been produced or collected in the context of WSIS.[15]

With respect to the promotion of an enabling environment for digital development, the starting point would be for all stakeholders to realize that any digital divide has specific ramifications for girls and women and disadvantages them in comparison to boys and men. For example:

- The digital divide between rich and poor disadvantages girls and women because they constitute two thirds of the world's poor, a phenomenon that has become more pronounced and that has been termed the "feminization of poverty".

- The digital divide between urban and rural areas disadvantages girls and women because they constitute the majority of people living in rural areas, particularly in developing countries such as in sub-Saharan Africa.

- The digital divide between formally educated and informally educated people disadvantages girls and women because they have less time and opportunities to receive formal education and to profit from it and build on it throughout their lives. This is an issue ranging from basic literacy to foreign languages to information literacy to technological skills.

Building on this insight of the gender-specific scope and impact of digital divides, it would be crucial to realize and to reaffirm that at issue is not a global "zero-sum-game" in which the genders are in an antagonistic position and the gains of one gender would necessarily translate into the losses of the other. At issue is instead development, in the sense of overcoming the imbalances as well as the current standard, not redistribution on the basis of the current standard. Thus:

- Fighting the feminization of poverty does not mean that more boys and men should experience poverty, but that poverty needs to be eradicated. Globally, this may require fundamental changes in the systems of trade, finance and debt as well as a fairer distribution of profits and risks. Locally and with respect to gender, eradicating poverty can only happen with an understanding of its gendered dimensions, which encompasses land rights and inheritance rights that disadvantage women, wage and career discrimination against women and the higher ratio of

---

[14] Quoted from paragraph 12 of the WSIS Declaration of Principles.
[15] The UN Division for the Advancement of Women (DAW), the International Research and Training Institute for the Advancement of Women (INSTRAW), the UN Inter-Agency Network on Women and Gender Equality and the UN Commission on the Status of Women (CSW) have all concerned themselves with synthesizing gender-sensitive analyses and recommendations for WSIS. Inside the WSIS process, the WSIS Gender Caucus and the NGO Gender Strategies Working Group have worked diligently to further attention to gender issues and commitment to gender equality among all stakeholder groups.
For a brief overview of central gender-focused meetings and the subsequent fate of gender mainstreaming efforts in preparation of the WSIS in Geneva, see Heike Jensen, "Gender and the WSIS Process: War of the Words." In: Visions in Process: World Summit on the Information Society Geneva 2003 - Tunis 2005. Ed. Heinrich Böll Foundation. Berlin 2003: 19-23. (Available at http://www.worldsummit2003.de/download_en/Vision_in_process.pdf.)

unpaid versus paid work that girls and women perform compared to boys and men.[16]

▪ Working towards a better balance between urban and rural areas does not mean that more women have to leave the rural areas or that more men need to return. It involves establishing fair systems of trade and commerce that allow farmers, ranchers and others to make a decent living in a sustainable manner that does not deplete the natural resources. It also requires a fairer distribution of infrastructure provisions between cities and rural areas. From a gender perspective, issues such as the sexual division of labor, the undervaluation of women's labor and production and differing degrees of mobility for men and women need to be overcome.

▪ With respect to formal education, the goal is not to achieve a gender balance by barring more boys and men from receiving education, but to increase everyone's access to and benefits from education throughout the life cycle. On the global level, this issue ties in with the poverty eradication and rebalancing just mentioned. On the local gender level, it requires an abolition of sex role stereotypes that are directly and indirectly related to formal education. In direct relation are those stereotypes that claim girls and women do not need formal education or only formal education in certain fields or up to a certain stage. In indirect relation are the sex role stereotypes that force women into circumstances where they do not profit from formal education or only profit from it to a limited degree, such as confining them to private spheres and informal or unpaid, unskilled labor, or preventing them from contributing to cultural and political life.

Within the framework of a true commitment to tackle global challenges and work towards sustainable development, non-discrimination and gender equality, digitalization and the new ICTs indeed hold great potential, as rightly affirmed by the WSIS Declaration of Principles and the WSIS Civil Society Declaration "Shaping Information Societies for Human Needs".[17] Yet, without such a framework to guide the spread and application of ICTs, even their availability does not necessarily constitute a source of empowerment. Thus it has been found that there is no correlation between the percentage of female Internet users and gender empowerment indices, and that gender empowerment does not necessarily rely on the use of ICTs.[18]

At the same time, many good practice examples have been gathered from all parts of the world that illustrate how ICT projects can empower girls and women, and in particular, girls and women who have experienced multiple forms of discrimination and violations of their human rights. To be sure, these instances at present only provide anecdotal evidence, often from grassroots projects, for the power of ICTs to contribute to sustainable development, non-discrimination and gender equality. But this is exactly why they need to be understood

---

[16] For an excellent overview, see Natasha Primo, Gender Issues in the Information Society. Paris: UNESCO, 2003.

[17] Available at http://www.worldsummit2003.de/download_en/WSIS-CS-Dec-25-Feb-04-en.pdf.

[18] Nancy J. Hafkin, "Some Thoughts on Gender and Telecommunications/ICT Statistics and Indicators." Paper from the ITU World Telecommunication/ICT Indicators Meeting in Geneva, 15-17 January 2003. (ITU BDT document WGGI-2/7-E from the Second Meeting of the Working Group on Gender Issues at ITU Headquarters in Geneva, 7-9 July. Pages 8-10.)

as model projects showing the way for future concerted efforts of all stakeholders. Following are some examples:

- ICT projects have successfully empowered women to rise out of poverty. Famous is the project of Grameen Phones, the first cellular phone network in Bangladesh, set up by Grameen Bank. The Bank has given some of its borrowers the chance to become village phone operators, providing them with phones as in-kind loans, which they could use to resell wireless phone services to their fellow villages.[19]

- E-government and e-governance projects[20] have provided women in rural areas with access to government services and to politicians. Electronic access to services, such as land registration in Andhra Pradesh in India, eliminates the financial and time burdens that rural women face when they have to travel to the agencies, thus mitigating infrastructural drawbacks. Access to politicians and their administrative apparatus, for instance through the electronic discussions with village governance institutions organized by the Indian Self-Employed Women's Association (SEWA)[21], allows previously marginalized constituencies to state their cases and be heard at the appropriate levels of the political apparatus, in turn giving politicians and administrators a clearer idea of these groups of citizens and their concerns. Such instances may lead the way to more transparent, participatory and fruitful e-democracy procedures.

- ICT projects concerned with education have focused on both ICT training itself and ICT use as teaching devices. SchoolNets projects in Africa have followed "training the trainer" models and have, thus, increased women's capabilities of utilizing ICTs for teaching. Additionally, they have also targeted pupils and have provided girls with opportunities to access these technologies.[22]

---

[19] See the report by Don Richardson, Ricardo Ramirez, and Moinul Haq, "Grameen Telecom's Village Phone Programme: A Multi-Media Case Study. Available at www://www.telecommons.com/villagephone/contents.html. See also Nancy Hafkin and Nancy Taggart, Gender, Information Technology and Developing Countries: An Analytical Study. Washington, DC: AED/USAID, 2001. As Kuga Thas, Ramilo and Cinco point out, a crucial requirement that often needs to be added to providing poor women with the ICT training and resources to set up a business is to assure "captured markets" for them, because they will initially lack business networks. Angela M. Kuga Thas, Chat Garcia Ramilo, and Cheekay Cinco, ICT and Gender. Bangkok: UNDP-APDIP, 2005 (forthcoming).

[20] I here use the distinction between e-government, e-governance and e-democracy employed by Martínez and Reilly. The first term refers to the ICT-based modernization of the state, the second to ICT-based improvements of a government's possibilities to identify and handle social needs, and the third one to ICT-enabled forms of strengthened democratic processes. The latter encompasses better possibilities for citizens to access information, to participate as stakeholders and to hold governments accountable. See the excellent study by Juliana Martínez and Katherine Reilly, "Looking Behind the Internet: Empowering Women for Public Policy Advocacy in Central America." UN/INSTRAW Virtual Seminar Series on Gender and ICTs, Seminar Four: ICTs as Tools for Bridging the Gender Digital Divide and Women's Empowerment (2-14 September 2002). Available at www.un-instraw.org/en/docs/gender_and_ict/Martinez.pdf.

[21] For these and other examples, see ICT and Gender by Kuga Thas, Ramilo and Cinco, referenced in full in footnote 35.

[22] See Shafika Isaacs, "IT's Hot for Girls! ICTs as an Instrument in Advancing Girls' and Women's Capabilities in School Education in Africa." UN DAW Expert Group Meeting on Information and Communication Technologies and their Impact on and Use as an Instrument for the Advancement and Empowerment of

These few examples illustrate that overcoming gender digital divides can indeed serve the purposes of addressing concurrent forms of discrimination and of contributing to a better fulfillment of the human rights of girls and women. In order to allow such projects to contribute to sustainable development more broadly, we need to move from understanding examples such as these as marginal aid initiatives for underprivileged fringe groups to turning them into paradigmatic instances that show ways towards development in general and digital development in particular. This shift is needed on the part of civil society no less than on the part of private enterprises, governments and international organizations.

What marginalizes initiatives such as these is a lack of collaboration within the larger social settings in which they occur, coupled with a lack of imagination and experimentation in these settings to explore how these initiatives could point the way towards more just and productive relationships on a much broader scale. Concurrently, a similar absence of imagination and will to change can be diagnosed on the supra-levels, from which initiatives such as these only appear as add-ons or special measures compared with a huge majority of programmes that bolster the exact same hegemonic structures against which these fringe initiatives may then exert their minimal influence. Only if all stakeholders agree on using their power and expertise to promote gender equality and non-discrimination as integral to promoting development can a truly concerted effort materialize. What does such a commitment entail for the different stakeholders with respect to ICTs?

Roles and Responsibilities of the Different Stakeholders

While many of the enabling factors for ICT use for gender equality and sustainable development have been identified[23], the shaping of information societies is an ongoing endeavour that will continuously draw on innovative approaches, vision, energy, commitment and skills of all involved. The following points, hence, are only to be taken as rough guidelines and are not meant to be exhaustive. Ensuing from the argument developed so far, they build on the strategies of gender mainstreaming, targeted intervention and women's empowerment for bringing about sustainable development with the help of ICTs. The United Nations, other international organizations and donors are then called upon to facilitate this development accordingly. All stakeholder groups need to ascertain that they are represented by women and men of equal numbers and that they do justice to the diversity of the people that are affected by their actions.

Governments and regulatory authorities need to devise ICT policy and regulatory frameworks that enable gender equality.[24] Central tasks are to bring about universal access and universal service for both women and men. This involves gender-sensitive infrastructure

---

Women. Seoul, Republic of Korea, 11-14 November 2002 (EGM/ICT/2002/EP.7, dated 5 November 2002). Pages 10-11.

[23] For comprehensive lists, see the documents cited in footnote 20.

[24] For an excellent overview of the different kinds of ICT policy issues and their gender aspects, see Nancy Hafkin, "Gender Issues in ICT Policy in Developing Countries: An Overview." UN DAW Expert Group Meeting on Information and Communication Technologies and their Impact on and Use as an Instrument for the Advancement and Empowerment of Women. Seoul, Republic of Korea, 11-14 November 2002 (EGM/ICT/2002/EP.1, dated 25 October 2002). As the basis for her overview, see Sonia Nunes Jorge, Gender Perspectives in Telecommunications Policy: A Curriculum Proposal. Geneva: ITU, 2000 (available at www.itu.int/ITU-D/gender/projects/GenderCurriculum.pdf). See also the Gender-Aware Guidelines for Policy-making and Regulatory Agencies developed by Jorge for the International Telecommunications Union (ITU) BDT Task Force on Gender Issues (TFGI-4/5 E, July 2001).

development and access point planning. It also involves regulatory frameworks that make the technology affordable and useful, for answering both practical gender needs that arise from traditional responsibilities of men and women and strategic gender interests that are related to furthering equality between the genders.[25] Licensing criteria need to reflect these considerations, and they should also promote women-owned companies and companies with women in high-ranking positions.

The private sector is concurrently called upon to abolish labor segmentation, occupational segregation and wage disparities arising from discrimination against women. The goals are that women are no longer severely underrepresented at the ownership and the decision-making levels, that they no longer earn less money as a group as well as at each occupational level for comparable work, and no longer hold the most insecure and exploitative jobs. The trend that new ICT industries and ICT-related forms of employment exploit these gender imbalances and hierarchies instead of working to overcome them needs to be reversed. Companies should also bring their business activities in line with larger social responsibilities towards workers, communities and the environment, and not just their philanthropic activities.

All professionals and individuals providing media and ICT content, and exercising their right to communicate through media and ICTs should let themselves be guided by voluntary codes upholding values such as gender equality, non-discrimination and respect for all human beings. This also requires respect for diverse voices and their input, and voluntary self-constraint on the part of those whose perspectives have dominated and drowned out or marginalized other constituencies. Women's views and concerns, and particularly those that have been most marginalized and discriminated against on account of racial, ethnic, religious, geographic, linguistic, age and other hierarchies and human rights violations, need to be heard and need to have an impact on the public sphere and on political decisions.

Useful media and ICT content as well as networking opportunities need to be provided by and for the respective constituencies, answering the needs for local articulations, diverse languages and non-text-based ICT interfaces. Media forms such as public media and community media, which may in the short run be best accessible for these constituencies, have to be promoted, for example by low licensing fees assigned on a sliding scale and by consciously integrating new and old ICTs and allowing them to synergize effectively. The goal is to close digital divides in order to facilitate private and public lives and communities enriched by a plurality of viewpoints, experiences and forms of knowledge, and to abolish knowledge and information as hegemonic tools. Correspondingly, a similar breadth of input needs to characterize not only the content and networks but also the technology itself. In particular, women need to be empowered to create the technology that best answers their needs, and they also need to be empowered to shape, as equal partners with men, the societies in which the technologies are to be integrated.

Civil society needs to promote the above goals in all contexts, be it in the shape of consumer advocacy groups, non-profit networks, unions and other workers' rights groups, partners in development projects as well as in global governance and e-democracy contexts. Civil society

---

[25] For more on practical gender needs and strategic gender interests, see ICT and Gender by Kuga Thas, Ramilo and Cinco, cited in full in footnote 21.

and all other stakeholders are needed to help monitor and assess all activities and their own contributions towards gender-equality, non-discrimination and sustainable development, so that adaptations can be made if need be. To enable such assessments, data need to be gathered that are meaningful in these respects, most notably data disaggregated by sex and any other form of social stratification that has a significant impact in each specific context. Quantitative data will have to be augmented by qualitative information to enable an understanding of a situation and its larger context.[26]

To enable an effective, widespread and sustainable use of ICTs for development, a strong commitment on the part of all stakeholders is required to let themselves be guided by shared norms and values. Taking into account that discrimination and human rights violations are at the root of the digital divides and other forms of uneven and unsustainable development, and that it is girls and women who are most adversely affected by these conditions, the decisive norms and values to follow toward sustainable development are the ones of gender equality, non-discrimination and the fulfillment of the human rights of all. On the basis of a shared commitment to these norms and values, all stakeholder groups need to set themselves targets and devise strategies to bring these norms and values to life, to empower girls and women as central agents of development in equal partnership with men. Starting from the lived realities of different groups of men and women, mainstreaming a gender equality perspective and devising targeted actions for women and men, girls and boys, will open the way. Within this enabling framework, ICTs can play an important role, and all stakeholder groups need to make sure that their ICT endeavours synergize to meet the challenge of creating cooperative and gender-equitable information societies.

---

[26] Of the points mentioned in this section, the WSIS Gender Caucus highlights the following six key recommendations: Gender must be a fundamental principle for action. Equitable participation in decisions shaping the Information Society. New and old ICTs in a multimodal approach. Designing ICTs to serve people. Empowerment for full participation. Research analysis and evaluation to guide action. For more information, visit http://www.genderwsis.org.

Section 2

Role of Stakeholders – Enabling Environment

LEVERAGING ICT FOR GOOD GOVERNANCE: VISION, ACTION AND THE ITALIAN EXPERIENCE

By Lucio Stanca, Ministry for Innovation and Technologies, Italy

During the last decades of the 20th century, the world went through unprecedented political and social changes that have impacted the lives of millions of citizens. Globalization, powered by the revolution in information and communication technologies (ICT), has marked these changes by rapidly propagating positive effects and by giving the international community a new sense of interdependence.

Nowadays, new technologies offer developing countries a unique opportunity to leapfrog into the future, to speed up their economic and social development and to benefit from the global information network.

Governments are confronted with a new reality and changed imperatives as a result of the diffusion of ICT throughout the world and within their nations as well as the associated change in expectations for the future. Governments respond to these new challenges and opportunities by actively harnessing and managing ICT, which demands a fundamental change in the way the state traditionally functions internally and how it interacts with its citizenry.

While highlighting the broad potential of ICT as an enabling tool in the service of development and the greater integration of developing countries in our globalized society, the international community has furthermore recognized the critical value of ICT in the area of public administration and governance

The World Summit on the Information Society (WSIS), during its first phase in Geneva, adopted a Declaration of Principles on December 12, 2003, in which member states affirmed, in Article 38: *"An enabling environment at national and international level is essential for the Information Society. ICT should be used as an important tool for good governance"*.

Furthermore, the WSIS Plan of Action, recognizing the importance of ICT as an enabling factor of new forms of governance, invites Governments to formulate national strategies, which include e-government strategies, to make public administration more transparent, efficient and democratic with the ultimate goal of establishing a dynamic information society.

ICTs are enabling tools but they are not a solution in and of themselves. They are neutral instruments that are as good or bad as the ideas they support. In applying ICT to government activities and processes and in addressing some of the preconditions for their success, benefits will be distributed to and enjoyed by other sectors seeking to apply ICT. The government can lead by example and, in acting as a champion, demonstrate the importance that it places on ICT as a fundamental tool for development.

Fostering Innovation

Innovation for Citizens

The fundamental challenge of ICT for development is to devise means to ensure that virtually all citizens have access to these technologies. As information is increasingly codified in digital forms, new skills are needed to operate the technology, to search for, organize and manage information and to use it to solve problems and create new knowledge and cultural products.

Information literacy aims to develop both critical understanding and active participation. It enables people to interpret and make informed judgments as users of information sources; it also enables them to become producers of information in their own right, and thereby to become more empowered participants in their societies. Digital media – and particularly the Internet – significantly increase the potential for active participation. Information literacy is part of the basic entitlement of every citizen to freedom of expression and the right to information. It is instrumental in building and sustaining democracy.

Internet usage is increasing across all socio-economic sectors, but access gaps – between men and women, employed and unemployed, high and low-incomes, highly educated and less educated, old and young – have grown in absolute terms over the last years. Digital exclusion is frequently cumulative, affecting various kinds of socially disadvantaged groups.

In Italy, great efforts have been made, especially in recent years, to accelerate the establishment of a sustainable and inclusive information society. The governmental policy to foster digital inclusion in the education system has proved to be effective: in 2004, Italy had 1 PC for every 11 students. Broadband access in schools has increased, during the same time-frame, from 20% of the total number of schools to the current 56%. In addition, the government has promoted policies to reduce digital exclusion by promoting bonuses for the purchase of PCs to disadvantaged families; information acclimatization of elderly people and in general for the distribution of broadband access to families, just to cite a few. The latter, in particular, has been significant: Italy has the second highest Internet growth rate in Europe (10% in the last 12 months) following Germany.

Innovation for Businesses

Electronic government could become a driving force in the implementation of national e-strategies, including online services offered by governments, e-business and e-payment operations undertaken through the public procurement process. There is an international common understanding of the importance of ICT for enhancing the competitiveness of small and medium-sized enterprises (SMEs). Many SMEs, even in developing countries, have Internet access and use it to communicate with suppliers and customers, to search for business information and to showcase their products.

In this field Italy has been particularly active. In 2004, 1,500,000 digital signatures have been attributed to an equivalent number of firms and a fund of 100 million euros for joint venture capital has been established in order to promote high-tech firms in the South of Italy, in the broader context of regional framework programmes. From a total budget of 690 million euros, 9395 firms received funding for e-commerce initiatives. These examples represent just a few of the overall national policy for the implementation of ICT in a competitive business sector.

Innovation for Public Administration

Governments are confronted with a new reality and changed imperatives as a result of the diffusion of ICT throughout the world and within their nations, and due to the associated change in expectations for the future. Governments must respond to these new challenges and opportunities by actively harnessing and managing ICT, which demands a fundamental change in the way the state traditionally functions internally and how it interacts with its citizenry, particularly in its dual function of meeting basic human needs and alleviating poverty.

It is a process that makes ICT a servant of the government's own effectiveness and efficiency as well as, via relevant government activities, a servant of good governance. Put differently, it is technology-enabled transformation of government services wrapped around customer/citizen's needs rather than administrative convenience and around transformation rather than automation.

In Italy, there are 10 million users of public administration online services every year. The government promoted 132 projects, which (for a total of 73 million euros) have fostered the involvement of citizens in public decision-making processes. Innovative public services have spurred over the Internet in recent years and many public agencies have digitalized their functions, internally and externally. Digital public administration protocols have increased from 6% of the total number of public protocols in 2002 to 83% in 2004. The importance of this fundamental change in the Italian public administration has been greatly appreciated by citizens as well as by civil servants.

The Role of Developed Countries in Bridging the Digital Divide: the Contribution of the Government of Italy

Governments of developed countries should contribute to ICT promotion in developing countries by transferring technology and capabilities, facilitating the creation of effective partnerships among all stakeholders and providing financial support for "added value" projects and initiatives. Bridging the digital divide requires that developing countries adopt concrete measures aimed at creating a free ICT market, thus attracting the necessary internal and foreign investments needed to develop their ICT infrastructure. Developed countries on their part need to assist with technology transfer, technical assistance and training. Financial support is therefore only one aspect of a wider range of measures that are needed.

Italy is strongly committed to provide the necessary assistance for specific projects, based on agreed objectives, particularly when there exists the potential for the beneficiary country to play a central role in the implementation process. In fact, the idea of assisting developing countries and countries with economies in transition in their efforts to implement e-government projects and services to foster transparency, efficiency and effectiveness in their governance systems started in 2001. In July, during the G8 Summit of Genoa, Heads of State and Governments approved an Action Plan to bridge the digital divide between developed and developing countries, thus initiating a promising process to increase access to the benefits of the Information Society through the widespread use of information and communication technologies. The Action Plan recognizes e-government as a critical factor to strengthen democracy and the rule of law, hence empowering citizens and improving efficiency in public service delivery.

On this occasion, Italy had announced for the first time its intention to realize e-government projects in developing and transition countries. A new priority for Italian Development Cooperation emerged: e-Government for Development.

In fact, the e-Government for Development Initiative is fully integrated into Italian Development Cooperation activities and its broad guidelines, in close collaboration with the Ministry of Foreign Affairs, are in line with European Union's and United Nations' policies. Due to the specific technical nature of the Initiative, the latter is expressly suited for the Ministry of Innovation and Technologies' mandate.

The Initiative has been formally launched at the two day International Conference on e-Government for Development, held in Palermo, Italy, on April 10th and 11th, 2002. The Conference, organized in collaboration with the United Nations Department for Economic and Social Affairs, witnessed the participation of 90 countries and 700 delegates. The Initiative was strongly welcomed, in particular by Albania, Jordan, Mozambique, Nigeria and Tunisia. On this occasion, the Italian Government stipulated essential agreements with the United Nations and the World Bank through the United Nations Department for Economic and Social Affairs and the Development Gateway Foundation respectively.

The following G8 summits of Kananaskis (June 2002), Evian (June 2003) and Sea Island (June 2004) confirmed Italy's role as a leading actor on global scale of this innovative form of international development cooperation to promote good governance through the use ICT for development.

As a result, the government of Italy stipulated Cooperation agreements, at the international and regional level, with the Inter-American Development Bank and the United Nations Development Programme.

The Initiative on e-Government for Development

The Initiative is an innovative development cooperation methodology aiming at the dissemination of e-government in developing countries and in countries with economies in transition through design and implementation of operative, result oriented and measurable projects.

The Initiative sets a series of ambitious goals: to contribute to economic growth and social development by means of a factual collaboration with international organizations on the basis of the general principles of good governance such as transparency, concreteness and co-sharing criteria in public administration activities.

The Government of Italy is committed to fulfill these goals through an innovative programme composed of attainable and measurable targets, which include a vast number of intermediate objectives, the realization of which builds the necessary basis for the overall success of each individual project.

In fact, an e-government for development project is not merely a reproduction of an abstract technological model meant to meet the needs of a given country. Rather, it is an application to redesign operational modalities of the public administration in order to enhance its overall transparency, efficiency and effectiveness. For this reason the project necessarily has to be participatory. The technical unit fully adopted this approach by working closely with representatives from developing countries and by putting to the fore comparable and measurable models of e-government implemented in Italy and elsewhere.

The logic underlying this initiative is that information will be transmitted between governments: the Italian Government transfers the experience of Italian Public Administration bodies to the beneficiaries. This modality ensures the sharing of the knowledge heritage not currently available on the market.

The innovative form of development cooperation demanded a long period of divulgation and consolidation of principles and models with regards to the potential beneficiaries and the international community at large. It is only with the support of a systemic approach that governments are able to spread the competences and create favourable pre-conditions for e-government. Having this in mind, the technical unit on e-Government for Development has dedicated part of its efforts to create a trusted framework for action, to build a culture of cooperation, to participate in various international events and to build partnerships and promising alliances.

Diplomatic action has been undertaken by the Presidency of the council of ministers, the various general directorates in the Ministry of Foreign Affairs concerned with e-government and the worldwide network of Italian embassies.

Main Achievements

Sixteen projects in 11 countries have been established, two of which, the Government Electronic Network in Iraq and Mozambique are already operative. Leaders of these respective countries have agreed to be part of the initiative, confirming the strategic importance of e-government in the process of state reform, growth and socio-economic development.

A promising collaboration has also begun within the Italian Public Administration, involving its relevant bodies in development cooperation projects. These bodies are: the Italian Institute of Statistics, the Accounting Department and the Land Management Agency.

The Projects

Adopting the principles and recognizing the immense opportunities provided by e-government does not imply underestimating the complexity, multidisciplinary and criticalness in transforming these principles into factual projects. First, technological aspects need to be addressed: selecting applications, integrating different information systems, defining standards and awareness of the varying nature of information and communication technologies.

Secondly, financial and economic aspects need to be considered: e-government applications must be supported by an economic plan that entails costing, savings, financial resources and an evaluation in real terms of the benefits attainable.

Ultimately, e-government means creating a good, modern administration and introducing innovations that simplify procedures and raise efficiency, transparency and effectiveness. As a result, e-government entails modifying the processes of administrative regulation. The methodology adopted by the e-Government Unit relies on the productive partnerships with Italian Public Administration bodies, which are experienced in the use of e-government applications.

In implementing the e-Government for Development Initiative, having taken into consideration the criteria described above, the Government of Italy has realized a number of promising results. For instance, the collaboration with the Government of Iraq started with a project implying technical and financial assistance for the establishment of a Government Electronic Network for the Iraqi Public Administration, a fundamental pre-requisite for the functioning of the modern central government. By October 2004, activities had started in Iraq with the testing of a technological solution and subsequently the training of personnel in Italy.

In the African region, the Gov Net Project in Mozambique started in January 2004 when the Technical Unit and the United Nations Department of Economic and Social Affairs jointly drafted the first proposal of a governmental intranet. On December 11th 2003, in Geneva, during the World Summit on the Information Society, the Mozambican Minister for Science and Technology and the Italian Minister for Innovation and Technologies together with the CEO of the Development Gateway Foundation signed an agreement for the realization of the government network. The project, now fully operational, is in line with the WSIS spirit with regards to the use of ICT to foster transparency and efficiency in Public Administration. Upon the project platform an important application has also been initiated: the electronic cadastre. This application will take advantage of the government's intranet and aims at the conversion of all paper information related to land use rights into digital forms. A national e-accounting project and a second project in conjunction with the Italian Institute of Statistics (ISTAT) on statistics and demographics in Nigeria have been initiated.

Additional e-government projects have been negotiated and activated in the Latin American and the Caribbean region, ranging from e-payments in Panama to the support for the establishment of an e-Taxation System, just to cite examples. The e-Government for Development Initiative has also been involved in supporting Eastern European countries, such as Macedonia and Albania, in the realization of e-government projects.

In the Middle East Region, the Initiative is involved in the implementation of two projects in Jordan: a project for the establishment of an e-procurement system and a National e-accounting System.

Conclusion

In the context of the WSIS Plan of Action, Italy is committed to the realization of e-government for development projects in developing and transition countries. The Ministry of Innovation and Technologies, through its Technical Unit on e-Government, has developed national e-government services in the various areas of competence mentioned before. In article 15, sub-comma c) the WSIS Plan on Action clearly states that governments should "support international cooperation initiatives in the field of e-Government in order to enhance transparency, accountability and efficiency at all levels of governments". Italy is in line with this objective and has raised awareness of numerous countries that formally demonstrated their interest in being part of the e-Government for Development Initiative. Moreover, in the process of implementing e-government services and applications on an international scale, Italy has created a network of partnerships with different international organizations experienced in international cooperation activities in the field of e-government. Due to the complexity of realizing e-government services in certain contexts and in particular where an enabling environment for the Information Society is still in an embryonic form, it is all the more important to build a more concrete and effective cooperation among all stakeholders.

LOWERING THE 'AFFORDABILITY LINE' TO ACHIEVE TRUE MASS MARKET PENETRATION

By Veli Sundbäck, NOKIA

Enabling half the world's population with access is a noble ambition. However, various barriers pose unfortunate – but addressable – threats. A more enabling environment is needed. This article explains why we need more active collaboration from committed and informed stakeholders.

Just over a year ago, at the first World Summit on the Information Society in Geneva, a commitment was made to build a people-centered and inclusive information society. It was agreed that access to information enables individuals, communities and societies to achieve their full potential, and in doing so, promotes sustainable development and higher quality of life. It is a challenging goal but an achievable one – to provide half the world's population, four billion people, with access by 2015.

It is clear that the grand objective will be achieved through a mix of technologies, each with its own virtues and challenges. This paper focuses on the role of mobile communications as the most cost-effective way to meet this objective.

There are significant logistical and economic problems involved with trying to hard-wire vast areas or spread this capability via satellites. These concerns are countered by the ability of proven and cost-efficient mobile networks to enable communications and information access via affordable personal mobile devices.

While the first services deployed to first time users are basic voice and SMS, this is only the beginning of what a mobile solution can be. Internet Protocol (IP) convergence in mobility is rapidly increasing the power of mobile devices. As this becomes more affordable, the advantages of data service, multimedia and Internet access will be possible in even the most remote parts of the world. As appealing a solution as mobile communications may be, its potential is hampered by several legacy factors. Today, in many countries there are no open and competitive markets. Custom duties keep mobile device prices out of the reach of too many people. There is too much of a tax burden placed on mobile devices and services. Interconnection charges are too high.

Overcoming Barriers

Clearly many stakeholders are needed to address the still-existing barriers and many other stakeholders will benefit from a more enabling environment. It is only by aligning these interests that progress will be made. What does this mean to all the stakeholders? They need to be committed to the noble ambition of a people-centered, inclusive society. On the government side this means being committed to change. On the regulatory side, this means being committed to competitive markets. On the private sector side, this means committing people, time and money to developing the appropriate technology, infrastructure and service offerings.

All stakeholders also need to be competent, in the sense that they are fully aware of all the dynamics of making the necessary changes. Governments have to understand the long-term socio-economic benefits. Regulators have to understand the ways to create and control open markets. The private sector has to understand the economic returns possible from investing in new market growth.

Finally, it takes collaboration, with all the stakeholders helping each other in creating a common understanding and pursuing a common goal.

New Learning about the 'Affordability Line'

The 'affordability line' is a function of disposable income and the total cost of ownership of a mobile device (the device itself plus the running costs). Lowering the total cost makes mobility affordable to people with lower disposal incomes. The impact is exponential: with every dollar saved in total cost, the market expands rapidly.

Think of a pyramid. The most affluent people are at the top peak. As we move down to lower levels of affluence, there are with each step down far more people. This dynamic is essential to the economic viability of widespread mobile communications. Mobile infrastructure and devices can be made more cost-efficient and operators can profit from lower average revenue per user (ARPU) when the underlying technology is geared for a mass market.

But costs continue to be higher than needed in many markets because of policies of regulators, tax authorities and operators. To better understand the impact of this, Nokia recently commissioned an internal study that quantifies the role of an 'enabling environment' in mobile penetration.

The result is 'The Affordability Line', a comprehensive review of 37 middle and lower income nations, analysed across 17 variables related to the availability of affordable terminals, the operator business model and the regulatory environment. The study looks at countries in Latin America, Africa, Middle East and North Africa, Asia, and Europe.

This study found that while the levels of personal income and overall economic development are the crucial drivers for mobile penetration, individual governments can initiate policy changes that allow mobile telecommunications to thrive within the boundaries of overall national wealth. Since telecommunications is accepted as being one of the main drivers in the development of national wealth, such initiatives can only create a cycle of mutual benefit.

The study investigated the factors affecting mobile penetration rates in emerging markets. Some possible barriers, which affect mobile penetration rates, that were examined in the study included the income levels, the availability of credit, tax and duty levels, call and SMS tariff rates, prepaid refill affordability and ease of access, interconnection costs, the availability of calling party pay schemes, population coverage, regulations and the state of market liberalization.

The study found that approximately 80% of the differences in penetration rate could be attributed to differences in average personal income levels between countries. This is intuitively clear: the more purchasing power individuals have, the more likely they are to have the possibility of entering the mobile telecommunications market as consumers. The study then factored out the effect of differences in average personal income levels between nations. The findings of the study suggest that countries, irrespective of income, can enjoy higher mobile penetration if barriers are lowered.

Regional Differences

Clear regional differences emerged from the study. The East and South-East Asian regions showed the highest penetration rates in relation to private consumption levels per head, followed by the CIS/ Eastern Europe, Latin America and the MENA region.

Within each region, certain 'star performer' countries showed much higher penetration rates in relation to private consumption levels per head than the average for the region, showing that regional differences may be resolved by the introduction of telecommunications friendly policies.

When looking for possible reasons for the success of the East and South East Asian regions, for example, it was found that many countries in this region have systematically favourable conditions and policies for mobile telecommunications expansion in place compared to other regions. These include specific issues such as: low custom duties on mobile handsets; reasonable taxation on mobile handsets and services; fair interconnection charges to enable affordable tariffs; encouraging conditions to increase coverage; healthy competition; and existence of independent regulator.

South Asia had the lowest current penetration rates in relation to private consumption per head despite having lower average tariff levels than any other region. The problem in South Asia, other than its low rate of urbanization, seems to be its limited calling party pay scheme availability, low population coverage by networks, a lack of competition and foreign direct investment restrictions. Countries in the region have also only recently begun to reduce customs rates. India has experienced an enormous growth in penetration since putting through reforms aimed at reducing many of these barriers.

Success Factors

The study then looked at common factors that might link the success of the nations showing the highest penetration rates relative to private consumption per head in each of the regions. The star performers in each region were the Philippines in East and South East Asia, Bolivia in Latin America, Kenya in Sub Saharan Africa, India in South Asia, Ukraine in CIS/Eastern Europe and Morocco in MENA.

The study found that the star performers consistently had lower than average call tariff rates than their region. They also showed lower than average minimum prepaid refill levels and a higher availability of e-refills than was normal for their region. Star performers all contained an average or greater than average number of network operators. They generally had lower levels of customs duties, lower absolute service tax levels and higher population coverage levels than the regional average. Bolivia, Ukraine and Morocco all allowed higher than average permitted FDI levels, whilst India had greater access levels to calling party pay schemes than its neighbors. The evidence clearly indicates that lower barriers do result in higher mobile penetration rates.

Star performer countries were all found to have proactive policies to support the development of telecommunications. For instance, Kenya has identified ICT as one of the five sectors it hopes will revitalize the economy.

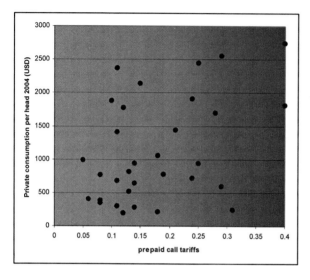

Figure 1: Wide variation in cost of ownership

When markets analysed in the study were plotted on an axis that compares private consumption versus prepaid call tariffs in US$, we see that there is a wide spread of tariff levels, and that tariffs are high in many low income countries (see Figure 1).

The Road to Development

Conditions for mobile expansion are unique in every country. It is not possible to pinpoint one universal policy change that would enable extraordinary growth in mobile communications. At the same time, the research proves that the overall level of market entry barriers does influence the rate of mobile penetration. Removing such barriers has a clear positive impact. The specific issues to consider when designing policies could include:

- How to bring down the price of mobile calls and SMS messages? The study shows that for optimal conditions to exist, most emerging market regions need to substantially reduce tariff levels in order for East and South East Asian levels of penetration to be achieved worldwide.

- How to bring down the overall tax and import duty burden on telecommunications equipment? Import duties should preferably be abolished in accordance to ITA recommendations.

- How to provide access to mobile terminal financing and affordable prepaid payments in consumer segments with low disposable incomes?

Furthermore, it is essential that a country has access to affordable, long term capital to enable it to invest at the realistic return and repayment conditions required in establishing and operating mobile telecommunications at optimal social and economic benefit levels. Thus, especially in countries that lack sufficient domestic capital, the opening of the telecommunications sector for foreign direct investment is important. It is also relevant that national policy favors the creation of a strong and independent regulator that guards the interests of the end consumer. For instance, these factors may be the key to bringing East and South East Asian levels tariff levels down to those existing in Latin America.

Huge Mass Market Potential

The study revealed that some 700 million people are today trapped below the 'affordability line' due to regulatory policies, taxation, and the resulting high total cost of ownership. This huge gap was identified by looking at what caused one of the most outstanding successes in lowering the 'affordability line'. This happened in the Philippines where an appropriate balance has been struck between terminal affordability, strong operator business models and a favourable regulatory environment.

The study explored what would happen if other markets reached the same levels of penetration – by addressing the underlying inhibiting factors. For instance, Nokia estimates that if all the other markets studied matched the success in the Philippines, some 700 million people would be able to afford mobility. Many markets in the study have achieved less than 40% penetration, when levels of 50-70% could be possible if addressable inhibitors were changed.

New technology, once deployed, dramatically increases the efficiency of networks and lowers the cost of subscriber maintenance. For instance, new and more efficient ways of transmitting voice communications enable operators to derive more capacity from the same infrastructure.

Micro prepaid makes it cost-effective for operators to gear their prepaid offerings to people who have a very slow cash flow. These users need to buy in very small increments, which cannot effectively be done through traditional prepaid scratch card methods. Enabling technology now gives operators a cost-effective way to service these low value transactions electronically. Users go to a local shop and by low-denomination top-ups, the vendor uses a mobile device to authorize the purchase, the user receives his top-up automatically. The results: minimal cost to the operator and a viable way to regularly buy mobile access for the user.

Commitment, Competence and Collaboration

Our mutual goal is a noble one: bringing access to billions of people who today have none. Through this action, we will create an inclusive information society that breaks down the current digital divide, and will enable richer lives and build stronger countries in terms of their socio-economic development. Additionally, we will take significant steps toward connecting people to essential information, a need highly underscored by the recent tsunami disaster. Imagine the difference in human cost if millions of mobile devices had been able to trigger timely evacuation warnings by SMS.

Clearly, the key issue is the 'affordability line' and the barriers to lowering it that remain in place today. Governments would do well to rethink how they generate revenues from customs duties and device/service taxation. Regulators could make great advances by opening up markets to lower costs through healthy competition and by lowering the costs of services and interconnection. The private sector can implement the tools that drive low total cost of ownership for subscribers.

Markets that have lowered the 'affordability line' have seen the positive results in every respect. The growth has been phenomenal and while we previously estimated that the two billionth subscriber would come on board in 2008, now we can confidently say this will happen in 2006. The upside potential is there for all stakeholders. A shared spirit of commitment, competence and collaboration will turn this potential into reality.

PRIVATE SECTOR ROLE IN DIGITAL CAPACITY-BUILDING

By Carlo E. Ottaviani, STMicroelectronics Foundation

In 2001, at the beginning of our collaboration with the United Nations ICT Task Force, Pasquale Pistorio, CEO of STMicroelectronics, proposed an initiative, "The Digital Unify", which we would like to reiterate here.

The initiative is based on the firm belief that, even though contributing to building infrastructure and provide Internet access is essential for overcoming the technological gap between the most advanced nations and the developing world, it is equally important that people are able to use the technology, understand its importance, and recognize the benefits it has to offer. It emphasizes the importance of education and training as vital tools for offering access to modern means of communication and information, and through them, to the immense multiplying effect of modern technology on human endeavour. Thousands of private enterprises throughout the world possess the know-how and the resources, and therefore could – and should – invest in training, tutoring and education.

The initiative proposed that medium to large corporations – namely firms with over 250 employees – should voluntarily donate up to 0.1% of their annual revenues and up to 0.1% of their employees' working hours to this cause. Such resources could be utilized for educational purposes, for the most part directly by the companies who have donated them, in agreement with local authorities, which could provide some logistical support.

While the amount donated by private enterprises would vary each year according to the actual financial performance of the corporations involved, the contribution of human resources – which, in our opinion, is the most innovative part of the proposal – even though not necessarily cheaper, would surely be less subject to market conditions and business fluctuations. It would also have the invaluable advantage of helping create a sense of belonging and team spirit among employees of participating enterprises.

Private Sector Role

Through the initiative, sponsored and coordinated by STMicroelectronics Foundation, we have begun working in this direction: we have launched an IT literacy programme in some of the countries where we operate, with particular focus on Morocco, Malaysia, Tunisia and India, and we aim to reach out to at least one million people in the next ten years. We have chosen to concentrate on countries where STMicroelectronics has a strong presence, where we feel we can and should contribute to the well-being of communities, and where there is a strong demand for this type of educational initiative.

Upon request of the Foundation, a group from the IT department at ST in Italy and ST University has created an introductory level course "Informatics and Computer Basics" (ICB) which is offered in Italian, French, English, and Hindi and is currently being translated into Arabic. The programme was launched in 2004, after an initial debugging phase in which we delivered the course to ST employees and family members in the countries mentioned above as well as in Italy and Malta, and we also began setting up external labs and cascading the programme to the local community.

The programme operates via a "cascading" process: volunteer ST staff cascade the "Train the trainer" course to external trainers who then cascade the computer literacy course to the local community. In some cases, ST staff will oversee initial cascading or even deliver a certain number of ICB courses per year. ST Foundation will set up a computer lab with Internet connections at predetermined locations where the courses will take place. To establish where to set up such labs, we identify and work closely with local partners who want to join in the implementation of the programme. ST Foundation contributes the lab equipment, organizes and runs the "Train the trainer" courses and supervises the initial cascading process. Local partners provide volunteer trainers, guarantee a safe and secure location for the lab equipment, agree to run a minimum number of courses throughout the year, and ensure access to the computer facility outside of course hours to allow participants who are taking or have completed the literacy course to use the Internet, applying the computer skills they have acquired.

Some examples of local partners are: local administrations in Italy, India, and Morocco; high schools in Italy and Morocco; universities in Morocco; and youth groups, NGOs, and women's associations in Morocco and India. Other examples include training for the police force in Malta and supporting schools in underprivileged neighborhoods in Southern Italy.

Today, the initiative counts over 250 volunteer trainers worldwide and more than 4000 people who have completed the Informatics and Computer Basics course. It is a small contribution on our side, but we are confident that, if this initiative were to meet a widespread positive response, it could mobilize human and financial resources sufficient to strike a significant portion of world underdevelopment at the roots.

A number of other companies, notably companies in the field of ICT, have engaged in similar educational efforts. We believe that with wider participation, and not just by companies from the high-tech sector, the impact on helping bridge the digital divide would be enormous.

It is important to emphasize that the uniqueness of the initiative is not only that it contributes financial resources, but also that it teaches how to use ICT, allowing people to become citizens of the digital era. We are employing human resources to transmit knowledge to ensure that a good part of the local community where we operate will be able to use and benefit from IT technology and be a part of the digital revolution.

We also believe that the direct contribution of working hours by a company's employees has unique and unrivalled advantages that make it more interesting for enterprises to contribute to these initiatives. Company employees can be identified directly by the beneficiaries of their activity as well as by the civil society around them. Secondly, a contribution of human resources, being a less common form of donation, also attracts attention and publicity which can help promote the programme.

A Win-Win Engagement

We believe that a company, by engaging in such a programme, not only benefits in terms of image, but also from the pride that such activities create in all the people who are offered the chance to devote some of their time to perform an active role in this important initiative.

Indeed, employee motivation is an even greater return on the sponsorship of community initiatives.

In our opinion, when companies engage in any activity of this kind that shows their commitment to promoting the well-being of the communities in which they work, they are improving the company's image, improving employee motivation, and gaining the acceptance by the local communities, thereby generating more value, not only for their shareholders, but for all stakeholders.

Lastly, in the long run, the more advanced economies will clearly benefit if, by contributing to the development of poorer parts of the world, new markets and new opportunities for trade and production are created. It would undoubtedly be beneficial for all corporations to have three billion potential new consumers instead of three billion people living in poverty.

Role of Governments

If all large companies (Fortune 500 companies) donated up to 0.1 % of their revenues to help bridge the digital divide, billions of dollars could be used to this end in programmes clearly defined by each corporation. The impact would be enormous. Nonetheless, efforts to help bridge the digital divide must also be shared by all stakeholders, the private sector, NGOs and governments.

The role of governments is fundamental both in creating a favourable environment to enhance the use of ICT within the country, as well as contributing the same know-how, expertise and tools to other governments. A good example is the government of Italy, which through a strong "e-government" programme, provides the tools and training in e-government and e-procurement to a number of developing countries. The benefits of e-government are well-known: lower risk of corruption, greater transparency, improvement of administrative management of developing countries, and an increase in efficiency of the bureaucracies. E-procurement, for example, can generate savings in purchasing and facilitate and accelerate management of purchasing operations. Governments of developing countries should follow the examples of other countries that are already benefiting from this digitalization of administrations and governments. Private stakeholders and NGOs can also share the costs and organization of such operations, and there are numerous examples of multiparty participation in projects of digitalization of governments and local administrations.

However, in the broader context of the Millennium Development Goals, there are many other actions that should also be undertaken by private enterprises, NGOs and, most of all, by governments.

Pasquale Pistorio, in a number of occasions when asked to share his views on the Tobin Tax, expressed how governments can contribute meaningfully to make the achievement of the MDGs possible. We feel governments could and should increase efforts to implement a better redistribution of wealth and, thus, alleviate poverty globally.

In the last decades, free market economies and globalization have created unprecedented levels of economic development. Nonetheless, alongside these positive phenomena coexists dramatic conditions of poverty. Eight million people die every year of hunger or malnutrition and over one billion people live on less than one dollar a day. Over one billion people do not have access to clean water and basic sanitation. People are suffering from the AIDS epidemic; millions of people and children are being exploited. The gap between the rich and poor countries only gets wider, just as in developed countries the gap between the richest segment of the population and the least fortunate is also growing.

Obviously, free markets and globalization are not the causes of these phenomena. It is the *lack* of a regulation in the world economy which could allow for a better redistribution of wealth that could mitigate excessive disequilibrium within each country and especially between rich and poor countries. Some of the phenomena that most affect world poverty are tied directly to the economic activities of rich countries and the power groups that influence their politics. It is important to mention the agriculture subsidies in rich countries which have denied poor countries the possibility of benefiting fully from their own internal agricultural resources. It is also important to mention the oligopolistic exploitation of many natural resources, both of food (cacao, coffee, bananas) as well as minerals (oil, copper) by multinationals that freely imposed their economic power and were supported by their governments in the process. There are also many financial crises generated or exacerbated by financial speculation that escape from any kind of political control.

In this sense, the Tobin Tax is a good example of a tool that can mitigate such phenomena. The objectives of the tax would be to 1) discourage financial speculation, 2) give back to governments the power to intervene in most dramatic speculative phenomena, and 3) use the revenues from this tax for development initiatives in developing countries.

For a multinational company with a strong sense of social responsibility, a tax of this type can only be welcomed. In fact, in its measure of 0.1% of all currency financial transactions, which is what the tax proposes, the tax would be inconsequential to the profitability of the company in the context of financial transactions associated to the normal industrial activity of the company. In addition, the tax is absolutely irrelevant for normal industrial operations (a manufacturing company transfers currency to finance its operational activities and not to speculate on currency).

The tax would have a marginal impact on the competitiveness of a company even if only applied to one country where such company operates. But if the tax is applied to a series of countries that represent an important quota of financial transactions worldwide, the competitive impact on the company would really be null. In fact, by discouraging excessive financial speculation and giving governments a tool to intervene (including the possibility of increasing the tax in specific cases of extreme speculation), implementation of such tax would contribute to improve international financial stability and indirectly favor conditions for more balanced and sustainable development.

Revenues from such a tax that will be devolved for developing countries could be regulated by an international organ of the United Nations subject to mechanisms of auditing and transparency that guarantee appropriate deployment of such funds for the development of poor countries. The Millennium Declaration defines priority areas of intervention and has the goal of halving extreme poverty by 2015. All countries have signed on to this declaration but, in reality, most are involved in a very limited way. Likewise, in the early nineties governments of developed countries pledged to contribute 0.7% of their GDP for the development of poor countries, but in reality their contributions average around 0.2 %.

Undoubtedly, the theory of the free market economy is the best economic theory tested by man to generate abundance in goods and services and, hence, in wealth. Globalization and the opening of markets can potentially offer access to ICT in all countries and to a new universal well-being. However, this process will not take place automatically – governments should strive to put humanity at the center of economics and place the economy at the center of humanity.

A cultural change is needed. The tools for the redistribution of wealth exist and they are sufficient to allow the achievement of the goals cited in the Millennium Declaration. These tools are the following:

1. Official Development Assistance (ODA). Effective application of developed countries' commitment to give 0.7% of their GDP to developing countries.

2. The Tobin Tax. Collecting 0.1% of all currency transactions (contribution by financial institutions, companies, individual investors that make international financial transactions, and central banks).

3. Environmental Regulation. Pollution and global warming create dramatic environmental disasters such as floods, hurricanes, deforestation and desertification with consequences especially severe in poor countries that have less possibility of protecting themselves. In fact, pollution, generated mostly by developed countries, is a "violent tax" imposed on poor countries. Governments should contribute to this objective by imposing stricter laws: companies should contribute by adopting conduct that promotes sustainable growth and development. Citizens should contribute with a new conscience of respect for the environment.

4. Debt Cancellation. Rich countries should cancel the public debt of poor countries (not only through a simple cancellation of the debt, but also by using those resources to make infrastructural investments in the indebted countries under the supervision of the creditor countries and/or international organizations).

Attribution, monitoring and auditing mechanisms need to be put in place in developing countries which receive economic resources to ensure proper use of funds to reduce risks of fueling corruption or useless bureaucracies.

Social Commitment of STMicroelectronics

In the context of these concepts, we would like to underline that any company today needs to place social responsibility amongst its fundamental priorities not only because it is an ethical duty but also because we are convinced that all companies that have a strong social responsibility generate better economic results creating advantages to their shareholders and all their stakeholders. STMicroelectronics has made social responsibility one of the fundamental pillars of its company culture and puts it in practice in its daily operations along three main areas:

1. Human globalization. In any part of the world where we operate, whether it is Italy, France, US, Morocco, Malaysia, India or China, we apply the same social commitment in terms of bringing technology, continuous training of human resources, creation of local added value with continuously more qualified staff, identical respect for the environment, and a variety of initiatives to promote social development in the communities where we operate.

2. Commitment to the environment. We are convinced that sustainable development is not contradictory to economic results. Our environmental commitment in all the countries we operate has demonstrated that we can protect the environment and increase profits in the process. The Kyoto protocol, for example, is an important step, but it is only one step and insufficient to save the planet. In fact, our goal is much more ambitious: reaching zero carbon dioxide emission by 2010 while continuing to grow at the same historical pace. To our knowledge, we are the only manufacturing company that took up this commitment 10 years ago. We are on target with our road-map and we have not had any negative impact on our economic result; we even created extra profits from our energy savings (results are available on our website).

3. Contribution to the reduction of the digital divide. As outlined above, our objective is to reach one million people in ten years' time. Again, this project and other similar initiatives are being coordinated by STMicroelectronics Foundation, a non-profit organization created with the mission of sharing and building on values of social and environmental responsibility and implementing worldwide corporate programmes such as the "Digital Unify" initiative.

MANAGING CHANGE IN THE KNOWLEDGE ECONOMY: HARMONIZING STAKEHOLDER INTERESTS IN A DEMOCRATIC PROCESS OF EFFICIENT, EQUITABLE AND SUSTAINABLE DEVELOPMENT[1]

By Danilo Piaggesi and Robert A. Vitro, Inter-American Development Bank

The predominant attitude towards information and knowledge defines, to a large measure, what a society is, how it will evolve and what it will become. If that attitude reflects a belief that information and knowledge are fixed and absolute, one type of society will evolve; most likely closed, doctrinaire and authoritarian. If the predominant attitude is open-ended and expanding, another type of society might evolve; most likely curious, deliberative and better able to deal with complexity. Clearly this is not an "either-or issue", but subtle shifts in emphasis in these attitudes can have profound implications for the kind of enabling environment that emerges as well as on the rate and character of development.

An expanding knowledge economy is a product of change, provokes change and is a vehicle for managing change throughout a society. This expansion contributes to and emerges from a democratic process of efficient, equitable and sustainable development. The increasing and diverse demand for information resulting from this process provides incentives for innovative applications of information and communication technologies (ICT). For knowledge economy expansion to reflect the values, needs, resources, conditions and aspirations of each society, diverse stakeholder interests need to be mediated and harmonized through an ongoing process of managing change. An enabling environment should enhance the capacity to manage change.

Managing change involves knowing when, how and with what resources to make and implement the decisions to change or not to change. The accumulated impact of these decisions shapes the character and size of the knowledge economy and the capacity of the society to manage change. Decision-making effectiveness depends on access to timely, reliable, relevant and complete information.

Creating a climate for change and developing a capacity to manage change in knowledge economy expansion have a significant impact on the contribution of information and communication technology applications to the rate and character of economic growth as well as on the degree to which the capacity to manage change permeates an entire society.

This paper discusses knowledge economy expansion as a common denominator for achieving the Millennium Development Goals (MDGs) and as a means for managing the change needed to achieve them. The discussion includes the role of cultural values and the character of information in defining the enabling environment and orienting the institutional transformation provoked by and resulting from ICT advances. The importance of political will and institutional transformation in ensuring the effective contribution of ICT to overarching development objectives, such as sustainable economic growth, human capital

---

[1] The ideas and opinions expressed in this paper are those of the authors and do not necessarily represent the official position of the Inter-American Development Bank (IDB).

formation and strengthening democracy, are also discussed. One section is devoted to how these processes are being reflected in initiatives that foster a more successful partnership between the Inter-American Development Bank and beneficiary countries in Latin America and the Caribbean. Strengthening this partnership can make enabling environments more effective, accelerate knowledge economy expansion, facilitate efforts to achieve the MDGs and strengthen the capacity of citizens to manage change in the personal, social, economic and civic aspects of their lives.

Information – the organization of data in image, text, audio and multimedia audio formats – is understood in this paper as an input that people use to construct knowledge in their mind. The quality of this "construction" is enhanced through the constant strengthening of learning skills and learning. When a person reproduces the knowledge in his or her mind – in print, text, audio and multimedia format – the product is information that others might use. This sharing of information contributes to a common knowledge base that shapes the sense of community that an enabling environment can leverage to mobilize resources for development.

Furthermore, knowledge economy expansion can be understood as reflecting the capacity of an economy to add value (increase the information content) to resources to create and distribute new wealth. ICT for development is understood in this document as the evolution of mechanisms and tools for matching supply and demand for a diverse and increasing volume of information, in text, audio and image formats, and communication services while ensuring that the institutional, legal and technological safeguards exist for all citizens to participate in and benefit from accessing needed information and the skills to use it to create and apply knowledge. This definition seeks to avoid an interpretation that more and more information is needed and explain to the reader why the phrase "information society" is not used anywhere else in this discussion. Finally, this perspective – humans as unique knowledge producers – underscores the fact that knowledge economy expansion and human development are inextricably linked. These and related terms will be elaborated throughout this document.

Managing Change: Cultivating Many Solutions

There is no one "solution" to development. An enabling environment can be defined by the degree to which they encourage the ongoing search for marginal and cumulative practical "solutions" about what works and what does not work to solve their individual and collective challenges (a culture for innovation). The cumulative impact of these decisions defines the character and rate of development. Creating such environments is as important as any specific change that is made.

The ongoing interaction of market, technological, price and competitive forces combines to drive constant change in the knowledge economy and underscores the need to manage it effectively throughout a society. An effective enabling environment that harmonizes stakeholder interests can facilitate adjustments to the constant disequilibrium these forces provoke in the knowledge economy and throughout society.

Knowing when, how and with what resources to change effectively is a core difference among people, groups, organizations, countries and regions. What one knows determines how one behaves. Consequently, creating conditions and mechanisms that facilitate timely access to relevant, precise and accurate information, whether in image, audio, text format, in order to apply knowledge, is at the core of development. More precisely, producing information on information and knowledge about knowledge are imperatives for any enabling environment and essential for managing change in the knowledge economy and enhancing the capacity to have an impact on the rate of change throughout society. More about this meta-information appears further on in this discussion.

Cultural Values: The Foundation of an Enabling Environment

Culture plays a critical but often under-estimated role in defining an enabling environment and managing change. Cultural values towards what is known and knowable play a crucial role in mediating stakeholder interests and managing change involving the deployment of information and communication technologies to achieve development objectives. To increase the rate of expansion and guide the character of knowledge economy growth, key cultural values that have an impact on the capacity to deal with change must be identified, understood and strengthened. Values define the enabling environment just as much, perhaps more, as its institutional, economic and human resource elements.

Numerous conference papers, speeches and studies propose very specific sets of activities that societies could carry out for deploying ICT for development. However, whether or not stakeholders actually carry out such activities often depends on cultural values such as: the balance between change and tradition, propensity for risk taking and willingness to explore the unknown though learning, without bias.

Change for the sake of change is not the issue. Any change must respect the roots out of which it emerges. To detach change from its roots often increases the risk of failure; even apparent "breakthroughs" have their history. The balancing point between tradition and change is in constant flux and shifts according to context. Mechanisms that facilitate constant dialogue among stakeholders promote greater understanding of this shifting balance. Expanding mechanisms for broadening this dialogue is a crucial component of any effective enabling mechanism.

Incomplete information and uncertainty inevitably determine the context for all decision-making. The effectiveness of the decisions depends on the quality, completeness and timeliness of the information that is accessible. Taking risks does not have to be too risky. When understood as a continuous process, involving learning and a willingness to decide what to do next, the "risk" in taking risks can be reduced. While taking large risks can lead to breakthroughs, the process of innovation can be understood as the accumulation of decisions that make marginal changes for improving processes and products.

Along with advances in information and communication technologies, groups of people emerge, who, for a variety of reasons, unduly increase risk by over-exaggerating what these tools can accomplish or under-estimating what is involved in finding out under what conditions deployment of them can be effective. Motivated by a desire to increase sales, manufacturers of these technologies can be prone to exaggerations in their capabilities. Numerous experts and supposed gurus emerging from academia, the consulting community and futurists sometimes offer exaggerated visions that either under-estimate the level of risk needed to achieve effective change or they over-estimate the capacity of the technology. Clearly, "vision" is needed to stimulate people to consider new possibilities. However, anyone offering simple solutions to complex problems should be treated with skepticism. The truth is that to know what kinds of innovations work under what conditions, one must take calculated and deliberate risks, make adjustments based on the results and move forward.

An enabling environment encourages deliberate risk taking. No one knows everything needed for making and implementing a decision. Questions function as a compass for navigating in the knowledge economy. Learning helps define the path. Being aware and admitting what one does not know are essential for finding out what one needs to know. In societies where such admissions are considered signs of weakness and not valued, change is less likely to take place. Consequently, an enabling environment for shaping the knowledge economy in development must facilitate a culture of learning in traditional and non-traditional learning environments by all stakeholders. A common knowledge base about the knowledge economy can increase the likelihood that the accumulation of individual and collective stakeholder decisions and their implementation will achieve their desired outcomes.

Cultural values such as these can amplify qualities of information that by their very nature demand communication and collaboration among diverse stakeholders.

Information Imperatives for Harmonizing Stakeholder Interests

Certain inherent qualities of ICT, information and knowledge drive the need for harmonizing stakeholder interests for carrying out knowledge economy expansion. An enabling environment that promotes widespread understanding of these qualities can contribute to facilitating stakeholder involvement and cooperation.

ICT Potential for Increasing Access

As advances in information and communication technologies, particularly digitalization, significantly increase the capacity of these technologies to store, process, distribute, transmit and access data in text, image, audio and multimedia formats, the per unit costs of accessing the technology and the content is reduced. Whether or not the corresponding shift in the costs of producing, distributing and accessing information and communication technologies as well as the information itself is translated into greater access for more and more people depends on the nature of the corresponding institutional transformations and incentives for innovation that evolve. Inevitably, the effective institutional transformation needed to liberate the potential of ICT advances requires an enabling environment that expands stakeholder participation and harmonizes their diverse interests.

Knowledge Economy Expansion as a Core of Human Development

As a general premise, an enabling environment that focuses on the contribution of ICT to human development is likely to be most effective. People affected by change should be involved in shaping that change. If the enabling environment is fair, open and accessible, these qualities will characterize the knowledge economy. There is an inextricable relationship between an enabling environment and the capacity for managing change. Since there are no simple solutions for growth and development, a combination of values, incentives and other mechanisms, is needed to create an environment that encourages the search for practical, viable and self-funding solutions. Within such a context, the degree to which a person or group can deal with changes in markets, technology, competition and prices, determines whether or not a country will be able to develop according to its own values, conditions, needs, resources and aspirations.

Furthermore, neither sex has a monopoly on creative and communications skills. Consequently, knowledge economy expansion levels the "playing field" for men and women and creates development opportunities for each. As women, indigenous and trade groups come to understand this dynamic process, their involvement in knowledge economy is likely to accelerate the expansion. Similarly, an effective enabling environment is crucial for mobilizing non-government stakeholders, inside and outside the ICT field, to shape the character of the knowledge economy.

Knowledge Application as Socializer

The type and format of knowledge that can effectively be part of a solution to any problem usually comes from a variety of people with different perspectives. No one person sees the entire "picture"; people must share their knowledge to approximate accurately the nature of the problem and consider their options for addressing it. This is true in all human endeavours, including the integration of knowledge economy expansion into development. Consequently, bringing different disciplines together is an unavoidable condition for achieving knowledge economy expansion.

Enhancing the Development Paradigm: Making the Invisible Visible

The call for a new development paradigm is being heard with increasing frequency. Yet advances in information and communication technologies reveal an historic truth about development: all economies are knowledge economies, they differ to the degree to which each society leverages conditions that facilitate access to information and the skills to use it to build and apply knowledge. Through knowledge economy expansion, the capacity of economies to add value (i.e., increase the information content of the factors of production) is enhanced so that more wealth can be created and distributed. A new paradigm may not be needed, a deeper understanding of the role that information and knowledge may play to help people see the familiar through a different lens.

Shaping a Shared Vision

A knowledge economy is not an end in itself. While it is a powerful tool for social transformation, the societal values out of which it emerges will always orient how ICT are deployed and the character of knowledge economy expansion. Consequently, the society must decide for itself what it wants to become: more efficient? more equitable? more sustainable? more just? The challenge for political leaders seriously concerned with the future of their country is to structure a process through which that vision can be refined and progress towards its achievement measured and, when needed, adjusted The use of information and communication technologies can mediate this process of shaping a shared vision as well as be an important element in that vision.

Interdependent Stakeholder Interests in Information and ICT

Public, private and civil society organizations have different, yet complementary, objectives and interests in shaping the structure of the knowledge economy. However, no single group can achieve its objectives without the collaboration and some degree of support from the other groups. Consequently, new platforms and patterns of communication and cooperation are essential to build consensus on common outcomes, outputs and indicators.

Meta Information Imperative: Defining and Measuring the Knowledge Economy Links in Development

Just as the effectiveness of all decision-making depends on access to precise, complete and accurate information on a timely and reliable basis, so, too, do decisions involving the integration of knowledge economy expansion into a democratic process of efficient equitable and sustainable development. Clearly, volumes of such information on information (meta-information) has been produced, much of it useful in understanding the phenomenon being experienced. However, if this meta information is to become an effective tool for managing change, much more of it, particularly in the form of economic statistical indicators, linking the role of information and knowledge to overarching development outcomes and outputs, needs to be produced.

Bringing Stakeholders Together: Forget about the "e"

Advances in information and communication technologies have not changed the basic nature of development challenges. They are, however, potentially powerful tools for addressing the challenges. Whether or not these technologies exacerbate or contribute to overcoming these challenges, and at what pace, depends on how they are deployed. In essence, the challenges continue to involve the creation and distribution of new wealth efficiently, equitably and in a sustainable manner, while carrying out a democratic process for formulating and implementing public policies to ensure that all citizens participate and benefit in the process. An increasing understanding of the functions of ICT deployment and knowledge economy expansion in identifying and addressing these challenges remains a crucial aspect in the effective management of change.

Building consensus on the contribution of ICT to over-arching development outcomes can be a means for achieving greater stakeholder collaboration in managing and implementing change. Often building consensus on such "macro" outcomes (the contribution of ICT to growth, employment and trade) can get lost behind the numerous and diverse "micro" ICT activities that take place in sector areas throughout a society. Consequently, an enabling environment should promote consensus on outcomes regarding the contribution of the knowledge economy expansion to shared, overarching development outcomes. This would complement and underscore the importance of the individual contributions to such outcomes.

The deployment of advances in information and communication technology is part of a process of the diffusion of innovation. In spite of the numerous changes that have already been provoked by ICT, many believe that the fundamental impacts have yet to be fully experienced. Regardless of where in the process of diffusion of innovation a society actually is, it is clear that continuing change is unavoidable. One aspect of this diffusion process has been the widespread addition of the letter "e" to almost everything: e-business, e-commerce, e-learning, e-government, e-health, et al. Although the use of the prefix "e" can be helpful in popularizing the use of ICT in development, its use may risk being interpreted as suggesting that technology is an end rather than a means. It may be time to return to basics and reassert the contribution of ICT to achieving overarching development objectives. In the process the potential of ICT may be better appreciated and more highly valued.

In other words, by not diluting common efforts, stakeholder involvement could be enhanced. Individual stakeholder are already doing a great deal, but the value of their effort could be enhanced if each was part of a consensus that link knowledge economy expansion to specific "macro" outcomes and outputs related to development.

Similarly, the emphasis on the "e" can obscure the distinctions and the relationship between the two areas through which ICT, information and knowledge economy expansion actually contribute to economic growth and development. The information sector, the core of a knowledge economy, has two parts, as defined by Marc Porat and Michael R. Ruben, in their groundbreaking work, "The Information Economy: Towards Definition and Measurement", published in 1981, and subsequently applied by the Organization for Economic Cooperation and Development (OECD). These parts are:

- Primary information sector (those economic activities involving the production, distribution and use of information). Those information and communications goods and services that are traded in the marketplace

- Secondary information sector (the application of ICT to specific sectors of macroeconomic activity). Those information and communication technology goods and services that are produced and consumed within non-information related economic activities.

These two parts of the information sector reinforce the need to integrate ICT in support of sector activities such as health, education, environment, modernization of the state, with the ICT intersectoral contribution to "macro" objectives. An enabling environment that respects these differences and the inextricable relationship between them can clarify the roles of the different stakeholders.

Furthermore, these two parts of the information sector might well turn out to have a crucial role in linking micro and macro-economic growth and development. All too often, macro and micro development efforts are incongruent: macro policies may not have the desired impact on micro-activities while micro-activities are not reflected in macro policies. Access to information and the application of knowledge are common and mutually supporting in the primary/macro and secondary/micro areas. Synchronizing primary and secondary information sector expansion could contribute to generating greater synergy between these efforts.

An enabling environment that focuses on achieving ICT/knowledge economy outcomes in three basic development areas such as creating wealth, distributing wealth and formulating and implementing strategies and policies through a democratic process for ensuring that all participate in and benefit from a process of efficient, equitable and sustainable growth, could contribute to greater harmonization of diverse stakeholder interests. The complementary character of the diverse activities and interests of stakeholders are likely to become clearer and serve as an incentive for bringing them together. Consider the following:

- ICT in sustainable economic growth (creating new wealth). Possible overarching outcome: increase the rate of sustainable economic growth by adding value to resources (i.e., increasing the information content). The functions of information and knowledge in economic growth and development are not yet sufficiently applied or appropriately integrated into development planning.

- ICT in building human capital (distributing new wealth). Possible overarching outcome: increase human factor productivity and local purchasing power through lifelong opportunities to access diverse learning environments. The crucial issue here is to focus on increasing human factor productivity through lifelong learning so that citizens can be more productive and have a better quality of life.

- ICT in governance (rule making for fairness, access and equity). Possible overarching outcome: Use ICT to build trust between citizens and the public sector representatives in order to ensure policies and regulations evolve to increase opportunities and ensure that all can participate and benefit from using ICT to create and distribute new wealth in a sustainable manner.

An enabling environment that clarifies overarching outcomes can assist individual stakeholders in identifying their special role in achieving them and facilitate their adjustment to change.

Even if an enabling environment is successful in linking knowledge economy expansion with overarching development outcomes, this will not be enough to achieve effectiveness. Since information flow defines all organizations, any change, technological or otherwise, that modifies how information flows will have a profound change on the structure of the organization, whether it be the family, firm, public agency, non-governmental group or the society itself. Consequently, enabling environments must anticipate the need for processes that lead to profound institutional transformations.

Translating Political Will into Mechanisms: Institution-Building

One key factor in translating theory into practice is the need for a society to build the political will and commitment to formulate, work towards and refine, over time, regardless of changes in government, a collective vision of what it wants to become. An enabling environment is defined by this vision and is the means for pursuing it. Without such a commitment, a great deal of ICT-for-development activity may be generated without contributing to any fundamental change that addresses the roots of poverty and inequality. In this context, it is important to remember that information has value depending on what is at stake in the decision it will be used to make. If the shared vision has value and is legitimate to all citizens, then the value of information and knowledge economy expansion as a means for achieving it will come into focus.

However, vision and political will are not enough. The second factor is how to organize for change when change is the only constant. This involves promoting, throughout the society, the creation of flexible learning organizations, capable of difficult deliberations and risk taking. Vision is constantly being refined and political will modified by shifts in priorities and new conditions created by collective deliberation and effort. The specific adjustment mechanisms within organizations will vary from context to context. What is important is that adjustment mechanisms be integrated into overall operations and that a culture of innovation emerges from them.

At the level of national government, it is important for ICT-for-development and knowledge economy expansion efforts to be mainstreamed as part of overall development planning. Within this context, stakeholders from different functional areas (i.e., economics, social development, governance, law, organizational development, et al) need to acknowledge their relationship with each other. This is why formulating and pursuing overarching outcomes, as discussed in the previous section, is so important.

Managing change does not mean changing for the sake of change but knowing what to retain, for how long. It involves finding new ways to do things as well as new things to do. This, of course, begs the question of who decides and when is a decision made. The answer to these questions is that there is no one answer: there are numerous answers. The most effective answers emerge, as stated previously, when an organizational approach – an enabling environment – if you will, permits involvement by all stakeholders in bringing about the change that inevitably will have an impact on all of them.

Many of the concepts and processes described in the previous sections of this paper are part of the ongoing adjustment of the Inter-American Development Bank (IDB) to "development" in the context of a global knowledge economy and between it and beneficiary member countries. The adjustment is ongoing with much needed learning still taking place. The following section highlights some aspects related to institutional evolution to strengthen the capacity to manage change.

Towards a Regional Partnership for Managing Change in the Knowledge Economy: the Role of the IDB

On various, public occasions, Enrique V. Iglesias, IDB President, and other senior Bank officials, have stated that knowledge economy expansion serves as a "bridge" between the two objectives of the Bank's institutional strategy: increase the rate of sustainable economic growth while reducing poverty and promoting equity. Such statements are intended to reflect the general direction of the partnership between the Bank and the countries in the region to strengthen capacity to manage change at all levels and, thereby, leverage the creative, communication and intellectual capacities of the people in the region to carry out a democratic process of efficient, equitable and sustainable development.

The countries of the region have been building a consensus in this direction over several years during high-level regional summits and inter-governmental as well as international meetings. However, not all countries have the same priorities nor do they have the same level of accumulated experience in accelerating the rate of increase of their knowledge economy. The IDB works with the countries in the region to build consensus on outcomes, outputs and indicators so that diverse country needs can be effectively matched with the Bank's resources and experience. Together, the Bank and the countries are seeking ways to deploy ICT to increase the rate of sustainable economic growth while reducing poverty and promoting equity. Generating synergy between activities that support the use of ICT in specific sectors and the intersectoral contribution of knowledge economy to consensual overarching goals is crucial to this effort.

The IDB has been following a deliberate process for strengthening its own capacity to manage change regarding knowledge economy expansion in development, in strengthening its working partnership with the countries in this area, and in harmonizing its cooperation with other international institutions. It seeks to improve the enabling environment for policy and development at all levels.

The IDB has a long history of funding ICT activities in sector projects. However, during the mid-1990s, the Board of Executive Directors completed a series of reports on ICT for development and made a set of decisions to strengthen its capacity to manage change provoked by the widespread use of ICT by beneficiary member countries in their development planning. At the end of 1998, IDB Board of Executive Directors created an Information Technology for Development Unit to provide added support and serve as a "change agent" in this area as well as promote synergies among the extensive and diverse ICT for development activities in Bank-funded projects. In so doing, the Board acknowledged institutionally that ICT was an intersectoral activity and included support of these activities in the Unit's mandate. Two years later, the Unit was upgraded to a Division in the Sustainable Development Department, in order to facilitate more effective mainstreaming of ICT and knowledge economy expansion into operations. The Bank is involved in strengthening the institutional capacity of countries to manage change in the areas of: ICT in sustainable economic growth, ICT in human capital formation and ICT in governance, much as described in a previous section of this paper.

A number of other institutional changes have been evolving as new patterns of cooperation emerge organically among the ICT for Development Division, the regional operations departments and other groups in the Bank. A Strategy Group on ICT for Development, presided by the Vice President for Planning and Administration and composed of the senior managers of the Bank's major departments, began to meet periodically to share information, refine the IDB institutional response and harmonize cooperation with other international organizations. This includes Bank involvement in ICT support for the Millennium Development Goals, preparations for the World Summit on the Information Society (WSIS) Second Phase – Tunis and involvement in the United Nations ICT Task Force, as well as preparations for the Summit of the Americas.

In addition, the IDB Consultative Meeting process on ICT for Development was continued in order to provide the ICT leaders in the government of each country to meet with their counterparts and with the Bank to explore ways for better align the needs of the countries with the experience and knowledge of the Bank.

Deployment of information and communication technologies and expansion of a knowledge economy are common denominators of the four pillars of the IDB institutional strategy mentioned at the beginning of the section. Competitiveness and regional integration are crucial elements in the Bank's efforts to promote sustainable economic growth. Access to information about resources, competition, prices and markets are essential for operation of a fair open and competitive market economy, conditions essential for improving productivity and competitiveness. Similarly, harmonization of national efforts to deploy information and communication technology and the concomitant expansion of the information sector of the economy, are being recognized as a sector that can reinforce regional integration of all other sectors. Human capital formation is the nucleus of a knowledge economy. Learning, whether it takes place in a clinic, community center, home, factory, office or farm, has always been the core of social development. With Latin American and Caribbean countries expanding their knowledge economy, access to traditional and non-traditional learning environments is becoming a cornerstone of social development. At the same time, human capital formation is slowly emerging as an essential framework for integrating educational reform and transformation of the labor force. Information and communication technologies are tools for administration, delivery and content of learning. In addition, to ensure that all participate and benefit from these new conditions of development, governments are evolving new patterns of dialogue and collaboration with civil society and the private sector. As expanded deployment of information and communication technologies transforms modernization of the state efforts into comprehensive e-governance programmes, opportunities increase for improving public administration, increasing efficiency and access to public services and making elected officials more responsive to citizens.

Similarly, the information Technology for Development Division has been working closely with the Regional Operations Departments of the Bank in order to mainstream national ICT-for-development strategies as part of development planning. Other outputs resulting from a commitment to greater intra-institutional collaboration include an Information and Communication Technology for Development Trust Fund for pilot projects and studies that expedite the translation of new ideas to concrete projects. Similarly, the Multilateral Investment Fund (MIF) and the Information Technology for Development Division created and recently carried out the second round grants that facilitate use of ICT by small and medium-sized enterprises to become more productive and competitive.

All of these and numerous related activities are being channeled into the formulation of the Bank's information technology for development strategy. This document, to be submitted to the IDB Board of Executive Directors, will recommit the Bank efforts to effectively work with beneficiary member countries to accelerate the rate of knowledge economy expansion as a means to carry out a democratic process of efficient, equitable and sustainable development.

Development Effectiveness and the Harmonization of Stakeholder Interests in the Knowledge Economy

Beneficiary countries, donors and international organizations are currently devoting much attention to the issue of development effectiveness. However, these discussions do not yet appear to adequately reflect the strategic role of knowledge economy expansion in the new paradigm of development. Perhaps this is due to too much fragmentation of approaches among the diverse stakeholders of various segments of the knowledge economy and insufficient dialogue about how to link their individual efforts as part of a collective effort for achieving a set of overarching "macro" development objectives.

In Latin America and the Caribbean, the economic, social and political reforms of recent decades increased the demand for information, knowledge and the deployment of the knowledge economy. It may well turn out that the called for "second generation" reforms will require the effective integration of a comprehensive approach to knowledge economy expansion into development planning. Clearly, this is a two way process – reforms provide incentive for knowledge economy expansion while knowledge economy expansion ensures that all participate and benefit from the reforms. However, subtle shifts of emphasis can have profound implications on development strategy and project design.

To validate this hypothesis, it will be necessary for the collective effort of all stakeholders in the ICT-for-development field to learn to speak the economic and financial language of finance ministers, policy makers, development planners and decisions makers. More specifically, it is essential to produce more economic statistics that link ICT and knowledge economy expansion to overarching development objectives.

Just as the Organization for Economic Cooperation and Development (OECD) began doing almost two decades ago, developing countries need to provide measures of the contribution of the information sector to gross national product, the number of information workers in the labor force and the percentage of information goods in total international trade. By the same token, collective stakeholder efforts are needed to produce measures that document the size of the human capital industry contribution to economic growth by understanding, testing and integrating methodologies such as the one developed by the Canadian Government agency, Statistics Canada, that links skills development to economic growth. Furthermore, governments should measure under what conditions ICT can contribute to overcoming the weakening trust and confidence between citizens and democratic institutions (as documented in the UNDP report on "Democracy in Latin America" and research carried out by the Chilean firm Latinobarómetro) – as the IDB is currently doing with the London School of Economics, in order to provide a framework for measuring the effectiveness of the ICT contribution to public sector transformation. Governments might also consider how their regional integration efforts could be strengthened by harmonization of knowledge economy expansion efforts. The members of the European Union made a political decision more than a decade ago that growth of an information industry in European had to be a strategic component for achieving economic, social and political integration.

The results of such measurements should promote stakeholder cooperation, add focus to debate on development effectiveness and facilitate the formulation of shared outcomes, outputs and indicators for knowledge economy contribution to overarching objectives involving growth, employment, trade and strengthening democracy.

Conclusion

The previous discussion has suggested that an enabling environment must strive to link effectively knowledge economy expansion with achieving overarching development outcomes. The effectiveness of such linkages depends, in large measure, on bringing stakeholders together to strengthen the institutional capacity to manage change and integrate into development planning a deeper understanding of the historical role of information and knowledge in carrying out a democratic process of efficient, equitable and sustainable development. The entire society is more likely to benefit when individual stakeholders are part of a collective effort to achieve this type of development.

ENABLING WIRELESS BROADBAND COMMUNICATIONS INFRASTRUCTURE DEPLOYMENTS: LESSONS FOR LOCAL AUTHORITIES

By Axel Leblois and Peter Orne, Wireless Internet Institute

Broadband Internet connectivity and the information access it brings unleash human capital and increase productivity as well as knowledge sharing in underserved areas where it has been most constrained. New wireless Internet technologies are ready to fulfill this promise, supported by universally accepted standards set by the Institute of Electrical and Electronics Engineers (IEEE) for both wireless local area networking (the 802.11 standards known as "Wi-Fi") and long-distance point-to-point connectivity (the 802.16 standards known as WiMax).

These two standards-based solutions are good examples of broadband-wireless technologies meeting different requirements that complement each other more often than they compete. Wi-Fi is ideally suited for providing coverage to limited areas where it can provide high data rates, secure access, and robust performance in the license-exempt spectrum with a very low capital expenditure. Base stations and customer premises equipment may be purchased for less than $100, though costs for external carrier-grade equipment may be considerably higher.

Mesh networks based on Wi-Fi can provide wider coverage by creating a wireless network among neighboring access points and cost-effective coverage for wider areas. Mesh networks do require the deployment of a dense network of access points, which may be difficult or expensive to maintain mostly because of right-of-way issues. Still, this technology can lower the cost of infrastructure while increasing the cost to users only marginally and provides welcome connectivity redundancy in dense areas.

Although often compared to Wi-Fi, WiMax is best suited to networks designed to cover large areas and that need carrier-grade service and advanced quality-of-service functionality. At first, WiMax will require a higher capital expenditure because base stations and customer premises equipment are more expensive, but WiMax requires fewer base stations over all.

A multitude of devices, software, and services currently on the market are designed to interoperate with unified protocols in the frequency spectrums defined by the Wi-Fi and WiMAX standards. In recent years, the definitions of unlicensed spectrum have normalized around two major sets of frequencies: the Instrument, Scientific, and Medical band at 2.4 GHz; and a newer allocation in the 5-Ghz to 6-Ghz range adopted by the World Radiocommunication Conference in 2003.

More and more devices are reaching the market with chip sets that will allow the instant detection and connectivity to local hotspots where they are available. Support for portability will be limited for a time because WiMax PCMCIA cards or laptops will not be available until 2006.

Nevertheless, fast declining costs promise to make broadband wireless solutions more and more affordable, especially as they are embedded in more devices, including "intelligent phones" and other hardwares that are able to automatically shift from a local 802.xx connection with voice-over Internet Protocol to a regular cellular service. Perhaps more important for developing countries is a new "smart" technology under development that will help to optimize spectrum use by automatically limiting interference, solving a potentially difficult issue in dense areas.

Technology Adoption

Deciding which technology to adopt can be difficult and requires a solid understanding of the technologies available as well as their core strengths and limitations. Even more importantly, public agencies and local government authorities should carefully identify and evaluate what network configurations they need, which applications they will run, whether support for portability or mobility is required, which devices will access the wireless network, and the funding available for the initial build-out and for long-term maintenance.

As any wireless access network eventually gets connected to the wired Internet, so it is important to understand the role of wireless with regard to wired parts of a deployment.

Wireless systems have a number of advantages of which the two most notable are the portability of the end systems and the ability to deploy without extensive laying of physical wires or fibers. At the same time, wireless systems will never be as high performance as a fiber deployment. Consequently, it is best to see wireless systems as complementing rather than replacing wired ones.

Ideally, fiber would be deployed as deeply into a process as affordable and practical. Whenever new "wires" need to be deployed to carry data, fiber systems are clearly the right choice. Wireless would then be used to extend this connectivity to a larger number of locations and ultimately to connect end systems to the network.

Sensible deployments will use good copper connections that may already be in place to feed wireless systems, and wireless-access systems can feed locations such as offices that have an internal wired Ethernet system in place. Thus, most real-world deployments will use both wired and wireless technologies in a cost-effective mix to reach the most users.

In the absence of wired infrastructure, wireless point-to-point connection can be used very effectively to provide inexpensive broadband access. But online interactive applications and voice-over IP require as little "latency" as possible. As the number of hops grows along a connection, so does latency. And the so-called multiple-hops configurations will often end up in a common link to a high-performance fiber backbone, presenting yet another potential bottleneck. Developing countries will need to establish a minimum level of performance based on the capacities of local infrastructure.

Because many developing countries are advanced in the adoption of wireless cellular telephony, the topic of the future convergence between IEEE 802.xx standards and cellular standards of the International Telecommunication Union is certainly important. WiMAX (802.16) was defined for broadband distribution to fixed points on reasonably large channel allocations, whereas mobile telephony standards are designed to transport voice on narrow bands. Both, however, are evolving toward the other's position: 802.16e supports some form of nomadic applications while 3G, with a high level of mobility, offers mid-bandwidth data services. 4G and 802.20 may still be at the conceptual level, but developing countries will need to remain well informed in order to optimize existing infrastructure, given that these technologies will continue to evolve.

Amid the fast pace of technological advance, regulatory authorities are faced with a number of issues. Defining international unlicensed bands in support of wireless Internet and other applications has been long and arduous, but the process has come to fruition thanks to the active role of several key constituents, including the US Federal Communications Commission, the European Union, the International Telecommunication Union, and the information technology industry.

THE IMPORTANCE OF BROADBAND WIRELESS STANDARDS

It is quite important to realize how important standards actually are. First, standards create a way for the best technical ideas from academic and industry developers to be combined and amplified. The process of creating the standard subjects the proposed ideas to broad review and generally results in considerable technical improvements on any individual company proposals.

Of great importance to purchasers of the final equipment, standards generally result in much lower costs much sooner. This is because the existence of a standard creates a common market into which competing companies sell. Furthermore, the size of that common market is larger than any submarket based on what proprietary approaches would be used. In the high-technology world, costs are strongly a function of volumes so the creation of a single high-volume market leads to much lower costs than a fragmented market would. Standards also permit higher degrees of integration of equipment, which also contributes to lower costs.

For communications gear, particularly mobile equipment, standards are critical to allowing users to move around countries and the world while still having their equipment work correctly. While this may not seem to be of direct importance to the use of communications equipment to connect the citizens of developing countries, it will, in fact, enable those citizens to more easily become part of the world economy and benefit from the resulting development. For example, while mobility may not be important for providing access to the residents of a farm, it may be important to the visiting business people who are negotiating for the exports of their crops or the introduction of new economic development projects to the area.

—Kevin Kahn is an Intel Fellow and Director of the Communications and Interconnect Lab, Corporate Technology Group, Intel Corporation. Adapted from "The Wireless Internet Opportunity for Developing Countries," co-published in 2003 by the infoDev Program of the World Bank, the United Nations ICT Task Force, and the Wireless Internet Institute.

Broadband Communications Infrastructure and the Regulatory and Telecoms Environment

While developed countries have started or, in some cases, already completed the deregulation of the communications markets, many emerging economies still run their telecom networks through a single, often state-owned organization. These monopolies are the *de facto* sole providers of interconnection both for telephony and for high-speed data networks and the Internet.

Over the years, these organizations have invested heavily in wire and cable communications infrastructure and are not yet ready to support broadband-wireless initiatives, much less to open the way to what may be perceived as potentially disruptive low-cost competition. This protective stance is often exacerbated by financial constraints because wire and cable infrastructure have been financed through debt. Quite often, incumbent telecoms also maintain tight control over the access to national Internet backbone resources, making it difficult, if not impossible, for new wireless Internet service providers to operate.

The pressure exerted by such organizations to limit the access to new technology and service providers is, in some cases, encouraged by political restrictions on information access. In most cases, the result is a wireless market strewn with procedural hurdles that can prevent new actors from entering the field.

Unlicensed Spectrum

Only 41 percent of developing countries allow unlicensed use of wireless Internet devices and/or spectrum, compared with 96 percent of developed countries. Most newcomers to the telecommunications field in emerging economies face red tape and then a series of fees to obtain licenses for equipment and/or spectrum use. For example, countries charge license fees for hotspot equipment or sites and one-time or annual license fees for access-point devices.

Most researchers, analysts and entrepreneurs see the need for a comprehensive regulatory framework for using limited spectrum. Presently, the unlicensed wireless spectrum was set around the 2.4-Ghz band. In June 2003, the International Telecommunications Union made available the 5-Ghz band for license-exempt technology deployment.

The 900-Mhz band, unlicensed in the United States, is presently used by the international GSM wireless phone standard, which is utilized in Western Europe and in many developing countries.

Within those internationally defined zones, national regulations vary widely, with more or less restrictions applying to radiation power. What is lacking is a comprehensive worldwide policy that would align countries and best practices among independent wireless Internet service providers around the world.

On March 20, 2003, marking a positive step toward greater international consistency, the European Commission issued a recommendation to encourage member states to provide license-exempt WLAN access to public electronic communications networks and services in the available 2.4-Ghz and 5-Ghz bands. This is not a binding commitment for member states, but it is consistent with the (binding) Authorization Directive, which requires all member states to allow license-exempt access to the spectrum when the risk of harmful interference is negligible. The Authorization Directive was scheduled to be implemented by member states on July 25, 2003.

The recommendation is important because it opens the way for using license-exempt spectrum for commercial purposes, creating large opportunities for service providers and showing how fast changes have occurred, given the amounts recently paid by mobile operators for access to the 3G spectrums. Here, access to the spectrum is free. But it also introduces new issues, which operators of radio systems did not have to deal with in the past, in particular, the obligation of noninterference already in place in the United States.

Unlicensed Does Not Mean Unregulated

Many analysts emphasize that unlicensed does not mean unregulated, and operators providing wireless services still need to maintain a no-interference working plan and a "good neighbor" attitude.

Conversely, licensing does not always promote the development of services. In the United States, for example, many licenses are attributed to providers that go no farther than the paper that they are printed on! Several countries have early on embarked on various options for licensing, such as class licensing and service (as opposed to equipment) licensing. Many of those experiments are still under way, and they hold the promise of opening access to actors in underserved areas through a less cumbersome regulated environment.

Whatever solutions are chosen, enforcing an orderly use of the spectrum and an acceptable quality of the systems may require setting up unbiased oversight bodies with legal authority and a clear charter to promote the broadest access possible to users at the lowest possible cost.

ISPs vs. Network Providers

The provision of unlicensed wireless services raises further questions because of the presence of two different kinds of actors in the field: network providers and Internet service providers. Of course, the two may be the same. When this is the case—that is, the ISP and network provider are affiliated—the two will jointly try to curb all competition. In countries where Internet service comes only from the incumbent telecom, competition is effectively curtailed, and a fair playing field is very hard to establish. Special interests will do everything in their power to hold on to their monopolies. This is particularly problematic when ISPs need to access the incumbent's network.

Consequently, both Internet-service entrepreneurs and end-users can argue for unlicensing altogether, letting markets drive both the choice of technology and the services offered. The rapid development of advanced wireless Internet technologies is compelling evidence of how robust markets quickly create a fair playing field. Both incumbents and newcomers must then adjust to the needs of the market, complementing one another rather than strictly competing.

Forward Agenda for Regulators

With both the North American and European markets taking more advantage of wireless Internet technologies using unlicensed spectrum, it seems ineluctable that wireless Internet solutions will gather great momentum and further benefit from economies of scale. Developing countries have the opportunity to assess when and how to transition toward similar unlicensed spectrum definitions.

To draft a forward agenda, both government agencies and the private sector should make a thorough analysis of market potentials and the technologies that best suit a particular setting. A strong push for dissemination of knowledge in the sector seems indispensable. Internet access in general, and wireless Internet possibilities in particular, are seldom at the top of the agendas of government agencies. A comprehensive catalogue of potential applications, especially in e-education and e-health, is needed to expand policymakers' awareness.

The same goes for available technology which remains in the somewhat guarded realm of technology wizards. Regulatory bodies need to be enlightened on the options for distance and proximity transmission equipments, and on the technical knowledge necessary for implementation and maintenance. This is particularly true in remote underserved areas where the expertise to sustain a working system may be unavailable. Technical education programmes should be delivered by providers on an ongoing basis, in cooperation with international institutions and regulatory bodies.

Last but not least, guidelines are needed to help assess the economic sustainability of wireless Internet access systems. Today's last-mile solutions can bring access to the most underserved and poor areas. The financing of such networks in itself does not constitute a major obstacle to implementation, but the financial aspects of content sale and use are still pretty much undefined. The legal and economic framework for existing providers and newcomers to develop those systems should be comprised of incentives for sustainable and financially sound programmes.

A competitive regulatory environment, free access to spectrum within guidelines, alliances between private sector and government bodies and between incumbent telecommunications providers and newcomers, and an international agreement on the basic framework available to wireless Internet systems can nurture the development of the networks and further bridge the digital divide. Multi-partner discussions are strongly encouraged, lest the market takes the lead.

Principles for Broadband Deployment and Experimentation

Wireless Internet technologies and applications are emerging in many different settings, often outside the operational landscape of traditional telecommunications services and with new types of participants from both the private and public sectors.

Those applications resulting from grassroots initiatives may be seen as disruptive and can hit unintended roadblocks in the form of local regulations and lack of understanding of their potential. Conversely, proper government support and incentives can accelerate their successful implementation with little cost and with significant immediate economic and social benefits for the poor.

Each country exhibits unique characteristics and conditions with respect to wireless Internet deployment from a geographic, social, economic, regulatory, and telecommunications infrastructure standpoint. There are, however, several regulatory and economic success factors that country authorities should consider. To facilitate such local review, the following guidelines to governments wanting to support the experimentation and early deployment of wireless Internet infrastructure applications are proposed.

1. **Identify, promote, and establish national consensus on the potential benefits of wireless Internet applications and local priorities**

A key factor of success for wireless Internet deployment is a generally supportive environment, a pre-requisite of which is adequate awareness of policy makers, the public and private sectors and the local media.

The United Nations Millennium Development Goal No. 8, Target 18, states that: "In cooperation with the private sector, make available the benefits of new technologies, especially information and communications." There is a general agreement that Internet access is a key success factor in making these new technologies work for development. In many geographic areas, however, the cost of expanding Internet connectivity with landlines or cable remains prohibitive for the foreseeable future, while available bandwidth is increasing exponentially in developed countries, furthering the digital divide.

Raising awareness and building national consensus on the benefits of low-cost broadband wireless Internet infrastructure solutions is, therefore, an important first step.

One complex challenge is to clearly differentiate the broadband capabilities of IEEE 802.xx-based technologies for fixed infrastructure from the low bandwidth mobile solutions offered by current cellular telephony and personal-devices networks.

Local governments may also inventory the applications that can contribute the most to bridging the digital divide, both from a geographic and social standpoint, and foster economic development, job creation, and productivity gains in all economic sectors. Of particular interest for developing countries are the opportunities in the 3 "e's": e-government, e-education, e-health (a fourth, e-commerce, is sometimes also included); rural-areas coverage, small business connectivity, the development of local ICT services, including private-sector ISPs and voice-over IP services.

Identifying leading applications, which may drive the initial use of wireless Internet infrastructure and distribution, will further develop support for wireless Internet solutions among key constituents.

2. **Adopt minimum regulations supporting the use of unlicensed spectrum and ICT industry standards**

A second critical success factor is the leverage of internationally recognized norms. Harmonization creates significant economies of scale for equipment manufacturers, software developers and off-the-shelf solutions. It is, therefore, in the best interest of countries to closely follow and support the norms and recommendations of the following organizations:

- For spectrum policy and standards references:
  - Institute of Electrical and Electronics Engineers (IEEE)
  - ITU World Radiocommunication Conference

- For manufacturers' standards compliance, interoperability, and quality assurance
  o Wi-Fi Alliance for 802.11 products
  o WiMax Forum for 802.16 products

The single most important step to support wireless Internet applications is to develop a spectrum policy that allocates bands for unlicensed applications, such as the 2.4 and 5-GHz bands currently unlicensed in a number of countries.

In a first step toward worldwide spectrum allocation to wireless Internet applications, the ITU, in its July 4, 2003 World Radio Conference communiqué, indicates that it "successfully established new frequency allocations to the mobile service in the bands 5150-5350 MHz and 5470-5725 MHz for the implementation of wireless access systems, including RLANs. Wireless devices that do not require individual licenses are being used to create broadband networks in homes, offices and schools. These networks are also used in public facilities in so-called hotspots such as airports, cafes, hotels, hospitals, train stations, and conference sites to offer broadband access to the Internet…."

"The lower part of the 5-GHz spectrum will be predominantly used for indoor applications with the first 100 MHz (5150-5250 MHz) restricted to indoor use. The use of these frequency bands is conditional to provisions that require interference mitigation mechanisms and power-emission limits to avoid interference into other radio communication services operating in the same spectrum range."

Each country may have existing spectrum allocations that need to be adjusted. A close monitoring of international regulatory activities and the adaptation of local spectrum policies is, therefore, recommended.

3. **Update telecommunications regulations to foster market opportunities, optimize existing infrastructure resources, and free competition among wireless Internet service providers**

    Although situations will vary greatly from country to country, four areas need careful attention from a telecommunication regulatory perspective:

    a. Access to an Internet backbone is a pre-requisite for a successful deployment of broadband wireless Internet services. To the extent possible, telecommunications regulations regime should foster a competitive Internet backbone market. Private- or public-sector entities outside the telecommunications industry should be allowed to contribute their backbone capacity. This is particularly important in regions with underused backbone capacity. As an example, GrameenPhone in Bangladesh was made possible by the collaboration of the National Railway System contributing access to its fiber-optic network. Conversely, if only a few backbone service providers exist, they should be obligated to open up their infrastructure to independent service providers.

b. If no backbone is available, alternative solutions should include broadband terrestrial wireless links, satellite stations and power grids. Appropriate incentives encouraging such solutions should be implemented.

c. At the final distribution level, Internet service providers, or ISPs, implementing wireless Internet solutions need to be facilitated by telecommunications regulations and operate in the context of free-market competition.

d. Legacy regulations concerning radio communications, some related to law-enforcement agencies or the military, can also create unintended obstacles for wireless Internet ISPs, including for the physical deployment of antennas and radio-communications equipment. These should be adapted to the specific needs of wireless ISPs as in such landmark cooperation agreements facilitated by the regulator between the private sector and the NTIA (National Telecommunications and Information Administration) on the use of unlicensed spectrum in the United States.

4. Identify key available resources and foster cooperation among potential actors

Wireless Internet infrastructure and services can leverage a number of existing resources in any given country:

- backbone operators and owners of fiber-optic networks, including governments, private-sector networks, telecoms, power-grid operators, and satellite communications operators;

- owners of real estate and high points with adequate power supply and security to install antennas, such as existing radio communications towers or possibly public-sector buildings such as post offices or other types of standard venues;

- systems integrators with the technical capabilities to install and maintain wireless equipment such as towers, cabling, hub-integrated antennas, wireless modems, control and network management systems, routers, cables, uninterruptible power supplies, racks, etc.;

- operators of similar services such as TV broadcasting, cellular telephony, computer maintenance organizations, and power distribution;

- financial-sector interested to fund start-up ISPs;

- community leaders eager to provide Internet access to their constituents;

- incumbent telecommunications operators; and

- providers of know-how and training services. It is recommended to support venues such as conferences or seminars on wireless Internet to increase awareness and initiate dialogues and cooperation among key decision makers from both the private and public sectors.

5. **Support the experimentation of new services and encourage the aggregation of demand for bandwidth**

Although wireless Internet initiatives can be perceived as disruptive and infringing on existing regulations, they are an important source of information to adapt regulations and develop public-sector strategies. Governments are encouraged to support early initiatives with interim measures until appropriate regulatory adjustments are made.

One of the most important factors of success for wireless ISPs is a rapid increase of initial demand for connectivity, which allows for a faster break even on operating expenses. This can be achieved through initial aggregation of demand based on applications for local public services such as schools, universities, health services and public administration. Business, agriculture and private uses will inevitably add to the mix once service is available. In very underserved areas, it is likely that initial viable aggregation will occur through the deployment of wireless Internet kiosks operated by small entrepreneurs.

Governments are encouraged to deploy applications in the areas of e-government, e-education, and e-health to leverage the use of Internet access by the general public. Governments should also encourage local public services to use the infrastructure of local wireless ISPs.

6. **Follow-up and support of wireless Internet developments at governmental and intergovernmental levels, including sharing of best practices**

It is anticipated that wireless Internet technologies and applications will continue to evolve rapidly, which makes them important for governments and private-sector leaders to remain abreast of other countries' experiences, regulatory work at the international level, best practices and latest innovations.

In Focus: Piraí, Brazil, Digital Programme and Local Economic Development

Eighty kilometers north of Rio de Janeiro sits the remote hill town of Piraí, population 23,600—a town that, in the course of one year, went from zero broadband Internet access to the possibility of broadband universal access. W2i visited Piraí in September of 2004 because of its pioneering success at using broadband communications infrastructure to bridge a rather sizeable digital divide.

Approaching his final year in office, Piraí's charismatic Mayor, Luiz Fernando de Souza, was determined to realize a vision for social and economic development through the installation of a broadband network. The mayor's primary motivation was to make Piraí more attractive to investors, with the goal of creating 4,000 jobs over the next several years. But to do this, he knew he not only needed a modern communications infrastructure but more efficient government and an educated workforce. Piraí currently supports some 1,700 government employees—more than 7 percent of the total population.

Over time, Piraí's citizens would become the main actors in producing, managing and enjoying the benefits brought by the new infrastructure—a hybrid system with wireless support (public/private-wireless/wired). The town created a management outline with four large activity areas, each one with a specific set of goals: .gov, .edu, .org, and .com. The first, .gov, was charged with developing e-government and electronic governance.

With the support of the Rio de Janeiro State Government, Piraí established an association with REDE RIO and got a 1 MB link, which was later expanded to 3 MB to support videoconferencing. In its contract with REDE RIO, Piraí agreed not to use the link for commercial purposes.

After two years of investment by the municipality and about a dozen stakeholders and public- and private-sector supporters, on February 6, 2004, the network became operational, integrating all public buildings, eight schools, one laboratory, two telecommunications centers and a computer terminal for public access. Broadband-wireless signals currently emanate from existing telecom base stations above the town, enabling throughput at a good rate of 14 Mbps.

Piraí has created a monitoring and evaluation system to identify how the population has incorporated the new network and technologies into its daily life, with the early goals of linking all public workers by e-mail (100%), connecting all schools (30%) and public buildings (100%), and installing telekiosks (1 out of 10 so far).

In phase two of the deployment—Piraí will focus on improving skills and expanding the numbers of technically skilled personnel to bring the telecenters and school laboratories towards technical-administrative autonomy.

GUIDEPOSTS FOR LOCAL-GOVERNMENT PROFESSIONALS

Imagine a day when all the residents of a community can walk about feeling perfectly secure; are able to work, learn and play no matter where they are; and can stay in touch with friends no matter the distance separating them. This is the promise of wireless broadband, and many local governments throughout the world are pursuing this dream using wireless-broadband technologies, which provide a magical, invisible umbilical cord connecting citizens to the rich world of the Internet and to one another. Moreover, acceptance of Wi-Fi by the consumer industry brings the citizen for the first time to the electronic doorstep of e-government, a bonus that may strengthen the business case for Wi-Fi deployment at the local level.

For those who decide to travel down this path of Wi-Fi deployment, several Guiding Principles have emerged as strong touchstones. They reflect the experiences of pioneers and pathfinders with bold new ideas, and they balance the technology potential with a more human approach to community development and networking. Instead of using one application—the infamous "killer app"—to line up necessary funding, establish a series of such Guiding Principles that are easy to appreciate and to support by technical experts as well as laypersons, and promote them as the foundation of your deployment effort. Five principles, in particular, are important to my own thinking and reflect the experiences of many local-government innovators. Each community may wish to develop its own based on the culture, incentive systems, and priorities inherent to its own circumstances.

The first principle is **interoperability**. Wi-Fi networks enable the connection of diverse devices such as laptops, PDAs, cell phones, and a host of other software and data platforms. However, for this connectivity to be realized, both operating systems and application protocols must be interoperable. This quality is not necessarily built into our devices today.

The second principle is the **diagonal imperative**. Many projects concentrate on vertical integration among levels of government or horizontal integration across agencies. Wi-Fi networks will offer the tantalizing potential of diagonal integration of all governmental systems toward a single focal point—the citizen. This will require substantial amounts of reengineering and painful acceptance of changes to the ways the public sector does its work. *(continued)*

The next principle is counterintuitive. If a government implementing a wireless broadband solution is to see a strong return on its investment, it must leave the comfort of city hall behind and **plunge into the community at large** to enlist fellow travelers; that is, community leaders, the nonprofit world and business networks, among others. The successful deployment plan will not be limited by a government service improvement promise but include uplifting the entire community through robust, new tools of economic development and the promise of democracy. And, thanks to the ubiquitous placement of Wi-Fi empowerment circuitry on consumer products, the tourism aspects, always an important contributor to the local economy, can now take on new intimacy.

Communication and outreach plans informing the traveling public about public as well as private opportunities for engagement is made possible through the magic of Wi-Fi.

Another important guiding principle arises from issues of ownership and the desire of winners to find ways to break out of win-lose models and launch win-win partnerships. Both public and private sectors bring undeniably strong assets to the table of wireless broadband deployment. Right-of-Way ownership and management, anchor tenants and long-term infrastructure financing capacity are important elements (necessary and yet not sufficient) that must be incorporated into a plan.

Weak efforts pit private and public sectors in never-ending cat-and-mouse games of one-upmanship. There is another way! In Europe, the development of **joint enterprises**, with shares owned by the public and private sectors alike, enables community-wide infrastructure efforts to move forward quickly, anticipating and taking advantage of the strengths of each partner.

Finally, social equity dictates that all members of a community benefit from a wireless broadband deployment effort. In the same way that highways became a public investment to be enjoyed by all, and the nascent TV industry in the 1950s adopted a financing model that permitted the deployment of educational and entertainment material to all, Wi-Fi stakeholders are poised to develop new models that could also guarantee to all this new essential good of the 21st century.

Against this set of Guiding Principles, each community can overlay its own program objectives and the serendipitous opportunities that drive so much of technology deployments today. Whether it is in education, homeland security or public works, the opportunities to rethink services and outcomes are far more robust with a wireless-Internet canopy to connect desirable and appropriate resources. Partnerships between diverse governmental agencies at the local, state, and federal levels could mean a sharing of the financial burden of network deployment and speed the magic point of cost recovery. It does take a lot of finesse and interpersonal skills to explore such partnerships, but the effort is well worth it.

How can we organize the energies of the diverse players into a coherent and mutually supportive strategy? We need to establish a non-threatening platform of action where diverse and oftentimes competing actors can come together and allow themselves to be guided by a trusted leader through the complexities of this major infrastructure deployment effort. Technical feasibility, market studies for new services, replacement strategies for sunk investments, and financing strategies in a rapidly changing regulatory framework are all aspects of the same business plan.

Instead of different stakeholders developing their own competitive business plans, perhaps a single, community-based business plan allowing each stakeholder to accomplish a major portion of a desired outcome, bringing feasibility and a good community-based return on investment can be a wiser strategy. To lead in this effort, one must find community leaders who can create and embrace a vision of change and success, educate them in the potential of Wi-Fi, and get out of the way! As magicians of change, our local-government elected officials are able to pass legislation and adopt investment strategies that can literally change the future overnight. The promise of Wi-Fi demands no less!

—Dr. Costis Toregas is President Emeritus of Public Technology, Inc. and a member of the Program Committee, W2i Digital Cities Convention.

Considerations for Local Governments Planning a Broadband Communications Infrastructure Rollout

- When planning a network, it is important to build consensus and get all stakeholders on board. Elected officials must ultimately respond to their constituents' needs and requirements. Does the municipality provide for universal access in its IT or telecommunications plan?

- One way to build consensus is through a needs assessment to determine the best kind of network for the government, city employees, business community, and residents. Needs with the highest priority may not necessarily be the needs that are the most beneficial to constituents, yet, they may be the priorities that allow the municipality to finance the network.

- Cities must determine whether they can deploy the network themselves or will need to bring in one or more private-sector partners. How knowledge-savvy is the municipality about such agreements? How long does it want to be in the broadband service business?

- The government and the private sector work on different time lines. Partnerships must examine how to accommodate the pace and style of both.

- Any business model must carefully consider the return on investment (ROI) from the network, whether through efficiencies gained and thus tax dollars saved, or through revenue generation from Internet-service-provider bandwidth leasing arrangements. Sources of investment should be explored at start-up and for future maintenance and expansion of the network. How will roaming agreements work?

- How does the broadband budget fit into the municipal budget? How does it compare, for example, with the roadwork budget? Which one gets priority?

- Is broadband communications infrastructure a utility such as water or electricity, where every single household gets access? It may be perceived as such but not charged in the same way.

- Can wireless Internet services be deployed in a fair way, using public property and public funds? As soon as permission is given to put an antenna on a water tower, does the municipality allow someone else to install one as well? How do you sign contracts with multiple service providers at one time?

LOCAL GOVERNMENT DEFYING THE SKEPTICS: THE ORIGINS OF WIRELESS HOUSTON COUNTY, GEORGIA, USA

Since August 2003, Houston County, Georgia, has been working with Intel, Siemens and Alvarion to deploy a countywide wireless network. Houston County is located in the geographic center of Georgia and is home to Robbins Air Force Base, the largest industrial complex in Georgia with more than 22,000 employees, civilians and military workers. The county also has great cottage industries and hundreds of other smaller companies with offices in the county using new technologies.

The regulatory environment in Houston County is fairly conservative, whereas the political leadership is very conservative. Houston is home to the first Republican governor of Georgia. He thinks that the public should be public and the private should be private, and that the two shouldn't be confused, which has an impact on how you deploy a network of this type. At the same time, we are a progressive community because of the infusion of Air Force people from around the world, and we have an international flavor of which we are very proud. *(continued)*

Fortunately, Houston is an "IT-ready" county. Siemens recently did a study for us, and more than 80 percent of our citizens have access to broadband. Access is not cheap, but it exists.

Project Origins and Political Will

Intel had partnered with one of our local high schools, putting wireless networks over laptop units. In August, they made a presentation on wireless networks, and a couple of us said: "Wow, this seems like a really interesting idea. We'd like to be a part of it. "In our mission to provide affordable wireless broadband access to all of Houston County, we have found that a tier approach seems to work best. Our provision first covers the government and then our businesses (especially our defense contractors). The ultimate goal is to position Houston County as one of the first mobile wireless broadband "hot counties" in the United States in the 2006 to 2008 timeframe—to have the infrastructure in place and easily upgraded.

We have taken a couple of steps in this process. First, we began with our own education. In the beginning, I did not know what WiMAX was. I would look at the presentation of how you build 802.11 (Wi-Fi) or 802.16 networks and it was like listening to another language. But now our citizens are working in community forums. They understand what WiMAX and wireless technology is and how it can be used.

Second, it is very important to build political support at every single level. We have received statements of support from both our city and county governments. Some of our representatives from the state government serve on our committee, and Governor Sonny Purdue has been briefed on the project and has had a vision for wireless. We are very excited about this. The reason why it is so important to get political support, especially at the state level, is because you must work with and sometimes against your incumbent telecommunications service operators. At first, we got a very interesting response from them. One telecom more or less patted us on the back and we had a really good idea. One time they called it "our little project," which indicated their level of interest. The telecoms are very powerful, and they have a good track record of outmaneuvering local initiatives at the state level because of the money and the lobbying power they have. It is important to bring them to the table, and it is also important to outmaneuver them first!

Third, we got some business and technology consulting work done. As a city councilman, I am more of a policy maker and a political leader than a technical person, and I think that is probably the case among most government leaders. We brought in Siemens Business Services and a gentleman named Greg Richardson worked with us. He did an outstanding job and came up with some very tricky solutions.

Fourth, you figure out how to deploy the network, and then you just do it. During each of these steps though, we constantly did two things that really formed the foundation of our success. We built and maximized relationships. Our partnership with Intel is long-term. They have been our strategic leader in this, kind of holding our hand. They have so much exposure. They also helped bring in Siemens's business circle to support this, along with Alvarion to deploy and test the network.

It is important to have those partnerships—some big folks in the room—because there can be lots of opposition at times. The other thing that we have done is to promote the project and our region throughout the country and the world. Consequently, I probably get three to four calls a week from reporters throughout the country wanting to know more about the deployment.

Applications

Currently, our police department uses Wi-Fi technology. Very quickly, with this technology, our police will be able to file a portion of their reports through our systems. They hate coming back to the station to do head work as much as we hate for the police not to be on the street keeping our citizens safe. And so, it has the effect of making them happy while increasing their productivity and their exposure.

Through wireless, they also can do real-time intelligence sharing at all different levels of government. Most importantly, because we have a military base, we feel we are perhaps more at risk for some kind of terrorist attack or something of this nature. But the network will allow communication with the Air Force base, military police, and civilian public-safety agency. At the same time, Robbins Air Force Base is not our target customer. They told us, "Yes, this is great, and you guys do what you need to do in the community", but we are not interested. We did find that they have a hospital in the base, and if soldiers in the compound want it, emergency calls are routed to the county 911 Center, through a 56K dial-up modem connection. *(continued)*

This is not very satisfactory for us, and it is one of the things we want to change to increase outward communication. It will also allow us to modernize home health-care systems, social work and public works. We also have some community colleges that will harness this technology as well. So that is how it started to change our community.

Cost and ROI

So how much does it cost? The capital expense to deploy two towers to cover our county is $362,000, and this includes 40 of the expensive (CPD) devices. Consequently, you are not looking at major expenses. Our county is large, 386 square miles, and it will cover all of that. Operating expenses for the first year are about $340,000, so it's taken about $700,000 to make this network happen. That is doable and it is doable for most communities even in tight times through bonds or loans. In terms of investment sources to go with the cooperative wholesale model, I am hoping that we can just get the city and county to cut a check and start moving on this, though we do have private companies and investors on deck.

So what is the return on investment? We should not pay taxpayer dollars for this. If we can cut that in half, which I think we can easily do, then ROI will come very quickly. Siemens says we can pay for the expense in 10 months, so our next step in Houston County is to decide on the business model. There has been some political heat, and some misunderstanding in the press, but that is just how it works.

Our next step is to measure the aggregate demand, to look at our customers, and how much they are paying right now. If we add that all together, what do we get? What contract should they have? A long-term agreement with telecoms? Can they break these contracts? What are the penalties?

Alvarion has been a tremendous partner, but there are other vendors out there as well. You can download Siemens's 40-page report feasibility study from our Web site. I think it has a great deal of national application and you get a sense of the tremendous work of Greg Richardson. We learned a lot.

I spent a lot of sleepless nights and then got up early in the morning just to be faced by a newspaper that got everything wrong. That is something to watch out for. There is a tension inherent in government working with private enterprises, especially vast, leading-edge companies. Those companies want immediate implementation. They want product stuff now, and network stuff now.

But at least, where I come from, we have had to work to change the institutional thought process about technology and about broadband, and that certainly takes time, or folks would not understand the value you are bringing.

It is also important to focus on recruiting those that do not just have political power, who are elected or those with economic power, but also those with social power, the social leaders in your community, your opinion leaders, to drive the project and to be involved.

And, finally, it is critical to have partners. In this day and age, with complex technology, doing it alone, I think, is probably nearly impossible, and it is certainly not as much fun and not as rewarding. At the end of the day, when you are trying to implement the technology, you have to realize that it is not about the technology, it is about people, about changing the way government provides services to people and then changing people's lives.

—Matt Stone is co-founder and government strategist for Civitium, a digital-cities consulting company. In 2003, Matt helped create the Wireless Houston County Committee and was elected its first chairman. (wirelesshoustoncounty.org). Adapted from "Wireless Internet and Municipal Public Safety," published by the Wireless Internet Institute (2004).

The Wireless Internet Institute's Global Municipal Government and Local Authorities Series

The Wireless Internet Institute's Global Municipal Government and Local Authorities Series aims to build consensus among local-government elected officials and agency executives, industry practitioners, and regulators involved in technology policy development and implementation through establishing the strategies needed to develop environments favourable to the broad deployment of broadband communications infrastructures in local communities.

The Series is overseen by a multinational, multidisciplinary steering committee and includes various high-visibility conferences, seminars, and interactive workshops around the world in 2004 and 2005, creating the conditions for informal dialogue and brainstorming with a focus on the following components:

- case studies and the role of various constituents;

- business models and partnerships in support of broadband communications infrastructure deployments;

- benefits to citizens, local government, and economic development; and

- the leadership role of mayors and local officials in promoting wireless Internet applications and developing progressive policies.

In November 2003, W2i joined forces with the City of Atlanta and the Atlanta Mayor's Office of Community Technology to co-host "The Wireless Internet and Municipal Government Summit." Primary findings from the Summit were captured in a report of the same name and presented in December 2003, at the first World Summit of Cities and Local Authorities on the Information Society in Lyon, France, as part of the World Summit on the Information Society in Geneva. They included the following:

- A majority of elected municipal officials view broadband wireless as a utility essential to the development of their community;

- The primary drivers for local government to adopt the wireless Internet include:

  o social services such e-health, e-education, and emergency response services,

  o government operations such as public safety and field workforce productivity,

  o local business and economic development;

- The primary challenges for local government to adopt wireless Internet include:

  o establishing citywide consensus,

  o identifying municipal needs and objectives,

  o exploring business models and funding mechanisms,

  o deriving a clear set of policies and regulations,

  o starting a city-officials and community-partners education programme.

The second conference in the Series, co-hosted in June 2004, with the City of San Mateo, California, brought together public-safety officials, regulators, field practitioners, and technology executives to explore how broadband communications infrastructure can enhance public safety, municipal workforce productivity, and economic development.

Major findings from this conference were that:

- there is emerging evidence that deployment of a broadband wireless infrastructure can be favorably cost-justified by increasing local-government workforce productivity and efficiency;

- as an ancillary benefit, the deployed infrastructure can be shared and provide low-cost Internet access;

- there is emerging evidence that innovative public-private partnerships and business models are a viable path for sustainable deployments.

The third conference in the Series was co-hosted in September 2004 in Monterrey, Mexico, in cooperation with the governor's office of the State of Nuevo León and Tech de Monterrey. It brought together local-government officials, industry stakeholders, regulators and academia to explore how the wireless Internet can bridge the connectivity gap at the root of the digital divide in underserved areas of Mexico; provide a new-age infrastructure fostering economic development and workforce productivity; and enable delivery of new social service-applications in areas of e-health, e-education and e-government.

Primary findings were that:

- there is a strong desire on the part of local officials to act upon these objectives;

- and for such local-government initiatives to blossom, the national regulatory agency must first establish a favourable regulatory environment.

Going forward for the remainder of 2005, W2i has launched the W2i Digital Cities Convention programme in the following four cities: Rio de Janeiro (February), Philadelphia (May), Shanghai (September), and Bilbao (November) with the goal of disseminating established best practices and accelerating the proliferation of local-government initiatives.

The W2i Digital Cities Convention programme will provide local government-technology stakeholders with high-level analysis, focused brainstorming sessions and an opportunity to build consensus on the issues surrounding broadband-wireless municipal-area networks. In the largest event of the programme, in Philadelphia on May 2-4, 2005, municipal elected officials, industry thought leaders, technology providers and systems integrators will participate in an interactive three-day programme to explore the full range of opportunities and roadblocks surrounding the planning and deployment of these networks.

Created as part of the Task Force and W2i's overall programme, and in cooperation with UNITAR, W2i maintains a comprehensive public knowledge base on opportunities and challenges for local communities in deploying broadband communications infrastructure, a

FINANCING ICT FOR DEVELOPMENT: A GLOBAL PUBLIC GOODS PERSPECTIVE

By Roberto Bissio, Instituto del Tercer Mundo and Social Watch

Back in 1990 when the preparation for the Earth Summit was starting with the very first PrepCom in Nairobi, African and southern NGOs came together about how they could participate in the Earth Summit. They released a statement saying, "We need the Earth Summit to use electronic communications in order to be able to participate. Please make sure it happens". At that time already more than 100 African NGOs were connected by email and that technology not only allowed them to receive information and documents cheaper and faster than fax or snail mail, but also acted as a mechanism for collective discussions.

The first email communications during a United Nations conference in New York, and probably one of the first email transmissions out of the United Nations building, was setup by technicians from Instituto del Tercer Mundo in Uruguay, part of the Association for Progressive Communications, during the fourth PrepCom of the United Nations Conference on Environment and Development (UNCED) in 1991. That was not for lack of technicians in the US that knew about email, but because of the technology being identified by civil society organizations from the South as relevant for then, even when it had not been understood as such by the System yet. The Earth Summit was the first summit that was connected to the Internet. The electronic communications for the Rio Summit were provided by Association for Progressive Communications (APC), an NGO, for the NGOs, for the official Summit and for the media.

When the Global Environmental Facility was being set up, the NGOs lobbied the World Bank, by stating "Please use email to communicate with us". Because if they sent a 100-page document by fax we would not even be able to pay for the thermal paper to receive the document; whereas, if they emailed it we would not have to pay anything, or just a very small amount. And the World Bank started to use its electronic communications to reach Southern NGOs by using the APC conferencing system before it adopted e-mail to communicate between its own offices.

At that time, every user of email or electronic conferences had to sign a statement promising that they would not make any commercial use of the network; it was absolutely forbidden to use it for non-educational or profit-making purposes. Why? Because it was an operation subsidized by the United States government. The US government subsidized the Internet for more than 20 years from 1970 to 1990. And until today you could claim that e-commerce is in a way heavily subsidized by the way of being exonerated from taxes that other brick-and-mortar commerce do pay.

So, to forbid the South from in any way subsidizing the development of ICT sounds a little bit of the kicking-the-ladder kind of strategy, once some people have arrived at the top. But the main point that directly relate to the issue of financing, is to consider and discuss information society and ICT as a global public good. That it actually is a good does not need much discussion: it is good for development, for international communications, for information dissemination, and more. That it is public in the sense of a public good, does need some discussion.

For a good to be public it has to be non-rival, meaning that access to it does not deprive others from access, non-depletable, and non-excludable, meaning that using it does not prevent others from using it. Knowledge reproduction on the one hand, but at the same time communication and access to the network, has all those characteristics, so it is a public good.

On top of being a public good it generates positive externalities. Every time an individual connects to the network, the value of the network increases instead of decreases. Jumping on a bus or a plane takes some other person's space. Driving a car on the highway crowds that highway such that the value for others decreases. But by connecting to the Internet the value for others increases because they can also connect to you. This is now a very well-known principle of a networked economy.

In a similar way, if a country connects or expands its connections to the global network, it generates a positive cross-border externality. So it is not just that this country is gaining access, it is also the whole of the world that gains access to that place. It is not just the people in the village being able to make phone calls, it is people around the world that are calling that village or tapping into that knowledge, basically increasing the value of the overall network. And the positive externalities are recognized by industry, and there is extensive literature recognizing these positive externalities of the expansion of the network. Among other things it generates markets for information products, knowledge products, computers, and services. But basically it also increases the value of the network in itself. So it is a public good; being cross-border, its a global public good.

Now, how can global public goods be financed? That is the major problem. The traditional mechanisms have limits. Foreign direct investment (FDI) only goes to the people who can pay for the communication, and it doesn't go to the poor unless it is subsidized, but that is another problem. In the case of domestic financing, countries have been asked to finance the expansion of the network because it would be good for them, which is fine, but, here there are free-riders, because it is good for the rest of the world also. And those free-riders, which are the more powerful countries, are not paying their way. Official development assistance (ODA), could provide finance, but the question is whether this would be appropriate. The answer is no – ODA is intended to support local development, not global public goods. If you use ODA to support a global public good you are actually subtracting from ODA that should go to national development priorities and not to global priorities.

Alternative mechanisms are therefore needed, and those mechanisms have been discussed in a paper that is available on the Internet on: www.apc.org[1]. (Financing the Information Society in the South: A Global Public Goods Perspective by Pablo Accuosto (ITeM) and Niki Johnson, APC, June 2004.)

This is a paper on Information Society as a global public good and how to finance. And the answer is through taxes. A lot of global taxes are being suggested currently, like a carbon tax,

---

[1] http://rights.apc.org/documents/financing.pdf

the Tobin tax, and an international tax on arms trade to control or limit public "bads". Back in 1990, the UNDP proposed a tax on e-mails that could not only have generated enormous amount of resources but also have limited a public bad which is spamming. That was one of the proposals that was ahead of its time. Today everybody would have understood the costs of spamming.

Who should pay a tax to fund the Information Society as a global public good? One of the ideas we propose is to look at the other end of the chain of production. There are millions of computer buyers and millions of computer outlets around the world, and it would be very hard to gather the money from there at, say, one dollar per computer. But there are only a handful of microchip producers, and microchips go into cell phones, into computers, into microwave ovens. Let's put the taxes at that end, at the producer's end, and not at one dollar but at one cent. That would still generate millions of dollars annually.

Voluntary contributions have also been mentioned and there is nothing to be said against voluntary funds. But voluntary contributions do not address the problem of the free riders, those who get the benefits without paying for them. Some kind of mandatory system needs to be put in place, and there are mechanisms for that, and we strongly encourage the United Nations ICT Task Force to look into this. This is all a popular issue now, and when presidents Lula, Zapatero Lagos and Chirac proposed new funding mechanisms, including taxes, they gathered forty Heads of States last September to support them and within twenty four hours they got the signatures of 110 countries. So it is not possible to say that taxes to fund global public goods are not popular around the world anymore. Moving this issue forward would quite simply make an enormous difference to achievement of the Millennium Development Goals. It is an issue that the UN ICT Task Force could pursue with great potential benefit this year through the MS+5 and the WSIS.

FINANCING ICTs FOR DEVELOPMENT: RECENT TRENDS OF ODA FOR ICTs

By Susanne Hesselbarth and Ichiro Tambo, Organisation for Economic Co-operation and Development

The transformation of business and social activities that Information and Communication Technologies (ICTs) have brought about in the developed world is now seen to offer potentially huge benefits also to the developing world. Although the private sector has led the investments for building ICT infrastructure, operating ICT networks and delivering ICT services over the last decades and provided the bulk of financial resources, public sector funding and official development assistance (ODA) play an important role in creating an enabling policy environment, channeling resources toward less commercially attractive regions as well as toward the poor, and supporting innovative financing mechanisms for ICTs for development. The falling trend in international aid flows over the 1990s provided the background for the decline in ODA commitments for ICT infrastructure from US$1.2 billion in 1990 to US$194 million in 2002. The rationale for most donors to withdraw from the provision of ICT infrastructure was linked to the expectation of an increasingly strong role of the private sector. However, in addition to providing funding for ICT infrastructure, most donors are engaged in bilateral ICT-specific programmes and contribute to international multi-donor initiatives for ICTs, and at the same time many also have integrated ICT components in their development programmes which are not reflected in the trends on commitments for ICT infrastructure. The renewed commitment of bilateral donors for ICTs for development, as documented by the OECD-DAC Donor ICT Strategies Matrix, suggests that the decline in bilateral ODA financing for ICT infrastructure has at least been offset by the increase in ICT-related flows included in other development programmes.

Financing ICTs for Development: The Background

Over the past decade or so, the dramatic revolutions in information and communication technologies have deeply transformed international commerce, social interaction, political relations and development issues. Today, the role of electronic communications as a tool and conduit for promoting development and opportunity is increasingly indispensable, and the scope and impact of initiatives demonstrating the value of ICTs to achieving key global aspirations such as the United Nations Millennium Development Goals (MDGs) are multiplying daily.

But ICTs offer far more promise for development than they have achieved to date. In spite of immense progress in expanding the reach of basic and new ICT services and applications in developing countries, the majority of the world's population still does not have access to telephone service, computers or the Internet; even broadcast signals are virtually unknown to millions. The challenges raised by these continuing gaps in access to ICTs and to the opportunities that they can foster, and particularly the overriding questions of financing ICTs for development, are a key focus of the development community, and are a major concern of the World Summit on the Information Society (WSIS).

This paper is based on a report focusing on trends in current donor practices and the development of bilateral donors' portfolios for ICT infrastructure elaborated as a collective contribution from the Development Assistance Committee (DAC) Members of the Organization for Economic Cooperation and Development (OECD) to the discussions of the United Nations Task Force on Financial Mechanisms for ICT for Development (TFFM) established on recommendation of the WSIS.[1] In the following three sections this contribution looks at the global trends in aid flows, the recent trends in bilateral ODA commitments for ICT infrastructure as well as the strategic orientations for donor support for ICTs.

Trends in Aid Flows

The 1990s generally witnessed a trend of decline in aid flows to developing countries from donors as measured by net official development assistance from countries that are members of the DAC of the OECD. Between 1992 and 1997, total net aid flows from DAC member countries to developing countries and multilateral institutions fell by over 20% from $60.9 billion (1992) to $48.3 (1997). After maintaining a steady course through the 1980s, the end of the Cold War and superpower rivalry in the Third World marked the beginning of the fall in aid flows as share of donors' national income. By 1997, and in three of the subsequent four years, it was at an all-time low of 0.22% of donors' combined national income. Aid flows recovered slightly in 1998 and 1999, but the increase reflected only temporary factors and did not signal a reversal of the declining trend in aid flows during the 1990s and into the early 2000s.

However, the last two years have been a turning point in the evolution of aid flows to developing countries. In the context of the 2002 Monterrey Conference on Financing for Development, a large number of DAC members committed themselves to significant increases in their ODA volume. As a result, the real increase in ODA of 12% recorded over the last two years has reversed the declines in aid of the previous decade and on current commitments, ODA is due to rise by an additional 27% by 2006.

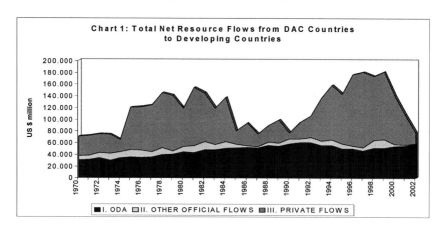

Chart 1: Total Net Resource Flows from DAC Countries to Developing Countries

[1] OECD (2005), Financing ICTs for Development – Efforts of DAC Members, A Review of Recent Trends of ODA and its Contributions, Report to the UN Task Force on Financial Mechanisms for ICT for Development (TTFM)

The sharp fall in private aid flows from the early 1980s – reflecting the collapse in international lending following Mexico's announcement that it was unable to meet its debt-service obligations – was reversed in the 1990s with a revival of private investment in developing countries in the context of falling interest rates and increasing profitability of investments.

Recent Trends in Bilateral ODA Commitments for ICT Infrastructure

In the 1990s, development assistance for ICT infrastructure experienced an even stronger downward trend than aid flows in general[2] and commitments for economic infrastructure in particular. In this paper, ICT infrastructure means "communications infrastructure" and is composed of three categories of activities: communication policy and administration management; telecommunications; and radio/television/print media.

Generally, bilateral ODA commitments for economic infrastructure (energy, transport, ICTs, irrigation, water supply and sanitation as well as infrastructure components of rural and urban development) have followed an overall downward trend since 1996, declining from \$15.175 billion to \$8.174 billion in 2002. Concurrently, the relative share of infrastructure allocations in total ODA commitments fell since 1997 from 26% to 14% in 2002 (Chart 2). Moreover, the requirement of dealing with the Asian, Latin American and Russian financial crises in the mid- to late 1990s, and a stronger focus on social-sector investments to reduce poverty, accelerated the move of donor assistance away from economic infrastructure.

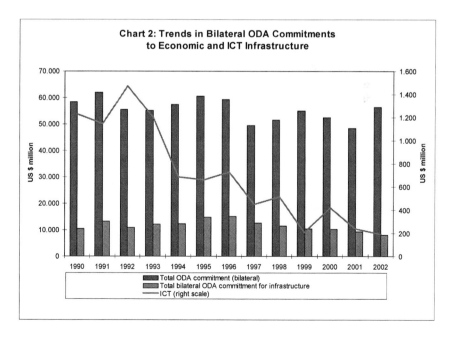

Chart 2: Trends in Bilateral ODA Commitments to Economic and ICT Infrastructure

---

[2] The analysis of the trends in bilateral donors' commitments to ICT infrastructure by sector and region is based on data in the DAC database as well as the OECD Creditor Reporting System (CRS) database and covers primarily the DAC bilateral donors.

The ODA commitments for ICT infrastructure show an even more dramatic decline over the period 1990–2002. From $1.2 billion in 1990, bilateral commitments increased slightly to around $1.5 billion in 1992, but since then declined steadily to $194 million in 2002. Chart 3 illustrates the magnitude of DAC bilateral donor commitments to the communications sector in total values and as a share of DAC countries' total bilateral sector-allocable ODA. Over the period 1990–2002, the share of aid for the communications sector dropped from a high of 4.5% of total bilateral sector-allocable ODA to a low of only 0.6% in 2002.

The rationale for the decline in commitments for infrastructure in general is also behind the dramatic decline in commitments for ICT. Given the dramatic shift of telecommunications infrastructure investment in particular from public ownership to the private, market-driven model, both multilateral and bilateral donors as well as the governments in the partner countries substantially reduced their role in funding capital investments in the sector.

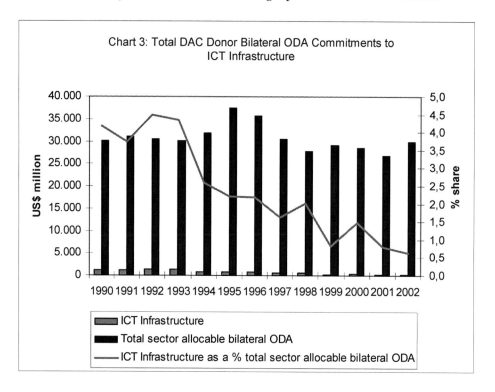

Chart 3: Total DAC Donor Bilateral ODA Commitments to ICT Infrastructure

ICT Infrastructure
Total sector allocable bilateral ODA
ICT Infrastructure as a % total sector allocable bilateral ODA

This declining trend in bilateral ODA commitments for ICT infrastructure has not been uniform across all bilateral donors. Chart 4 presents the commitments to ICT infrastructure by individual donor and shows the drastic decrease between 1990 and 2002. The strong decline in commitments for ICT infrastructure from an annual average of around $1,200 million during 1990–93 to an average of $500 million for 1994–98 and to $266 million for 1999–2002 can be traced back mainly to the strong reduction of a focus on infrastructure by some of the countries.

Japan, by far the largest donor over the years with a share between 30% and 68% of total allocations between 1990 and 2000, sets the downward trend. Overall commitments from Japan have declined from a high of $550 million in 1991 to a low of $40 million in 2001. In 2002, commitments to ICT from Japan showed a slight increase to $52 million but were still far below their absolute volumes in the early 1990s. While in value terms the global downward trend is mainly linked to Japan, the chart shows that there were similar substantial decreases for the majority of donors.

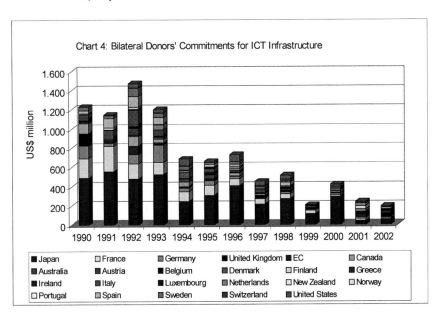

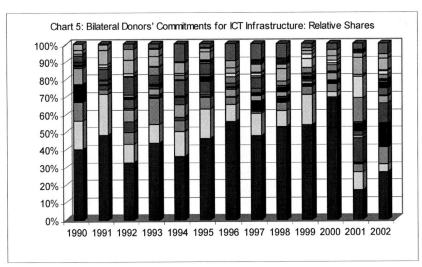

Commitments from France dropped from a high of $264 million in 1991 to a low of $9 million in 2002, and their relative share of total bilateral donor commitments declined from 23% to 5% over the same period. A similar trend can be observed for Germany with a decline from $178 million in 1993 to $19 million in 2002.

Taking a closer look at the relative share of bilateral ODA commitments for ICT infrastructure illustrated in Chart 5 highlights the role of Japan as the most important donor in infrastructure in terms of volume, followed by Germany, France and the EC.

Sectoral Structure

The stronger focus on social-sector investments to reduce poverty has contributed to the decline of donor assistance for economic infrastructure. However, also within the commitments for economic infrastructure, a reorientation in focus can be observed. The sectoral disaggregation of bilateral ODA commitment (Chart 6) highlights transport as the leading sector in 1990–2002, with 37% of all bilateral commitments for infrastructure. Aid flows for energy account for 27% of total commitments, followed by water and sanitation (20%) and ICT (6%). Irrigation, rural and urban development account for around 2–4% of total commitments.

Comparing 1990–98 with 1999–2002, a shift in the sectoral focus is clearly discernible, with decreasing allocations for energy (from average of 29% to an average of 20%) and ICT (from 7% to 3%) on the one side and increasing relevance of the transport (from 36% up to 42%) and the water sector (from 19% to 22%) on the other.

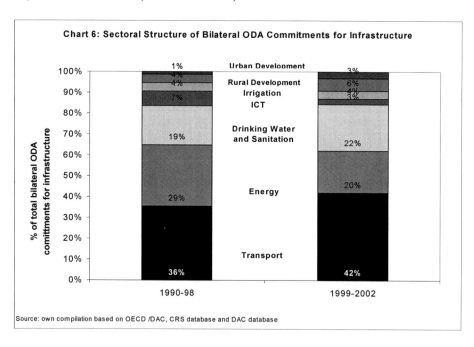

Chart 6: Sectoral Structure of Bilateral ODA Commitments for Infrastructure

Source: own compilation based on OECD /DAC, CRS database and DAC database

Behind these figures lies a slightly different picture for the changes in focus in the individual donor portfolios. In fact, a large number of bilateral donors have moved out of transport and energy in favour of water and sanitation sector. The overall increase in relevance of the transport sector can be explained in part by a move of some donors from energy to transport and by the increase in allocations to the transport sector by other donors such as the European Commission (EC) which together counterbalanced the shift of a number of smaller donors towards water and sanitation. In this case, the assumption that multilateral institutions such as development banks or the EC would massively take up investments in the sector – which led many bilateral donors, particularly in Europe, to move out of it – proved correct.

With regard to the importance of the different activities classified under ICT infrastructure, telecommunication accounted for 82% of total commitment in 1990–98, whereas communications policy and administration management and radio/television/print media received only smaller shares of total commitments. Yet there has been a dramatic shift towards an increased importance of radio/television/print media in recent years, their share accounting for 40% of total commitments during 1999–2002 with a parallel decline in commitments for telecommunications (Chart 7).

Chart 7: Structure of ICT Commitments

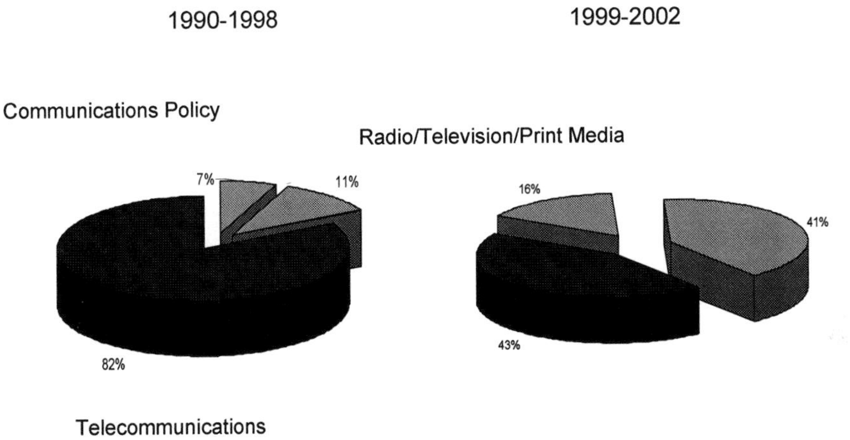

1990-1998

1999-2002

Communications Policy

Radio/Television/Print Media

7%   11%   16%   41%

82%   43%

Telecommunications

Regional Structure

The bilateral ODA commitments for ICT infrastructure are regionally concentrated on Asia, with an average of 50% of all commitments during 1990–2002 (Chart 8). Second in importance is Sub-Saharan Africa with shares varying between 10% (1990) and nearly 40% (1997) over the period. Between 10% and 20% of all commitments have been allocated for the Middle East and North Africa (MENA) region, and a slightly lower share to Latin America and the Caribbean. Commitments to the Southern and Eastern European countries gained in importance over the period, but represent only a tenth of all commitments.

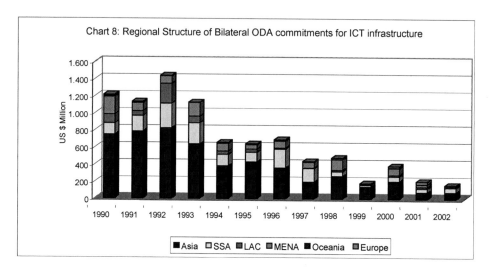

Chart 8: Regional Structure of Bilateral ODA commitments for ICT infrastructure

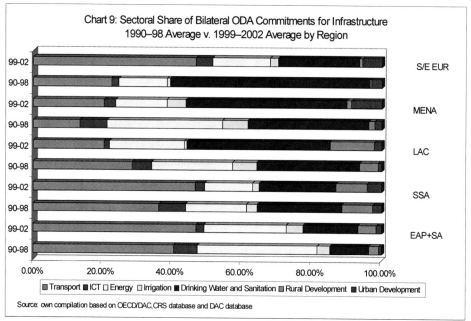

Chart 9: Sectoral Share of Bilateral ODA Commitments for Infrastructure 1990–98 Average v. 1999–2002 Average by Region

Source: own compilation based on OECD/DAC,CRS database and DAC database

The sectoral disaggregation of ODA commitments for infrastructure by region reveals diverging compositions. Whereas transport infrastructure was the leading sector, with over 40% of all commitments and an increasing trend in Asia and Sub-Saharan Africa, its relative share in commitments for infrastructure in Latin America only reached an annual average of 20% during 1999–2002, down from an average of 28% during 1990–98. Both the MENA region and Europe have experienced a strong relative increase in transport allocations, from 13% to 20% and 24% to 47% respectively.

Drinking water and sanitation, with an average of 46% (1999-2002) and 35% (1990-98) of all commitments, receives the largest share of ODA commitments in the MENA region as well as Latin America and the Caribbean (increase in average from 29% to 41%). It is interesting to note, that for the developing countries in southern and eastern Europe allocations for drinking water and sanitation – which accounted, on average, for 57% of total yearly allocations in 1990-98 – have been replaced by transport as the leading sector and their relative share has declined to an average of 23%.

With the exception of southern and eastern Europe, where on average ICT allocations have more than doubled their share between 1990-98 (2%) to 1999-2002 (5%), all regions show the trend of decreasing allocations for ICT (Chart 9).

Financing Mechanisms

In terms of specific financing mechanisms, bilateral ODA commitments for ICT infrastructure in general have shifted in recent years. Chart 10 breaks down the bilateral ODA commitments for ICT infrastructure by type of funding, i.e., loans, grant, technical cooperation and equity.

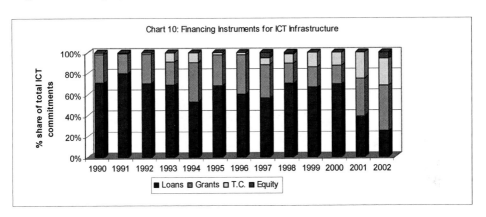

The relative importance of loan instruments has fallen considerably from an average of around 60% during the 1990s to a low of 38% in 2001 and 23% in 2002. Over the same period, grant funding has gained in relevance, nearly doubling its share of total commitments from 20% in the early 1990s to 40% in the early 2002s. Also funding for technical cooperation has increased steadily over the period. Equity has only played a minor role with small allocation in 1997 and 2002.

ODA Financing Instruments

Grants: transfers made in cash, goods or services for which no repayment is required.

Loans: transfers for which repayment is required. Only loans with maturities of over one year are included in DAC statistics. The data record actual flows throughout the lifetime of the loans, not the grant equivalent of the loans. Data on net loan flows include deductions for repayments of principal (but not payment of interest) on earlier loans. This means that when a loan has been fully repaid, its effect on total net flows over the life of the loan is zero. *(continued)*

Technical Co-operation: includes both (a) grants to nationals of aid recipient countries receiving education or training at home or abroad, and (b) payments to consultants, advisers and similar personnel as well as teachers and administrators serving in recipient countries (including the cost of associated equipment). Assistance of this kind provided specifically to facilitate the implementation of a capital project is included indistinguishably among bilateral project and programme expenditures, and is omitted from technical cooperation in statistics of aggregate flows.

Equity investment: Direct financing enterprises in the country receiving aid which does not (as opposed to direct investment) imply a lasting interest in the enterprise.

Other Donor ICT Assistance

Donor assistance to ICT infrastructure is by no means the entire picture of the role of ODA in ICT for development. Most OECD donors are engaged in bilateral ICT-specific programmes and contribute to international multi-donor initiatives for ICT, but many also have integrated ICT components into their development programmes. The scope of individual contributions as well as the degree of involvement in ICT assistance varies considerably across bilateral donors.

The OECD-DAC Donor ICT Strategies Matrix compiles information on the strategic orientation and policies in donor support for ICTD as well as information on funding for ICTD.[3] The Strategies Matrix, published in February 2003 and revised in late 2003, provides a general overview over donor support for ICTD and highlights good practices. According to the Matrix and related information compilation, there are three main categories of donor assistance for ICT for development:

- Bilateral ICT-specific programmes: These initiatives have mainly been designed to improve the flow of information and knowledge, increasing access to a range of information and communication technologies (from traditional to the most advanced) and enhancing the variety and quality of content. ICT infrastructure is the typical example. They include e-governance in Senegal (France), e-government for development initiatives (Italy), the Imfundo Partnership for IT and Education (United Kingdom), and many others.

- Contribution to international multi-donor initiatives: Multi-donor approaches have been created in order to pull together strengths and competencies while limiting duplication of effort as well as funding. Among the most prominent initiatives are the World Bank's Information for Development Programme (*info*Dev) and Global Development Learning Network (GDLN), Development Gateway Foundation, Global Knowledge Partnership (GKP), Bellanet, and many others.

- Mainstreaming ICTs into development programmes: Recognizing the cross-sectoral function of ICTs and their role as a tool to reach development goals more effectively and efficiently, donors have increasingly engaged in mainstreaming ICT components into their development assistance. Examples are the health and family planning sector programme in Vietnam supported by German financial

---

[3] Information compilation was conducted by Mr. Benoit D'Ansembourg, former independent consultant to OECD.

cooperation which comprises, among other things, the establishment of a computer-based logistical management system to improve stock-keeping, order processing, and the distribution and monitoring of drug flows. Another example is the Basic Education Programme for the Pacific region supported by the European Development Fund, which contains a large e-learning component.

Whereas the bilateral ICT-specific programmes and partly also the contributions to international multi-donor initiatives are covered by the data analysed in the preceding section, it proves difficult to provide an overall figure for the investment of bilateral donors in ICT for development and embedded ICT components are generally not reflected in the data for a number of reasons: the partial coverage and mix of multi-year commitments in the information provided to the DAC, the fact that many initiatives are built on partnerships and therefore specific contributions made by various partners are difficult to reconcile, but primarily the shifting of development assistance from providing technology to fostering development which led donors to consequently "mainstream" ICTs in their development assistance programmes in order to more effectively and efficiently achieve development goals, particularly the Millennium Development Goals are all the factors responsible for the incomplete data. As a result, the ICT component of projects is integrated into sector programmes in a variety of ways which is neither separately identifiable nor quantified.

Although the available data do not provide sufficient information to measure the volume of funding flowing into mainstreamed ICT components, the renewed commitment of bilateral donors for ICTD as documented by the OECD-DAC Donor ICT Strategies Matrix suggests that the decline in bilateral ODA financing for ICT infrastructure described in the preceding chapter has at least been in part offset by the increase in ICT related flows included in other development programmes.

Private-Sector Development

The role of private-sector initiatives for ICTD, especially local ones, has increasingly been recognized and strengthened in recent years, with wide acceptance of their effectiveness in promoting effective use of ICTs, strengthening local production capacity and creating jobs. In the future, local actors, initiatives and content should also be emphasized in ICT-for-development initiatives.

Fostering the provision of ICT infrastructure and access led by the private sector requires a proactive role from governments and donors. To extend the reach of ICT to poor and rural populations they must create appropriate policy and regulatory frameworks, build human capacity to implement policies and programmes, and develop innovative and flexible forms of public financing to leverage private investment.

Because the private sector is instrumental, perhaps even critical, in expanding ICT-for-development access and applications, and since a wave of privatization has been seen as a reality in developing countries since the 1990s, DAC members have extended their ICT for development support, directly or indirectly, through their financing instruments (not always ODA) for private-sector development (PSD). These activities are complemented by other donor support to the building of an enabling environment (through the establishment of an effective regulatory framework and capacity building). ICT projects are anchored locally and harness local capacity, including the private sector and non-governmental organisations. In all these efforts, however, special attention should be paid to using ICT to address the gender dimension of poverty. Examples for donor support for private sector development are:

- Denmark – an information technology joint-venture business start-up in Uganda through its PSD programme.

- EC – in addition to financing telecom projects, the European Investment Bank (EIB) has supported small and medium scale enterprise (SME) projects investing the adoption of computer technologies or providing ICT services.

- France – the subsidiary of Agence Française de Développement (AfD), the Société de Promotion et de Participation pour la Coopération Economique (Proparco) has a current exposure of €70 million in the ICT sector.

- Japan – the Japan Bank for International Cooperation (JBIC) provides untied loans to create local sector finance funds, including ICT funds.

- Netherlands – FMO, the Netherlands Development Finance Company, has been active in the telecom market in roughly 20 countries and works closely with local partners; the majority of the funding consists of loans to mobile operators.

- Norway – the Norwegian Investment Fund for Development Countries (NORFUND) formerly the industrial and commercial facilities of the Norwegian Development Cooperation, extended grants, loans and guarantees to GrameenPhone Ltd. in Bangladesh for the support of Village Phone Programmes (a grant of $5 million and a loan of $7.5 million; see also Box 8).

- Sweden – Sida, the Swedish development agency, promotes the PSD through donor support of risk mitigation and guarantees. In this regard, Sida has over the years developed a specific financing mechanism called GuarantCo., which is a financial entity to facilitate the provision of infrastructure and its services through sub-sovereign financing without the necessity of sovereign guarantee, though it has not yet specifically been applied in any ICT project.

- Switzerland – the State Secretariat for Economic Affairs (SECO) participates in Swiss and international risk-capital funds for ICT activities, and provides financial support for the Swiss Organization for Facilitating Investments (SOFI) in favour of SMEs.

- United Kingdom – the 100% DFID-owned Commonwealth Development Corporation (CDC) is a substantial investor in technology companies in developing countries. In 2003, CDC investments in the telecoms, media and technology sector accounted to some £111 million (approximately $200 million), about 10% of the CDC total portfolio. Major investments include Celtel, Digicel and GrameenPhone.

- United States – many collaborations with the US private sector are made possible by funds from the Global Development Alliance (GDA), a programme initiated by the USAID. The GDA facilitates agreements among stakeholders that maximize benefit of USAID assistance dollars. These alliances bring new resources, ideas, technologies and partners to bear on ICT problems in developing countries.

Multi-Donor Initiatives and Partnerships

Multi-donor initiatives provide important assistance to ICTD through a variety of approaches and financing instruments. New forms of multi-stakeholder partnership – linking governments, the private sector, NGOs and international organizations in informal co-operation – can bring flexibility and creativity to the ICT-for-development effort. But they require clarity about objectives and outcomes and their relationship to formal initiatives and institutions.

Public-private partnerships (PPPs) play a key role in harnessing ICT for development given the scale of the resources required. ICT can have a catalytic role in fostering growth in a variety of sectors of the economy. Encouraging growth in the ICT sector – as well as ICT-led growth in other sectors – requires a proper enabling environment, balancing risk and regulation, and new forms of partnership.

At the same time, donors and developing countries must do more to share information and coordinate efforts with a particular focus on evaluation, and learning from both successes and failures. Donors should focus on competing for impact, not for volume. Best-practice examples should focus not simply on which projects have succeeded but on the factors that were critical for success, including demand, cost, capacity and content. It is time to move beyond experimentation to a more rigorous, coordinated, results-oriented approach to ICT that will make them a more effective tool for sustained growth and poverty reduction.

The OECD has been playing a major role in sharing the experiences of its member countries with the "new economy", providing a forum to develop action plans, set benchmarks and monitor progress, and coordinating donor programmes, with more use of ICT within them to reduce inefficiencies. Jointly with the United Nations and the World Bank, the OECD DAC has so far organized two Global Forums: the first, in March 2001, examined the role of ICT in helping achieve shared development goals and cooperation in bridging the "digital divide"; and the second, in March 2003, aimed, among other things, at integrating ICT in donor programmes in support of countries' own development plans and addressing the policy challenges and opportunities of ICTs for development.

The rationale for the establishment of these multi-stakeholder initiatives thus lies not only in the joint financing of ICTD initiatives but also in providing a platform for exchange of experiences and learning among donor institutions. Given the fast advance in technology in the ICT sector, learning and sharing of experience is a critical factor in success and the scaling-up of pilot experiences to broad-based assistance for development requires co-ordination and co-operation between the different stakeholders. Some of the important multi-donor initiatives are described below.

The **Public Private Infrastructure Advisory Facility (PPIAF)** is a multi-donor facility that works with the central and municipal governments of developing countries to improve the enabling environment for private-sector involvement in infrastructure services. The PPIAF currently has fourteen contributing donors and undertakes a broad range of activities, including the development of legislation and regulatory systems, sector-reform strategies, the training of regulators and assistance with facilitating transactions. The telecommunications sector accounts for about 11% of PPIAF expenditure.

In 2002, the DFID (United Kingdom), SECO (Switzerland), Sida (Sweden) and DGIS (The Netherlands) formed the **Private Infrastructure Development Group (PIDG)** with the aim of mobilizing private investment in infrastructure for growth and the elimination of poverty. The World Bank has also subsequently joined the PIDG.

The **Building Communications Opportunities (BCO)** Alliance is the follow-up to the Building Digital Opportunities (BDO) programme. Five bilateral agency partners and five others support the BCO. The former include the Canadian International Development Agency (CIDA), the UK Department for International Development (DFID), the Dutch Directorate-General for International Cooperation (DGIS), the Danish Ministry of Foreign Affairs (DMFA) and the Swiss Agency for Development and Cooperation (SDC). Other partners are: the Association for Progressive Communication (APC), Bellanet, IICD, OneWorld International (OWI) and Panos.

The BCO Alliance, like the BDO Programme, is not a legal entity; rather, it is a framework by which donors and other stakeholders can coordinate their work more effectively and realize useful partnerships. Frequent consultation and learning will strengthen co-ordination and limit duplication of content and activities as well as funding. In the previous BDO Programme, the transparency of funding relationships between the donors and the NGO partners was not optimal. As part of the BCO Alliance, more concerted effort will be made between the donors to coordinate funding flows among the NGO partners. Joint financing of some organizations and activities will likely be the result. Legal relationships between NGOs and donors remain bilateral. There will be no "pooling" of donor funds through the BCO Alliance, as it is not a legal entity.

Conclusion

The transformation of business and social activities that information and communication technologies have brought about in the developed world is now seen to offer potentially huge benefits also to the developing world.

Although the private sector has lead the investments for building ICT infrastructure, operating ICT networks and delivering ICT services over the last decades and provided the bulk of financial resources, public sector funding and official development assistance play an important role in creating an enabling policy environment, channelling resources towards less commercially attractive regions as well as towards the poor, and supporting innovative financing mechanisms for ICT for development.

Donor support for ICT for development as well as overall ODA show clear trends in recent years. After the decline in the volume of ODA observed in the 1990s, the aid flows have recovered in recent years and reached their highest level of US\$ 61 billion in 2003. However,

ODA has fallen substantially as a percentage of donor countries' GNI over the past two decades, from 0.35% to 0.25%.

Parallel to the fall in overall aid flows, ODA commitments for ICT infrastructure have declined strongly from US$1.2 billion in 1990 to US$194 million in 2002. The rationale for most donors to withdraw from the provision of ICT infrastructure was linked to the expectation of an increasingly strong role of the private sector. However, donor assistance to ICT infrastructure is by no means the entire picture of the role of ODA in ICT for development. Most donors are engaged in bilateral ICT-specific programmes and contribute to international multi-donor initiatives for ICT, and at the same time many also have integrated ICT components in their development programmes which are not reflected in the trends on commitments for ICT infrastructure.

The renewed commitment of bilateral donors for ICT for development, as documented by the OECD-DAC Donor ICT Strategies Matrix, suggests that the decline in bilateral ODA financing for ICT infrastructure has at least offset by the increase in ICT-related flows included in other development programmes.

Future orientations and challenges for ICT for development as recognized by governments and donors in their ICT strategies and policies highlight the importance of the regulatory environment and policy frameworks for attracting the private sector investment for ICT for development. New forms of multi-donor partnerships are appearing not only as a joint financing mechanism but also as a platform for exchange of experiences and learning among donor institutions.

ICT AND NATIONAL INNOVATION SYSTEMS

By Motoo Kusakabe, European Bank for Reconstruction and Development

There is a common understanding among academics and development practitioners that the creation of a knowledge economy is the key for sustainable economic growth within developed and developing world, and that ICT has a strategic importance in achieving this knowledge economy. If we look at the ten countries that achieved the highest growth in the last 20 years, most of these countries are highly successful creators of social and economic systems, which allow innovation and entrepreneurship and ICT-enabled businesses.

However, the relationship between ICT/knowledge and economic growth is not straightforward. If we calculate, using the data of 131 countries, the correlations between per capita income growth in the past two decades and the indicators relating to knowledge, such as tertiary education enrolment, research and development (R&D) expenditure, number of engineers, patent applications by residents, teledensity, Internet and personal computer penetration, no meaningful correlations exist.

On one hand, these knowledge/ICT related indicators have a high correlation with income levels. In turn, economic growth rates are highly correlated with basic indicators such as a primary education completion ratio, financial market development, regulatory quality and other governance related indicators, and export growth. Export performance is also closely linked to ICT-related exports.

These seemingly contradicting data indicate that knowledge and ICT usage do not automatically translate into higher economic growth, unless there is a system in place, which transforms knowledge into competitive production capability in knowledge-intensive goods and services, through good governance, regulatory frameworks, and workforce discipline created by basic education. In this stage, technologies used are often "borrowed technologies" supported by a high learning capability, efficient management systems and process innovation. We call such system a "basic innovation system".

While succeeding in achieving higher growth for limited periods of time, these countries face diminishing returns as their labor costs increase and technologies become mature. They need to transform their economy to a higher stage, which relies more heavily on the creation of knowledge through R&D and product innovation. For a country to be competitive in maintaining these high-income standards as well as high productivity growth, it needs to create a system to foster knowledge. This system requires more ICT usage, higher education, R&D expenditure and linkage of knowledge creation to business creation. We may call such a system as "Advanced Innovation System". Technologies at this stage are cutting edge and often subject to an increasing rate of return. R&D is more devoted to product innovation. The positioning of R&D resources to strategically important technologies is more important than the learning capability. Many countries have created their own unique advanced innovation systems.

What are the implications of such an understanding for the evolution of innovation systems?

- A fragmented approach to mechanically increase the usage of ICT or higher education does not work. For most developing countries, there must be a clear objective to create a basic innovation system.

- As many elements of the basic innovation system are related to governance, regulatory frameworks, and financial systems, national ICT development strategy should be closely linked to the national poverty reduction strategy, which addresses these issues.

- Higher education, ICT diffusion, and R&D capacity will not develop overnight, and it is important for developing countries to start systematic efforts in creating such capability with a longer-term perspective and vision.

- In both stages, the creation of the total ecosystem to promote innovation and entrepreneurship is essential. Particularly, a network of universities, an entrepreneur education system, technology transfer organizations, joint research programme with academic and business sectors, technology incubators and science parks, and financial infrastructure for early stage financing mechanism are important components of the system. But more important is the networking of all these components to work together to support the entrepreneurs.

- For latecomer countries, which try to create such an innovation system, the government's role is more important. Ireland, Israel, Taiwan, Korea, Malaysia, and Estonia, all created a unique advanced innovation system with different roles of the government.

What Countries Grew Most Rapidly?

Within the last 10-20 years, a group of countries has shown remarkable growth in per capita GDP, while most of the developing and transition countries suffered set-backs in economic growth.

The table below lists the top 10 countries in average growth rate per capita in the last 11 and 21 years. What are the common factors, which explain such high growth in these countries? There are many studies in the recent 40 years analyzing the source of the growth in developing and developed countries. China, Korea, Ireland and Singapore are all famous for their information and communications technologies (ICT). Are ICT an engine of growth?

In the 21 years to 2001 we have seen growth rates of:

China	8.2%	Thailand	4.6%
Korea	6.1%	Mauritius	4.5%
Ireland	4.8%	Singapore	4.4%
Botswana	4.8%	Bhutan	4.2%
St. Kitts & Nevis	4.6%	Cyprus	4.2%

What are the High Income Countries?

These are the top twenty countries in terms of GDP per capita PPP (Purchasing Power Parity). They are a different set of countries compared to those with the highest growth rates. Therefore, the common factors explaining a high level of income will be different from the factors behind higher growth.

There are several countries in this list, which have achieved a high degree of ICT development at 2001. Are ICT a determinant for the level of income for, the following countries:

Luxemburg	Netherlands	Italy
U.S.	Canada	Finland
Ireland	Austria	Sweden
Iceland	Belgium	U.K.
Norway	Germany	France
Denmark	Japan	
Switzerland	Hong Kong	

How to Find the Factors that Explain Growth and Income Level?

The author calculated correlation coefficients between major economic indicators and the GDP per capita growth for the last 21 years or GDP per capita of 2001 using the data of 131 countries from World Development Indicators and Governance indicators compiled by the World Bank. In order to clarify the role of knowledge, innovation and entrepreneurship in economic growth, indicators are selected from the following categories: education, ICT use, innovation, infrastructure, finance, governance, export, and capital flows.

The role of knowledge, innovation and entrepreneurship certainly differs depending on the stages of economic development. The author found that there is a significant difference in the correlation patterns between the lower-middle income countries and upper-middle income countries. (Threshold is USD 3,000 GDP per capita -1995 prices). Therefore, in the following tables, correlation coefficients are shown for four groups of countries:

1. All countries for which data is available,

2. "Lower income" countries which consist of low-income countries and lower-middle income countries,

3. "Higher income" countries, which consist of upper-middle income countries and high-income non-OECD countries, and

4. OECD countries.

For OECD countries, correlation coefficients are shown in two forms; one is the correlation to GDP per capita growth rates in the last 21 years ("growth") and the other is the GDP per capita PPP in 2001 ("income levels"). Among OECD countries, income growth and income levels are in general inversely correlated and due to this fact, the two sets of correlation coefficients behave differently. Correlations to income levels often provide more useful policy implications in the case of matured economies such as OECD countries than those to growth rates.

Is Education the Engine of Growth?

Education is thought to be the most important determinant of economic growth. Many high growth Asian economies are also known to put strong emphasis on education. In the era of the knowledge economy, the relevance of higher education has become more significant.

However, the famous paradox known to development economists is that statistically there is almost no correlation between education indicators and economic growth rates (see all countries in Table 1), this is particularly true for tertiary education. As shown in the Table 1, in lower income countries, only small correlations are found in the primary education enrollment and primary completion rates, but negligible or negative correlations between indicators representing higher level education and quality of education.

Why do education indicators have such insignificant correlation with growth in lower income countries? The most plausible answer would be that education is effective only if other factors are present: good job opportunities for school graduates, economic incentive system to reward better education, etc.[1]. In most of the lower income countries, such opportunity or incentive systems do not exist. Furthermore, the quality of education is not satisfactory to improve the economic productivity of these countries.

Table 1. Education					
	Correl to Growth				Correl to Income
	All Countries	Lower Income	Higher Income	OECD	OECD
Expenditure per student, Tertiary (% of GDP per capita)	26.9%	-8.4%	22.1%	16.7%	79.4%
Expenditure per student, secondary (% of GDP per capita)	27.3%	-7.1%	21.5%	17.7%	81.1%
Expenditure per student, primary (% of GDP per capita)	28.4%	-6.2%	23.5%	14.7%	76.4%
School enrolment, tertiary (% gross)	25.5%	-1.9%	11.2%	-11.1%	-42.1%
School enrolment, secondary (% net)	44.3%	14.5%	29.7%	16.1%	-35.6%
School enrolment, primary, male (% net)	38.1%	28.7%	30.0%	4.6%	-25.0%
School enrolment, primary, female (% net)	39.7%	28.1%	41.6%	44.2%	-19.7%
Primary completion rate, total (% of relevant age group)	43.1%	32.5%	64.5%	77.8%	
Illiteracy rate, adult total (% of people ages 15 and above)	-9.0%	-6.8%	10.9%	-67.0%	1.7%
Illiteracy rate, youth total (% of people ages 15-24)	-2.0%	-1.9%	20.4%	-70.5%	7.3%
Pupil-teacher ratio, primary	-25.1%	-10.5%	-1.7%	-9.0%	-10.1%
Repetition rate, primary (% of total enrolment)	-34.8%	-36.3%	-9.4%	-70.5%	-30.3%
Personal computers installed in education (per mil GDP)	-4.7%	-32.7%	60.9%	-15.0%	29.9%

---

[1] Pretchett, Lant. Where Has All the Education Gone? The World Bank Policy Research Working Paper 1581

In the lower income countries (low-income countries and lower-middle income countries), indicators relating to primary education have a positive but insignificant correlation with economic growth. All other indicators, particularly those relating to tertiary education show negative correlations.

However, in higher income countries (upper-middle income countries and high-income non-OECD countries) we can see a different picture. Indicators relating to primary education show much higher correlations with growth, particularly the primary education completion ratio, which has statistically significant correlations. Indicators relating to secondary and tertiary education show fairly high correlations.

In the case of OECD countries, there are strong correlations between secondary and tertiary education indicators and income level. Higher level education is both cause and result of the higher level of income, which is synonymous to a knowledge-based economy.

Is Infrastructure the Engine of Growth?

Physical infrastructure is considered an important determinant of economic growth. A few decades ago, the World Bank and other aid agencies were focusing on investing in infrastructure project in order to increase the growth rate of the economy. Even now in many developing and transition countries, insufficient physical infrastructure such as power and transportation represents a severe limitation for any business environment.

However, again ironically, indicators relating to infrastructure, such as road paved or electric power consumption (kWh per capita) have almost no correlations to the growth rates in lower income countries. Correlation of telephone density to growth is also small (12.9%).

As Table 2 shows, indicators which represent the quality of management of infrastructure, such as electric power losses and telephone waiting time before installation have a more significant correlation with the growth in lower income countries. This result has some implications when considering how to improve infrastructure; namely that increase in supply of physical infrastructure by inefficient suppliers may not significantly impact on growth but improving management of infrastructure by competitive pressures from the market may have much better impacts on economic growth.

Table 2. Infrastructure					
	Correl to Growth				Correl to Income
	All Countries	Lower Income	Higher Income	OECD	OECD
Telephone mainlines (per 1,000 people)	39.0%	10.5%	45.6%	-0.7%	48.7%
Fixed line and mobile phone subscribers	39.5%	12.9%	40.6%	3.5%	41.8%
Telephone Mainlines Waiting Time (years)	-44.6%	-32.1%	-38.8%	-19.3%	-39.4%
Roads, paved (% of total roads)	35.3%	15.0%	30.7%	12.4%	3.9%
Electric power consumption (kwh per capita)	9.7%	0.2%	3.0%	28.7%	16.6%
Electric power losses (% of output)	-25.7%	-20.4%	-30.3%	-46.7%	0.8%

Looking at the column of higher income countries in Table 2, infrastructure indicators have much more significant correlations with growth and also significant correlations with income levels in OECD countries. It is noteworthy that telecommunication-related indicators show the highest correlation with the growth in higher income and OECD countries.

Is Financing the Engine of Growth?

The financial sector is also relevant to economic growth. There are three indicators representing the volume of the financial sector in the economy: Quasi money (M2) which represents liquid obligation of the banking sector (such as cash and demand deposits), domestic credit to the private sector by the banking sector, and stock traded (all relative to GDP). There are strong positive correlations between these indicators and the economic growth as shown in Table 3 for both lower income and higher income countries.

It is well-known that all high growth countries have relatively developed financial markets; Hong Kong, Malaysia, Thailand, Singapore, China and Korea have almost as deep a financial market as Japan, Switzerland, US, and UK , both in the banking sector and capital markets.

These indicators show only quantitative aspects of the financial market, but qualitative aspects, such as regulatory quality and efficiency of the market would show equally or even more important implications for the economic growth. This will be covered by the following section. As for OECD countries, correlations between M2, stocks traded and income levels are negative. This is probably because at this stage of economic development, indicators which represent only the volume of the financial market are not relevant to growth and income levels.

Table 3. Financial Market					
	Correl to Growth				Correl to Income
	All Countries	Lower Income	Higher Income	OECD	OECD
Money and quasi money (M2) as % of GDP	38.1%	26.4%	48.0%	31.5%	-34.0%
Stocks traded, total value (% of GDP)	31.4%	67.9%	45.4%	-8.7%	-5.1%
Domestic credit to private sector (% of GDP)	50.2%	52.5%	43.0%	17.8%	17.5%

Is Governance the Engine of Growth?

Governance is increasingly being emphasized as the key factor for economic growth. As can be seen from Table 4, governance indicators reveal a strong correlation with economic growth. Recently, after 50 years of less than satisfactory experience of growth in the developing world, the development community has realized the importance of governance factors, and put highest priorities to governance issues. Basically, all the statistical studies show that there are no positive impacts of economic aid on growth in developing countries, unless the countries demonstrate good governance.

Table 4 shows six indicators compiled by Danny Kaufman and his group in the World Bank: voice and accountability, political stability, government effectiveness, regulatory quality, rule of law, and control of corruption. All these indicators have strong correlations with growth.

It is noteworthy that among the six indicators, government effectiveness has the highest correlation with growth (51%), followed by regulatory quality (48%), rule of law (48%) and control of corruption. (48%).

Table 4. Governance					
	Correl to Growth				Correl to Income
	All Countries	Lower Income	Higher Income	OECD	OECD
Voice and Accountability	36.2%	6.7%	44.3%	-0.7%	22.8%
Political Stability	45.7%	27.5%	49.3%	15.8%	38.2%
Government Effectiveness	51.4%	50.2%	46.2%	9.3%	44.1%
Regulatory Quality	48.1%	35.9%	31.2%	28.1%	28.2%
Rule of Law	48.9%	39.8%	52.4%	1.1%	37.3%
Control of Corruption	48.0%	37.9%	54.6%	-3.4%	28.0%

It is interesting that governance indicators have an almost equally strong correlation with the growth and income levels in lower income countries, higher income countries and OECD countries. Fostering economic growth and maintaining high income levels build on a high standard in all aspects of governance, including government effectiveness, high regulatory quality, rule of law, and control of corruption.

Is ICT Usage the Engine of Growth?

One of the key finding is that the usage of ICT, such as Internet usage, number of PCs, and Internet servers per 1000 people, have a positive but insignificant correlation with the economic growth in lower income countries (see Table 5). This does not mean ICT are unimportant in lower income countries. But it has some implication for policy makers, when they formulate an ICT development strategy in their countries. Policies targeted for simply increasing the number of ICT users may not have a significant impact on creating higher economic growth.

Table 5. ICT Usage					
	Correl to Growth				Correl to Income
	All Countries	Lower Income	Higher Income	OECD	OECD
Internet Users (per thousand people)	31.4%	13.1%	41.6%	-3.6%	20.6%
PC (per thousand people)	32.7%	7.1%	40.1%	6.2%	63.0%
Secure Internet Server (per million people)	30.2%	11.7%	39.7%	-1.7%	36.2%

When we look at the higher income countries, the correlation between ICT usage and growth becomes much clearer, and the income level in OECD countries is correlated to the PC penetration in a significant way. This could mean that starting at certain income levels, high ICT usage produces higher productivity growth and contributing to keeping high levels of income or both.

Why are there such small correlations between ICT usage and economic growth in lower income countries? One hypothesis is that although ICT are an important ingredient for the growth, ICT effectively stimulates economic growth only if some other factors are available or some conditions are met. In lower income countries where such other factors or conditions do not exist, ICT cannot ignite growth.

In conclusion, it is more likely that ICT usage itself is not an engine of growth for lower income countries but when the income level reaches a certain level, ICT usage has a strong correlation with economic growth and with maintaining high income levels.

Is Innovation the Engine of Growth?

Innovation and scientific knowledge are thought to be the essential factors for growth particularly in the information age and in a knowledge-based economy.

As shown in Table 6, in lower income countries, the statistical correlations between science and innovation related indicators and growth are low or even negative, except for science and technical journal articles per GDP. In lower income countries, scientists and engineers in R&D, and patent applications by residents (per GDP) have negative correlations with economic growth.

This means that the simple promotion of science and technologies does not guarantee higher economic growth. This is a typical phenomenon in CIS countries: the world leaders in the number of patent applications by residents per GDP are Moldova, followed by Korea, Ukraine, Georgia, Mongolia, and Japan. Even though these countries are good at science and technologies, they have not been successful in commercializing the patent, due to lack of institutional support to entrepreneurs.

Promoting innovation and scientific and engineering capacity is key to maintaining high-income level as shown in Table 6. Top countries in terms of scientists and engineers per 1000 population are Japan, Finland, Iceland, Sweden, Norway, US, and Switzerland, all of which are well-known high-tech countries.

Table 6. Innovation					
	Correl to Growth				Correl to Income
	All Countries	Lower Income	Higher Income	OECD	OECD
Research and development expenditure (% of GDP)	17.8%	8.6%	36.1%	-26.5%	42.4%
Scientific and technical journal articles per $1000 of GDP	35.1%	19.0%	14.3%	27.4%	95.1%
Scientists and engineers in RandD (per million people)	3.0%	-36.3%	31.6%	-28.1%	49.8%
Patent applications, residents (per thousand GDP)	-4.5%	-28.1%	37.2%	2.3%	-5.5%

Looking at the figures in higher income countries and OECD countries (correlation to income levels), innovation-related indicators become positive and show much higher correlations. At this income level, innovation becomes an important factor for achieving economic growth and maintaining high income levels.

Is Export the Engine of Growth?

So far we looked at indicators which have little correlation with economic growth in lower income countries. Then, what are the factors that matter for the economic growth in lower income countries? There are three broad categories which have significant correlations with economic growth: exports, finance, and governance.

Table 7 below shows that export growth has a high correlation with economic growth (62%) for all countries, exhibiting the highest correlation coefficient among the various indicators of the correlation has been calculated. This finding is consistent with many previous studies, which show that trade, especially export, is the most important determinant of economic growth.

Table 7. Exports and Capital Flows					
	Correl to Growth				Correl to Income
	All Countries	Lower Income	Higher Income	OECD	OECD
Export Growth in 21Years (constant 1995 US$) (mill)	62.5%	61.5%	53.5%	81.5%	23.3%
Hi-Tech Export Performance	48.9%	61.7%	42.1%	72.5%	44.7%
Gross foreign direct investment (% of GDP)	30.3%	11.1%	25.7%	19.6%	0.1%
Private capital flows, net total (DRS, current US$ per thous GDP)	24.2%	13.3%	20.9%	5.1%	

Why do exports have so important an association with economic growth? Because the rapid growth of exports requires the combination of a good business environment, entrepreneurship, management and marketing skills, and quality of product etc., growth of export represents the outcome of effective market-based economic system.

Foreign direct investment (FDI) is also an important strategic factor for economic growth. But its correlation with growth (30%) is much less compared to that of export growth. Private capital flows should have a great impact in the economic growth, but in reality, due to the various impediments and imperfect market, private capital flows do not have significant correlation with the growth in developing countries.

What Factors Explain this High Export Growth?

What are the factors which explain the high performance in export growth in these countries?

In Table 7, the correlation between hi-tech export performance indicator and economic growth is calculated. Hi-tech export performance indicators are defined as the geometric average of the share of the hi-tech exports[2] to the total export in 1995 and the average annual growth rate of hi-tech export during the past seven years to 2002. This indicator has a strong correlation with the economic growth of both lower income countries and higher income countries.

Table 8 lists the ten top performers in export growth. They are mainly East Asian Tigers, plus Ireland, Mexico, and India. The common theme among these countries is that they export highly income-elastic hi-tech products, particularly, ICT-related exports.

Table 8. Top 10 countries with highest export growth and ICT exports		
1. China	13.7%	OO
2. Korea	12.5%	OOO
3. Thailand	11.5%	OO
4. Ireland	11.0%	OOOO
5. Malaysia	10.8%	OOO
6. Hong Kong	10.6%	O
7. Bangladesh	10.0%	
8. Mexico	10.0%	OO
9. India	9.1%	
10. Syria	8.8%	

The World Trade Center (in a study jointly sponsored by UNCTAD and WTO) published performance indicators of ICT-related exports in four categories: electric machineries and equipment, electronic equipment and components, office machinery and supplies, and telecommunication equipment. The circle marks in the left column indicate that these countries are among the top twenty performers in WTC index in those 4 categories. It shows very clearly that high export performance in these countries depend heavily on ICT-related export performance.

India is a good performer of ICT-related service exports, namely software services, which is not included in the ITC's exercise (focusing only on manufactured exports), but clearly India also represents a high export performance based on ICT.

ICT-related goods are no longer a minor part of total exports of emerging-market economies. Data shows that emerging-market economies account for 25 percent of total ICT exports and 35 percent of total ICT imports. In the area of office machinery, including assembled computers, Mexico's export share is twice as much as Canada's and the value of exports from Hungary was twice that of Switzerland.

Summary of Findings

In summary, the factors which have strong correlations with economic growth in lower income countries (low-income countries and lower-middle income countries) are: export growth, particularly high-tech export; primary education; financial markets development; governance (particularly government effectiveness and quality of regulation); and telecommunication infrastructure and its management.

---

[2] High-technology exports are products with high R&D intensity, such as in aerospace, computers, pharmaceuticals, scientific instruments, and electrical machinery. Source: United Nations, COMTRADE database.

On the contrary, the factors which have little correlation with economic growth in lower income countries are: higher education, ICT usage, innovation related indicators, and level of infrastructure.

As for the higher income countries (i.e. upper-middle income countries and high-income non-OECD countries), the factors which have strong correlation with economic growth are: ICT usage, such as Internet users, number of PCs and servers; education-related indicators, such as those related to secondary and tertiary education and quality of education; indicators related to innovation, such as number of scientist/engineers, number of academic journal articles, and R&D expenditure per GDP; infrastructure, especially telecommunication infrastructure; financial market and governance-related indicators and export growth, particularly hi-tech exports.

Two Stages of Knowledge-Based Economic Growth

How can we interpret the results of the correlation analysis of the previous section? For both lower income and higher income countries, export of the high-technology goods and services plays an important role in economic growth. This is consistent with the usual export-led growth strategy recommended by neo-classical economists. It is striking that even in lower income countries, hi-tech exports have a strong correlation with economic growth. However, technologies used in the lower income countries and higher income countries may have the following differences:

Lower Income Countries: "Commodity" Technology-led Growth

In the case of lower income countries, technologies used are mostly matured technologies "borrowed" from abroad through purchasing the patents or copying and learning. As these technologies mature, the availability of cheap and abundant labor will provide multi-national corporations the advantage to shift their production base to these countries. At this stage of economic growth the contribution of total factor productivity is relatively minor and increase in labor and capital inputs explain the major part of economic growth. The technologies are subject to diminishing rates of return.

"Innovation" Technology-led Growth

In higher income countries, after an exploitation of the relatively abundant and cheap labor, they have to rely more on the newly created technologies through their R&D efforts. Innovation and entrepreneurship become more important elements of competitiveness. The pattern of growth is relying more on total factor productivity growth than growth of labor and capital inputs. At this stage the technologies are often characterized by an "increasing rate of return".

"Commodity" Technology Export-led Growth and Basic Innovation Systems

Let us look more closely at the first stage of economic growth based on "commodity" technologies in low income countries. Even at this stage, economic growth is strongly correlated to export growth particularly hi-tech exports. However, the technologies used are mature technologies, such as assembly of consumer electronics, PC and peripherals, software programming and coding, and business process outsourcing. These technologies, when they were first invented, were innovative and knowledge intensive technologies, but after mass production and mass sales, these technologies became mature and are better transferred to lower income countries.

However, not every country can absorb such technologies and efficiently produce goods which are competitive in global markets. Technology transfer requires certain skill sets within these countries to allow for absorption. First, high learning skills are needed to understand and reproduce technologies, which require basic engineering and production skills. Secondly, there should be highly efficient entrepreneurs to undertake the task of producing and selling such hi-tech goods. Third, a well-educated and well-disciplined workforce, which produces high quality goods and services is needed. In order to be competitive in the market, workers need to be innovative with the production process.

To have such skills developed and applied and to create efficient hi-tech export industries, we need a highly integrated social and economic system that can be called a "Basic National Innovation System", which is comprised of governance, a regulatory framework, an efficient government system, primary education, financial systems, and entrepreneurship.

"Innovative" Technology Export Growth and Advanced Innovation Systems

After decades of high growth led by commodity technologies, per capita income of countries increases, and when they reach income levels which are above those of upper-middle income countries, they are faced with hurdles imposed by "diminishing rate of return", such as declining surplus labour, scarcity of middle management, increasing competition from the lower income countries and declining rates of return on the investments.

They can no longer be competitive by simply using commonly available technologies. In order to overcome such problems, when countries reach the upper-middle income stage, they have to transform their economy into a different paradigm; namely, "innovation" technology-led export growth. They have to innovate on technologies and commercialize such innovative technologies. As they can no longer rely upon borrowed technologies, they have to create a system to produce new technologies through R&D and incentivize the system to support entrepreneurs that will develop and adopt these new technologies. Innovation is addressed to both "process" and "product" innovation. In order to encourage such innovation, intellectual property rights need to be institutionalized.

At this stage, required skills or factors include highly educated innovative persons, managerial skills for large R&D projects, strategic positioning/selection of new R&D activities, management skills to start up an enterprise and to undertake innovative ideas as well as a culture that encourages innovation and entrepreneurship.

In order to develop such skills and coordinate the skills to create competitive hi-tech export businesses, a new type of social and economic system becomes necessary that can be called an "Advanced National Innovation System". The new system may have different characteristics county-to-country. However, it must include universities and higher research institutions, entrepreneurial education and an IPR system, R&D capability, technology transfer organizations, business incubators and science parks, venture capital funds, angel investors, and various professional services for entrepreneurs.

How did Countries Make the Transition from Basic to Advanced National Innovation Systems?

The United States of America, as the leading industrial country in mass production, suffered from stagnant productivity growth in the 70s. As a response, the country developed the Silicon Valley model during the 80s and 90s based on the creation of spin-off innovative small businesses using close relationships with universities and research institutions. Venture capital funds and angel investors' networks were developed to support entrepreneurs. This model was proliferated throughout the United States and significantly contributed to the recent increase in productivity growth.

Japan is one of the largest R&D spenders relative to GDP. However, this R&D is mostly conducted by large corporations. The university-business relationships have been relatively weak until recently, but there is a highly developed cluster of small hi-tech metal and plastic manufacturing companies in the Keihin district in Tokyo that facilitate prototyping and small lot large variety production.

Taiwan developed a large number of small- and medium-sized companies in manufacturing PCs and its peripherals during the 70s. In the 80s, the government undertook a joint initiative with the government research institute to develop advanced integrated circuit technologies. The Hsing Chu Science Park, located south of Taipei, was created. Spin-off IC foundry companies were created during the 80s to provide an OEM production of advanced IC chips. In the science park, there are close relationships among companies, universities, and research institutes. IC companies are specialized in design, manufacturing, and testing, etc. to have a horizontal division of labor.

Ireland suffered from stagnant economic growth and brain drain after World War II. The government initiated an active industrial policy to attract multi-national companies. During the 1980s, most of the foreign investments were oriented toward low value-added business process outsourcing and programming jobs. But the government started to promote innovation and entrepreneurship in knowledge-intensive industries, thus creating a hi-tech industry clusters and venture capital funds. In 1998 the government created Enterprise Ireland which coordinates all these activities. Through such government efforts, Ireland successfully created a National Innovation System and showed remarkable economic growth in recent decades.

India invested in tertiary education from the early 60s on, creating six Indian Institutes of Technology. Initially the most capable graduates of IITs went abroad, particularly to Silicon Valley to study, and created innovative enterprises. Bangalore attracted MNCs' research institutes due to abundant supply of highly educated software engineers. Eventually entrepreneurs successfully established in Silicon Valley came back to Bangalore to establish software companies mainly to export software services to the US and Europe. These companies apply a rigorous quality control mechanism to upgrade their software house to world-class and top-quality standards.

Conclusion

There are different types of National Innovation Systems depending upon the country's history, and economic and social conditions. The roles of the government, the private sector and universities are different in each system. However, it is important to create an integrated system to support innovation and entrepreneurship. If a country is successful in creating such a system, the country will achieve higher growth and in a world of increasing rate of return, this country can enjoy such advantages for a long time. Developing countries should focus more on the creation of such systems, and could learn from the experiences of the countries in similar situations. Also, development agencies should put more emphasis on providing strategic advice for developing countries in the formation of an Innovation System or regional ICT clusters as the total system, rather than providing fragmented support for individual sectors without a vision of a total eco-system to support entrepreneurs.

Section 4

Case Study

ICT DEVELOPMENT IN SMALL ISLAND DEVELOPING STATES: THE CASE OF SAMOA

By Gisa Fuatai Purcell, Samoa's National ICT Committee

All governments face difficulties in trying to ensure the full participation of every citizen. The further citizens are located from the centre of power and administration, the less engaged they are likely to be. This phenomenon can be observed at both national and international levels. At the global level, countries located in close proximity to major world markets are more likely to have well-developed ICT services than more marginally located countries, particularly those with low population densities. This is true of the small island developing states floating in the Pacific Ocean which are remotely located from major world markets and have very low population densities.

Within individual countries there is a marked variation between rural and urban areas both in terms of access to available infrastructure and uptake by citizens (Parker, 2000). In general, the more remote the location and the smaller the population density, the lower the rate of participation. This can be observed even in the most highly developed countries. For example, the Japanese government often struggles to provide the elderly residents of remote islands with government services (Hayashi and Hori, 2002). In small island developing states (SIDS) like Samoa, which are some of the most remotely located nations in the world with underdeveloped economies and with low population densities, ensuring citizens' participation is particularly challenging.

ICT now make it possible to connect a citizen in even the most far-flung location directly to central government services. A notable example of a remotely located country that has highly developed ICT, especially in implementing its e-government, is New Zealand. Despite having only four million inhabitants, and being placed on the other side of the world from the major world markets of Europe and the USA, in 2001 New Zealand was nominated by the United Nations as the country with the third most advanced e-government system in the world (Boyle and Nicholson, 2003). In comparing New Zealand to Samoa and other small island developing states in the Pacific, the marked difference is in the level of economic development.

This paper describes the efforts of the Samoan Government in developing a national ICT strategy. From the experience of Samoa, lessons can be learned about the way ICT can help overcome the advantages of distance and low population. The insights gained from sharing information on Samoa's National ICT development are relevant worldwide; even the most economically developed countries have pockets of population that are hard to reach. This paper will help bridge the gap in ICT for development between the small island developing states and highly populated developing countries.

Background

Samoa is an independent island nation in the South Pacific, with a long history of political and economic stability. The country has a land area of approximately 2,938 square kilometers, and a population of approximately 178,000. The Samoan economy is sustained by agriculture, fishing, handicraft production, small manufacturing goods, and one automobile-wiring firm. Tourism has recently become a valuable contributor to the Samoan economy, and since 1990 has been the top foreign exchange earner. Small and medium enterprises (SMEs) or micro small enterprises (MSEs) are central to Samoa's economic well-being comprising over 99% of the Samoan economy. The markets are small and limited to national and regional markets. However with the development of ICT, it has been noted that even the smallest NGO with only 32 members have already received handicraft orders through their website. This is an encouraging sign, and it shows that ICT can have an impact on the social and economic development of the poor.

Samoa is a small country with a simple governance structure. Though the central government consults with village mayors (Pulenu'u) and presidents of the village women's committees, there is no local government as such. This means that current systems of government are relatively easy to automate. Samoa has a low population density, which has its advantages, such that ICT-based strategies can be implemented more quickly than in a larger country. However, a small population often means that there is a lack of appropriate skills to implement such policies (Comnet-IT, 2002). Although Samoa has its own university and the educational level of the population is high, with a 96% literacy rate and two thirds of 15 to 19-year-olds receiving education (Purcell and Toland, 2004), there is a shortage of relevant ICT skills.

Recent research (Curthoys and Crabtree, 2003) has found that many governments have poured resources into developing ICTs, especially e-government systems, with only patchy results. Despite the extensive development of e-government services in the UK most citizens have continued to interact with government by traditional methods; as of 2002 only 11% of UK citizens had used a government online service. The conclusion that can be drawn from this is that to be successful, e-government must be popular with its actual users, the citizens themselves. Governments need to consult with their citizens in order to identify services that citizens are actually likely to use online. Samoa has taken careful steps to involve rural as well as urban citizens in the development of its new ICT policy and strategic plan. The policy was built up through a bottom-up process of consultation at the village level.

Currently, most government departments in Samoa have web sites (Purcell, 2003). Generally, however, they are still at stage one of the UN/ASPA 2001 model and are limited to advertising and information sharing. Like other Pacific countries, government departments in Samoa use the Internet mainly for email. The technology has not yet begun to contribute to efficient and effective procurement, as it does now with governments in developed countries.

ICT Development in Samoa

New ICT have considerable potential to raise a country's economic performance and improve people's daily lives. For instance, the use of plastic EFTPOS cards helps avoid bank queues and foreign exchange queues in countries like New Zealand or Australia. E-mail enables offices to stay in touch with employees continuously even when they are traveling, allowing them to work from anywhere in the world.

These examples point to a defining feature of ICT, in terms of their potential influence. They constitute what economists call 'general purpose' or 'enabling' technologies. As the names suggest, these technologies are of general application, provide a platform for many other innovations and can have pervasive economic effects. These examples are some of the reasons why the Government of Samoa decided to develop ICT at the national level.

In 2000, a National ICT Steering Committee, composed of members from the government and the private sector, was established to develop a national ICT strategy. It took the steering committee two years to develop the national ICT policies and twelve months to develop the national ICT strategic plan. Once the strategic plan was approved, the Cabinet established a National ICT Committee (note the removal of the word "steering") to act as a higher level decision-making body reporting directly to Cabinet on the implementation of the national ICT strategy.

Samoa's national ICT strategy is built on the guiding principles outlined in the overall plan for the South Pacific region developed by the Ministers of Communication of member countries of the South Pacific Forum (CROP, 2002). The Samoan national ICT strategic plan has six guiding principles: improve the skill set up of human resources, develop infrastructure, facilitate cooperation between stakeholders, improve policies and regulations, develop content and applications, and promote good governance.

The champion of ICT Development in Samoa is the Prime Minister, Hon. Tuilaepa Sailele Malielegaoi who played a critical role in raising awareness among government members on the potential of ICT to contribute to Samoa's economic development.

The interpretation of the role of ICTs is important because the major waves of accelerated growth through history have generally been related to the introduction, evolution and dissemination of enabling technologies. While the advent of the steam engine fueled the first industrial revolution in the United Kingdom (1760-1830), Robert Gordon from Northwestern University attributes the second industrial revolution, the American Golden Age (1913-1972), to a suite of enabling technologies invented 20 to 50 years before then. These enabling technologies include electricity and the internal combustion engine. The interesting question now is whether the ICT revolution is the harbinger of a third industrial revolution. For Samoa, ICT are truly a third industrial revolution. Once its national ICT strategy is fully implemented, Samoa will be much closer to the rest of world, and there will be increased participation in global markets.

ICT Issues

In recent years, the United Nations and other organizations recognized that there is a notable gap in ICT access and development between the developed and developing countries. The International Telecommunication Union (ITU) was given the task of studying and recommending to the United Nations the best possible solution of addressing this gap at the global level or what is now generally known as the "digital divide". The end result was the birth of the World Summit of the Information Society (WSIS). More information about the WSIS can be found on http://www.itu.int/wsis.

There were three preparatory meetings before the first summit in Geneva, December 2003. Samoa participated in these preparatory meetings as well as the Summit. There was so much to be learnt from this participation and it made it easier for Samoa to develop its own national ICT strategic plan without assistance from international organizations as was the case with development issues of small island developing states. However, Samoa does need a lot of help in terms of financial support and expertise to carry out its strategic plan.

The ICT development issues identified by the WSIS were and are still relevant to Samoa. The Samoan strategic plan takes into account the issues and ICT concerns in the WSIS Declaration and Plan of Action. In developing its ICT strategy, Samoa benefited from its participation in the WSIS process and other international conferences on ICT for development. It is now a priority of Samoa's government to ensure that it is represented in future conferences, workshops, seminars, and meetings at the international level in order to acquire the necessary knowledge and leapfrog to proven methodologies and technologies.

A number of issues are currently being addressed by the Government of Samoa in implementing its ICT strategy. These issues include:

- general awareness of ICT benefits and potential threats

- access to ICTs especially the Internet in rural areas

- limited ICT skilled personnel

- capacity to use ICTs effectively by the general population

- high cost of hardware

- poor infrastructure

Poor telecommunications infrastructure is a common barrier among the developing countries. Samoa is no different. The poor condition of the infrastructure is due in part to the condition of the cables being used. Both the underground and aerial cables are old and deteriorated. The national telecommunications provider, Samoatel, is working on improving this situation by laying down fiber-optic cable in Apia, Samoa's capital. Currently about 80% of Samoans have access to at least a basic telephone, and Samoatel plans to achieve 100% connectivity by the end of 2005. New developments in wireless technology open up the possibility of providing access to ICT without the development of costly infrastructure (Caldow, 2003). Telecom Samoa Cellular provides wireless communication in Samoa, and the prepaid mobile telephone is proving to be a popular method of communication (Vaa, 2003). In the most remote villages of Samoa, wireless telephones have already been installed.

A key issue in establishing ICT connectivity between small islands is affordability. Travel in these countries is expensive often involving a combination of bus and boat journeys. Although sending an email may be relatively expensive, the cost compares very favorably with the cost of a journey to the nearest government office. A long journey can be undertaken to reach the nearest telephone, only to find that the telephone is not working or a trip to the office can be a waste of money if the official that you want to contact is out of the office.

The Impact of ICT on Economic Performance

The particular contribution of ICT to Samoa's economic performance comes from their ability to reduce radically the costs of storing, accessing and exchanging information and increase its markets. In the US, transaction costs have been estimated by American researchers as amounting to over 40 per cent of the value of the national income (North, 1990), so the potential for economic gains from their reduction would seem considerable. While Samoa is still very much a cash economy, more and more people are starting to trust the plastic cards and are now using the EFTPOS machines reducing queues in the banks. They are also starting to use EFTPOS to pay for purchases. The first money machine was installed in Samoa in 1999. What was notable was the speed of the uptake of bank money machine cards by workers which has in turn allowed the banks to achieve efficiency gains.

There are a variety of avenues for ongoing efficiency gains. Some involve improved production processes within individual firms. Just as electricity enabled development of the continuous production line processes that Henry Ford used to such effect, the decentralized availability of information through ICT allows the reduction of hierarchical structures within firms and greater empowerment and capabilities for work teams and individual workers, who can do their own monitoring and make their own adjustments to production, and reap the rewards through performance-based remuneration systems (themselves ICT-based). For Samoa the use of ICT to achieve efficiency gains is developing slowly. All government departments now have access to computers and have their own websites. One of the main projects that is being developed is the implementation of a financial management information system to be used by all government ministries, departments and corporations, which will dramatically change processes and achieve efficiency gains.

ICTs also allow leaner and timelier inventory management, as sales data are continuously and accurately monitored and communicated in turn transforming relations between firms and their suppliers. This is one of the issues in Samoa and the reason why the shortage of key products for consumption is common. As mentioned earlier, these developments have shown the impact of ICT on social and economic developments.

Evidently, ICTs can also transform a firm's relations with its customers, providing (among other things) increased scope to tailor products to individual requirements. (It is perhaps not surprising that a pioneer in this area has been an entrant to the IT sector itself – namely Dell.) And consumer sovereignty is enhanced by the ability of consumers to scan markets more quickly and effectively over the phone line either directly or via the Internet. Access to the Internet and the skills to use it are most needed by SMEs and MSEs in Samoa and will allow the business sector to participate more in the global markets. It is one thing to provide access to ICTs especially the Internet, it is another to provide people with the capacity to use it to their advantage. Capacity-building is one of the priority projects arising out of the national ICT strategy. As evident from the current pilot of ICT development in an NGO, even those who have limited education can now use the computer to record their production and sales. The aim of the national strategy is to move Samoa towards the knowledge economy by training people on using computers, especially email, to communicate with families living overseas. All these can contribute to the economy of the country as a major contribution to the economy of Samoa are the remittances from the Diaspora.

The Internet, an enabling technology in its own right, has dramatically enhanced the efficiency of searching for information of all kinds including investment opportunities and jobs.

International ICT Projects

In its major cross-country study, The Growth Project, the OECD (Organisation for Economic Cooperation and Development) concluded that: "ICT is important for growth but having an ICT-producing sector is not a prerequisite."

The previous discussion of the transforming potential of ICT as an "enabling technology" would also suggest that it is in achieving effective use of these technologies that many of the gains in efficiency and productivity are to be derived. This is not to deny that there may be some useful synergies between production and use, or between producers and users of ICT. For example, as Harvard's Michael Porter has argued, sophisticated customers may foster the development of more sophisticated production, and the reverse is also possible (Porter, 1998). However such potentialities need to be placed in perspective. As the OECD warns: "… only few countries will have the necessary comparative advantages to succeed in ICT output."

In its 1998 Inquiry into Telecommunications Equipment, Systems and Services, OECD found that the international pattern of revealed comparative advantage in telecommunications and Internet use per inhabitant suggested, if anything, a negative correlation between intensity of use and manufacturing capability (IC, 1998, p88-9). International comparisons demonstrate that a country can have thriving and efficient telecommunications services, without domestically manufacturing the constituent parts (and vice versa).

The extreme competitiveness within the ICT sector has seen equipment prices fall like a stone since the mid-1990s – and with them the share prices and workforces of some of the leading manufacturers (like Ericsson, Lucent, Alcatel and Fujitsu) which have been restructuring and closing down plants. Intel, the icon of the ICT industry, has seen its share price fall by about 65 per cent over the past year.

While Samoa cannot be seen as an example of the impact of ICT development as explained here, reduction of ICT hardware costs are already evident now compared to the last five years. One major factor that has helped in reducing hardware costs is the reduction of duties and import tax approved by the Government.

The fall in ICT prices has been to Samoa's advantage, being a predominantly importing small island developing country because it helps raise its terms of trade and boosts the real income of Samoans. The dramatic fall in ICT prices in Samoa (although they are still more expensive than in New Zealand and Australia) also helps explain the recent rapid growth in the number of SMEs trading in ICT goods and services.

While reforms have brought significant efficiency gains unrelated to ICT through better management and work practices, they have also created the incentives and capacity for enterprises to adopt and adapt to the new technologies in ways which appear to have yielded additional gains, for instance, the use of email instead of the telephone to communicate with customers or family members living overseas.

E-commerce is one ICT application that can have a huge impact on the productivity of SMEs in Samoa. However, the lack of assets of SME owners to secure credit cards, and a central payment system to verify credit cards has become a key issue in developing e-commerce.

Policy Issues in Getting the Most out of ICT

Ensuring that Samoans can maximize the benefits from the "ICT Revolution" demands a wide-ranging policy agenda to ensure that Samoans have access to new technologies, as well as the incentive and capacity to use them most productively and effectively. There are a host of policy issues that have to do with removing obstacles to the use of these new technologies which are posed by redundant laws and regulations, or conversely, preserving and re-casting regulations or social institutions that are affected by the new technologies.

One of the key principles of the national ICT strategy is legislation. Rules of commerce and other laws formed in a pre e-commerce environment have to be adopted. For example, laws have to be passed that recognize the validity of electronic transactions. Samoa does not yet have an "Electronic Transaction Act". There is also a need for protection of privacy, although this has to be weighed against compliance cost issues and the value that comes from sharing information (for example, in getting better medical or job outcomes). As the OECD observed:

"Countries that moved early to liberalize telecommunications have much lower communications costs and wider diffusion of ICT than countries that were late to take action."

With advances in digital technology, telecommunications, broadcasting and the Internet are converging rapidly in Samoa. They are being redefined in terms of what they are, who provides services, and how they are produced and delivered offering consumers and producers of services enormous opportunities. It is not possible to predict and describe what direction the digital revolution will take. The directions and speed of convergence are unclear, but the inevitability of continuing change in the media and telecommunications industries is certainly evident in Samoa. In such an environment, regulation must be flexible enough to deal with uncertainty and change. And it should not benefit some technologies or producers at the expense of others. An important implication of convergence is that regulatory regimes that could once remain relatively distinct now need to be coordinated.

The convergence of telecommunications and broadcasting accentuates the pro-competitive emphasis of policy towards the former and the protective pall of regulation that shrouds the latter. So policy makers need not fear any lack of important challenges! That said, in sketching this broad canvas of policy issues, it is not that legal problems related to ICT are intrinsically new. To a large extent, the policy agenda is the same agenda that needs pursuing to get the most out of an "old" economy, in terms of prudent reform of institutions and processes that stifle opportunity. A stable macro economy, openness to trade, and building human, social and intellectual capital will remain fundamental policy tenets, even if their particular manifestations differ. The new era also suggests an increasing importance for international negotiation and agreements — representing a natural evolution of the General

Agreement on Trade in Services within the WTO, and other international agreements. It should be noted here that Samoa is in the process of joining the WTO, and some researchers have argued that it is not going to be cost effective for such a small island developing state to join. Others argue that there will be no economic benefit for Samoa to do so because the WTO does not differentiate between small island developing states and other highly populated developing countries.

History has shown that enabling technologies have much to contribute to the living standards and well being of society. History also tells us, however, that the extent to which particular countries benefit depends critically on their institutional and policy receptivity.

Conclusion

While Samoa has not yet reaped the many benefits of ICT that more developed countries such as NZ, UK, USA, and Australia have experienced, Samoa is in a favourable position in that it can learn from mistakes of others and can leapfrog to proven technologies and ICT models of development. Industrialized countries have made a substantial investment in developing ICT and enhancing its regulatory environment. And that has delivered significant returns in higher productivity and income growth including more widespread and effective use of ICT. The economic opportunities in these countries, made possible by the Internet and e-commerce, make it imperative that Samoa, a small island developing state in the Pacific, sustains its ICT development at the national level to achieve its strategic goal of "ICT for every Samoan" and its national strategic goal of "a better life for every Samoan."

Before ICT can be fully developed and implemented, the Government of Samoa recognized that there was an urgent need to develop a national ICT strategic plan to ensure that any ICT development – including e-government – is aligned with the country's overall national strategic goals. In 2004, the Samoan Cabinet approved a national ICT strategy. The overall vision is "information and communications technologies for every Samoan" (SICT, 2004). The development of an appropriate telecommunications infrastructure is of particular challenge for small island developing states, due to their low population densities, and the vast distances to be covered. The goal is to open up regulatory frameworks to allow competition, and encourage private sector participation in infrastructure development. A key role for the government will be to act as a role model in its own use of ICT to link up government departments and corporations. This should encourage the private sector and NGOs to expand their use of ICT in interacting with their stakeholders (SICT, 2004). National ICT strategic plans can most effectively be developed and implemented by drawing upon partnerships among organizations, and collaboration among people across organizational borders.

References

Comnet-IT (2002), Country Profiles of E-governance, UNESCO http://www.comnet-IT.org [retrieved from the Internet 16/03/2004]

CROP ICT Working Group (2002), Pacific Islands Information and Communication Technologies Policy and Strategic Plan, Ref JCO141 http://www.sopac.org/tiki/tiki-sopac_reportsindex.php [retrieved from the Internet 19/07/2004]

Curthoys, N. and Crabtree, J. (2003), SmartGov: Renewing Electronic Government for Improved Service Delivery, iSociety http://www.theworkfoundation.com/research/isociety/smartgov-main.isp [retrieved from the Internet 16/11/2004]

Ernst and Young and Cap Gemini Ernst and Young, 2001, Business Redefined: Connecting Content, Applications and Customers, Communications Week International, Issue 266, 4 June

Hayashi, K. and Hori, H. (2002), JBIC Institute, Presentation at Development Research Symposium: South Pacific Futures, Brisbane, 22-24 July 2002

North, D. C., 1990, Institutions, Institutional Change and Economic Performance, Cambridge University Press, Cambridge USA

OECD (Organization for Economic Cooperation and Development), 2001, The New Economy: Beyond the Hype, Final Report on the OECD Growth Project, Executive Summary, Meeting of the OECD Council at Ministerial Level, 2001

Parker, E. B. (2000), Closing the Digital Divide in Rural America, Telecommunications Policy 24, 281-290

Porter, M. (1998) Competitive Advantage: Creating and Sustaining Superior Performance Free Press, 1998 (1985)

Purcell, F. (2003), E-commerce Adoption in the South Pacific: An Exploratory Study of Threats, Barriers and Opportunities for e-commerce in SMEs in Samoa, MCA dissertation, Victoria University of Wellington

Purcell, F. and Toland, J. (2004), Electronic Commerce for the South Pacific: A Review of E-Readiness, Electronic Commerce Research, Vol 4 pp. 241-262

SICT, (2004) The National ICT Strategic Plan of Samoa Apia, Samoa

PART II

TOWARD THE
MILLENNIUM DEVELOPMENT GOALS:
E-STRATEGIES, UP-SCALING, INDICATORS, INNOVATION AND
INVESTMENT

UNLEASHING THE POTENTIAL OF E-STRATEGIES: WHY ASSESSING THEIR IMPACT AND MONITORING THEIR IMPLEMENTATION IS KEY TO THE SUCCESSFUL BUILDING OF INFORMATION SOCIETIES AND TO THE ATTAINMENT OF THE MDGS

By Bruno Lanvin, The World Bank[1]

At the end of the first phase of the World Summit on the Information Society (WSIS) in December 2003, political leaders made a commitment to develop national e-strategies by the time the world convenes for the second phase of WSIS in November 2005.[2] This represents a major challenge for individual countries, as well as a significant risk for many of them.

A first risk is that individual e-strategies will be launched in the absence of a common reference framework, which will make it difficult to evaluate their impact, compare their achievements, and consolidate them at sub-regional or regional levels. A second risk is that errors of the past might be repeated: over the past decade, many countries have spent significant time, energy, and resources to design e-strategies which often remained blue prints, or white elephants because no systematic set of indicators had been agreed upon and established to monitor and evaluate their implementation.

It is hence of paramount importance that monitoring and evaluation ('M&E') should not be an 'ex-post facto' component of an e-strategy, but a vital part of its design and implementation, and a condition of its effectiveness. Developing M&E components of e-strategies is a means to ensure that the strategies are explicit and realistic with regard to what they aim to achieve, and that their implementation is regularly assessed and realigned to ensure the efficient use of scarce resources, particularly in terms of the opportunity costs of those resources when they might alternatively be used for poverty reduction, healthcare, or non-ICT infrastructure.

This chapter is mostly a summary version of the 'E-strategies Monitoring and Evaluation Toolkit' recently developed by the World Bank. It is divided into three sections. The first one offers a general view of the ways in which e-strategies can be designed as a core element of development strategies, with specific references to the Millennium Development Goals (MDGs) and the WSIS Plan of Action. The second section describes the methodology proposed by the toolkit, focusing in particular on linkages between e-strategies monitoring on one hand and the so-called 'logical framework' on the other. Eventually, section III considers one specific application of the toolkit methodology, namely in the area of e-government.

---

[1] Senior Advisor, e-Strategies. The views expressed here should be considered as the author's own. They do not necessarily reflect the views of the World Bank or of its Board members.
[2] Article 8 of the WSIS Plan of Action states that the "Development of national e-strategies (…) should be encouraged by all countries by 2005." See http://www.itu.int/wsis/docs/geneva/official/poa.html

SECTION I – E-STRATEGIES AS CORE COMPONENTS OF DEVELOPMENT STRATEGIES

Any e-strategy, however far-reaching and broad-ranging, cannot be a substitute for a development strategy (d-strategy). From an 'M&E' point of view, this has important practical consequences, including the following:

- Formulation

    Some indicators (especially regarding 'Impact') will have to be formulated at a level of decision making which is higher than that of an e-strategy (namely that of the country's overall development strategy – d-strategy) or even that of its socio-economic policy; the designers and promoters of e-strategies should hence refrain from 're-inventing the wheel' when such M&E indicators already exist, and focus on making them a fully integrated component of their own efforts.

- Linkages

    The M&E indicators should be related to each other in a way that reflects the sequencing of objectives at the various levels of decision making. For instance, if an e-strategy includes initiatives regarding distance education, it will be important that such activities (and their outputs) be connected not only to broader e-strategy objectives (such as promoting e-literacy or enhancing the use of ICT in education), but also to 'd-strategy' objectives (e.g. developing ICT usage in general), and more generic policy objectives (which could be in this case a diversification of the economy from traditional sectors into newer ones).

This is illustrated in the following diagram:

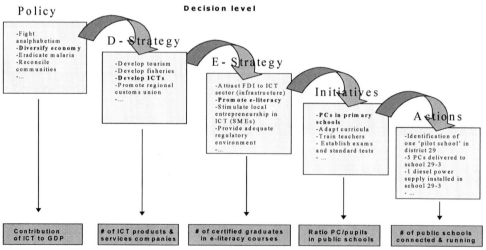

E-strategies vs. Information Societies

Over the last few years, an increasing amount of international effort has been devoted to the building of information societies.[3] Still, evidence shows that there remains a limited awareness about the potential role of ICT in the fight against poverty.[4]

Even in the significant and cross-sectoral intellectual effort mobilized behind the objectives of the Millennium Declaration, ICTs appear largely as a second thought, and a relatively minor tool to reach the Millennium Development Goals (MDGs). In spite of the myriad of findings regarding ICT projects in the field, such evidence has not yet been aggregated or scaled up in a way that would easily convince decision makers at the policy level. To a large extent, the case for ICT for development (ICT4D) still needs to be made[5].

M&E indicators and processes have a crucial role to play in this respect. This role however, will not be fully realized unless the following objectives are clearly recognized as priorities, both at the national and international levels:

M&E Integration. When selecting e-strategy M&E tools and indicators, the designers and promoters of e-strategies should make them as compatible as possible with existing objectives and targets regarding development in general, and the building of information societies. This may include a search for homogeneity in terminology, or more importantly, possibilities to establish causal linkages between objectives and indicators; this will enhance their ability to receive international support for their efforts, and to benefit from existing or emerging best practices in the field.[6]

Indicator Quality. Every effort to enhance the quality, coverage and detail of ICT and e-economy indicators should be pursued. Major gaps currently exist for data regarding applications and usage, i.e. about all indicators beyond physical measurement of tele-density, connectivity, equipment or information traffic flows. In most cases, the first step will consist of strengthening local statistical and data collection capacities.[7]

M&E Compatibility. As underlined earlier, M&E instruments attached to e-strategies should be made as compatible as possible with those existing for 'traditional areas of d-strategies'. This will be necessary to (a) achieve consistency in pursuing overall national policy objectives, and (b) obtain the support and 'buy-in' or those parts of government and civil society who might otherwise see e-strategies as a fad or a distraction from other, more fundamental development objectives.

---

[3] Chief among those are the European Union's 'e-Europe Initiative', the G-8 DOT Force (Digital Opportunity Task Force), the United Nations' ICT Task Force (UNICTTF), and the whole process of the World Summit on Information Society (WSIS).

[4] Recently, a survey carried out by OECD/DAC underlined the remarkably small proportion of PRSPs (Poverty Reduction Strategy Papers) mentioning ICTs. See '*Role of Infrastructure in Economic Growth and Poverty Reduction – Lessons learned from PRSPs of 33 countries*', www.oecd.org/dataoecd/57/60/33919674.pdf.

[5] See for example K. McNamara "ICT for Development: What Works & What Does Not" (*info*Dev, 2003).

[6] Not to mention the significant impact that it would have on countries' abilities to benchmark their efforts vis-à-vis those of other economies.

[7] Capacity building at the local/national level is a priority; considering the expected cost of such efforts, coordination at the international level (such as the one advocated by members of the '*Partnership on Measuring ICT for Development*') is likely to receive increasing attention.

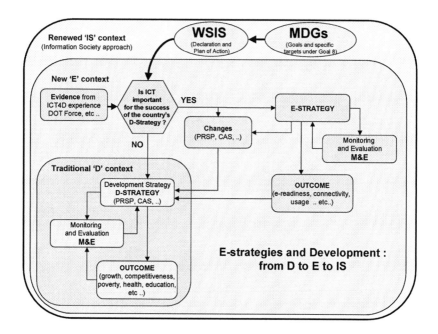

E-readiness vs. Access and Usage

The M&E component of an e-strategy should reflect the fact that ICT is only a tool and not an end for development. In other words, the number of telephone lines, personal computers, or even Internet hosts available in one country are not the ultimate indicators to be used to assess whether or not an e-strategy has been successful. On the other hand, while the economic and social value that people will derive from a greater use of ICTs is clearly a much better indicator of such success, it is also much more complex to measure, monitor, and evaluate.

If it is clear that usage is a better indicator than access, it remains equally obvious that there will be no usage if there is no access. Moreover, both access and usage will depend heavily on the legal, regulatory, and other economic and social frameworks within which information and information technologies can be accessed and used, and on whether government, business, schools, and individuals are interested and able to access and use them. Such elements are generally understood as being part of 'e-readiness'.

E-Readiness

Most business strategies begin with a review or assessment of the current state of business. They focus on key elements of the business – such as its customer base, its operations, and its product line – and describe where the business stands with regard to each of these areas, what it has achieved in the recent past, and highlights areas of relative strength, weakness, and opportunity. The assessment of how well (or badly) things are working now for a business drives the degree of change that will be required in the future.

A similar approach is required for the development of national e-strategies. Understanding where the country stands with regard to key elements of its ICT development agenda must form the base from which a national e-strategy is developed. Fortunately, this has already occurred in a number of countries. E-readiness assessments have been conducted in over 137 countries.[8]

E-readiness assessments are central to the ability to formulate e-strategies, in two key ways:

- *What to do.* E-readiness assessments provide the basic information from which to determine the themes or sectors on which to focus the country's e-strategy. They provide information on where a country has made good progress and help to identify areas of continuing weakness. Oftentimes this is done through comparison to other similar countries, so as to provide context in which to understand the country's current position.

- *How much of it to do.* E-readiness assessments also facilitate the process by which a country develops targets on how far to go in pursuit of each key objective (i.e. once it has been decided what to do, how much of it to do). They provide data regarding the current level of ICT development for a specified country, baseline data against which the progress of the e-strategy can be measured.

Country comparisons play an important role in selecting strategic priorities and establishing growth targets. If a comparator country is considerably 'more ready' in an area of importance, for example ICT infrastructure, then strategists may choose to put more emphasis on this area. It is also on the basis of such a comparison that reasonable estimates of growth targets can be established. If a comparator country previously grew its infrastructure, measured by tele-density for example, at a rate of X percent per year, strategists may chose to establish the same (or a slightly more ambitious) target for their own ICT infrastructure development.

Depending on the specific context of a particular country, e-readiness may also give different emphasis to issues regarding, for instance, security and privacy, consumer protection, or 'digital divide' issues.[9]

Access and Usage

Access (both physical and economic) is only one dimension of possible 'digital divides.' It refers to whether or not the connectivity and equipment provided (to businesses, local governments, schools, hospitals, community access points, or individuals) will actually be used in a productive and sustainable fashion that will determine how ICTs actually contribute to local and international development objectives. Beyond access and usage, it will also be important to assess the economic and social value that are derived from e-strategies,

---

[8] One can even consider such efforts as excessive (or at least redundant) in a certain number of cases: 55 countries have been assessed for e-readiness at least 5 times, and 10 countries at least 8 times. See http://www.bridges.org/ereadiness/where.html

[9] 'Digital divide issues' refer here to disparities among various groups of the national population, between urban and rural areas for example.

which has much more to do with 'outcomes' than with 'outputs', and requires reference to pre-existing values in a society.

Summary

Readiness, access, and usage constitute the three layers against which the chances of success of an e-strategy can be rated. It will hence be important, from an M&E point of view, to link indicators (whether they concern impact, outcome, or specific deliverables) to at least one component of the following three sets of elements:

- Readiness

    o Legal, regulatory and overall institutional framework (rule of law, IPR regimes, trade and investment openness, regulatory framework, competition framework, etc.)

    o Society's support (at all levels) for innovation, reform, and ICT

    o Human resources (education in general, e-literacy in particular)

    o Perceptions about security/privacy[10]

    o Digital divide issues (e.g. rural/urban)

- Availability/Access

    o Infrastructure (e.g. telecom) and network penetration

    o Equipment (computers in business, administrations, schools, homes)

- Usage

    o Applications (e.g. e-government, e-business, e-education, e-health)

    o Specific usage modalities (e.g. community access points)

    o Specific sectoral or policy objectives (e.g. export competitiveness)

---

[10] Security concerns have received increasing attention in the recent past. They are no longer restricted to digital signature, encryption, consumer protection, or intellectual property issues. Topics such as cyber-crime, identity theft, phishing or spam are progressively finding their way into e-strategies. E-security is hence expected to be addressed as a separate item in future editions of the M.E.T.E.R. toolkit.

Moreover, the more the indicators chosen under each of those three sets are compatible with internationally agreed objectives and targets (such as those attached to the MDGs), the easier it will be to generate international support for particular e-strategies, benchmark national efforts vis-à-vis those of other countries, and encourage foreign direct investment.

---

e-Strategies and the MDGs

In order to reach the targets set by the MDGs, countries can either increase the resources they allocate to specific objectives, or increase the efficiency with which they use their available resources. At the core of the discussion about ICT and MDG is the question of whether ICT can contribute to improving efficiency in delivering the MDGs.

Figure 9. **Investing in ICT to Reach MDG**

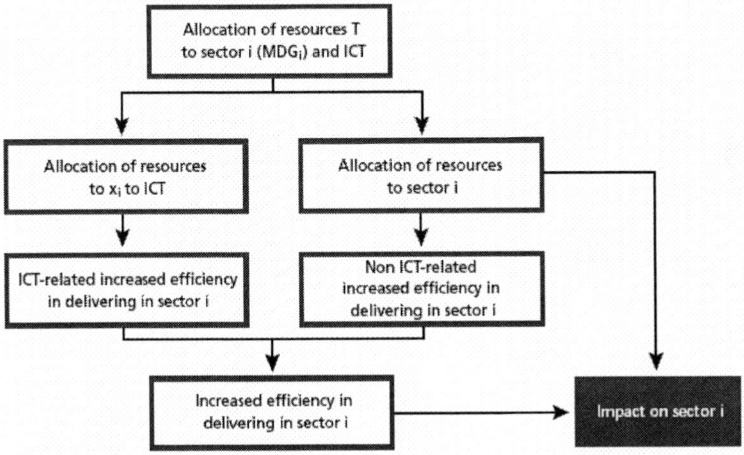

This way of representing ICT investment as a source of increased efficiency in pursuing MDGs 2 to 7 (and hence MDG 1) opens a number of policy and strategic avenues. Additional efforts will be required from statisticians and econometricians to help quantify the relevant elasticities and dynamic linkages between multiple variables, which may vary from one country to another. International efforts are hence required to collect relevant data at the local, regional, and global levels.

Excerpt from Lanvin, B. and Qiang, C. 2003. 'Poverty "e-Readication" - Using ICT to Meet MDG:', in 'Global Information Technology Report, 2003-2004.' INSEAD-WEF-*info*Dev, 2003.

SECTION II – E-STRATEGIES MONITORING AND EVALUATION – A POSSIBLE METHODOLOGY

In order to facilitate the monitoring and evaluation of e-strategies, and to ensure that such evaluations are internationally comparable, the World Bank recently launched its 'M.E.T.E.R. toolkit' (see box below). This toolkit is organized as a series of modules. In addition to background and methodological modules, the toolkit offers a selected number of thematic modules, reflecting the most common priorities among the e-strategies reviewed[11].

---

[11] The list of the e-strategies considered is provided in an Annex.

Toolkit Structure

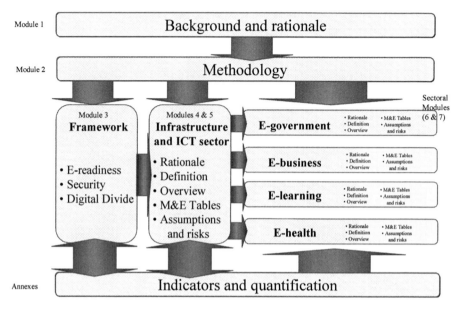

Each thematic module is based on a common format, and includes the following sections:

Rationale. Why the theme under consideration was selected as a module of the toolkit.

Definition. What is understood by the specific theme being addressed, and how it will be covered in the module.

Overview. How e-strategies have addressed this theme to date.

M&E tables. The M&E framework is applied to a selected number of the strategic interventions that are commonly undertaken under the theme considered. The matrices thus developed provide examples for users to develop similar matrices for areas that the module does not cover. The tables form the heart of each module.[12]

Assumptions and risks. Some key assumptions and risks that are commonly related to the theme are addressed, in particular regarding how they may affect e-strategies targets and ways to reach them.

---

[12] The tables focus on strategic priorities that relate to each thematic area. The choice of focus areas is driven by: (a) what is found in similar components of over 50 e-strategies reviewed by the authors (i.e. common strategic priorities); (b) the complexity of the M&E challenge (i.e. where possible, tables are developed for areas that are more challenging to monitor and evaluate than others). No formal value judgment is attached to the selection process. However, there is an implicit acceptance that such priorities are at least useful, and no tables are developed for initiatives that the authors think potentially ineffective.

M.E.T.E.R.

Monitoring and Evaluation Toolkit for e-Strategies Results

The World Bank chose the Berlin Meeting of the UN ICT Task Force (November 2004) to launch a preliminary version of its '*E-Strategies Monitoring and Evaluation Toolkit*' *, also known as 'METER: Monitoring and Evaluation Toolkit for E-Strategies Results). The focus of this toolkit is premised on the fact that effective Monitoring and Evaluation (M&E) is integral to the design and implementation of effective e-strategies. Developing M&E components of e-strategies is a means by which to ensure that the strategies are explicit and realistic with regard to what they aim to achieve, and that their implementation is regularly assessed and realigned to ensure the efficient use of scarce resources. In many respects, the credibility and efficiency of e-strategies depends on their having a strong M&E spine.

Based on a review of some 50 e-strategies conducted by the authors, this toolkit advances a framework by which to integrate M&E into e-strategies. The M&E framework expands on indicators that relate to core elements of the strategy formulation process, namely the development of policy goals, strategic priorities, and key initiatives and actions that are embodied by e-strategies. This toolkit is targeted at anyone who is involved in, or even just has an interest in, the development of national e-strategies. This includes decision-makers and staff from government agencies, development practitioners from international and non-governmental organizations (NGOs), members from the private sector involved in ICT development, and the interested general public.

This toolkit should be regarded as a 'living document' which will evolve with time. In future editions, the M&E framework applied in the current version to several of the key thematic areas on which national e-strategies commonly focus (namely infrastructure, ICT sector and e-government) will be deepened in other similarly important domains such as e-health, e-education, and e-business. This initial version of the toolkit simply gives an overview of these areas. As the toolkit benefits from users' feedback, and as additional evidence becomes available about various e-strategy players' experience with M&E, the online version of the toolkit will attempt to capture best practices and offer additional tools for monitoring and evaluating progress in the implementation of e-strategies.

* Prefaced by Mohsen Khalil, Director, GICT, the Toolkit was written by Aref Adamali and Bruno Lanvin, under the general direction of Robert Schware. Additional research and writing support was provided by John Coffey and Charles Watt. Mark Wahl developed the web site and edited the document. The toolkit is available on-line at http://www.worldbank.org/ict/

A Simple Framework to Monitor and Assess e-Strategies

An 'e-strategy pyramid'

The Logical Framework Pyramid

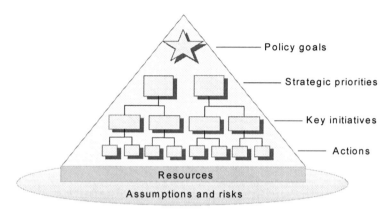

Based on the 'Logframe Handbook' developed in the World Bank, the M&E approach offered in the toolkit refers to a rather simple way of considering the inter-relationship between policy, strategy, and implementation. The overall policy of a specific country will determine how and why themes such as 'building an information society' or 'implementing a national e-strategy' are priority objectives. Notwithstanding the reasons why a particular country may select such objectives, this toolkit considers that in any particular sector or area, policies, strategies, and implementation are the respective responses to three main questions: Why? What? and How?

Policy	–	Why
Strategy	–	What
Implementation plan	–	How

The implementation level will itself be divided into two operational levels, namely 'key initiatives' (how certain objectives will be implemented), and 'actions' (which will be more specific to one area of responsibility – e.g. institutional or geographic).

Moreover, the inputs and resources required to implement the e-strategy need to be addressed. These can be institutional structures, staff, or financial resources. A clear understanding of resource requirements is an important link between the strategy and its implementation, and forms the base upon which all elements of the strategy depend.

Finally, a strategy may need to consider elements that are outside the focus of the strategy and will affect its implementation. Identifying the assumptions and risks on which the strategy is based is critical to setting parameters around which to measure its success or failure. It is also the only means by which to begin developing risk-mitigation measures and, where possible, incorporating these into the strategy itself.

Where does M&E Fit?

M&E applies to all 'layers' of the strategy pyramid introduced above. However, various levels of the pyramid will clearly require different types of indicators. For example, policy objectives, which will typically be longer-term and society-wide have traditionally been assessed in terms of 'impact', i.e. in rather broad and largely unquantified ways. One of the ambitions of this toolkit is precisely to offer simple ways to attach indicators to such objectives.[13] Strategic priorities have proved more amenable to quantification. However, such quantification has often remained limited to broad aggregates (e.g. percentage of the national population that has reached a certain level of ICT education); one will hence consider 'outcomes', which will typically be society-wide indicators. By contrast, once one reaches the implementation layers of key initiatives and specific actions, indicators will be easier to design and use, referring respectively to outputs (e.g. number of computers installed in classrooms) and deliverables (e.g. so many computers installed and connected in so many schools in a certain region).

From LogFrame to M&E

Whatever the level of the e-strategy pyramid one may wish to consider, each and every one of the indicators selected is potentially a basis for an M&E component. However, for reasons of practicality and in order to account for local specificities, an efficient M&E approach will often have to be designed and implemented in a customized fashion.

---

[13] If a country happens to adopt a policy objective such as 'to become a knowledge society within twenty years', or 'to stimulate the growth of the national ICT sector', various strategic goals will need to be articulated to assess progress in achieving them. Such goals could include, respectively 'provide primary education to 80 percent of a class age by a certain date', or 'generate a certain percentage of national income through the ICT sector by a certain date', for example.

The thematic modules of the M.E.T.E.R. toolkit will provide practical ways to exercise such selectivity. However, it is important at this stage to examine in greater detail what each of the indicators mentioned in the diagram above (namely: impact, outcomes, outputs, and deliverables) might mean for the institutions and individuals involved in each of the respective levels of the e-strategy pyramid.

A Strategic Approach to Monitoring and Evaluation

As mentioned earlier, the way in which an M&E model and its indicators are incorporated in an e-strategy will influence its feasibility and hence its credibility and wider application. It is therefore important that the M&E system be designed in such a way as to make it comprehensible and usable by domestic participants (government, ministries, enterprises, and civil society) as well as external stakeholders (investors, donors, partners).

If understood in that manner, M&E ceases to be a mere component of the e-strategy. It becomes a powerful instrument to make such a strategy more meaningful and convincing for those who will have the task to implement it and to support it. Designing the M&E component of an e-strategy hence requires that priority attention be given from the start to two of its main aspects, namely:

- Methodological aspects, and

- Institutional and strategic aspects

The methodological context of M&E refers mainly to the ways in which it will offer relevant tools to monitor and evaluate progress made vis-à-vis the various levels of decision-making mentioned earlier (policy goals, strategic priorities, key initiatives) and to their expected results (impact, outcome, output). On the other hand, the institutional and strategic context of M&E will include the ways and means by which the M&E model can best be adapted to local constraints, and maximize ownership and 'buy-in' from the various players/stakeholders involved.

Methodological Context

(a) Policy Goals/Impact indicators

At the top of the strategy pyramid is the policy or vision that the strategy ultimately attempts to fulfill. The indicators by which such policy goals will be measured are generally development-focused indicators, pertaining to the country's economy and society as a whole, and not necessarily ICTs in particular. For example, a policy that seeks to grow the country's ICT sector to make it a leading growth factor in the economy may choose to measure this by GDP growth, total employment growth, or total productivity growth. These indicators are considered to be *impact indicators*.

Impact indicators are often the most difficult to assess. This is due to two key factors:

- Time horizons. Impact indicators often only show change after a considerable time lag. This may be years after the e-strategy has been undertaken. Positive changes to these indicators may be of limited concern to the original formulators or implementers of the strategy, as they may have moved on to other duties by the time the impact of their efforts begins to show on the key indicators. Due to the time delay, such indicators are seldom monitored on a regular basis.

- <u>Establishing causality</u>. Changes in impact indicators are likely to be influenced by interventions undertaken as a part of the e-strategy, but almost certainly not as a result of these interventions alone. Therefore establishing causality between the e-strategy's interventions and the changes in an impact indicator is difficult – many other factors come into play, making it hard to establish whether or to what degree an ICT strategy or intervention is responsible for indicator change. For example, GDP growth is clearly driven by a vast array of factors, of which the ICT-producing sector may be just one.

(B) Strategic Priorities/Outcome indicators

Converting a policy or vision into tangible change on the ground requires choosing what initiatives to undertake and establishing goals for how far to advance in each particular initiative. Choosing what to do also implies undertaking the difficult task of choosing what *not* to do. Equally important, is the process of establishing how far to go in pursuit of any given objective. This requires establishing indicators to track achievement against core objectives that the strategy prioritizes. This requires clarifying what will be the tangible outcomes of the strategy. The decision of what to do (and not do), and how much of it to do lies at the heart of e-strategy formulation.

For example, if a country has selected the growth of its ICT sector as a policy goal, it will have to make choices among a number of possibly viable strategic priorities, such as:

- Develop ICT infrastructure

- Develop high-bandwidth technology parks

- Encourage high-tech foreign direct investment (FDI)

- Increase the stock of locally trained ICT professionals.

For example, should the country choose to increase the stock of ICT professionals among its key strategic priorities, it will require a number of *outcome indicators* to assess its progress towards this objective. This may include the number of people graduating from tertiary and professional education institutions or the number of people employed by the high-tech sector. The last indicator could be segmented by domestic or foreign firms to provide meaningful data for FDI-related strategic objectives.

Since the time required for change to be reflected in outcome indicators is likely to be shorter than for impact indicators, causality will be somewhat easier to determine. Though the stock of locally trained ICT professionals may only show an increase some time after the initiation of the strategy, such time should not be expected to be more than a few years.

Therefore, outcome indicators are easier to monitor than impact indicators, as they are likely to show the results of the e-strategy intervention over a shorter time horizon. However, there is still a key role for evaluation, in assessing to what degree the interventions are responsible for a certain outcome, and in assessing what would have been the outcome had the intervention not occurred.

(C) Key Initiatives/Output indicators

To meet the strategic objectives outlined above, a number of distinct initiatives can be undertaken. For each initiative, the key deliverable, or *output indicator*, should be specified in the strategic plan. For example, increasing the number of qualified ICT workers will require a variety of initiatives, all of which will generate outputs or products that should be qualified in terms of their number and level of quality. Qualification is achieved through the selection of key indicators that measure both the quantity and the quality of the deliverables or outputs.

For example, increasing the stock of ICT professionals will require a number of interventions, each of which will create different outputs. These may include:

- Improvement of capacity of ICT-focused learning institutions
- Increase in demand for ICT education/training
- Improvement of quality of ICT education at tertiary/vocational level.
- Assessing success or failure of an initiative may require establishing measures for the capacity, demand, and quality of ICT-focused education[14].

The table below provides some examples:

Output	Quantitative indicator	Qualitative indicator
Capacity of ICT-focused learning institutions improved, e.g.: - a measurable improvement of teachers' qualification in such institutions, - quantified support to teachers responsible for introducing computers in classes and curricula, - similar output for the business sector (on-the-job training)	- Teachers of general and vocational schools trained in basic ICT skills and use ICT in teaching increases by X% - In-service training of managers in the use of ICT in educational settings increases by X% - Training programs and materials for in-service training staff designed and applied increases by X % - Funding provisions to institutions increases by X% - Number of professional teaching staff increases by X% - Number of students graduating increases by X% - % of graduates that are women	- Rating of graduates' capabilities by private sector increases by X points - Rating of institutions by standards agency increases by X points *(continued)*

---

[14] Appropriate indicators will be both quantitative and qualitative.

Demand for ICT education/training increased	• Number of students applying to technical institutions increases by X%	• Secondary curricula places greater emphasis on ICT-focused subjects
Quality of ICT education improved at tertiary/vocational level	• X number of partnerships formed with private sector • X number of partnerships formed with foreign institutions • Distance education services, extend access to X number of students to a full curriculum • X number of students graduating with recognized certification from accredited ICT-training institutions	• Tertiary/vocational curricula includes market-leading techniques and knowledge • An established information environment that provides a range of support systems through use of ICT. • Hot-line services established to support teachers and advisors in their use of hardware and software.

Aside from measuring the quantity and quality of outputs, initiatives should also be assessed for how effectively they have been undertaken, both immediately after implementation is complete as well as during implementation. This will entail conducting periodic assessments of distinct initiatives. This will allow the implementation team to understand areas of comparative strength to build on further, and to incorporate them into other elements of the strategy. It will also allow the team to address areas of relative weakness, to make necessary adjustments, or even bring them to an early close. Mid-stream evaluation plays a key role in ensuring that the strategy is implemented well and resources are spent efficiently. It will ultimately help to ensure that the strategy meets its intended goals.

(D) Actions/interim deliverables indicators

Details of each initiative in terms of its main stages, dependencies, and resources required for each stage of implementation should be included in the implementation plan. The strategy should present an overview of the actions involved in each initiative, as well as key milestones by which to gauge their progress.[15]

At this layer, the indicators are the *interim deliverables* or sub-products that are generated by each key task of the initiative. They are closely tied to how the initiative is designed and the specific approaches selected. They serve as milestones against which to track the progress of the project through its various stages, with shorter completion timeframes than impact, outcome, or output indicators.

For example, building the capacity of ICT learning institutions requires a number of interrelated activities. They may all comprise part of a single initiative, or a number of separate initiatives that coalesce to meet a larger capacity-building objective. Depending on how the project is structured, some action or activity indicators could be:

- Assessment of capacity needs of higher educational and technical institutions. Assessments completed of X percent of institutions by month A

---

[15] This is particularly important in the case of ICTs as many of the initiatives being proposed will be unfamiliar to policy-makers and reviewers of the e-strategy. Details of the actions required to implement the initiatives will make them more tangible and therefore comprehensible.

- Program to provide grant funding to institutions established by month B, of amount of $X

- X percent of grant facility funds disbursed to eligible institutions by month C

- Recruitment criteria for staff completed. Staffing needs for X percent of institutions completed by month D.

Many of the initiatives undertaken as part of national e-strategies are related to creating institutions or building the capacity of existing ones. For example, an ICT infrastructure component of a strategy may focus on establishing a regulatory agency to ensure an open and competitive telecommunications market. Monitoring and evaluating the success of institution building will focus on some of the key elements that starting and running a well-functioning organization requires. This can range from the development of a physical location for the institution, to whether it has been staffed, to the sustainability of its financing.

(E) Resources/Input indicators

The resources required to undertake these projects, and ultimately meet the strategic and policy objectives, should be specified in the strategy. These make up the project's inputs, or *input indicators*. Inputs take a variety of forms. They can be institutional structures, including the mechanisms required to implement initiatives or supervise the over-all strategy. They will include staff, oftentimes highly skilled professionals with expertise in ICTs as well as in the area of thematic focus (such as e-education or e-health). Financial resources are undoubtedly a key input. A clear understanding of required financing and, importantly, its source, is the link between the strategy and its implementation. It therefore forms a base on which all elements of the strategy depend.

Assessing the outputs, outcomes, and ultimately the impact of a strategy must be conducted relative to the level of resources that have been dedicated to the strategy. Clearly some countries have more resources to dedicate to their e-strategies than others. Therefore, assessing the outputs of an e-strategy, and therefore its success, cannot be done in absolute terms alone, but requires integrating the resources that have been dedicated to the strategy into the indicators themselves as a common denominator. For example, the performance measures of an ICT sector incubator may include the number of firms launched that are financially sustainable after a certain number of years. However, they should also assess how many financially sustainable businesses were launched for a given amount of money invested in the incubator.

The definition of required resources also plays a role in facilitating communication with regard to the e-strategy. Many of the initiatives contained in the strategy will have little precedent to go by. Therefore, understanding the scale of the activities will not come naturally to a number of stakeholders. Financial resource requirements are the most basic means by which a variety of stakeholders will be able to understand the scale of the e-strategy and the activities it embodies. It can serve as a common language to provide the necessary context for what may otherwise be a number of unfamiliar activities.

(F)   Assumptions and Risks

The development and implementation of an e-strategy is necessary to bring about effective ICT development across a range of sectors. But it is not sufficient in itself. There are a number of other factors on which ICT development is dependent, but over which both the formulators and implementers of the e-strategy have little control. Many of these factors relate to the political, economic, and social environment in which the strategy exists, that when combined with the outputs of the strategy lead to the outcomes and impact that the strategy intends.

These environmental factors are often pre-requisites or assumptions that strategy-makers take for granted in developing their targets and goals. At the most general level, strategy-makers may assume that a country remains politically stable. Without political stability, the strategy is unlikely to attain its overall outcomes or impact, no matter to what degree it delivers on its outputs.

A change in the assumptions on which the strategy is based necessitates re-evaluating the goals that the strategy sets. This need not be negative. A strategy that focuses on ICT sector development for export purposes may assume an export market of a certain size, of which the country intends to generate revenues worth $Y million. However, should the market suddenly boom, the country may revise its revenue targets to say $Y million plus 20 percent.

While many assumptions on which a strategy is based are outside the control of the strategy, this is not always the case, particularly at the component level. For example, ICT sector development initiatives may be dependent on the advancement of e-government programs, based on the assumption that the government will be a major source of demand for locally developed ICT products and services. Reductions or delays in e-government initiatives will therefore adversely impact the development of the ICT sector.

Similarly, the ICT sector is also dependent to a large extent on the establishment and enforcement of an intellectual property rights (IPR) regime to safeguard investments in knowledge intensive products. Creation of an IPR regime may be covered as part of a component of legislative reform. However, strategy-makers may choose to make the development and enforcement of an IPR regime an element of an ICT sector component, thereby wielding better control over the outcome of related initiatives and 'internalizing' the risks associated with them.

Incorporating activities on which the success of the strategy is dependent into the strategy itself is one way to mitigate risk. However, the ability to do this is usually limited. It is also for the most part inadvisable, as the strategy will become excessively fragmented as it strives to control the bearing of a wide array of factors, many of which have little to do with ICTs. Other risk mitigation measures, such as monitoring progress or change in certain key areas on which the success of the strategy is dependent may be all that can reasonably be done.

Institutional and Strategic Context

(A) M&E mechanisms and institutions

All major initiatives pertaining to an e-strategy's key objectives require clear definition in the strategy. The strategy should also specify which agencies will take lead responsibility for each project, and estimate the resources required to complete the projects. Unambiguously stating implementation responsibility and resource requirements in a strategy is an important means by which to ensure that the projects actually get done. A lack of clarity on responsibility and budget reduces the chances of the strategy moving forward to the implementation phase.

The same applies to M&E activities. An e-strategy should clearly define the roles, responsibilities and financing options for M&E. The choice of which institutions should take primary responsibility for the M&E effort will depend on (a) which 'layer' of the strategy is being addressed, and (b) existing national M&E capacity.

In general, as one moves down the strategy pyramid from the apex to the base, the location of the M&E capabilities should move closer to the agencies responsible for project implementation. In some cases there may be an existing agency that can take primary responsibility for M&E-related activities, while in others a team may have to be established for this purpose. Selecting which agency should take lead responsibility, or where to locate a new team, should be determined by striking a balance between ownership, access, and capacity.

> Ownership - M&E activities are conducted to inform and guide e-strategy decision-making and implementation processes. They also serve to encourage accountability and transparency of the processes of public office. Agencies responsible for making decisions and undertaking implementation should see the M&E information gathering and analysis as an integral component of what they do, and develop a sense of ownership for that component. Should M&E be conducted by an external agency, there is a risk that the agency will be seen as an external auditor. It may face resistance in so far as its ability to gather data and information and, worse still, parties responsible for implementation may not act on the M&E findings. The benefit of being able to make adjustments and improvements mid-stream through implementation will therefore be lost.

> Data access - The ability to conduct good M&E is dependent on access to data. Some data is available at a national level, and so gathering and analyzing it can be effectively conducted by a national organization. This would apply more commonly to M&E relating to policy and strategic objectives (impact and outcome data). Some of this data may reside with a National Statistical Office (NSO), or with a line ministry. For example, the NSO may have data on the growth of the ICT sector (a policy objective), while the ministry of education may have information on the number of locally trained ICT professionals (strategic objective). Lower down the pyramid, the relevant M&E data is more likely to reside with the project team that is responsible for implementation.

Pyramid Layer	Objective	Indicator	Responsibility for gathering and analyzing M&E data
Policy goals	Grow the country's ICT industry	▪ Total sector revenues ▪ % contribution to GDP growth	NSO or Ministry of Trade & Industry
Strategic priorities	Increase stock of locally trained ICT professionals	▪ Number of people graduating with ICT-related qualifications ▪ Number of people employed in ICT sector	Ministry of Education
Key initiatives	Improve capacity of ICT-focused learning institutions	▪ Funding provisions to institutions increased by X% ▪ Number of professional teaching staff increased by X% ▪ Number of students graduating increased by X%	Ministry of Education or Project Team
Actions	▪ Conduct capacity needs assessment ▪ Create grant program ▪ Establish staff recruitment criteria	▪ Assessments completed in X% of institutions by month A. ▪ Established by month B. X% of grant facility funds disbursed to eligible institutions by month C. ▪ Staffing needs for X% of institutions completed by month D.	Project Team

<u>Capacity leverage</u> - An efficient means by which to conduct e-strategy M&E may be to use established M&E agencies and institutions such as National Statistical Offices, leveraging their data gathering and analytical capacity. However, ICT is a comparatively new field, and thus there may be little existing data and limited applicable capacities[16].

(B) Where should the 'M&E team' be located ?

It is clear that the institutional location of the team that will eventually be responsible for formulating and discharging M&E responsibilities may have a significant impact on its ability to do so. On one hand, such a team should not be seen by the operational entities involved in the e-strategy as 'a remote judge and censor'. On the other hand, if the team is too close to implementation tasks, it runs a distinct risk of becoming 'judge and party', and losing credibility in the process.

---

[16] Building the capacity of National Statistical Offices is clearly a priority in this area, and remains complementary to efforts made by certain organizations (such as ITU and the World Bank) to maintain worldwide databases on connectivity or ICTs for example. Such efforts will require significant financing. One way to optimize the use of the resources and knowledge available is to enhance coordination and cooperation among the various agencies involved. This is precisely the purpose of the 'Partnership on Measuring ICT for Development', launched during UNCTAD XI (Sao Paulo, June 2004) by ITU, OECD, UNCTAD, UNESCO's Institute for Statistics, the UN Regional Commissions (UNECLAC, UNESCWA, UNESCAP, UNECA), the UN ICT Task Force and the World Bank. See http://measuring-ict.unctad.org.

To perform its work efficiently, the 'M&E team' will need to receive its legitimacy from the highest levels of government, i.e. above the level of specific ministers involved in the strategy.[17] It will also need to exercise its responsibilities with the necessary levels of visibility and transparency. Whether this is performed through the establishment of a 'special' centrally-located government unit, or through a more flexible network of individuals involved in various aspects of the formulation and implementation of the strategy will heavily depend on the pre-existing local institutional framework and work habits of government, business, and civil society. In any case, the efficiency and credibility of the M&E team will require that it base its work on the highest technical and methodological standards.

Key Activities of an e-strategy M&E Agency

Management
- Develop a formal plan and business processes, including a budget and goals/targets for staff
- Develop human resource management systems, assessing training needs of other agencies
- Conduct regular training on ICT-related M&E
- Develop internal communications and team building.

Indicator development
- Assess existing data sources and their relevance to the strategy and implementation plan
- Recommend improvements in specific data series in terms of timeliness, coverage, or level of disaggregation
- Develop and publish new data series
- Ensure compliance with international standards for specific data items
- Create new data products, for instance, presenting existing data in new ways, or including new types of analysis and discussion
- Improve response rates for specific surveys.

Outreach
- Establish regular consultations between users and providers of statistical data
- Establish processes to receive regular feedback from customers
- Update statistical legislation
- Establish links with the media.

Source : Adapted from Achikbache, B., Belkindas, M., Eele, G., Swanson, E. "Strengthening Statistical Systems." *PRSP Source Book*. World Bank.

SECTION III – A PRACTICAL EXAMPLE OF HOW TO APPLY THE M.E.T.E.R. METHODOLOGY: E-GOVERNMENT

For many government officials concerned with extending the benefits of information and communication technologies (ICTs) to their country, e-government is a natural point of entry, and is a core element of most e-strategies designed so far.[18] E-government has the potential to greatly and rapidly improve how government operates internally and how it serves its customers. At the very least e-government can bring cost savings to businesses (e.g. faster business registration), and time savings to citizens (e.g. online tax returns). The best e-government implementations however address the ways in which internal government processes are executed, as well as how government transacts with society as a whole. The

---

[17] An increasing number of countries has chosen to pursue a 'CIO' approach, whereby a personality (often issued from the private sector) is given high visibility (and sometimes significant powers) to promote national e-strategies.

[18] E-government development is the most frequently cited (over 60%) focus area of the strategies surveyed.

potential of ICT in government should therefore be understood as a paradigm shift that improves how government operates and how society interacts with and views government.

More than many other components of an e-strategy, e-government efforts must be measurable (and generally visible) in order to attract support from civil society at large.[19] Hence, any failure to meet deadlines or reach milestones will be more damaging in e-government than in most other areas. Offering transparent ways to measure progress (through benchmarking, and more generally through M&E) will therefore be vital to for success in e-government. In its approach, the M.E.T.E.R. toolkit focuses on the range of 'best practices' that emerges from the relatively broad array of experiences available in this area.[20]

Definition: What is e-government?

E-government consists of a set of activities and instruments through which ICTs are fully or partially integrated in some of the core functions of governments, administrations, and public service entities. The purpose of such integration is generally a combination of the following:

Efficiency - Greater efficiency in delivering government services to citizens and businesses as well as improved intra-government services

Provision - Development and delivery of new services to the population, or provision of services to populations previously underserved, especially in rural or less densely populated areas.

Responsiveness - Increased responsiveness of governments to the needs of their citizens, including new possibilities for citizens and governments to interact with each other.

Accountability - Greater transparency and accountability of governments and administrations, including in the area of public procurement.

Participation - Higher levels of citizen participation in public decisions and management, hence strengthening democracy.

Understood as such, e-government is much more than a tool for improving cost-quality ratios in public services. It is also an instrument of reform and a tool to transform government. Thus, e-government is not primarily about automation of existing procedures (which may or may not be effective), but about changing the way in which government conducts business and delivers services.

---

[19] Some internal (G2G) transactions may remain invisible (if not hidden) from the end user; however, even in such cases, civil society may require transparency (as in the case if the French Legislation 'Informatique et Libertes', which limits some linkages between various governmental databases)

[20] This best-practice approach was already the starting point of the 'E-government Handbook for Developing Countries', published by *info*Dev and the Center for Democracy and Technology, in November 2002 (see www.infodev.org). Many of the items described in this module refer to the classification used in this milestone publication.

Overview of e-government Strategies

E-government strategies vary considerably in terms of their focus and the degree of change they aspire to undertake. However, most e-government strategies include the following elements:

- A precise identification of the prerequisites for success (and possible indications on how to meet these prerequisites if necessary)

- A clear definition of the objectives being pursued (output and outcome), ways of measuring success, and a time horizon within which such success is expected

- A set of M&E indicators, linked to specific objectives, levels of responsibility, and milestones embedded in the e-government strategy.

Prerequisites

The achievement of e-government goals requires that ICTs in a country are developed to a sufficient level to allow measurable changes to take place in the way government functions and citizens are served. The ability of citizens to access ICTs will depend on the existence of infrastructure (e.g. Internet access), affordability of access (which will itself critically depend on the existence of a competitive regulatory environment), and of the availability of basic knowledge (e-literacy) across society.

Moreover, since e-government is not just about saving money by computerizing procedures, but also about reforming and improving government, other prerequisites include (a) the political will of government authorities to reform and improve government processes, and (b) the support and engagement that such efforts will gather from civil society as a whole.

Although many of the prerequisites relevant to e-government also happen to be necessary conditions for the development and successful implementation of e-strategies as a whole, one cannot over-emphasize the importance of <u>adequate legal, regulatory, and institutional environments</u> as necessary conditions for success in e-government. Whether such frameworks are designed and enforced at central or local (i.e. sub-national) levels, they have proven to be the single most important pre-condition for the successful and society-broad use of information technologies, mainly because they have allowed cost and prices to diminish. In areas in which public entities (i.e. governments, administrative departments, or state-owned enterprises) remain major players (as in e-government), the creation of such environments becomes particularly critical (and visible) because government is both on the supply side (e.g. for on-line services to citizens) and on the demand side (e.g. for e-procurement) of the equation.

Such prerequisites can be summarized by the 'ABCDE' of e-government:

Prerequisite	Concern	Activity (typical indicators)
Access	Infrastructure, costs, competition/ regulation (hence includes proper regulatory and competition frameworks)	▪ Equipment (PCs, kiosks, community centers) ▪ Teledensity ▪ Rule of law ▪ Pro-competitive ICT regulation (tariff and non-tariff barriers, competition in the ICT sector) ▪ Cost (fixed line calls and Internet access) ▪ Access for disadvantaged or excluded
Basic Skills	Basic education, vocational training, ICT awareness	▪ Literacy (alphabetization rates) ▪ E-literacy ratios per age/group/sex/region ▪ Vocational training
Content	Value to government and citizens	▪ Questionnaires on value to users/citizens and government ▪ Content in local languages
Desire	Political leadership and will to reform	▪ Public statements/decisions ▪ Laws and regulations (perceptions of quality of legal system)
Engagement	Commitment of all components of civil society	▪ Broad involvement of civil society (questionnaire/survey) ▪ Local awareness of ICT potential for development (questionnaire/survey)

Expected Outcomes and Sequencing

Depending on their own development goals and available resources (financial, technological, and human), governments may have different levels of ambition regarding e-government. It is generally recognized that three types (or layers) of e-government may be considered as part of a national e-strategy, namely:

- Publishing information (one-way communication: (G2B, G2C)

- Interacting with the citizen (two-way communication: (G2B, G2C)

- Contracting with citizens and government on-line: (G2B, G2C, G2G)

Although those three layers undoubtedly correspond to increasing levels of institutional, legal, and technological sophistication, they should not be seen as stages in a required strategy 'sequence'. Various layers may coexist within e-government, some services being more advanced than others at any point in time.

	Publish	**Interact**	**Contract**
Rationale	Bring information quickly and more directly to citizens	Engage civil society in reform process and generate support	Offer cost-effective government services anywhere, anytime
Focus Area	Rules, regulations, documents, forms, institutional structures, processes and procedures	Two-way communications (e.g. e-mail), feedback forms and online discussion fora	Services such as ID cards, certificates, land ownership titles, registrations (automobiles, change of address, public procurement tenders), tax and fine collection
Good Practices	<ul><li>Strategy to get information online, with appropriate milestones</li><li>Post information of value to people in their daily lives, and emphasize local language content</li><li>A mandate that all agencies publish a specified range of information online</li><li>Design sites so they are easy to maintain, and sustain funding to ensure that information is updated regularly</li><li>Focus on content that supports other goals, e.g. economic development, anti-corruption, attracting FDI</li></ul>	<ul><li>Show citizens that their engagement matters, by informing them of the outcomes of their online comments</li><li>Break down complex policy issues into easy-to-understand components</li><li>Be proactive about soliciting participation - use traditional media to publicize online consultations</li></ul>	<ul><li>Enlist the support of those who will be using the site</li><li>Integrate e-government with process reform, streamlining and consolidating processes before putting them online</li><li>Address the concerns of government workers whose role will change as a result of the innovation</li><li>Recognize that initial investments in transaction systems can pay off over time in terms of cost savings and increased revenue</li><li>Create a portal for transaction services</li></ul>

An important point needs to be made regarding the level of government at which an e-government strategy is being considered. Since social consensus is often less difficult to generate at the local (e.g. state or municipal) level than at the national (e.g. federal) level, e-government strategies are in general most productively designed and implemented by local governments (state or cities). E-government strategies, whether national or local, will involve virtually all parts of government. As the e-strategy is formulated and customized, this should be reflected in its objectives and relevant M&E instruments.

The e-government components of an e-strategy should consider various best practices, depending on which level of governance they focus upon. The table above provides an initial basis for their identification in a possible 'e-government roadmap'.[21]

---

[21] Based on elements from in the E-government Handbook for Developing Countries. *info*Dev and CDT, 2003. Web: http://www.cdt.org/egov/handbook/2002-11-14egovhandbook.pdf

M&E Frameworks

It is important to note that e-government initiatives have commonly been incorrectly conceived, haphazardly applied and rarely measured in terms of their relative success.[22] The most common mistake is the use of IT to automate existing processes when what is required is a comprehensive business case to define how technology can positively impact government and society in the short and longer terms, and a corresponding M&E system to reflect progress and return on investment.

More than many other components of an e-strategy, e-government efforts are highly visible. To attract support from civil society at large, they are required to establish clear objectives and be transparent with regard to their implementation.

Failure to meet deadlines or reach milestones may be more damaging in e-government than in many other areas. The specification and design of indicators and methodology must therefore be rigorous and precise, while also leaving a reasonable margin for adjustments during implementation. They also require a high level of commitment and endorsement from relevant authorities.

For each of the three types of e-government approaches, an appropriate set of M&E indicators needs to be implemented. The following tables offer proposals in this regard. It is up to each decision maker to select and adapt those indicators best fitted to their needs and constraints.

It should be noted that many of the initiatives and actions that are covered in the tables relate to putting information and services on-line, therefore focusing to a large extent on the 'front-end' of e-government. However, substantial 'back-end' or organizational changes are required to undertake many of these initiatives. Information must be shared across government departments, requiring (at the very least) standardization in collection and processing. Processes and procedures have to be adjusted – even completely overhauled – to respond to the different requirements of online service provision. Staff skill requirements are also likely to change, necessitating adjustments to staffing and hiring practices; such organizational change is taken into account in the M&E frameworks that follow. Indicators to track progress and measure success of this change will be required as well.

E-government Level 1: Publish

It can be particularly challenging to develop indicators to measure progress made in putting government information online and to evaluate the degree to which people are accessing it. At the initiative (output) level it is possible to simply count web sites. However, assessing the strategic value of this outcome is considerably more difficult. Counting website visits is of limited help, as this cannot be tied back to the number of users (or percent of the

---

[22] http://www.e-devexchange.org/eGov/topic1.htm

population). Conducting surveys of the population would be an effective way to gauge usage, but this can be costly.[23]

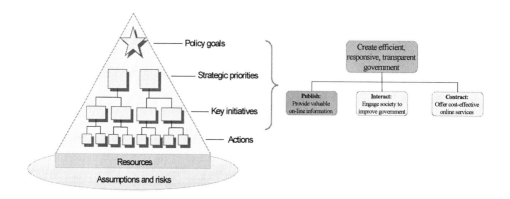

E-government and Efficiency: Examples from Singapore and India

Advances in information technology, including the Internet, are paving the way for investment climate improvements that reduce demands on public administration, enhance transparency, and ease compliance burdens on firms. Approaches to business regulation in Singapore and land titling in India's Karnataka state illustrate the potential.

The e-government initiative launched by Singapore in 2000 included business registration and licensing procedures. It provides an online application system for business registration and licensing and a one-stop online application system for certain special licenses (for example, building and construction permits) that previously required separate submissions to as many as 12 regulatory authorities. The integrated approach reduced the cost of incorporating a new company from anywhere between S$1,200 and S$35,000 (around $700 to $20,000) (depending on the capital of the company) to a flat fee of S$300 ($175). What used to require two days now requires less than two hours. Streamlining the submission process for construction permits saves applicants more than S$450 ($260).

India's Karnataka state introduced an electronic land-titling system, Bhoomi, in the late 1990s.The online system is delivered through kiosks installed in all land offices of Karnataka. These kiosks provide copies of a Record of Rights, Tenancy, and Crops (RTC). Obtaining an RTC once required up to 30 days, and typically a bribe of as much as Rs. 2,000 (about $43). Land records could be deliberately "blurred" for fees of Rs. 10,000 ($220).These records were not open to the public, and it sometimes took two years for the records to be updated under the manual accounting system maintained by 9,000 "village" accountants - state employees responsible for three to four villages each. Today an RTC can be obtained for a fixed fee of Rs. 15 ($0.32) in 5 to 30 minutes. The records are open for public scrutiny. Citizens can now request that land titles be updated quickly through the kiosks, a process that has increased the number of annual applications for updates by 50 percent.

Source: Tan (2004); Bhatnagar and Chawla (2004); and Lobo and Balakrishnan (2002). Quoted in 'A Better Investment Climate for Everyone' *World Development Report, 2005,* The World Bank. (Box 2.16, '*E-government and the investment climate'*)

---

[23] One way to minimize costs would be to include relevant questions in national household and business surveys, carried out by NSOs. Efforts in this area should ideally be developed with a view to collect data in a way that would ensure international comparability.

Pyramid Layer	Objective	Indicator	Data source
Policy goals	Create an efficient, responsive and transparent government	Perception of overall administrative burden Perception of government effectiveness	Office of Government and Ministry of Local Government
Strategic priorities	Bring valuable information online to the public, anytime anywhere [a]	• Perception of government online presence • % pop. using govt. sites • Usage growth rate	E-government CIO's Office
Key initiatives	• Roll-out of online information services [b] • Raise public awareness through online and offline channels	• No. of agencies with web sites • % of agencies with web sites • % of information services rolled-out on time	E-government CIO's Office
Actions	• Establish an independent central e-government group and M&E unit [c] • Establish selection guidelines for information/content to be posted, including nature and volume • Assess technology and organizational needs/requirements • Develop online information platforms • Offer information services on line, including local language content • Develop publicity campaign to promote new e-government initiatives • Solicit feedback on usability and usefulness of online government services	• Central e-government team and M&E unit established by month A • Guidelines for M&E established by month B • Relevant information sources identified by month C • System functional requirements completed by month D • Mid-term implementation review conducted by month E • Public awareness survey results	Project team or Central M&E unit

(a) There should be a clear linkage between the type of content that is brought on-line and larger development goals, such as economic development, anti-corruption, and attracting FDI.
(b) Criteria used for information publication should be related to cost and time savings and envisaged productivity gains.
(c) Central e-government group responsible for interoperability and inter-agency consistency of e-government services, security, consolidation of records, and M&E.

E-government Level 2: Interact

Measuring levels of interaction is similarly challenging to publishing-focused initiatives. Indicators can focus on the types and number of interactive channels available (such as e-mail or discussion fora) and the government's responsiveness. As the sophistication of the online services increases, the indicators should be disaggregated to reflect progress made by individual government agencies.

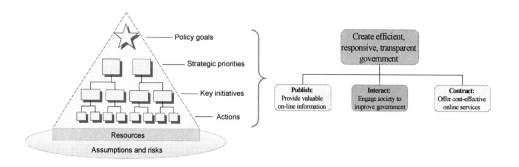

Pyramid Layer	Objective	Indicator	Data source
Policy goals	Create an efficient, responsive and transparent government	Perception of overall administrative burden Perception of government effectiveness	Office of Government and Ministry of Local Government
Strategic priorities	Engage society to improve government, and enhance efficiency of delivery of government services	Perception of government online presence No. of improvements to government services resulting from public suggestions	E-government CIO's Office
Key initiatives	Deploy online interactive tools Raise public awareness through online and offline channels Examples: e-mail Q/A, threaded discussions, feedback forms, 'Ask the policy maker'	% govt. agencies with interactive sites No. of online interaction channels (by agency) % of possible reforms/policy issues that have interactive tools (by agency)	E-government CIO's Office
Actions	▪ Establish selection guidelines for opportunities for interaction ▪ Assess technology and organizational needs/requirements ▪ Develop online interactive platforms ('interact' stage), integrating with information platforms ('publish' stage) ▪ Publish government contact information ▪ Develop publicity campaign to promote new e-government ▪ Solicit online public consultation through other media ▪ Publish deliberations of questions/queries from the public in FAQ, to show that engagement is taken seriously ▪ Solicit feedback on usability and usefulness of online government services ▪ Link to other online government services	▪ Guidelines for selection established by month A ▪ Relevant opportunities for interaction identified by month B ▪ System functional requirements completed by month C ▪ Mid-term implementation review conducted by month D ▪ Public awareness survey results	Project team or Central M&E unit

E-government Level 3: Contract

At this level of e-government, quantitative M&E indicators become easier to use. These may include the number of agencies and functions online, average time for processing citizen requests or applications, number of complaints about the level and quality of government services, or depending on the e-government initiative, reduction in government costs for service delivery (procurement), increased revenue (tax collection) and better governance (voter turn-out). Indicators at this level will not only be agency-specific, but also focus on individual online services.[24]

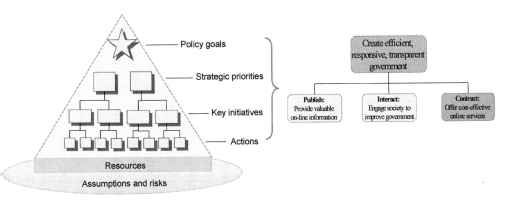

Pyramid Layer	Objective	Indicator	Data source
Policy goals	▪ Create an efficient, responsive and transparent government	▪ Perception of overall administrative burden ▪ Perception of govt. effectiveness	Office of Government and Ministry of Local Government
Strategic priorities	▪ Offer cost-effective online government transactional services anywhere anytime	▪ Perception of govt. online services ▪ % govt. agencies with transactional sites ▪ % of possible services online (by agency)	E-government CIO's Office
Key initiatives	▪ Create online versions of offline services (to cut costs and redeploy resources more efficiently) ▪ Raise public awareness through online and offline channels *Examples: ID cards, certifications (death, birth, marriage, divorce), land ownership titles, registrations (automobiles, change of ownership), public procurement (tenders), tax and fine collection*	▪ No. of online services ▪ % of possible services that are online (by agency) ▪ % of total customers transacting online (per service)[25] ▪ Usage growth rate (per service) ▪ Time to complete transaction (per service)	E-government CIO's Office *(continued)*

---

[24] See also M&E table in module 4 on development of an online business registration portal.
[25] Available from 'Weblogs' generated by the computers that 'host' the e-government website or portal.

Actions	<ul><li>Establish guidelines for selecting online services</li><li>Establish mechanism for interagency coordination and system integration</li><li>Assess technology and organizational needs</li><li>Develop online transactional platforms, integrating with interactive and informational platforms</li><li>Address the concerns of government workers whose roles will change</li><li>Provide necessary feedback and possible training</li><li>Build confidence in security and privacy</li><li>Develop publicity campaign to promote new e-government</li><li>Solicit feedback on usability and usefulness of online government services</li><li>Benchmark processing times for individual services and transactions</li></ul>	<ul><li>Guidelines for selection established by month A</li><li>Relevant services identified by month B</li><li>Interagency mechanisms and procedures established by month C</li><li>System functional requirements completed by month D</li><li>Mid-term implementation review conducted by month E</li><li>Staff and user training complete by month F</li><li>Public satisfaction survey results</li></ul>	Project team or Central M&E unit

Summary

The incentive to undertake e-government development is based not in technology itself, but rather in the real benefits that can be realized over the short, medium, and long term, in particular where e-government goals are aligned with larger governance objectives.

The drivers for the success and sustainability of e-government are true government commitment to improving administrative processes, increasing productivity and generating savings, and building public confidence in the government's ability to execute the necessary reforms and transformations. Developing effective indicators to monitor such change and evaluate the means by which e-government initiatives are delivering on their promise is particularly important, as e-government is often the most visible (and closely watched) component of an e-strategy.

Conclusion

Considered as a central part of development strategies, e-strategies have the potential to stimulate many changes in the way governments, business and other stakeholders function together and contribute to growth, competitiveness and development.

However, to achieve such potential, e-strategies will need to respect two major imperatives, namely:

- they should not be designed (even less implemented) in isolation from other strategies and policies aimed at addressing 'fundamental' development priorities (e.g. health, education, etc.); they should be fully used to pursue other objectives such as transparency and good governance;

- they should include, since the earliest stages of their design and implementation, the monitoring and evaluation components necessary to measure progress made, assess the efficiency with which resources are being used, and take corrective action as required.

As a vital component of the objectives of WSIS, and as a potential catalyst and accelerator of the pursuit of MDGs, e-strategies conceived in that fashion will constitute not only the epitome of national efforts to make the best of local and global digital opportunities, but also a pool of international experiences and best practices, which will contribute to our collective ability to address imaginatively and forcefully some of the major challenges of development and poverty.

Case: Benchmarking e-government in Europe

The e-Europe Plan of Action for 2005 establishes 7 targets which are specific to e-government:
- Interactive public services accessible to all
- Electronic procurement for a significant part of public procurement
- Public Internet Access Points (PIAP's) for all citizens, preferably with broadband connections
- Broadband connections for all public administrations
- Interoperability for e-government services
- E-services to promote culture and tourism
- Secure communications between public services for the exchange of classified government information.

With regard to the first target, 20 recommended services are listed (12 to citizens and 8 to businesses):

Public Services for Citizens	Public Services for Businesses
Income taxes	Social contribution for employees
Job search	Corporation tax
Social security benefits	Value Added Tax
Personal documents	Registration of a new company
Car registration	Submission of data to statistical offices
Application for building permission	Customs declarations
Declaration to the police	Environment-related permits
Public libraries	Public procurement
Certificates (birth, marriage)	
Enrollment in higher education	
Announcement of moving	
Health-related services	

Monitoring and evaluating progress achieved in establishing these online services is based on a five stage framework that assesses the level of maturity or sophistication of each e-government service. While the definition of each stage of maturity varies depending on the service being assessed, in general terms they translate as:

Stage 0 – No online presence
Stage 1 – Information (on-line information about public services)
Stage 2 – Interaction (downloading of forms)
Stage 3 – Two way interaction (processing forms, including authentication)
Stage 4 – Transaction (case handling, decision and delivery)

Based on this classification, member states are scored for the maturity level of each of the 20 e-government services. This allows them to compare their levels of maturity relative to one another, as well as progress made in different groupings of services, such as services for citizens versus services for businesses. Because the framework has been in existence since 2001, it also allows member states to compare changes over time.

Though this framework is very useful, it has limitations. First, it only applies to Internet-based electronic services, and not those delivered through other channels such as mobile devices or call centers. Second, it focuses only on the front-office of e-government, and does not account for important back-offices changes that e-government entails, such as process redesign and system integration. *(continued)*

Sources

E-Europe. 2001. "E-government Indicators for Benchmarking E-Europe."
http://europa.eu.int/information_society/eeurope/2002/action_plan/pdf/egovindicators.pdf

E-Europe. 2002. "E-Europe 2005: An Information Society for All."
http://europa.eu.int/information_society/eeurope/2005/all_about/action_plan/index_en.htm

E-Europe and Cap Gemini Ernst & Young. 2003. "Web Based Survey on Electronic Public Services: Report of the Fourth Measurement, October 2003."
http://europa.eu.int/information_society/eeurope/2005/all_about/benchmarking/index_en.htm

Annex - List of e-strategies considered

The following e-strategies (national or sub-national) were reviewed as part of the background research for this toolkit.

Country (or region)	Web address at which the strategy can be found
Albania	http://www.undp.org.al/?elib,428
Angola	http://www.uneca.org/aisi/nici/Angola/angola.htm
Azerbaijan	http://www.nicts.az:8101/
Bangladesh	www.bccbd.org/html/itpolicy.htm
Bhutan	http://www.dit.gov.bt/bips/documents/documents.htm
Bolivia	http://www.aladi.org/nsfaladi/ecomerc.nsf/0/E8147919B55D97A403256BEA004D2EDA/$File/lineamientos.pdf?OpenElement
Chile	http://www.agendadigital.cl/agenda_digital/agendadigital.nsf/vwDocumentosWebLink/27363116E8E6631704256E5800549FE3?OpenDocument
China (Hong Kong)	http://www.info.gov.hk/digital21/eng/strategy2004/strategy_main.html
Colombia	http://www.agenda.gov.co/
Czech Republic	http://www.micr.cz/scripts/detail.php?id=1288
Dominican Republic	http://www.edominicana.gov.do/interfaz/contenido.asp?Ag=1&CategoriaNo=3
Egypt	http://www.uneca.org/aisi/nici/Egypt/egypt.htm

Finland	http:::://www.tietoyhteiskuntaohjelma.fi/esittely/en_GB/introduction
Ghana	http://www.uneca.org/aisi/nici/Ghana/ghana.htm
India (National)	http://www.gipi.org.in/ITPolicyInIndia.php
India (Andhra Pradesh)	http://www.gipi.org.in/state_policy/andhra.pdf
India (Delhi)	http://delhigovt.nic.in/icetpolicy.pdf
India (Haryana)	http://www.gipi.org.in/state_policy/haryana.pdf
India (Orissa)	http://www.gipi.org.in/ITPolicyInIndia.php
Indonesia	http://www.sdnbd.org/sdi/issues/IT-computer/policy/indonesia.pdf
Ireland	http://www.taoiseach.gov.ie/index.asp?locID=181&docID=1773
Jamaica	http://unpan1.un.org/intradoc/groups/public/documents/CARICAD/UNPAN009931.pdf
Japan	http://www.kantei.go.jp/foreign/policy/it/index_e.html
Jordan	http://www.reach.jo/
Korea	http://www.ipc.go.kr/ipceng/public/public_view.jsp?num=2007&fn=&req=&pgno=3
Mauritius	http://ncb.intnet.mu/ncb/downloads/Downloads/Reports%20and%20surveys/Others/finalntp.doc
Mozambique	http://www.markle.org/downloadable_assets/mz_final_ict_strategy.pdf
Namibia	http://www.uneca.org/aisi/nici/Documents/ICT%20Policy%20Document%20Ver%208.2.pdf
Nigeria	http://www.uneca.org/aisi/nici/Documents/IT%20policy%20for%20Nigeria.pdf
Norway	http://odin.dep.no/nhd/engelsk/publ/rapporter/bn.html
Poland	http://www.informatyzacja.gov.pl/_d/files/projects/epoland-the_strategy_on_the_development_of_the_information_society.pdf
Romania	http://unpan1.un.org/intradoc/groups/public/documents/UNTC/UNPAN016044.pdf
Russia	http://www.e-rus.ru/eng
Rwanda	http://www.uneca.org/aisi/nici/Documents/rwanpap2.htm

Singapore	http://www.ida.gov.sg/idaweb/aboutida/infopage.jsp?infopagecategory=&infopageid=I226&versionid=2
Slovenia	http://unpan1.un.org/intradoc/groups/public/documents/UNTC/UNPAN015723.pdf
South Africa	http://www.tsicanada.com/documents/Strategy.pdf
Tanzania	http://www.tanzania.go.tz/pdf/ictpolicy.pdf
Thailand	http://www.nectec.or.th/intro/e_nationalpolicy.php
Trinidad & Tobago	http://www.gov.tt/nict/
Tunisia	Hard copy only
Ukraine	http://www.e-ukraine.com.ua
United Kingdom	http://e-government.cabinetoffice.gov.uk/assetRoot/04/00/60/69/04006069.pdf
Venezuela	http://www.mct.gov.ve
Viet Nam	http://mpt.gov.vn/english/introduction/?thucdon=in

References

Achikbache, B., Belkindas, M., Eele, G., Swanson, E. "Strengthening Statistical Systems." *PRSP Source Book*. World Bank. http://www.worldbank.org/poverty/strategies/sourcons.htm

Association for Progressive Communications. 2003. "ICT Policy: A Beginner's Handbook." APC

bridges.org. 2001. "Comparison of E-Readiness Assessment Models." Bridges.org. http://www.bridges.org/ereadiness/

bridges.org. 2002. "E-readiness Assessment: Who is Doing What and Where." Bridges.org. http://www.bridges.org/ereadiness/

Commonwealth Business Council. 2001. *E-government – Modernizing Commonwealth Governments*.

De Wulf Luc and Sokol, Jose B., eds., "Customs Modernization Handbook" (Washington, DC: The World Bank, 2004).

Digital Opportunity Task Force. 2001. *Digital Opportunities for All*. http://www.g7.utoronto.ca/summit/2001genoa/dotforce1.html

E-Europe. 2001. "E-government Indicators for Benchmarking E-Europe."
http://europa.eu.int/information_society/eeurope/2002/action_plan/pdf/egovindicators.p
df

E-Europe. 2002. "E-Europe 2005: An Information Society for All."
http://europa.eu.int/information_society/eeurope/2005/all_about/action_plan/index_en.h
tm

E-Europe and Cap Gemini Ernst & Young. 2003. "Web Based Survey on Electronic Public
Services: Report of the Fourth Measurement, October 2003."
http://europa.eu.int/information_society/eeurope/2005/all_about/benchmarking/index_e
n.htm

ESIS Report. 2000. "Public Strategies for the Information societies in the Member States of
the European Union."

Grace, J., Kenny, C. and Qiang, C. "Information and Communication Technologies and
Broad-Based Development: A Partial Review of the Evidence." World Bank Working Paper
No. 12. World Bank. http://poverty.worldbank.org/files/10214_ict.pdf

Hanna, N. 2003. "Why National Strategies are Needed for ICT-Enabled Development."
ISG Staff Working Papers. World Bank.

*info*Dev and CDT. 2003. *The E-government Handbook for Developing Countries.*
http://www.cdt.org/egov/handbook/2002-11-14egovhandbook.pdf

G-8 Kananaskis Summit, 2002. "The Italian Initiative on E-government for Development."

Kenny, C. and Qiang, C. 2003. "ICT and Broad-Based Development." *ICT and Development:
Enabling the Information Society.* World Bank.
http://lnweb18.worldbank.org/ict/projects.nsf/WSISPublications#ictDev

Lanvin, B. and Qiang, C., 2003. "Poverty 'e-Readication': Using ICT to the Meet MDG."
The Global Information Technology Report 2003-2004. Oxford.
http://www.weforum.org/site/homepublic.nsf/Content/Global+Competitiveness+Progra
mme%5CGlobal+Information+Technology+Report

National Audit Office. 2002. "Government on the Web II." http://www.nao.org.uk/pn/01-
02/0102764.htm

NORAD. 1999. *The Logical Framework Approach.*
http://www.baltichealth.org/customers/baltic/lfa/LFA%20handbook.htm

Nordic-Dutch Trade Union Centers. 2003. "Handbook of Participatory Project Planning."
http://www.fnv.nl/download.do/id/100001160/

OECD. 2003. *The E-government Imperative.* OECD.
http://www1.worldbank.org/publicsector/egov/E-GovernmentImperative.pdf

Prennushi, G., Rubio, G., Subbarao, K., "Monitoring and Evaluation." *PRSP Source Book*. World Bank. http://www.worldbank.org/poverty/strategies/sourcons.htm

Qiang, C., Pitt, A., with Ayers, S. 2003. "Contribution of Information and Communication Technologies to Growth." World Bank Working Paper No. 24. World Bank. http://lnweb18.worldbank.org/ict/projects.nsf/WSISPublications

Schware, R. 2003. "Information and Communications Technology (ICT) Agencies: Functions, Structures, and Best Operational Practices." Emerald. http://hermia.emeraldinsight.com/vl=12696689/cl=14/nw=1/fm=docpdf/rpsv/cw/mcb/14636697/v5n3/s1/p3

Schware, R. and Deane, A. 2003. "Deploying E-government Programs: The Strategic Importance of 'I before E'." World Bank. http://www1.worldbank.org/publicsector/egov/ReinventingGovWorkshop/Deployingegovt.pdf

Tan, Eng Pheng. 2004. "The Singapore E-Government Experience." Paper presented at Foro Internacional: Hacia una Sociedad Digital. Panamá City, Panamá. April 6.

UNCTAD "E-commerce and Development Report (Geneva, 2004) http://www.unctad.org/Templates/WebFlyer.asp?intItemID=3084&lang=1

UNPAN. Benchmarking E-government: A Global Perspective - Assessing the Progress of the UN Member States. http://www.unpan.org/egovernment2.asp

World Bank e-government web site: http://www1.worldbank.org/publicsector/egov/

World Bank. *The LogFrame Handbook*. World Bank.

World Bank. 2002. *ICT Sector Strategy Paper*. World Bank. http://info.worldbank.org/ict/ICT_ssp.html

UP-SCALING PRO-POOR ICT POLICIES AND PRACTICES

By Richard Gerster and Sonja Zimmermann, Gerster Consulting

Information and communication technologies (ICTs) can make a difference in reducing poverty and in contributing to reaching the Millennium Development Goals (MDGs). The pioneer of appropriate technology, E.F. Schumacher, said many years ago: "The gift of material goods makes people dependent. The gift of knowledge makes them free"[1]. Practical experience, as well as the lessons learned around the globe, demonstrates the great potential of ICTs for enhancing empowerment, opportunity and security. This potential, however, contrasts with the relatively modest impact attributed to ICT as a general enabler in reaching the MDGs. Untapped opportunities exist to multiply and scale up successful pilot projects and approaches, by harnessing ICT's potential for dynamic knowledge sharing and networking, building on economies of scale, and drawing on a broad range of approaches that can be used as a catalyst for local adaptation. Up-scaling poverty reduction with ICT means increasing outreach and deepening impact.

On this background, the MS Swaminathan Research Foundation (MSSRF) and the Swiss Agency for Development and Cooperation (SDC), launched a process in 2004 to identify the potential and constraints of up-scaling pro-poor ICT policies and practices. The process was organized in coordination with and supported by the Global Knowledge Partnership (GKP), OneWorld South Asia and the United Nations Development Programme (UNDP). This process consisted of four steps: (1) A draft study on up scaling – drawing on desk research – was made by consultants and widely shared. (2) The draft report served as the starting point of an international workshop, jointly hosted by MSSRF and SDC in Chennai, India, on November 17-19, 2004, with a wide range of experts participating, including grassroots practitioners as well as policy makers. That workshop resulted in a 'Chennai Statement'[2], containing the main messages in a nutshell. (3) Taking into account the insights of the workshop and the Chennai Statement, a revised final paper[3] was published and disseminated in 2005 jointly by MSSRF and SDC. (4) Based on the published report on "Up-scaling Pro-poor ICT Policies and Practices" a side event of the WSIS PrepCom II was jointly hosted by SDC, MSSRF and GKP in Geneva on February 18, 2005 in the form of an international panel on "Promoting WSIS – MDGs Synergies".

The following pages summarize the lessons learned, the MDG implications and the messages for WSIS as outcomes of this process.

Lessons Learned

A participative ICT approach, involving people from the needs assessment to monitoring, makes a difference[4]. When scaling up, this experience presents a major challenge, as the danger of embarking on

---

[1] Schilderman 2001.
[2] See Global Knowledge Partnership, with the option to comment: http://202.144.202.75/gkps_portal/index.cfm
[3] Gerster Richard/Zimmermann Sonja, Up-scaling Pro-Poor ICT Policies and Practices: a Review of Experience with Emphasis on Low Income Countries in Asia and Africa, SDC/MSSRF, Berne/Chennai 2005, hard copies available at ict4d@deza.admin.ch. Download at
http://www.deza.ch/index.php?navID=689&userhash=23091110&lID=6
[4] Batchelor 2003.

a top-down and supply-driven expansion is ever present. The information gap lies not only on the poor people's side and the fact that they lack relevant information to improve their lives. Equally, there is an information gap with decision makers who are not sufficiently informed about poor people's situation and concerns. This makes participation in decision-making essential.

Leadership matters, as does institutional ownership. A large number of successful pilot programmes using ICTs for poverty reduction are driven by committed individuals[5]. When up-scaling, this human component must not be lost and this may be the most difficult challenge. Making use of ICTs for poverty reduction results in more than a traditional business relationship. However, relying only on committed individuals significantly limits[6] the up-scaling potential, because there has to be an institutional base to extend outreach and to increase the number of people involved without moving away from the poor as the primary target group. Up-scaling may also imply increasing benefits.

Adopting a community approach in ICT access has a number of important strengths[7]. It is a cost-effective way of up-scaling connectivity outreach. It allows for the combining of a multitude of functions of public interest (media, banking, other) and facilitates the integration of traditional and new media. A collective learning environment is created and a social space for interactions provided. The Philippine model of community e-centres[8] provides a demand and content-driven reference framework for linking up community services with private sector involvement. The UNESCO CMC programme builds on radio as a key facilitator for community access.

ICT centres expand users' social networks[9]. They do this in several ways: (1) They provide legitimate spaces to socialise and work with different people in free and interesting situations; (2) The centres act as 'hubs' where different social networks can intersect; (3) Centres are connected to larger organisations and attract visitors, giving a sense that the locale is connected to a wider world. Restricted social networks reflect social norms that narrow people's mobility (often women's), access to information and resources, and their ability to interact with others to gain support and to organise themselves collectively. ICT access produces increased face-to-face communication within local social networks.

Multi-stakeholder partnerships are a promising and appropriate response. They respond to the complexity of tasks, to the need for resources to scale up, and to the fact that development is a shared responsibility of all sectors of society. A successful partnership has clear and mutually understood objectives, is based on mutual respect and trust of partners, involves pooling of resources, responsibility and benefits, and combines the diverse strengths of partners[10].

---

[5] Beardon sees this also as a weakness of the bottom-up process: "There is an inevitable reliance on committed people with integrity to ensure that the participatory process is properly followed." (Beardon 2004, p. 20).
[6] Hagen 2004.
[7] Jayaweera 2004.
[8] Pena in: UNDP/APDIP 2003.
[9] Slater/Tacchi 2004; Jayaweera 2004.
[10] Greener 2004.

Information and communication involve costs. Comprehensive and transparent budgeting provides a sound basis for decision-making and sustainability. Public funds should focus on the production of public goods. Costing should distinguish between investment and operational costs, between pilot and replication costs, between commercially viable parts and the production of public goods. Eventually, community contributions in cash and kind are to be included. The design of cost recovery mechanisms should take into account the economic situation of the users.

A threshold level of physical and human infrastructure is required to make effective pro-poor use of ICT. For low income Asia and the Pacific it was observed that a country's income level, adult illiteracy and population density are guides to its capacity to adopt advanced forms of ICTs[11]. This lesson is also valid at the sub-national, e.g. the village, level. The low literacy level, as well as the weak infrastructure, in sub-Saharan Africa puts this region at a clear disadvantage in adopting ICTs compared to low income Asian countries. In decision making on public or private investment priorities, in project design, and in the choice of technology options (that are supposed to serve the poor) the physical and human infrastructures are determining factors.

An adequate choice of technology largely co-determines potential pro-poor effects[12]. There is no such thing as technology neutrality. The distributional effects of different technology options have to be considered carefully. For example, the use of community radio provides local solutions to local problems without referring to external solutions. An intervention based on the Internet, however, enhances external solutions – if it is accessible at all by the poor. The combination of the Internet with other ICTs, radio in particular, has a significant potential for poverty reduction purposes. "What is needed is a judicious blend of traditional and modern technologies depending on what would work best in a given situation."[13]

Content should receive as much attention as access.[14] The poor have to be at the centre of all the efforts, which must be people-centred[15], demand-driven and in local languages. Physical access is just one element along the road to effective access and use. Investment in hardware should be matched by investment in local content creation and capacity-building: as a rule, at least one third into hardware, two thirds into software including capacity-building.

Pro-poor effects are more likely if ICTs are embedded in a larger, demand-driven effort[16]. Ownership in defining the problem, as well as the solutions, is essential to avoid ineffective supply-oriented interventions. Technology should follow community needs. One-sided ICT-driven programmes are likely to fail. Effective efforts combine a number of elements to deal with an issue holistically. An example: ICT-supported information on AIDS-prevention or treatment may not have the desired effects if there are no condoms or drugs available or if people simply cannot afford them.

---

[11] Curtain 2004.

[12] Gerster in: Weigel/Waldburger.

[13] Swaminathan in: Weigel/Waldburger 2004, p. 209. See also UNESCO 2004.

[14] Swaminathan in: Weigel/Waldburger 2004.

[15] Beardon shows that the information needs of three communities in Uganda and Burundi are quite different and influenced by their surroundings (such as continuous conflict in Burundi). Furthermore the needs differ depending on gender and age (Beardon 2004).

[16] Gerster in: Weigel/Waldburger 2004.

Those countries mainstreaming ICTs effectively into their productive sectors gain dramatically in competitiveness, often to the disadvantage of others. It is a matter of economic survival to make appropriate use of ICTs. Therefore, the application or non-application of ICTs in an economy affects people living in poverty, both directly and indirectly.

South-South exchanges and partnerships can be an efficient and effective way of learning[17]. Based on touring in South Indian villages, MSSRF has acquired a wealth of practical experience in sharing experience with interested partners in African, Latin American and Asian countries. It is an option to avoid the built-in bias towards Northern models. Moreover, MSSRF, together with OneWorld International, created the Open Knowledge Network (OKN), which connects villages on different continents by using World Space Radio. OKN is still in its experimental phase.

Negative impacts need to be taken into account[18]. As mentioned earlier, benefits of ICT supported interventions may be unequally distributed and may deepen economic, social and cultural divides, instead of reducing poverty.[19] Moreover, an ITU report lists negative effects such as e-waste, environmental problems, and others (electromagnetic fields, muscular pain from poor posture, poor eyesight, 'infostress', spam etc.). While some of these are mainly of concern to developed countries, spam has been described as "a significant and growing problem for users, networks and the Internet as a whole."[20] Apart from such negative effects as decreasing confidence and trust in online activities, losses in productivity and financial costs are felt by all alike, since "expecting that […] all become power users and keep up to speed with the latest user side filtering and MS [Microsoft] security patches is unrealistic."[21]

MDG Implications

There is an explosive increase in publications on relevance of the ICTs in reaching the MDGs and how to make use of them. Noteworthy is a pioneering stocktaking exercise in Asian countries to promote ICTs for human development in view of the MDGs.[22] The United Nations ICT Task Force, in preparing the ground for the United Nations high-level meeting in 2005 on the Millennium Declaration, has published a report on mainstreaming ICTs for the MDGs[23]. It is not the intention to repeat the findings of these major efforts but rather to add and underline selected specific effects that are important in relation to up-scaling poverty reduction through ICTs.

In order to maximise their targeted contribution to attaining the MDGs, decision makers (governments, donors, others) should shift their attention from bridging the digital divide to pro-poor policies and practices. The digital divide is a symptom of different levels and modes of development, not a cause. Bridging the digital divide, therefore, is treating symptoms. With limited public funds available, allocating ODA to bridge the digital divide

---

[17] Arunchalam 2004.
[18] Gerster/Zimmermann 2003; Mathison, 2003.
[19] The example of Bhutan is well analysed in Faris 2004
[20] ITU/WSIS 2004.
[21] Drake 2004.
[22] UNDP 2004.
[23] UN ICT Task Force 2004.

carries the danger of crowding out competing poverty reduction programmes. Focusing on the digital divide is as misleading in the information society as the trickle down assumption has been in economic growth.

Most of the (urban) policy makers lack knowledge about the local context of the rural and urban poor. Talk of a knowledge gap usually means that the rural poor lack access to information and knowledge. However, in terms of developing meaningful policies and programmes, related information is crucial. It is much more difficult to raise funding to remove the former divide than to refill the latter gap.

More traditional ICTs are often considered to be less attractive than the latest technologies, such as the Internet. Unfortunately, the basket of MDG 8 on partnership for development contains, under target 18, an explicit reference to new technologies: "In cooperation with the private sector, make available the benefits of new technologies – especially information and communications technologies." This might explain why radio especially has a more difficult position in the entire debate – despite its comparatively rich track record in poverty alleviation. The choice of an appropriate information and communication technology is directly relevant for poverty reduction.

Since the MDGs are the key framework for development cooperation, there is a need to mainstream ICTs in all forms of programme assistance, including sector-wide approaches (SWAPs), and poverty reduction strategies (PRS) based budget support. Mainstreaming[24] means that evaluating the ICT potential and incorporating ICT options is not left to the knowledge and preferences of individual desk officers (of government, donors or other organisations) but is built in at an institutional level. Mainstreaming includes explicit terms of references, training, and exchange of experience. At the country level, options should favour the involvement of local pro-poor ICT policy makers and NGOs.

The Tsunami catastrophe of December 26, 2004 in South Asia highlighted the life saving potential of using ICTs in disaster prevention and relief. A warning system and communication network in the Indian Ocean similar to that in the Pacific could have reduced the death toll by thousands of people. Complementary to such international preventive measures, grassroots knowledge centres proved to be extremely well positioned to mitigate the effects of the disaster. Village knowledge centres, supported by MSSRF[25] disseminated the tsunami warning without delay once they had received the information. The fishing villages with such knowledge centres suffered a comparatively low loss of lives, despite an enormous destruction of fishing boats and houses. Again, the knowledge centres played a crucial role in organising relief measures in an orderly way. Ownership of the information and communication system by the village community is crucial, so that they are aware of the potential and know-how to handle it – in the case of these fishing communities, loudspeakers and sirens were more important than the Internet.

---

[24] See also the mainstreaming checklist in Curtain 2004, pp. 50-54.
[25] See the remarks in the preface by Professor MS Swaminathan, MSSRF Chairman, and Walter Fust, Director-General SDC, to the up-scaling study (see note 3), as well as reports on the MSSRF website: http://www.mssrf.org/.

Messages for WSIS

The tangible products of the WSIS 2003 are the Declaration of Principles and the Action Plan. The principles expressed in the Declaration, however, are not always carried through to the policy proposals of the Action Plan[26]. Nevertheless, despite its weaknesses, it is politically unlikely that the debate on the Declaration of Principles and the Plan of Action will be reopened[27]. What matters now is how to address implementation and monitoring.

Box 1: WSIS – Open Issues for Discussion

Debate around key issues in the use of ICT for development reached a first peak at the WSIS in Geneva – with a rather disappointing outcome for Southern governments. The two issues of Internet Governance and a Digital Solidarity Fund[28], upon which no decisions were taken due to basic disagreements, are not the only ones that affect the disadvantaged. Equally relevant is the debate around issues of intellectual property, which was hardly addressed and was subsequently inappropriately treated in the official declaration of the summit. "Needless to say, it will return in a bigger way in the future as questions are raised whether the Summit's aims and plans can be implemented if the current intellectual regimes continue and expand"[29]. Based on the unresolved conflicts of Internet governance and financing, the issues in implementing the action plan are therefore the following: (1) building infrastructure with no additional public funding; (2) securing human rights and (3) extending global knowledge commons[30]. It seems that "civil society [... is] positioned best to advance a development and human rights agenda for ICTs. [...An agenda] not dominated by concerns of governance and profitability."[31]

A successful up-scaling of poverty reduction through ICT flourishes on the basis of (1) an enabling ICT policy environment; (2) conducive conditions for poverty reduction; (3)

---

[26] For example, the first article of the Declaration affirms "our common desire and commitment to build a people-centred, inclusive and development-oriented Information Society, where everyone can create, access, utilize and share information and knowledge, enabling individuals, communities and people to achieve their full potential in promoting their sustainable development and improving their quality of life." But in its first article, the Plan of Action limits this vision to "promoting the use of ICT- based products, networks, services and applications" to achieve development goals. Similarly, the targets contained in the Action Plan, to be attained by 2015, are almost all related only to ICT connectivity. "In summary, most actors in the process will be able to find language that they can use as support for their agendas, and to leverage support from governments and international institutions, even though the documents are not binding [...] the simple fact of having opened a space within the multilateral framework of the UN to initiate a debate on these issues is not a negligible step, at a time when there is an increasing trend towards the privatization of policy and the imposition on the rest of the world of agreements made among Northern governments." (Bruch, 2003).

[27] The website http://www.itu.int/wsis/gfc/index.html presents the process and documents originating from the Group of Friends to the Chair, leading up to the second phase of WSIS in Tunis. In the longer run, the power geography is likely to evolve. The recent agreement between the governments of India, Brazil and South Africa to co-operate on a broad range of issues after the failure of the Doha trade round at Cancun could be extended to include producing a global e-strategy. The three governments could work co-operatively with a number of leading ICT civil society organisations based in developing countries to formulate the global e-strategy (Currie 2003).

[28] A WSIS Task Force is exploring how to use existing financing mechanisms in a more effective way.

[29] Khor 2004.

[30] Böll Foundation 2004.

[31] Currie 2004. A similar concern was voiced in discussions among promoters of free software: "There was a clear message that the movement to them was about much more than software, and more about true sharing and partnerships, treating everyone as an equal, rather than one to be exploited in the name of market theories (and coincidentally making those on the top ridiculously rich and powerful", see http://wsis.ecommons.ca/node/view/156.

appropriate technology choices; (4) mobilization of additional public and private resources. This chapter follows in part the Chennai Statement that reflects these requirements.

Enabling ICT Environment

An enabling ICT environment for up-scaling includes respect for freedom of expression, diversity, the free flow of information, supporting infrastructure – such as electricity, Internet connectivity – and a reasonable level of basic education. The acceleration of the introduction of competition in ICT infrastructure provision, including in the last mile, is key. Competition lowers prices, which is of a particular importance for the access of people living in poverty. It should be associated with investment in service development, including local content, to drive the demand for infrastructure. Enhancing the adoption of free/open source solutions (FOSS) and strengthening user groups are key.

The use of FOSS has impacts on all three aspects of the discussed poverty concept – empowerment, opportunity and security. It supports the notion that of all ICTs, software (and the Internet) are open to, and powered by amateurs in a way that other technologies are not. People can build technologies on top of existing ones and in doing so provide products for others to build on. One of the main hindrances to the spreading of FOSS seems to be a gap in communication (and understanding) between the FOSS community and CSOs[32] and governments, as well as a lack of awareness of the benefits of FOSS[33]. Since governments have a crucial role to play in promoting FOSS, informing and sensitising policy makers is key. Some of the issues that need to be addressed in this process are: (1) procurement – equal opportunities need to be given to both FOSS and proprietary products; (2) change management (migration) where existing proprietary software infrastructure is used; (3) licensing and legal issues; (4) localisation – opportunities and costs. The International Open Source Network (IOSN) is a regional centre of excellence in the Asia-Pacific region. Such initiatives should be strengthened. In South-South networking, cooperation with African institutions, such as the FOSSFA, should be encouraged.

To achieve pro-poor outcomes, such an enabling ICT environment has to be combined with targeted pro-poor policies and measures.

Priority for Poverty Reduction

Targeted pro-poor regulations and policies as part of an enabling ICT environment may include:

- Building up strong, independent regulators through capacity-building measures and the provision of resources to finance any resultant legal cases; supporting research and awareness raising throughout civil society.

- Transforming the policy environment through more deregulation in favour of local communities: (a) Licensing of air waves to grass roots level institutions; (b) Representation of grass roots level institutions on regulatory bodies.

---

[32] Schout 2004.
[33] Wong 2004.

- Fast-track licensing for innovative solutions, such as Voice over Internet Protocol (VoIP), Wireless Fidelity (WiFi) and Very Small Aperture Terminal (VSAT), and licensing of community-based electronic media, in particular broadcast radio.

A pro-poor emphasis is also required for the provision of infrastructure and content development. They should include:

- The introduction of lowest-cost and transparent demand- and supply-side subsidies to ensure that access costs are affordable.

- The use of voucher systems could be an appropriate option for promoting private partnerships in subsidised public access provision to address the needs of those in poverty.

Furthermore, mainstreaming ICTs in poverty reduction strategies (PRS) is a key issue. The implementation of PRS can play an important role in achieving the MDGs and empowering people living in poverty. ICTs can be used to facilitate the PRS process. ICTs should be mainstreamed into the implementation of sectoral components, complementing the poverty-reducing priorities of the national ICT strategy. PRS are more relevant in the African context. Most of the countries that have a PRS in place have included ICT as an independent strategic component, or they mention it as an enabling factor or a component of infrastructure. Most of the PRS date back to the last two to three years. Since there is agreement that much of the challenge of PRS lies in their implementation, the coming years will be crucial. Particular attention should be paid to the regular progress reports. Furthermore, the effects of the implementation should be followed closely, especially with respect to ICTs, in order to learn more about the different factors of the overall enabling environment and their effects.

Meaningful poverty reduction must be based on participatory needs assessments related to empowerment, opportunity and security of people living in poverty. ICT applications embedded in poverty reduction strategies should support demand-driven, solution-focused initiatives for, and with, disadvantaged people, characterised by applications and content that are highly contextualised.

Technology Choices

Economic history shows that technological innovation has often exacerbated the rich-poor divide. Exploiting technology in the interests of poor people requires deliberate technology choices. In the field of ICTs, technological progress reduces costs dramatically and lowers access barriers, which is of particular importance to people in poverty. When making a technology choice, information about the latest technological developments is only as useful as remembering 'old' ICTs. What counts is to choose simple, context-related solutions that may not require high connectivity or high-level human capacity. "Simpler technology often produces better results."[34] Flexible platforms, combining the strengths of complementary technologies, such as radio and Internet, have often proved particularly appropriate.

---

[34] Batchelor 2003, p. 82.

It has been stated repeatedly that ICTs are not only about technology and that people should stand at the centre of any ICT-related activity. However, in order to maximise the benefits that ICTs can bring, sound technological knowledge is needed, especially by policy makers. Health interventions are only successful if specialised know-how on issues such as reproductive health or HIV/AIDS is taken into consideration. Similarly, ICT interventions need to be based on solid expertise. This is not only necessary because of rapid technological progress, which constantly changes the available opportunities, but also because many of the issues raised in this paper, such as regulation, FOSS, or localisation, are interconnected with technical issues. The digital divide is not the only one that needs to be addressed, equally relevant is the divide between development specialists and technologists. A common understanding needs to be found between the worlds of MDGs, SWAPs, PRSPs and of TCP/IP, LAN and BCB.

An issue that includes all of the above mentioned elements – an enabling environment, a priority for poverty reduction and appropriate technologies – is that of localisation. It is a key issue in up-scaling, since up-scaling implies changing contexts, which in turn require localisation. On the one hand, this is very much a technical issue (translations in local languages depend on the availability of fonts and encoding as well as input methods). On the other hand, gender roles, cultures of communication and personal attitudes determine access to, and use of, ICT. Whereas the first can be supported by specific policies (such as strengthening investment in the local ICT sector or ensuring that technological and linguistic pre-requisites are provided to developers), the latter is more complex. This is also reflected by the fact that localisation is very often reduced to the issue of language. However, up-scaling is not merely translating content. It is important, therefore, to learn from ongoing up-scaling activities (expansion of CMCs in Africa, Mission 2007 in India) what the key issues in localisation are from a cultural perspective.

Resource Mobilisation

Up-scaling to reach the MDGs requires additional investment. Public resources are severely limited at the national, as well as the international, level. Despite the Monterrey Consensus, it is unlikely that official development assistance (ODA) will be increased substantially. The search for new sources of development financing (NSDF) is still in its initial stages. The options discussed include a byte tax, a licence fee on electromagnetic waves, a taxation of domain names, and other ICT-related sources[35]. Such NSDF are not likely to materialise in the near future. Other sources have to be tapped.

In order to ensure the best use of scarce public resources, maximum mobilisation of private investment is vital. Depending on the enabling regulatory framework, the existing infrastructure and the development potential, private investment can be mobilised, to a certain extent, even in remote regions. The microfinance movement demonstrates that banking for people in poverty is feasible. Similarly, there is an untapped market for the private sector in general and for social entrepreneurs in particular, to bring connectivity, services and content to those in poverty.

National ICT licensing obligations should include funding mechanisms, resulting in a hybrid form of private-public sources, to mobilise finance for appropriate community initiatives,

---

[35] Carron 2004.

and to address the financing gap for small and medium enterprises (SMEs) interested in starting ICT businesses. Regulators must have the political backing and the capacity to enforce compliance with universal service obligations (USOs) and to evaluate the effectiveness of the use of funds.

Financial, social and ecological sustainability is the triple bottom line for successful ICT-supported projects. Sustainability is contextual and dynamic.[36] In a poverty-stricken rural context, appropriate technology choices favouring social sustainability are as important as financial sustainability and require a focus on local content creation. From a longer term perspective, the question of profitability should be embedded right from the start when designing and planning poverty reducing projects with ICT use. The drive for up-scaling and sustainability can itself become a challenge, as it may cause a drift away from a focus on the poorest.

Box 2: Sustainability at the Hindukush?

In Hunza, Northern Pakistan, the Karakoram Area Development Organisation (KADO) aims at alleviating poverty. More than 50% of the population live on less than US$ 1 a day. Among many activities, this regional NGO established a Mountain Institute of Computer Sciences to promote computer education and related enterprises. This pioneering vision of the knowledge society at the Hindukush is faced with many challenges: Hunza is 800 km away from the next urban centre, villages are scattered, and infrastructure cost is high. Half of the population of 50,000 is reached by the KADO institute through ICT training, distance education, increased sales, access to information, etc. Despite local contributions, investment costs of US$ 60,000 and annual running costs (including website updates) of US$ 60,000 are mainly covered by donor funding. Since this environment is not attractive to private investors, the KADO will have to continue to rely on external funding for some years to come. The yardstick of success will rather be poverty reduction, and social rather than financial sustainability, the private institute being part of the public infrastructure.

Source: Communication by Javed Iqbal, KADO, Pakistan

Technological progress reduces costs[37] dramatically and lowers access barriers, which is of particular importance to people in poverty. When making a technology choice, information about the latest technological developments is necessary in order to choose simple, context-related solutions that may not require high connectivity or high-level human capacity. Flexible platforms, combining the strengths of complementary technologies, such as radio and Internet, have often proved particularly appropriate.

Mainstreaming ICTs pays off even when budgets are stagnating or shrinking. ICTs can be used as a strategic tool for development. They also merit, and receive, growing attention for their instrumental value in implementing pro-poor policies. The deployment of ICTs increases the effectiveness and efficiency of all endeavours to reach the MDGs whatever the resources available.

The Way Forward

There are significant challenges in the transition to scaling-up poverty reduction through the use of ICTs, in terms of retaining local ownership, capacity building in local communities,

---

[36] Mathison 2004.
[37] World Bank 1997; Lal in: Weigel/Waldburger 2004; Aro and Campbell 2001.

developing sustainable business models and defining the level of institutional and public sector support. Successful scaling-up, therefore, needs support from different levels:

- National level advocacy is key for up-scaling poverty reduction through ICTs. The added value of global declarations, including the Chennai Statement, depends on the extent to which they are heard by governments, civil society, and the private sector. In particular, the policy makers and the younger generation should be reached.

- Global coalitions advancing the empowerment, opportunity and security of people in poverty, including gender equality, education, health and democracy, are an effective and efficient channel for taking up-scaling concerns forward. In particular, intensifying South-South networking and dialogue should be pursued systematically, as this strengthens the voice of Southern countries in the international dialogue.[38]

- South-South exchanges and partnerships can be an efficient and effective way of learning. Instead of looking to the affluent Western societies and expecting solutions from the North, poverty stricken environments and challenges create empathy and facilitate transfer of knowledge while recognising the differences between SSA and LIACs, and even within the two regions. The MS Swaminathan Research Foundation (MSSRF) is implementing a successful model in the form of a travelling workshop directly linking the Indian grass roots experience with the experience of the workshop participants from Asia, Africa, and Latin America.

- Recognising the complementary roles of governments, the private sector and civil society, building multi-stakeholder partnerships (MSP) becomes a priority in implementing and monitoring an inclusive information society based on the WSIS' vision and inspired by the Millennium Declaration. The GKP unites multi-stakeholder partners and promotes such partnerships as a priority.[39] At the grass-roots level, the capacity of community structures, such as self-help groups and other intermediaries, should be tapped and enhanced.

References

Aro, Pekka and Campell, Duncan: The new information and communication technologies: genuine potential and real constraints, chapter 2 in: The World Employment Report 2001: Life at work in the information economy, Geneva 2001

Arunchalam, Subbiah: Information and communication technologies and poverty alleviation, in: Current Science, Vol. 87, No. 7, 10 October 2004, pp. 960-966

---

[38] This is particularly relevant in the context of the WSIS where there seems to be a strategy divide between South and North. While developing countries may emphasise basic telecoms and access to the Internet, developed countries may be more concerned with privacy, broadband networks and intellectual property rights. This strategy divide needs to be taken into account when global priorities are created in international forums such as WSIS (Currie, 2004).

[39] See their webpage for more information: http://www.globalknowledge.org.

Batchelor, Simon et. al.: ICT for Development – Contributing to the Millennium Development Goals. Lessons Learned from Seventeen *info*Dev Projects, Washington 2003, http://wbln0018.worldbank.org/ict/resources.nsf/0/4b6fa1c490ea367d85256e750061182e/$FILE/CaseStudies.pdf (September 2004)

Beardon, Hannah: ICT for development: empowerment or exploitation? Learning from the Reflect ICTs project, no year given, presumably 2004, http://217.206.205.24/Initiatives/ict/resources/publication1.pdf (January 2005)

Böll Foundation: Positioning for second summit phase has begun, http://www.worldsummit2003.de/en/nav/14.htm (March 2004)

Carron Joelle: Possibilités de financement dans la société de l'information: recherche de données sur la Suisse, October 2004, in French only, http://www.ppp.ch/cms/IMG/2004_-_10_pre-etude_financement.rtf (January 2005)

Currie, Willie: E-strategies and the World Summit on the Information Society, APC, May 2004, http://rights.apc.org/documents/estrategies.pdf (September 2004)

Curtain, Richard: Information and Communications Technologies and Development: Help or Hindrance? http://www.developmentgateway.com.au/jahia/webdav/site/adg/shared/CurtainICT4DJan04.pdf (October 2004)

Drake, William: Spam and IG meetings in Geneva, Contribution to Politech Mailing list, http://www.politechbot.com/2004/07/13/un-spam-report/, (October 2004)

Faris, Christopher B: ICT and Gross National Happiness: Advancing Bhutan's Development Goals, in: I4D, December 2004, pp. 15 –18

Gerster, Richard and Zimmermann, Sonja: Up-scaling Pro-Poor ICTPolicies and Practices. A Review of Experience with Emphasis on Low Income Countries in Asia and Africa, Berne/Chennai 2005, http://www.gersterconsulting.ch/fs/fs_main.asp?kt=2&skt=5 (March2005)

Gerster, Richard and Zimmermann, Sonja: ICTs and poverty reduction in Sub-Saharan Africa. A Learning Study, The Hague 2003, http://www.gersterconsulting.ch/docs/Synthesis_report.pdf (September2004)

Greener, Paul: Multi-Stakeholder Partnerships in ICT Enabled Development, Presentation at the GKP South Asian Regional Meeting 2004, http://www.globalknowledge.org/sarm2004/ (December 2004)

Hagen, Ingrid: Going beyond a project approach: Embedding ICT support in a wider development context, Capacity.org No. 23, October 2004, http://www.capacity.org/Web_Capacity/Web/UK_Content/Navigation.nsf/index2.htm?OpenPage

ITU/WSIS: ITU WSIS Thematic Meeting on Countering Spam, Chairman's Report, http://www.itu.int/osg/spu/spam/chairman-report.pdf (October 2004)

Jayaweera, Wijayananda: Scale-up, Presentation at the GKP South Asia Regional Meeting 2004, http://www.globalknowledge.org/gkps_portal/view_file.cfm?fileid=2449 (January 2005)

Khor, Martin: WSIS skirts three key issues, Third World Network, April 2004, http://www.crisinfo.org/content/view/full/267 (September 2004)

Mathison, Stuart: Digital Dividends for the Poor – ICT for Poverty Reduction in Asia, Kuala Lumpur, 2003, http://www.globalknowledge.org/gkps_portal/view_file.cfm?fileid=435 (September 2004)

Mathison, Stuart: ICT for Poverty Reduction: Upscaling and Sustainability, ppt-presentation October 2004, at: http://www.globalknowledge.org

Schilderman, Theo: Can ICTs help the Urban Poor Access Information and Knowledge to Support their Livelihoods, Marrakech 2001, http://www.unhabitat.org/programmes/ifup/conf/Theo-Schilderman.pdf (October 2004)

Schout, Loe: Why civil society is not embracing FOSS, in: i4d, Vol. II, No. 10, October 2004

Slater, Don; Tacchi, Jo: Innovation and research in South Asia? in: i4d, Vol. II, No. 5, May 2004, pp. 6-11

United Nations ICT Task Force: Mainstreaming ICTs for the Achievement of the MDGs, draft report for the conference in Berlin 18-20 November 2004

UNDP: Promoting ICT for Human Development in Asia 2004: Realising the Millennium Development Goals (Summary), New Delhi 2004, http://hdrc.undp.org.in/APRI/Publication/PBriefings/summary-web%2008-01-2004.pdf (September 2004)

UNDP/APDIP: Asian Forum on Information and Communication Technology Policies and e-Strategies – Abstracts, Kuala Lumpur 2003, http://www.apdip.net/projects/2003/asian-forum/abstracts (October 2004)

UNESCO: CMC website, http://portal.unesco.org/ci/en/ev.php-URL_ID=1263&URL_DO=DO_TOPIC&URL_SECTION=201.html (January 2005)

Weigel, Gerolf and Waldburger, Daniele (eds.): ICT4D – Connecting People for a Better World. Lessons, Innovations and Perspectives of ICTs in Development, Berne 2004, http://www.globalknowledge.org/ict4d

Wong, Kenneth: Free/Open Source Software Asia Pacific Free/Open Source Software Asia Pacific (FOSSAP) Consultation Report, Kuala Lumpur 2004, http://opensource.mimos.my/tech_wshop/slides_2004/18Mac/fossap_mimos_report.pdf, (January 2005)

World Bank: The Drivers of the Information Revolution—Cost, Computing Power, and Convergence Private Sector note 118 by James Bond 1997. http://cbdd.wsu.edu/kewlcontent/cdoutput/TR503/pdf/infodrivers.pdf

THE MILLENNIUM DEVELOPMENT GOALS AND INFORMATION AND COMMUNICATIONS TECHNOLOGY[1]

By the United Nations ICT Task Force Working Party on ICT Indicators and MDG Mapping

I.   Making the link between ICT and MDG

As we approach the five year measure of progress toward the achievement of the Millennium Development Goals (MDGs), international development organizations are taking stock of what progress has been made. Results to date are showing some countries are progressing well toward achieving the MDGs. Yet others are much further behind and certain countries have even regressed compared to their development levels at the turn of the century. As international development organizations and developing countries endeavour toward meeting the MDGs, world wide attention is being focused on the status of the developing world. This development focus has in turn encouraged collaboration on strategic multi-lateral efforts to address current and urgent development challenges of the new millennium.

ICT are an important catalyst in this multi-lateral collaborative effort to achieve the MDGs, not only in furthering communication and exchange of information, but also in support of specific development initiatives. International organizations are increasingly mainstreaming ICT into the development process. The United Nations Millennium Project was tasked by the Secretary General with identifying how countries can best achieve the MDGs and set up a specific task force to examine and report on the role of science and technological innovation (STI) in furthering development. The report examines past successes in using STI to achieve specific development objectives and secondly, outlines a number of key areas for further action by policy-makers.

Initial analysis in this report, and other similar reports, has demonstrated that ICT have an important role to play in furthering development, yet ICT are not widely used for this purpose. The diffusion, uptake and access to ICT are unequal across nations and within borders. This so called "digital divide" is a reflection of a deeper historical divide along socioeconomic factors such as income, education and geographic location. Although ICT may catalyse development, the reverse effect can also occur when ICT exacerbates pre-existing inequalities between the rich and the poor.

There is a need to proceed cautiously when on the one hand not investing in ICT may further marginalize developing countries from developed ones yet, investing in ICT can be quite costly and is a long-term effort. Further analysis of where ICT can have the greatest impact is required, rendering it even more important to develop appropriate tools for measuring, reporting and analyzing the real impact of ICT on development. A collaborative effort, bringing together key players from international development organizations, national governments, development workers and national statistical offices is needed to develop effective ICT impacts measuring and monitoring tools.

---

[1] This paper was first presented during the UN ICT Task Force Global Forum on Enabling Environment in Berlin, Germany. It is still a work in progress and comments can be sent to Johnston.jennifer@ic.gc.ca.

At the World Summit on the Information Society (WSIS), in Geneva in 2003, world leaders, national governments, civil society, and the private sector discussed what measures need to be taken for countries to transition toward a people-centered, inclusive and development-oriented Information Society. The Summit culminated in a declaration of principles and action plan which outlined a clear role for ICT. The action plan called for every country to develop a national e-strategy with specific targets to benchmark progress toward an Information Society. In the WSIS follow-up, discussions are continuing on how countries can benchmark their progress. This paper is a contribution to this dialogue.

Under the auspices of the United Nations ICT Task Force, and in collaboration with international development organizations such as the United Nations Conference on Trade and Development, the World Bank and the International Telecommunication Union, the Working Party on ICT Indicators and MDG Mapping has continued efforts to identify how ICT are being used to catalyse development. This paper presents some of the work to date to identify where ICT have had a direct and measurable impact on development. This has been a challenging task as ICT impacts on development are often not measured and, even less so on a quantitative front.

The purpose of this paper is to examine more closely where ICT has had a measurable impact on development. As data is still being gathered on ICT impacts measurement, this paper examines some of these measurement gaps and highlights some of the work completed to date to address these gaps. Section two proposes a measurement framework for capturing the impacts of ICT on development. This draft framework aims to identify a process that can be used to capture qualitative and quantitative impacts of ICT on development. As the measurement methodologies of specific case studies are reviewed, indicators selected from each of the case studies will be added to the framework. The final section of the paper presents case studies where ICT has had a clear and important impact on four development areas: economic development, education, health and the environment.

In a previous paper entitled "Tools for Development: Using ICT to Achieve the MDGs", we examined the link between ICT and the achievement of basic development objectives. The paper also included a matrix mapping ICT indicators and targets to each of the MDGs. This was an important step toward strengthening the link between ICT and the MDGs and providing preliminary evidence to policy makers on the catalysing role of ICT in development. This was a small step in a much lengthier process to measure where and when ICT are effectively and successfully deployed in support of specific development initiatives.

This initial draft of the United Nations ICT Task Force paper on ICT Impacts Measurement is a work-in-progress. It will be circulated more widely for comment in the coming months. A preliminary version was presented at the United Nations ICT Task Force meeting in Berlin in November 2004. Subsequent versions of this paper will take a more in depth look at the measurement methodologies used in each case study. Case study inputs or suggestions are particularly welcome. The framework proposed in this paper will be revised based on feedback received and will be part of the United Nations ICT Task Force contribution to key international events such as UNGA and WSIS 2005.

II. Analyzing ICT Impacts

Beyond the Digital Divide

Since the release of the 2001 United Nation's Report Making Technologies Work for Human Development, international organizations, national governments and non-governmental organizations have studied and reported on the effects of information and communication technologies on development. These studies examine the diffusion, uptake and access to ICT as well as highlight the catalysing role of ICT in furthering development. These are important tools in determining our progress toward bridging the digital divide on an international and domestic scale. Many of these reports also examine some of the related policy issues. For policy makers to effectively address these issues, additional measurement tools are needed to provide an adequate assessment of the impacts of ICT on countries' socio-economic development.

An even greater number of research activities and reports have been undertaken to measure and report on developing countries' progress in improving social and economic development. Most recently, dozens of developing countries, in cooperation with the United Nations, are compiling annual reports on their progress toward achieving the MDGs by 2015. Current analysis indicates that some countries are progressing well, whereas, other countries have actually regressed from the initial levels of development in 2000 and may not achieve the targets set for 2015. ICT can play a key role in bringing countries on target toward achieving the MDGs.

The concept of ICT as an enabler for development (ICT4D) has been explored by many development organizations and was analysed more thoroughly in a previous paper produced by the United Nations ICT Task Force Working Party on ICT Indicators and MDG Mapping entitled "Tools for Development: Using ICT to Achieve the MDGs". As illustrated in this paper, ICT and development are directly correlated. Our collective challenge is to measure more precisely the impact of ICT on development and from this analysis, determine how ICT are best used to catalyse development and further the achievement of the MDGs.

Defining ICT Readiness, Access, Use and Impact

The following table provides a typology of four different categories of ICT indicators: readiness, access, use and impact. Definitions of these four types of indicators differ between the various measurement organizations. For greater clarity, the table provides a general definition of the four types as well as provides usual indicators used for each category. For the most part, ICT measurement has traditionally focused on the first three, ICT readiness, access and use. Impacts indicators are still in the developmental stage and have yet to be applied in many countries therefore they are subject to significant variations depending on who is collecting the data.

Category	Measurement	Types of Indicators
ICT Readiness	What appropriate and effective elements have been put in place to ensure the rapid adoption and widespread use of ICT?	Infrastructure Policy framework Enabling environment
ICT Access	How widely diffused and accessible are ICT across all regions and sectors of society?	Diffusion (ICT per capita and geographic dispersal) Real access based on proximity, affordability and appropriate skill level
ICT Use	How is ICT being used by business, government and civil society? What innovative e-applications are being developed and used?	Number of users for specific technology Purpose of use ICT uptake rate across regions, user profiles Profile of user groups
ICT Impacts	How is ICT an enabler for social and economic growth? What effects does ICT have on development? How is ICT enhancing development opportunities at local, national and international levels?	Identification of enabling factors: human development factors, skill levels, literacy rate, education level, Impact on specific development goals (sector specific, country specific, global)

Some of the current efforts to measure ICT readiness, access and use are highlighted below. In some instances, impact indicators have been suggested but less effort has been dedicated to this area than for the first three types of indicators. Each report examines various aspects of the information society and has different objectives depending on the particular focus of the report. For example, certain reports are more focused on the infrastructure whereas others focus more on the enabling environment which is still, as of yet, difficult to quantify. Often different measurement methodologies are used to measure ICT access, readiness and use.

Data on access, readiness and use of ICT are sometimes scarce in developing countries and not always collected or compiled consistently from country to country making it difficult to compare between countries. As more consistent and internationally comparable data becomes available from developing countries, additional countries are included in the reports. Certain reports use a more limited set of indicators and can therefore cover more countries, whereas others focus on a limited number of countries and provide more comprehensive indicators. Most of these reports are recent of the past few years and, are still refining their measurement methodologies so it is sometimes not possible to compare each report's results from year to year.

A number of reports allow comparison between years as their measurement methodology and countries covered hasn't changed significantly to affect the results. For example, the International Telecommunication Union (ITU) has consistently collected and compiled data on telecommunications penetration since the 1990s and continues to add countries each year. Both the World Bank and the United Nations have published more than 15 annual reports ranking more than 150 countries' human development. Each report also now includes indicators on access to the information society. In the following section, we briefly highlight what these selected reports cover.

- The International Telecommunication Union has closely tracked global telecommunications penetration since the early 1990s. This research is compiled into the annual ITU Telecommunications Development Report which includes telecommunications indicators on more than 100 countries. These indicators are mainly focused on measuring access to telecommunications infrastructure via penetration rates for certain technologies and services such as the number of telephone lines per 100 inhabitants. Last year's report introduced a Digital Access Index used to measure actual access and use to ICT in 178 countries. The index was aggregated from 8 indicators in 5 categories: infrastructure, knowledge, affordability, quality and usage, each weighted and averaged leading to a country ranking. The report also included a chapter with examples of ICT impacts on specific development initiatives and proposed specific roles for ICT in supporting each MDG.

- The World Economic Forum's and INSEAD's Annual Global Information Technology Report includes a composite index for Measurement of Readiness for the Networked World and examines the overall policy framework for building an Information Society (102 countries were measured in 2003-2004). This report has been published annually since 2001-2002. The readiness index is composed of 3 separate indices: environment, readiness and usage each broken down into sub-categories with indicators for each sub-category. Based on the results of the 3 indices, countries are then ranked annually on their readiness for the networked world.

- Orbicom/UNESCO released a report last year including a composite index for measuring ICT readiness, use and access. The report, "Monitoring the Digital Divide and Beyond" is mainly focused on analyzing the extent of the domestic and international digital divide and measures the state of e-readiness for 192 countries, access for 153 countries, and use for 143 countries. This data was aggregated into a composite measure of the Info-state for 139 countries. The indicators used are mainly to measure ICT diffusion, uptake and real access as determined by skill level and literacy rates. An initial framework was released in 2001-2002 followed by the first annual report in 2002-2003. This report covers the evolution of the digital divide over a five year period from 1996-2001 allowing comparison between countries and from year to year.

- The Organization for Economic Cooperation and Development (OECD) recently released a report on the "Measurement, Evidence and Implications of the Economic Impact of ICT" based on its significant efforts to measure and monitor the information economy for OECD member countries and examine many of the related policy issues. The report analyses data from 80 OECD indicators on size and growth of the ICT sector and its contribution to economic performance.

- The Center for International Development at Harvard University developed an e-readiness guide for self-assessment of a community's networked readiness. This guide can be used to examine ICT readiness, access and use and provides measures for 19 different categories, covering the availability, speed, and quality of network access, use of ICT in schools, workplace, economy, government, and everyday life, ICT policy (telecommunications and trade), ICT training programmes, and diversity of organizations and relevant content online. The analysis is based solely on qualitative assessments.

- The United Nations Development Programme (UNDP) publishes an annual report with a quantitative and qualitative analysis of more than 150 countries' development progress. This year's report also measures progress toward the achievement of the MDGs. The HDI – human development index – is a summary composite index that measures a country's average achievements in three basic aspects of human development: longevity, knowledge, and a decent standard of living. Longevity is measured by life expectancy at birth; knowledge is measured by a combination of the adult literacy rate and the combined primary, secondary, and tertiary gross enrolment ratio; and standard of living by GDP per capita (PPP US$).

- The World Bank Annual World Development Report is a comprehensive measurement, both quantitative and qualitative, on the status of countries' development. This year's report measured 152 countries and includes approximately 800 indicators with specific ones for measuring basic ICT infrastructure. The 2004 report also includes a qualitative analysis on how countries can achieve the MDGs.

- UNESCO has developed a database of international and national indicators for ICT use in education. The website provides methods for collecting indicators, comparisons of indicator themes in selected countries as well as several case studies on the use and impact of ICT in education. UNESCO has also compiled a list of national ICT indicators on education for approximately 30 developing and developed countries. The indicators are not as of yet comparable between countries.

- The United Nations Development Programme measured the use of ICT to further the Millennium Development Goals in nine Asian countries in its latest Regional Development Report on Asia. The report measures the extent to which ICT can further the MDG in nine countries: China, India, Indonesia, Malaysia, Mongolia, Pakistan, Sri Lanka, Thailand, and Vietnam. The report introduces an ICT index for human development and points to the difficulty of applying such an index globally due to varying data collection methodologies. The aggregate index reflects the overall progress a country has made in promoting ICT in the context of goals for human development. Data is collected from mostly publicly available sources in four categories: availability, efficiency and speed, and targeting vulnerable groups.

- The Conference Board of Canada has developed a Connectedness Index that includes measures of technological infrastructure (including information and communications technology), access, affordability, usage and socio-economic impact. 150 indicators are compiled for 10 developed countries.

- An increasing number of national statistical organizations are collecting national data on ICT access, use and readiness but not on the impact of ICT on the economy and society.

Building on these earlier measurement efforts, the United Nations Conference on Trade and Development (UNCTAD) recently launched an ICT4D partnership with the World Bank, United Nations ICT Task Force, ITU, UNESCO and the United Nations Economic Commissions at the annual UNCTAD XI conference in Brazil in June 2004. The regional purpose of the partnership is to gain consensus on a common set of core ICT indicators to be used by international organizations and national statistical offices in their data collection and analysis. Some of the issues to be addressed through this partnership include data collection methodologies such as self-assessment versus census or survey assessment; collection at the individual, household and business level; and standardization of data collection methods.

The agreed upon set of ICT indicators will be fed into a global indicators' database. This is an important step toward developing comprehensive and internationally comparable ICT-for-development indicators. However, more work will need to be undertaken to develop ICT impacts indicators. Each of these studies mentioned above provides quantitative and qualitative measures of ICT readiness, access and use, whereas the impact of ICT on development is measured mostly in qualitative terms. Although many of these reports use separate indicators for measuring access, readiness and use, the three are directly correlated. Readiness is often assessed from indicators on access and use because higher access and use indicators point to the likelihood that the country is "e-ready". On the other hand, the higher the enabling environment factors, the more probable that a country is e-ready, that is able to quickly and effectively increase access to and use of ICT.

One of the challenges in measuring access and use is to effectively determine who has access and how are ICT being used. This is in part due to the inherent anonymity on the demand side of ICT. It is much easier to measure the supply (production) of ICT then quantify the demand. For example, data on number of Internet Service Providers (ISP) is readily available whereas data on the number of e-mail accounts is quite difficult to obtain. This discrepancy has resulted in an abundance of indicators and data on the supply of ICT but a dearth of indicators on the demand side. Lack of data on the demand side of ICT makes it even more challenging to derive impacts indicators from access and use indicators.

The impacts of ICT are directly correlated with and often derived from ICT readiness, access and use. The more people that have access to and the ability to use ICT, the more numerous will be the impacts. Nonetheless for ICT to have a meaningful and profound impact on development it is clear that other factors must be in place. Much of the impacts of ICT depend on the context and purpose for which they are used. This is why measuring ICT impacts on development poses such a challenge. It is not sufficient to correlate ICT readiness, access and use with development goals but rather necessary to quantify and qualify the effects of ICT on development. In order to do this, it is necessary to first identify how ICT enables development and secondly, quantify how ICT catalyses development.

It is important to note that indicators on access, readiness and use are very useful tools for benchmarking progress in ICT deployment and use and adapting policies and programmes accordingly. Our particular focus on impacts is to take measurement efforts one step further by providing policy makers with concrete evidence of where ICT are best deployed and used to further specific development initiatives and goals. The first three measurement areas will often provide an overall picture of what elements are in place or need further attention whereas impacts measurement will demonstrate more clearly what has been successful so far.

Defining ICT as an Enabler for Development

Certain e-ready countries with well-developed ICT services, widely available access to technological services and widespread use have experienced important impacts of ICT. Some of these more generalized effects of ICT on development include increased access to information, greater capture of knowledge, improved efficiency in service delivery, reduced service delivery costs, new service delivery methods, better monitoring and therefore improved processes and greater opportunity for wider consultation and participation. These effects occur across organizations, whether government, business or civil society, and transform how society interacts. For these transformations to take place though, the human factor of ICT is critical.

People must have the appropriate skill level and access to the technology. Even if the infrastructure is in place, many people may not have "real access", especially the poor who often live in rural and remote areas, with insufficient training to effectively use ICT. Furthermore, even those that do have access to ICT may not be in a position to use them for development purposes such as job searching, expanding market access or e-learning.

Bridges.org, a non-governmental organization that researches and measures ICT and development, has developed a definition of "real access" that incorporates the human factor into the measurement methodology. "Real access" is measured through 12 criteria: physical access, appropriate technology, affordability, capacity, relevant content, integration, socio-cultural factors, trust, legal and regulatory framework, local economic environment, macroeconomic environment and political will. The use of such indicators that measure real access will be important indicators in assessing ICT impacts on development.

"Providing access to technology is critical, but it must be about more than just physical access. Computers and connections are insufficient if the technology is not used effectively because it is not affordable; if people do not understand how to put it to use or if they are discouraged from using it; or if the local economy cannot sustain its use." (www.bridges.org)

Measuring ICT Impacts

An essential component of measurement is identification of instances where ICT have had an important impact on development. An increasing number of international development organizations are examining when and where ICT have had impacts on development projects and programmes. Recently the World Bank, the *info*Dev Programme, the United Nations Development Programme and a few national development and cooperation agencies such as the United Kingdom's Department for International Development (DFID) and the United States Agency for International Development (USAID) have compiled case studies that identify and analyse the impacts of ICT on development. On a more macro level, many of these same international organizations and development agencies have revised their programming strategies and policies to define a supporting role for ICT along with expected impacts.

Even though many international and national development organizations are integrating ICT into their development strategies, few currently have measurement frameworks in place which monitor the specific and direct impacts of ICT on their development initiatives. Certain development organizations, in addition to their combined efforts already underway to adopt a common set of internationally comparable ICT indicators, are beginning to adapt their development programme measurement frameworks to capture the impacts of ICT.

For example, DFID is proposing to survey how information and communication is furthering their development projects and subsequently devise a comprehensive framework to measure the impacts. The International Telecommunication Union also included a selection of case studies demonstrating the impact of ICT on development along with a possible set of ICT impact indicators. *Info*Dev has plans to develop a measurement and evaluation framework that will be tested over the coming year on a select group of pilot projects. The framework will include the development of general analytical models and evidence-based best practices tool kit.

These organizations are addressing the need for appropriate mechanisms to measure and monitor the impact of ICT on development, both quantitatively and qualitatively and on a regional, national and local scale. At this stage, after investing in ICT infrastructure and deployment for a number of years, these organizations have recognized the need to step back and examine what has been successful so far and determine where ICT are best used as a catalyst for development. However development of measurement processes and their implementation will be a timely process. In the interim, until the impacts of ICT can be measured on a more quantitative basis, we need to continue to gather a body of evidence demonstrating the impact of ICT in development on a qualitative level.

Much work has been done to gather qualitative evidence of ICT impacts, yet it is still difficult to isolate the impacts of ICT on a specific development area as the impacts are cross-cutting and often interdependent. For example, using Geographic Information Systems (GIS) to map and monitor the spread of malaria in Africa will increase the effectiveness of malaria-reducing programmes, thereby improving overall health and the status of the environment in the area. Distance learning provides an opportunity to reach students that otherwise might not have access to education. This will improve their skill level leading to employment opportunities that may reduce poverty in the region in the long run.

The advantage of isolating the impacts of ICT on one development area is to demonstrate clearly how ICT can be used to support specific development initiatives and subsequently replicate the success. In the following section, we have attempted to extract the impacts from selected case studies and define more precisely how ICT have had a direct and measurable impact in four specific areas: economic development, education, health and the environment.

ICT have a central role to play in supporting gender-based development initiatives; however, these initiatives are often multi-faceted as gender is a theme that affects each of the above mentioned development areas. For this reason, instances where ICT have had a significant impact on improving girls' and women's development will be included within each of the four categories.

For illustrative purposes, the following table identifies specific impacts of ICT on the four development areas: economic development, education, health and the environment. The impacts have been derived from common, generalized ICT focused activities (outputs) and associated outcomes. For the most part, the impacts are quite generic and are provided for demonstrating how ICT can catalyse development. In the longer term the table will include indicators and impacts synthesized from specific case studies.

(Generic Outputs, Outcomes and Impacts)

Development Area	Impact	Outputs	Short Term Outcomes	Long-term Outcomes
Economic Development	Increased prosperity and reduced poverty	Business presence on the web B2B links (telephone, e-mail, Internet) B2C links (telephone, e-mail, Internet) ICT in product and service management ICT utilized in product development Access to online market information e-support for SME ICT products manufacturing (software engineering, hardware, cellulars)	Increased marketing to new clients Reduced supply and transaction costs Increased efficiency in business processes Better quality products New opportunities for businesses and clients Improved decision-making ability for business and clients with access to information on a long-term and sustainable basis Increased capital mobility	Increased sales Expanding market access Economic growth Greater participation in the global market Better matching between clients and business Increased employment opportunities Increased investment opportunities
Education and Training	Better trained teachers and better educated students	e-learning (software) Distance learning for primary, secondary and post-secondary education Distance training for teachers Collaborative learning, development of new learning tools and methods e-testing e-support for schools and teachers ICT in administrative processes	Greater access to learning materials Improved teaching and learning methods Better monitoring and evaluation of students' progress Improved efficiency in administration	IT literate population Increasing access to education Increased reach of education
Health	Improved patient care Healthier population	Research and Collaboration through communities of practice, e - records Health networks ICT for illness/epidemic tracking Remote diagnostics in rural areas ICT in administrative processes	Improved research on health conditions/problems Improved monitoring of health conditions Increased reach of health services Better management of health care systems	Better diagnoses Increase in remedies/health solutions More efficient delivery of health care services Greater reach
Environment	Cleaner environment Greater sustainability and more efficient use of environmental resources	Environmental monitoring (climate, natural and man made disasters) ICT for controlling and responding to environmental disasters ICT for dispensing resources e.g. water purification and processing Environmental impact assessments and scans using ICT IT for pollution reduction Access to information on environmental challenges/problems	Reduced impact of human activities on environment More efficient use of natural resources Greater prevention of environmental damage More efficient response to natural disasters Greater awareness of how to protect the environment Reduction of environmental impact	Greater access to vital environmental resources, Better monitoring of environmental disasters, citizen empowerment and participation re environmental status

Case Studies

In this section, we present some of the important impacts of ICT on the four previously noted areas as analysed in a preliminary selection of case studies. We have also highlighted how ICT have been used in each of these case studies. The case studies were chosen where the impacts were seen to be strongest and most relevant to one of the four development areas.

One of the challenges we encountered in our initial case study analysis is lack of up-to-date and consistent data to substantiate the impacts. Furthermore, definition of impacts varies greatly from case study to case study. The long term aim will be to continue to collect and compile case studies where ICT have had an important and measurable impact on development. Subsequently, we will examine the impacts and measurement methodologies used for each case study. Once an initial analysis of additional case studies has been completed, impacts and indicators will be compiled and included in a revised table attached at the end of this section.

We have noted that the impacts of ICT and, especially their measurement, vary depending on the development area targeted and the region. In a sense, the impacts of ICT are more remarkable at a local level but often more pronounced when part of a larger regional or national type of initiative. Measurement methodologies will differ depending on the scale and scope of the project. This is due in part to ICT acting more as a catalyst for development and directly dependent upon the cultural environment and context in which they are used. For example, an ICT-focused educational project implemented in a small community in Vietnam will have very different impacts than a national initiative to introduce computers into schools in Costa Rica. Wherever possible, we have included case studies from each of the regional, national and local levels and selected from the following regions – Africa, Middle East, Latin America, Eastern Europe and Asia.

Economic development (Goals 1, 8)

The 21st century economy

Drivers of economic development are rapidly changing in the 21st century. National economies are becoming increasingly global, digitized and dependent upon the effective use off knowledge and information to conduct business.

"Information and Communication Technologies (ICT) have become a key element in this new economy by improving and changing business processes and organizational structures, leading to higher productivity and a competitive advantage for firms, industry sectors and national economies. By overcoming barriers of time and space and shrinking entry costs, ICT have led to the creation of a truly global marketplace." (Government of Canada, 2004)

Yet, developing countries' position in this global marketplace is uncertain. On the one hand, developing countries are able to leapfrog utilizing ICT more effectively without having to invest in some of the earlier and now obsolete technologies. However a critical mass of infrastructure and skill level must be in place for developing countries to become full participants in a global and increasingly digital marketplace. Developing countries are reluctant to push for adoption of ICT given the cost and the potential to disrupt traditional employment sectors. The impacts of ICT on the economies of the early adopters are being closely watched as developing countries make the transition to the new economy.

Economic growth

The ICT industry has emerged as the most dynamic economic sector in certain Asian countries that were early adopters of ICT in the 1990s, notably China and Korea. Yet some of these early adopters suffered a tremendous setback during the turn of the century. ICT sector investment, as part of a national strategy for economic growth, can achieve more immediate results. However, this approach may not be the most appropriate strategy for emerging economies especially, considering that some countries already have the advantage of time and competition in the ICT sector is increasing. Even though there is concrete evidence that ICT can make a significant contribution to the economy as a sector, ICT is emerging as an even more important pillar to traditional economic sectors.

"Reliance on ICT now extends far beyond the few industries like telecommunications, software and computer services that are traditionally associated with the technology. In fact the use of ICT, like electricity, has infiltrated virtually the entire economy. This has created an e-economy, in which firms, organizations and governments make effective use of ICT to spur on product and process innovation across all sectors of the economy." (Government of Canada, 2004)

The link between ICT investment and economic growth is strong in developed economies. The Economist Intelligence Unit produced a cross-section analysis of 60 countries that confirms the general view that ICT is strongly linked to economic growth in developed countries. However, the report cautioned that the same impacts might not occur in emerging markets. "At the same time, the impact of ICT is weak in emerging markets and (our) analysis suggests this may be because ICT begins to deliver GDP per head growth only after a certain threshold of development is reached. The research also supports the widely held notion that ICT deployment and use will begin to affect economic growth only after an adjustment period." (EIU, 2004)

There is an important caution in these words. On the one hand, ICT have emerged as an important pillar to many sectors of the economy leading the transformation to an e-economy, and spurring economic growth in developing countries and developed alike. On the other hand, certain developing countries may not benefit unless a certain threshold of development is reached and, secondly, may only notice the impacts after a period of adjustment.

How are ICT and Economic Development Related?

An ICT-driven economy or e-economy can present a barrier to the poor who may not have access to the infrastructure nor the skills to use ICT. For developing countries to reap the benefits of an e-economy, ICT investment needs to be considered as part of a larger national strategy where barriers to effective access and use are addressed. The WSIS action plan calls for countries to integrate ICT as a core component of their development strategies. Before doing so, countries need concrete evidence on how ICT best fit within development strategies and policies and specifically, how ICT can be used to increase economic prosperity and reduce poverty.

The World Bank has assisted developing countries in devising national poverty reduction strategy papers (PRSP) to aid in the design of effective policies and programmes to benefit the poor. A recent survey demonstrated that of 34 countries PRSP analysed, only 13 countries (Albania, Azerbaijan, Cambodia, Cameroon, Chad, Georgia, Ghana, Mali, Mongolia, Niger, Rwanda and Sri Lanka) define or position ICT as a strategic component for poverty reduction and discuss it as an independent item in their PRSP. The other countries had not included ICT as an independent strategic component. However, the strategies do mention telecommunications sector development as an "important factor for rural/agricultural development" or as "one of the components of the infrastructure for economic growth". (OECD, 2003, p. 2)

This should not be construed as an indication that many developing countries are not investing in ICT. On the contrary, many countries are investing significantly in ICT, yet have not necessarily linked ICT to national development goals or poverty reduction strategies. ICT investment and national development goals need to be interlinked for ICT to have a significant impact on development. This link needs to be made right from the very planning process. Developing countries are in a position to devise combined strategies where ICT investment is targeted to the most urgent and prioritized development areas such as health care and education.

Pro-Poor Economic Growth

Research is showing a direct correlation between tele-density and GDP per capita (Gartner, 2002). This is an indication that ICT infrastructure, in this case broadband connections, is an important element in supporting economic activities. It still remains to be proved, though, exactly to what extent investment in ICT infrastructure may increase economic growth and, particularly, economic growth that benefits the poorest members of society. Intensive investment in ICT can actually exacerbate the divide between rich and poor along geographic, income and skill levels.

"While improving information and communication flows, and infrastructures, within a society might foster economic growth at a macro level, the benefits of that growth can be distributed very unequally within society. Therefore, addressing the information and communication needs of the poor must form one important component of a wider strategy to tackle poverty." (DFID, 2002, p. 9)

ICT-related economic growth may not be sufficient to spur pro-poor economic growth. A recent paper by the OECD on the use of ICT for pro-poor economic growth noted that "There is very little evidence to demonstrate that the future impact of any ICT activities that encourage and affect general economic growth, would be more pro-poor than our current experiences – unless policies are introduced to ensure such an affect." (OECD, 2004).

This paper does demonstrate the complementary role of ICT in three sectors that have potential to enhance pro-poor growth: infrastructure, private sector development, and rural livelihoods. It concludes that pro-poor growth can be found where infrastructure services help to enhance the productivity of the poor. ICT can lead to market efficiencies and attract greater investment. Access to infrastructure combined with relevant content can further promote pro-poor growth. Some of the examples used include ICT leading to the development of new markets and the increase in remittances (money transfers using ICT) from expatriates to their homelands.

Impacts of ICT on Economic Development

In the following examples, we demonstrate how ICT can be a key component of development strategies and initiatives designed to stimulate economic growth and reduce poverty. Some of the impacts include fostering new employment opportunities, providing training opportunities, increasing market access, making business processes more efficient, and enabling better business decisions through access to timely market information. In order for these impacts to occur though, a prerequisite is often an ICT-literate society where the intended beneficiaries have access to the infrastructure. This is where ICT and economic development interrelate with ICT and education.

An initial review of selected case studies where ICT have had a direct and measurable impact on economic development demonstrates that ICT initiatives that incorporate training along with access to ICT have a higher rate of success. Often training is required before the intended beneficiaries can effectively use ICT for a specific economic opportunity. The following are a few examples where ICT have had an important impact in furthering economic development.

Grameen Village Phone Programme

The Grameen Village Phone Programme has had a direct impact on the livelihood of women and the poor in rural areas in Bangladesh. The programme, in operation since 1997, provides a small repayable loan to a member of a rural community to purchase a cellular phone and services. The Community members, often rural poor who would otherwise not have subscriber phone access, can use the phone for a small fee. Two research studies have found that the introduction of Village Phones has made a "tremendous" social and economic impact in the rural areas, creating a "substantial consumer surplus" for the users. As of October 2003, there were more than 39,000 Village Phones in operation. These Village Phones are operating in nearly 28,000 villages of some 58 Districts. The Village Phones presently provide access to telecommunications facilities to more than 50 million people living in remote rural areas. The average revenue per user of Village Phone subscribers is double than that of the average business user.

PeopleLink

PeopleLink has connected local artisans and producers in developing countries to a Global e-Commerce Network of Grassroots Producers and Artisans that provides access to the global market. The network links artisans with worldwide buyers and the underlying catalogue generating software (CatGen) provides artisans with an easy method of displaying their wares virtually. As a result of the project, between 1996 and 2000, 55 producer groups were trained in website development and 5,000 crafts were made available to buyers online. Although data on the number of sales has not been consistently collected, the most popular CatGen web sites have attracted 2,000-3,000 visitors, generating sales of tens of thousands of dollars. (*info*Dev, 2003)

NetCorps Jordan

The NetCorps Jordan programme is an important example of how the combination of training and access to ICT has had an important impact on economic opportunities within the local community. This programme goes beyond just access to ICT through community centres by providing training in specific ICT applications to improve community development. The tele-centres are staffed with ICT trained youth interns. The interns develop training programmes for the community in ICT use as well as specific applications that relate directly to the community needs. For example, as part of the Jordanian Education Initiative, interns will be placed in selected schools to work as teacher assistants and to start up ICT focused community projects with the students. To date 111 interns have trained over 1,225 community members in 44 locations in Jordan. Over 50% of Interns and 60% of participants are women. Although a detailed analysis of the impacts of ICT training has not yet been conducted, anecdotal evidence has demonstrated that ICT projects initiated by interns and led by community members have had a direct impact on improving participants livelihood.

Education (Goals 2, 3)

Skills development for the future

ICT has shown a positive impact on education in two different areas. First, ICT can be seen as an important tool in increasing the reach and quality of education. Secondly, the integration of ICT into education is key to ensuring that the next generation has the appropriate skills and knowledge for an increasingly competitive and knowledge-based economy and society. ICT are pervading more and more economic activities on a global scale. Exposing children to ICT through the school system is one of the most effective ways to ensure that they can fully participate in the global economy. Even more importantly, ensuring that children and youth have access to a solid education will help secure their future. However, the two approaches are interdependent.

Integration of ICT into the school system is contingent upon overcoming the first hurdle: ensuring that education is accessible and of high quality. Yet integration of ICT into the school system can help achieve this second goal. We can conclude that one approach does not need to precede the other, but rather ICT can perform both roles simultaneously. In the next section we examine how integration of ICT into the school system can increase access to and the quality of education in a variety of ways and better prepare children for a knowledge based economy and society.

Access to education

The most remarkable impacts of ICT so far have been in extending the reach of education, both through infrastructure and improving service delivery. Similar to the effect of ICT on business processes, ICT can improve the efficiency of the administration of education at the regional, national and local levels whether through greater access to information, better tracking of student records and performance monitoring, increased exchange of information between administrators, teachers and students. In the long, run an improvement in the efficiency of school administration will increase access by allowing schools to admit more students.

In addition, both distance education through ICT and e-learning can provide methods for reaching students outside the traditional education system. Many potential students, because of gender, distance or other factors, are unable to physically attend schools. ICT such as radio and television have been successful in bridging the distance gap and sometimes cultural gap thus allowing a greater number of people to have access to education. Some children may have their education disrupted and are unable to keep pace with the traditional system. Self-paced ICT learning tools can offer an opportunity to integrate these children into the school system. Extending the reach of education and the development of ICT-based learning tools can also offer an opportunity to reach adults that were unable to access an education as youth.

Quality of Education

An area that has yet to reach its full potential is the use of ICT in the development of learning and training material. This lag is partly due to the requirement that teachers and learners be ICT literate before appropriate and relevant ICT-based learning material can be developed and used.

The potential of ICT to increase collaborative learning and the exchange of learning material, is quite large. More and more educational systems are taking advantage of free learning material available through the Internet. For example, geography can be taught by using some of the many free mapping programmes available through the Internet. Organizations are posting free training courses on the Internet in a variety of subjects. However, access to this material is the second important barrier to preventing the use of ICT to develop and deliver learning and training material. It is a "Catch 22": ICT skills are needed to develop the material, yet the material is needed to develop ICT skills.

Teacher Training

A key focus of education projects is capacity development of teachers. ICT can be an important tool for extending and enhancing teacher training programmes. If teachers are first trained in the effective use of ICT they are in a much better position to transfer this knowledge effectively to students. However, teachers often have limited time to learn new skills. One of the challenges with ICT training for teachers is ensuring that this does not add to the burden of teaching but rather enhances and supports the teachers' approach. Regional learning networks are providing teachers with a means to develop their own ICT skills as well as discover ways in which ICT can be integrated into their teaching methods and often, at their own pace.

ICT for Specialized Training

ICT can provide an alternative means of delivering an education or training to targeted sections of the population. ICT such as computers and interactive e-learning software offer a more flexible approach for training sectors of the population that may need to upgrade their skills but are already outside the education system.

Educational Informatics Programme in Costa Rica

The Omar Dengo Foundation has been implementing programmes to integrate ICT into Costa Rican primary schools since 1987. The educational informatics programme, implemented in partnership with the Ministry of Education, has been placing computers in schools since 1988 and training teachers and students in the use of ICT. The programme has focused on schools with limited resources, often in rural areas.

As a result of the programme, over the past decade more than one million children, teachers and community members have been introduced to computer technology. In 2002, almost one out of every two K-6 children attending public education in all regions of the country participated in the programme. A significant number of one-teacher, isolated, rural schools have also joined. An additional, 103,117 high school students also participated in the programme. After-school hours and during weekends, computer labs are used in training programmes for parents and other local citizens. The programme goes beyond simply introducing computer technology to students by developing their capacity to use the technology to improve learning skills.

Qualitative analysis shows how students have been empowered by the technology independently of their socio-economic backgrounds. Furthermore teachers – most of them women – have also achieved command of computer skills and culture while changing important aspects of their professional practice. This has been the result of extensive and long-term training, not only technical but professional as well, and, of follow-up activities that ensure sustainability.

Long-term impacts, as noted by the Omar Dengo Foundation, extend beyond the education system. The foundation attributes the programme with "catalysing a change in the country's productive structure previously agriculturally-based and now has become more technology driven. This in turn has had an effect on the attraction of foreign investment, particularly in areas such as microchip and software production. The Costa Rican experience shows that the cost-effectiveness of computers in schools must be seen not only in terms of their use as effective teaching tools or computer literacy skills, but also within the context of the more complex and far-reaching issues of quality of education, human rights and democratic participation in more productive and innovative job markets." (Omar Dengo, 2004)

SchoolNet Africa

SchoolNet Africa facilitates the integration of ICT into the curriculum of African schools by providing access to information and knowledge on the use of ICT to further education. SchoolNet Africa also brings together partners and donors from the education for the development community to support ICT projects or initiatives to improve education in Africa. Since its launch, SchoolNet Africa has supported the establishment of national SchoolNet networks in 34 countries. Through the network, educators can access learning material and share best practices on the use of ICT to improve education.

Long-term plans include providing computers and Internet access to schools that are members of the network. Although an evaluation of the SchoolNet continent-wide network and national SchoolNet initiatives has not yet been conducted, preliminary results from project-level evaluations indicate that access to information has assisted educators in making more effective use of ICT in the classroom. This has led, in certain cases, to schools being able to provide better and additional learning material to students and teachers.

Rwanda World Links SchoolNet

Reaching over 200,000 teachers and students in 22 developing countries, the World Links Programme provides sustainable solutions for obtaining equipment, training, educational resources and school-to-school, non-governmental organizations and public-private sector partnerships required to bring students in developing countries online. During an evaluation of the Rwanda SchoolNet project, data were collected from more than 500 teachers in 140 schools regarding pedagogical activities, use of computers to support these activities, implementation of the World Links programme, impediments to implementation, and assessment of the impact of computer use on student learning. (*info*Dev, 2003)

The project's main goal is to increase students' awareness of the importance of ICT and develop basic computer literacy in Rwandan primary schools. The project provides access to ICT as well as training. As a result of this initiative, 2,170 primary schools are equipped with a computer each and, at least two teachers are trained in the use of the newly acquired equipment and integration of educational materials that will improve the quality of teaching and learning in the classroom. So far, 13 schools in Rwanda, one in each province and two in Byumba, have benefited from World Links' SchoolNet. Each of the 13 schools has a computer laboratory with 16 computers and printers. Although the impacts on learning were not measured quantitatively, qualitative evidence showed an improvement in teachers' use of learning materials and a significant improvement in students' and teachers' ICT skills.

Health (Goals 4, 5 and 6)

ICT are transforming the delivery of health care in developed and developing countries alike. On a regional scale, ICT are increasing access to health related information exponentially. Developing countries can now access many health related journals online and for free. Reliable information on the treatment and prevention of diseases such as tuberculosis, malaria and HIV/AIDS are being disseminated through ICT based networks using e-mail, web sites, web portals and even hand held ICT devices. All these networks are increasing the rate and speed of exchange of information between researchers and health practitioners allowing for greater collaboration and diagnosis of epidemics and treatable diseases. More and more disease specific communities of practice are being established worldwide fostering greater collaboration between developed and developing countries.

On a national scale, developed countries have used ICT to increase the efficiency of and reduce costs for patient monitoring and disease tracking. ICT show promise in achieving the same efficiencies and potential cost reductions in developing countries. Access to health information, networks and diagnostic tools remains the biggest impediment to their effective use in developing countries. Nonetheless, television and radio, both more widespread ICT in developing countries have successfully been used to raise awareness on disease preventing strategies and decrease the incidence and spread of diseases such as HIV/AIDS.

ICT have also been successfully used to perform remote diagnostics whether through cellular phones, PDAs or more sophisticated equipment used for patient surveys in rural and remote communities. This has led to an increase in underserved populations' access to health care practitioners. We have yet to see how ICT have transformed administrative processes in developed or developing countries but this remains an area where ICT could dramatically increase efficiencies and reduce costs. By far the most important impact of ICT on health in developing countries has been tracking the spread of particular diseases such as AIDS/HIV and malaria. The following examples highlight where ICT have had a measurable impact on the delivery of health care in developing countries and impacted the overall health of the population.

Satellife

The Satellife project provided physicians, medical students and community volunteers with portable and handheld computers, for example PDAs, in different settings in order to demonstrate their viability and usefulness, especially for the collection of health data and dissemination of medical information. The handheld computers were first used in Ghana in December 2001 for field surveys on an American Red Cross project to track a measles immunization campaign. In Uganda the PDAs were used by medical practitioners to conduct an epidemiological survey on malaria as well as to use certain medical reference tools and texts.

Students in Kenya used the PDAs to collect field survey information, and access and use certain medical reference tools and texts as part of their studies. Overall, the handheld computers proved to be a useful and viable technology in the healthcare environments in Ghana, Uganda and Kenya for each of the three types of health practitioners. An evaluation of the project conducted by Bridges.org noted the effectiveness in using the PDA for the dissemination of information and subsequent improvement in the delivery of health care. The evaluation also noted the difficulty in obtaining relevant and useful health information for the PDAS (Bridges.org, 2003).

Mapping Malaria Risk in Africa (MARA)

MARA is an excellent example of a collaborative network of researchers, health practitioners and policy makers effectively using ICT to control and diminish the spread of malaria. The MARA collaboration was initiated to provide an atlas of malaria for Africa with relevant information for policy makers and health practitioners. Scientists from across Africa map the spread and risk of malaria. This information is used to support malaria control planning and programming activities and has led to greater prevention of malaria and more efficient allocation of resources in Africa.

The project was launched in 1997 and has been expanding ever since. Results to date include collection of data from 10,000 points across Africa using GIS. MARA scientists have produced over 2,000 maps from this data. These maps have been used for spatial modeling of malaria distribution, seasonality and endemicity. Relevant information is then disseminated to national and international policy makers, health practitioners and other end users. Throughout the project, local capacity has been developed to use the MARA system. To date 129 health workers and researchers have also been trained on GIS and database systems. Indicators on how these activities have reduced the spread of malaria are not yet available.

Environment (Goal 7)

ICT has proven to be an effective tool for countries and organizations working toward a cleaner and safer environment and more sustainable use of natural resources. In the following examples, ICT is shown to have a direct and measurable impact on the environment by promoting awareness of environmental challenges, increasing access to and the diffusion of environment related information and knowledge, increasing the efficiency and scope of environmental monitoring and response systems, and enabling better resource management.

Access to timely and relevant information underpins the success of many environmental initiatives. Awareness of current and potential environmental challenges is a first step toward engaging people to address them. Many environmental organizations have used ICT to gather support for and raise awareness of specific environmental problems such as extinction of species and non-sustainable use of natural resources. There are countless web sites showcasing specific environmental initiatives to address environmental problems. Various ICT have also been used to collect relevant data on the environment. For example, weather-monitoring systems provide essential information for farmers wanting to know what crops to plant and when is the most appropriate time. Although there is a significant amount of relevant environmental information available through ICT, the challenge remains to provide access to the ICT.

The communications component of ICT is quite significant for many environmental initiatives as they often require wide-spread collaboration and a very timely response. The Com+ alliance is an example of a partnership of international organizations and communications professionals from diverse sectors using communications to advance a vision of sustainable development that integrates its three pillars: economic, social and environmental. The alliance also offers access to ICT to members to share expertise, develop best practices and create synergies with the aim of furthering sustainable development.

Global Information Systems, both an information and communication technology, is an important example of a specific ICT that has become a key component of many environmental initiatives. GIS is an effective tool for quickly gathering information on a particular geographic location or environmental phenomena. However, one of the impediments to wide-spread use of GIS in environmental development initiatives is the significant cost of equipment and reliance on satellites for data capture. Also a specific skill set is needed to use the software and hardware. GIS is not a readily accessible tool yet, essential in mapping important environmental phenomena and environmental degradation such as the progress of natural and man-made disasters, climate change, desertification and deforestation.

Global Information and Early Warning System on Food and Agriculture

The Global Information and Early Warning Systems on Food and Agriculture (GIEWS) is a network of 115 governments, 61 non-governmental organizations, and numerous trade, research and media organizations involved in food production and management. Established in the 1970s, GIEWS has integrated ICT into core operations. ICT has enabled even greater access to information and extended the reach of the network. Furthermore, ICT has increased the efficiency of the early-warning system by improving data collection and enabling a more timely response to a food crisis.

The system provides policy makers and analysts with quick and accurate information on food supply and demand. The system synthesizes data collected from various organizations and emits regular bulletins on food crop production and markets at the global level. ICT is a critical element of operations whether for data collection, information dissemination or when responding to a food crisis. As an example, GIEWS has developed a computer workstation for data management and early-warning analysis, ranging from crop monitoring using up-to-date satellite images to estimating food import requirements. The system has centralized data collection processes and enabled better analysis of essential information on crop monitoring. Although an in-depth analysis of the impacts of ICT on GIEWS service delivery has not yet been done, the above example demonstrates how integration of ICT into the network operations has furthered GIEWS goal to diminish food crises across the globe.

GIEWS was recently an important tool in responding to the locust epidemic in Africa. The system provides regular updates on the migratory pattern and breeding habits of the locust in the various affected regions in Africa. This enables policy makers and development organization to better determine a preemptive response to the epidemic.

Central African Regional Programme for the Environment

The Central African Regional Programme for the Environment (CARPE) is a long-term initiative by the United States Agency on International Development to address the issues of deforestation and biodiversity loss in the Congo Basin forest zone. CARPE aims to reduce the rate of forest degradation and loss of biodiversity through increased local, national, and regional natural resource management capacity. Intermediate results to be achieved in order to reach this objective will involve implementing sustainable forest and biodiversity management practices, strengthening environmental governance, and monitoring forests and other natural resources throughout the region. ICT are used to monitor land use, logging activity, deforestation, and forest access throughout the region using remote sensing. ICT are also used to disseminate information on the above activities to the appropriate decisions makers and advocacy groups who can ensure appropriate action is undertaken. Access to timely information on the status of the environment in the region has led to more efficient use of the resources.

References

Bridges.org (2004) "Real Access" http://www.bridges.org/digitaldivide/realaccess.html

Bridges.org (2004) "Evaluation of the Satellife PDA Project, 2002; Testing the use of handheld computers for heath care in Ghana, Uganda, and Kenya".

DFID (2002) "The significance of information and communication technologies for reducing poverty". Phil Marker, Kerry McNamara and Lindsay Wallace.

Economist Intelligence Unit (2004) "Reaping the Benefits of ICT: Europe's Productivity Challenge"

Gartner Dataquest (2002) "The Payoff of Ubiquitous Broadband Deployment". Behram Dalal, Jin Shen, Ron Cowles and Kathie Hackler.

Government of Canada (2004) "The Challenge of Change: Building the 21st Century Economy". Conference background paper "e-Commerce to e-Economy Strategies for the 21st Century" Ottawa, 27-28 September 2004.

*info*Dev (2003) "ICT for Development: Contributing to the Millennium Development Goals – Lessons Learned from Seventeen *info*Dev Projects"

OECD (2003) "ICT and Poverty Reduction Strategy Papers", Development Assistance Committee. http://www.oecd.org/dataoecd/53/54/2499909.doc

OECD (2004) "The Contributions of ICT to Pro-Poor Growth". Development Assistance Committee (DAC) Working Paper. Ichiro Tambo.

Orbicom (2003) "Monitoring the Digital Divide and Beyond", National Research Council of Canada.

UNESCO Portal on ICT in Education indicators - http://portal.unesco.org/ci/en/ev.php-URL_ID=12438&URL_DO=DO_TOPIC&URL_SECTION=201.html

UNDP (2004) "Regional Development Report on Asia"

UNDP (2004b) "Human Development Report". http://hdr.undp.org/reports/global/2004/

World Bank (2003) "World Development Report"

World Economic Forum – INSEAD, *info*Dev (2003) "Global Information Technology Report"

Case Studies

Global Information & Early Warning System, http://www.fao.org/giews

NetCorps Jordan, http://www.dotrust.org/countries/jordan.html

Omar Dengo Foundation, http://www.fod.ac.cr

PeopleLink, http://www.catgen.com/catgen/EN/

Schoolnet Africa, http://www.schoolnetafrica.net/

Village Phone Programme http://www.grameenphone.com/village.htm

World Links Rwanda, http://www.world-links.org/rwanda/

INNOVATION AND INVESTMENT: INFORMATION AND COMMUNICATION TECHNOLOGIES AND THE MILLENNIUM DEVELOPMENT GOALS

Report Prepared for the United Nations ICT Task Force in Support of the Science, Technology and Innovation Task Force of the United Nations Millennium Project[1]

By Denis Gilhooly, United Nations ICT Task Force and United Nations Millennium Project

1. Executive Summary

The intersection of information and communication technologies (ICTs) and the Millennium Development Goals (MDGs) forms a critical nexus for the future of sustainable human development and poverty eradication. Yet the great paradox of the information age - the persistence of scarcity in a digital era of near-ubiquitous and superabundant capacity – remains the greatest single challenge to the networked and development-rich economy and society. This paper argues that while the means to meet the challenge for scaling up innovation and investment in ICT for Development are actually close at hand, the so-called "digital divide" has shifted perilously in recent years to the detriment of the poorest and Least Developed Countries (LDCs), with missed opportunities for the achievement of the MDGs.

To address this issue and unleash the full potential of ICTs as an enabler of economic and social development throughout the developing world, global and prioritised policy and practice breakthroughs are urgently required. Increasingly, the relevance and importance of such breakthroughs as part of an integrated development approach is being viewed within government, business, civil society and international organizations through the lens of the MDGs. For with the strategic, intensive, widespread and innovative use of ICTs in development policies and programmes the ambitious agenda of the MDGs becomes that much more possible to realize. Further, the scale of deployment and catalytic role played by ICT can in turn help to make such investment in ICT sustainable.

With the five year review of progress toward the achievement of the MDGs planned at the United Nations General Assembly/Millennium Summit + 5 (MS+5) in New York in September 2005 and the second phase of the World Summit on the Information Society (WSIS) in Tunis in November 2005, overarching issues and interests are set to converge. A unique and virtuous opportunity exists both to identify bottlenecks and gaps and to strengthen synergies and inter-linkages between the MDGs and ICT. By galvanising political will and action in 2005, the essential breakthrough criteria can be framed to meet the desired objectives of all interested players in the common cause of poverty reduction, sustainable development and good governance.

---

[1] The views expressed in this report reflect those of the author and not necessarily those of the Unted Nations ICT Task Force or any other United Nations organizations.

There is already a strong correlation between ICTs and the MDGs based on a mutually shared objective: namely, the efficient, scalable, affordable and pervasive delivery of goods, services and information flows between people, governments and firms. Significantly, of all the MDG targets it can be said that ICT has made the most rapid progress to date and is "on-track". Ultimately, however, despite the obvious benefits to economic growth, including pro-poor growth, of the global explosion in ICT supply and demand, it is as a *generic platform technology* and *enabler* for the achievement of the other development goals (Goal 1-7), within a broad and integrated development approach, rather than simply as a stand-alone production sector (Goal 8) that ICT will most profoundly impact the MDGs.

In order for ICT to positively foster development goals, it must be employed where relevant, appropriate and effective. In addition, perennial cross-sector complexities and issues must be overcome within existing approaches to ICT for Development to create an enabling environment for innovation and to prioritize a focus on investment and development uses of ICT. Specifically: full demonstration of development impact; integration and prioritization within national development and poverty reduction programmes and strategies; policy realignment on basic infrastructure deployment; improved government and donor coordination and cooperation; increased private sector engagement; and, enhanced mechanisms for resource mobilization.

Once ICT for Development policies and programmes are embedded within the overall development process, even subordinated in the service of the MDGs, many unresolved challenges and untapped opportunities are thrown into relief: policy and regulatory frameworks for ICT investment that can help to achieve the right balance between investment promotion and meeting the needs of low-income customers; profitable business models that engage the private sector in the local delivery of affordable ICTs to rural and urban areas; coordination and cooperation between government, business, civil society and international organization initiatives; and, financing mechanisms that realistically and effectively address the funding deficit in bridging the digital divide. By setting clear development priorities resource allocation to the kind of grassroots, south-south and multi-stakeholder ICT partnerships needed to achieve the MDGs can be pressed far more robustly.

Similarly, the massive scaling up and low cost delivery of public and private services to the world's poorest citizens inherent in meeting the MDGs also focuses attention on innovative and breakthrough approaches to ICT delivery that exploit the enormous variety of communication technologies. These approaches must allow access to information that is most relevant to people's multi-dimensional livelihoods. It requires forms of ICT transactions that achieve the optimal division of risk between the public and private sectors, and that afford the necessary flexibility for operators to deliver pro-poor services over time. It recognizes the importance to livelihood security of social capital, identifying those ICTs that contribute most to building this asset. And it implies knowledge and information delivery critical to sustainable livelihoods that reach the right people at the right time at the right price.

ICTs and the MDGs both blur the once obvious borders and boundaries between the technical and political, the social and economic. Moving decisively towards an inclusive information society requires, as an indispensable initial building block, a shared understanding of the nature and scope of challenges and opportunities, and developing broad common approaches to dealing with them. Today, however, the stark reality is that building such consensus is an evolving process at a very early stage of development. The developed and developing countries; governments; the private sector; civil society; international organizations; as well as the development, ICT, trade and foreign policy communities – all have yet to come to a common understanding and prioritization of issues, as well as agreement on the approaches, governance structures and implementation mechanisms for moving forward.

In this regard, the phenomenon of the grand stakeholder alliances and collaborations of the mobile and Internet network revolutions show the way ahead. For the successful scaling up of innovation and investment this model must be combined with a number of key elements. A prerequisite will be the recognition of national and regional differences and needs and to prioritize action and implementation accordingly. The importance of the establishment of basic innovation systems leading to advanced innovation systems in developing countries must also be recognized and prioritized by donors and countries themselves. Establishing an enabling environment for the scaling up of pro-poor ICT policies and practices is also an essential prerequisite. Finally, scaling up of ICT deployment for the achievement of the MDGs will clearly require additional investment and resource mobilization.

Here, whatever emerges from MS+5 and WSIS must also this time be backed up by concrete and realistic financial commitments that draw from complementary local resources, bilateral donors, multilateral donors and private investment. All parties must take responsibility to make realistic commitments and deliver on them. Given the great challenge of the MDGs and the resource constraints that are likely to continue even under the most optimistic growth scenarios, particularly in ODA, more attention must be paid to maximising synergies among existing resources and using aid strategically as a catalyst for private investment.[2] With evidence of *impact* in place, it will then be possible to *prioritise* in taking the *risk* to *innovate* and *invest* in new *global initiatives and partnerships* for ICT and the MDGs toward 2015.

2. ICT and the MDGs - Converging Fields, Common Interests

Information and Communication Technologies (ICTs) can play a critical role in sustainable human development and poverty eradication. Yet the field of ICT for Development is at a turning point. At one level, the past decade has witnessed the most dramatic growth in the history of global computing and communications, with the potential for near-ubiquitous spread of mobile telephony and the Internet. At another level, progress in narrowing the gap between those developing countries now empowered by the fundamental right of access to local and global networks of knowledge and information, and those developing countries still impoverished by the practical denial of that right, is widening and as stark as ever.

This central paradox – the persistence of scarcity in a digital era of superabundant capacity – is perhaps the greatest single challenge to the networked economy and society. This paper argues that while the means to meet this challenge are actually close at hand, the so-called "digital divide" has shifted perilously in recent years to the detriment of the poorest countries, most notably the Least Developed Countries (LDCs). Today, a chronic paucity of affordable access to network infrastructure and services endures in many of the LDCs. To address this network deficit, and unleash the full potential of ICT as an enabler of economic and social development throughout the developing world, a global and prioritised policy and programmatic breakthrough is urgently required.

Increasingly, the relevance and importance of such a focus is being viewed through the lens of the Millennium Development Goals (MDGs). Agreed by world leaders at the United Nations Millennium Summit in 2000, the MDGs are intended to catalyze sustainable human development and halve the number of the world's poorest citizens by 2015. In essence, with the strategic, intensive, widespread and innovative use of ICTs in development policies and programmes, the ambitious agenda of the MDGs becomes much more possible to realize. Without this laser-like focus and vision, scaleable, replicable and sustainable implementation of the MDGs in many instances may well be impossible.

The stakes could not be higher. The outcome of the Millennium Summit in adopting eight specific goals comprising eighteen targets and forty eight indicators for the first time established a globally agreed political and time-bound benchmark for measuring the progress of development at the national, regional and international levels (Table 1). In parallel, two major multi-stakeholder initiatives were launched at this time – the Group of Eight Digital Opportunity Task Force (G8 DOT-Force) and the United Nations ICT Task Force (UN ICT Task Force) – in ground breaking attempts to address the growing digital divide and its repercussions for economic and social development.

With the five year review of progress toward the achievement of the MDGs planned at the United Nations General Assembly/Millennium Summit + 5 (MS+5) in New York in September 2005 and the second phase of the World Summit on the Information Society in Tunis in November 2005, overarching issues and interests are set to converge. A unique and virtuous opportunity exists both to identify bottlenecks and gaps and to strengthen synergies and inter-linkages between the MDGs and ICT. By galvanising political will and action in 2005, the essential breakthrough criteria can be framed to meet the desired objectives of government, business, civil society and international organizations in the common cause of poverty eradication, sustainable human development and good governance.

Table 1 – Millennium Development Goals and Targets –
ICT Applications Map to the MDGs for Economic and Social Opportunity, Youth and
Education, Gender Participation and Empowerment, Healthcare, and Environment

Goals	Targets
1. Eradicate extreme poverty and hunger	1. Halve, between 1990 and 2015, the proportion of people whose income is less than one dollar a day.
	2. Halve, between 1990 and 2015, the proportion of people who suffer from hunger.
2. Achieve universal primary education	3. Ensure that, by 2015, children everywhere, boys and girls alike, will be able to complete a full course of primary schooling.
3. Promote gender equality and empower women	4. Eliminate gender disparity in primary and secondary education preferably by 2005 and in all levels of education no later than 2015.
4. Reduce child mortality	5. Reduce by two-thirds, between 1990 and 2015, the under-five mortality rate.
5. Improve maternal health	6. Reduce by three-quarters, between 1990 and 2015, the maternal mortality ratio.
6. Combat HIV/AIDS, malaria, and other diseases	7. Have halted by 2015 and begun to reverse the spread of HIV/AIDS.
	8. Have halted by 2015 and begun to reverse the incidence of malaria and other major diseases.
7. Ensure environmental sustainability	9. Integrate the principles of sustainable development into country policies and programmes and reverse the loss of environmental resources.
	10. Halve, by 2015, the proportion of people without sustainable access to safe drinking water.
	11. Have achieved, by 2020, a significant improvement in the lives of at least 100 million slum dwellers.
8. Develop a global partnership for development	12-17. Separate targets for developing trading and financial systems, addressing the special needs of LDCs, SIDS and land-locked countries, debt sustainability, youth employment, and providing affordable drugs.
	18. In cooperation with the private sector, make available the benefits of new technologies, especially information and communications.

Note: For a list of the 48 MDG indicators see the Millennium Indicators Database at:
http://millenniumindicators.un.org/unsd/mi/mi_goals.asp.
Source: Adapted from the United Nations Development Programme (UNDP) Human Development Report, 2003

2.1 - Network Revolution

The network revolution has forced a radical transformation of business and development models in both developed and developing economies and societies. New network economics and dynamics have combined multiple "positive feedback mechanisms" and "network effects" with disruptive and discontinuous change. This change encompasses: fast decreasing technology costs with volume and innovation; vastly increased system development costs, risks and timescales; new competitive market forces; heightened user expectations; uncertain industry restructuring and financial market behaviour; as well as standardisation that is often non-proprietary in nature. In addition, there has been the onset of nascent "network externalities" with major implications for the future of electronic commerce.

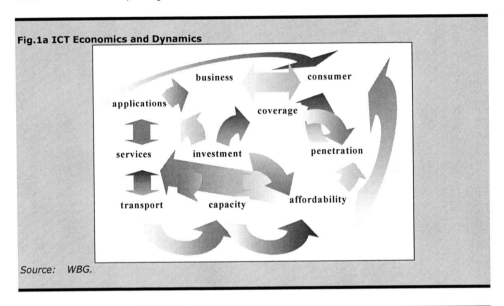

Fig.1a ICT Economics and Dynamics

Source: WBG.

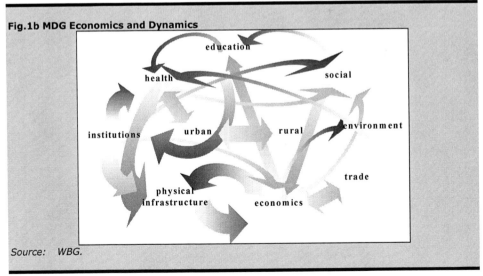

Fig.1b MDG Economics and Dynamics

Source: WBG.

Fig.1c Interaction of ICT and MDG Economics and Dynamics

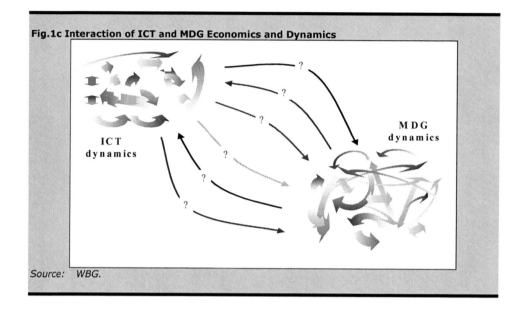

ICT dynamics

MDG dynamics

Source: WBG.

At many levels, the new network economics and dynamics remain complex and only partially understood. The complexity of development economics and dynamics is equally daunting, so that the assessment of the interaction of network (ICT) and development (MDG) economics and dynamics becomes highly subjective (Figure 1). Like poverty, ICT are multi-dimensional in nature. It is primarily for this reason that the debate over poverty eradication and the broad and systematic use of ICT in development policy and programmes has until quite recently been polarized between sceptics and enthusiasts.

While some have viewed ICT akin to an exotic luxury in relation to pure development needs and priorities - from clean water and food security to basic education and healthcare - others initially viewed it almost as a panacea for perennial development problems. Now, in parallel with the "dotcom" crash and the subsequent return of the ICT sector has come a shift from anecdotal exuberance to a focus on the empirical evidence of its full development impact. A more balanced perspective has emerged where ICT are no longer seen as an end in itself but rather as a critical enabler in the development process, increasingly in the context of the MDGs.

There is already a strong correlation between ICTs and the MDGs based on a mutually shared objective: namely, the efficient, scalable, affordable and pervasive delivery of goods, services and information flows between people, governments and firms. In addition, while ICT cuts across all seven Millennium Declaration goals targeted at specific objectives in promoting development and improving people's daily livelihoods – including income poverty, food security, healthcare, education, gender equity and environment – it also appears as an MDG itself within the eighth goal, "Develop global partnerships for development", focussed on how to achieve the objectives themselves.

Within Goal 8 Target 18 thus proposes that "In cooperation with the private sector, make available the benefits of new technologies, especially information and communication". It further suggests indicators in terms of telephone, mobile, personal computer and Internet users worldwide. It is against this background that the Task Force on "Science, Technology, and Innovation" was created within the United Nations Millennium Project to propose strategies for harnessing the pervasive and profound potential of modern science and technology in achieving the MDGs.

Significantly, of all the MDG targets it can be said that ICT has made the most rapid progress to date and is "on-track". The ITU estimates that access to telephone networks in developing countries tripled in the ten-year period 1993-2002 from 11.6 subscribers per 100 inhabitants to 36.4 (Figure 2). By the end of 2002, there were more mobile cellular subscribers than fixed telephone lines in the world. Growth has been particularly strong in Africa where almost all countries now have more mobile phones than fixed telephones.

Growth in personal computers and the Internet has been equally impressive. By the end of 2002 there were an estimate 615 million computers in the world, up from only 120 million in 1990. From only 27 economies that had a direct connection to the Internet in 1990, the figure grew to almost every country in the world by the end of 2002, corresponding to some 600 million users. Again, growth has been most rapid in developing countries where 34 per cent of users resided in 2002, up from only 3 per cent in 1992.[3]

Ultimately, however, despite the obvious benefits to economic growth, including pro-poor growth, of the global explosion in ICT supply and demand, it is as a generic platform technology and enabler of the other development goals (Goal 1-7) rather than a stand-alone production sector (Goal 8) that ICT will most impact the MDGs: through the creation of new economic and social opportunities for poverty eradication; by increasing the efficiency, accountability and delivery of public services in healthcare, education and environment; and, with the promotion of greater participation in development policies and processes. In all these areas, the potential of ICT for Development has yet to be fully realized. Critical to unleashing this potential is the need to recognize the unique characteristics of ICT and the MDGs.

---

[3] See "ICTs and the Millennium Development Goals", Chapter 4, *World Telecommunications Development Report 2003*, International Telecommunication Union, 2003. http://www.itu.int/ITU-D/ict/publications/wtdr_03/material/Chap4_WTDR2003_E.pdf

Fig.2 A decade of ICT progress
Total teledensity (main telephone lines and mobile users per 100 inhabitants), in 1992 and 2002, in developing regions

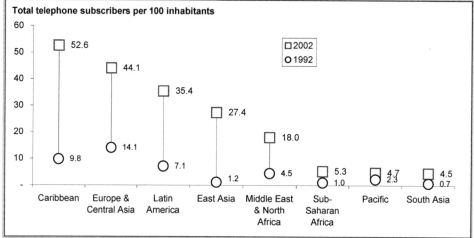

Total telephone subscribers per 100 inhabitants

Note: Developed countries are excluded. For definitions of regions, see: www.worldbank.org/data/countryclass/classgroups.htm.
Source: ITU World Telecommunication Indicators Database.

2.2 - Unique ICT and MDG Characteristics

There are a number of important ways in which ICT is differentiated from other development sectors and technologies, and this is not simply because of its status as a lucrative source of revenue and taxation for business and government. As accelerator, driver, multiplier and innovator, the unique character of ICTs, both established (radio, television, video, compact disc) and emerging (wireless, Internet, broadband), make them a powerful if not indispensable tool in the massive scaling up and inter-linkage of development interventions and outcomes inherent in the MDGs.

ICT are a powerful enabler of development goals because it dramatically improves communication and the exchange of knowledge and information to strengthen and create new social and economic networks. Its uses and applications are pervasive and cross-cutting and can be applied to the full range of human activity from personal use to business and government. It propitiates an acceleration factor through the power of the network that becomes ever more powerful and useful the more people are connected to it, thus creating network externalities or exponentially increasing returns as network usage increases. And it fosters the dissemination of information and exchange of knowledge by separating content from physical location and overcoming distance.

Crucial in the poverty context, ICT can also radically reduce transaction costs. Replication of content is virtually free regardless of volume, and marginal costs for distribution and communication are near zero. Central to the MDGs, ICT's power to store, retrieve, sort, filter, distribute and share information can lead to substantial efficiency gains in production, distribution and markets, and benefits for social processes. And ICT are global in nature, transcending cultural and linguistic barriers as they challenge current policy, legal and regulatory structures within and between nations.

Analogously, the uniqueness of the MDGs lies in two dimensions. First, by defining the goals in terms of development targets, as opposed to inputs and outputs, the MDGs draw attention to the multi-sectoral and inter-linked determinants of development targets. Second, the MDGs focus on the achievement of quantified and time-bound targets, providing both opportunities to make progress in combating poverty and risks of non-attainment. However, given current rates of progress many countries and regions are to date "off-track" and will be unable to meet the MDGs by 2015.[4]

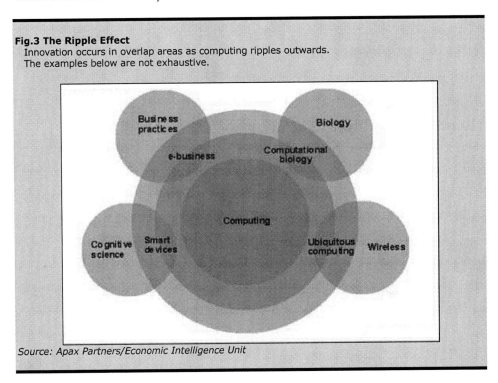

Fig.3 The Ripple Effect
Innovation occurs in overlap areas as computing ripples outwards.
The examples below are not exhaustive.

Source: Apax Partners/Economic Intelligence Unit

To catalyse progress, entirely new models and modalities of operation and implementation are therefore required in key areas ranging from policy to partnership to resource mobilization. Here, it is as a fundamentally generic platform technology that ICTs will likely have the most far-reaching impact on the achievement of the MDGs, because they anticipate and foreshadow many of the critical socio-economic growth and development models and modalities of the future. Even within the science and technology community itself, the seismic changes and tectonic shifts continuing to occur in the fields of computing and communications are still often underestimated.

---

[4] See "ICT & the MDGs: A World Bank Group Perspective", World Bank Group, 2003.
http://wbln0018.worldbank.org/ict/resources.nsf/InfoResources/99CB4E54A845DF9D85256E01006426AA

For example, progress in computing is providing the foundation for innovation in adjacent industries as far a field as wireless communications and genomics. This "ripple effect" (Figure 3) will continue to expand with the exponential growth of processing power, storage capacity and networking bandwidth. Today, processing power available at a given price doubles every eighteen months; storage capacity per unit area is doubling every year; and the amount of data that can be squeezed down a fibre optic cable is doubling every nine months. The impact of this technological progress has only just begun to be felt, but it will continue to be utterly pervasive and profound.

The Internet is a case in point. The ripple effects from the Internet are at an embryonic stage of development. Already the fastest growing communications medium in history, the Internet marks the beginning of the great discontinuity of technological convergence between telephone, television and computer. Reversing the relationship between quality, functionality and price it has already turned telecommunications orthodoxy on its head (Figure 4). Today, the Internet is being run on top of the telephone network. Tomorrow, all telephony will end up running on top of the Internet.

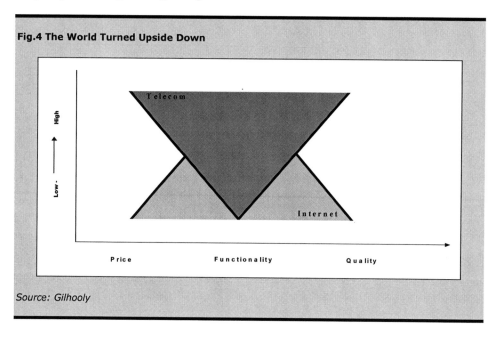

Fig.4 The World Turned Upside Down

Source: Gilhooly

Not only is an almost entirely unregulated network threatening to topple its highly regulated predecessor, but the Internet also embodies many of the elements of the future communications marketplace – the arrival of local-global calls, the onset of freeware, the separation of networks and services provision, the availability of affordable mass access, and the provision of scalable broadband communications. The implications for developing countries, whether early or late technology adopters, of an impending global Internet utility or grid - cheap, reliable, and always-on – will be too compelling to ignore indefinitely in applying knowledge across all development processes and projects. [5]

2.3 - Missing ICT and MDG Links

Ironically, the great self-sustaining, self-replicating and multi-stakeholder enterprise that in 2005 constitutes the global wired and wireless Internet seems almost by accident to have acquired the attributes of a global public good. Yet it is no coincidence that the innovative and breakthrough elements of the Internet value chain not only mirror the missing links in the development value chain, they also impinge on precisely the areas of difficulty and contention faced by the MDGs in meeting the 2015 agenda: namely, intellectual property rights; integration of legal, regulatory and physical infrastructures; youth and gender empowerment; and, viral growth models for very large scale projects and initiatives. In this regard, most experts concede that the MDGs can be attained if, and only if, ambitious yet realistic nationally-determined priorities and initiatives are also promoted and advocated at the global level. And these globally supported goals and initiatives must embed growth models based on just the kind of sustainable, self-replicating and multi-stakeholder business models and partnerships as evidenced in Internet-based efforts today.

In the meantime, the fact that the unique characteristics of ICT if conceived as means and not ends can, in theory, act as powerful development enable does not mean that it will necessarily do so. In order for ICT to positively foster development goals, it must be employed where relevant, appropriate and effective. And this means not in isolation or sector by sector, but as part of a truly integrated and multi-stakeholder development approach.[6] In addition, perennial cross-sector complexities and issues must be overcome within existing approaches to ICT for Development. Specifically: *full demonstration of development impact; integration and prioritization within national development and poverty reduction programmes; policy realignment on basic infrastructure deployment; improved government and donor coordination and cooperation; increased private sector engagement; and, enhanced mechanisms for resource mobilization.*

Key to making the case for the strategic deployment of ICT to support the achievement of the MDGs is the potential to demonstrate scalable impact. There are currently few studies or strategies that outline a strategic programmatic vision with regard to integrating ICT and assessing its impact through appropriate benchmarks, goals and indicators for its deployment in developing countries. It is generally agreed that the indicators proposed by Target 18 of the MDGs - number of telephones, personal computer and Internet users – are wholly inadequate if they are to also serve as a measure of development impact in the use of ICTs in poverty reduction, health, education, empowerment or environment. Here, major work is now being undertaken by the United Nations Partnership on Measuring ICT for

---

[5] See "Innovation: Applying Knowledge for Development", Task Force on Science, Technology and Innovation, UN Millennium Project, 2005. http://bcsia.ksg.harvard.edu/BCSIA_content/documents/TF-Advance2.pdf

[6] See "Investing in Development: A Practical Plan to Achieve the Millennium Development Goals", Report to the UN Secretary General, UN Millennium Project, 2005. http://www.unmillenniumproject.org

Development, United Nations ICT Task Force and the World Bank Group with findings due in 2005.[7]

The awareness of the development potential of ICT are often not fully reflected in the formulation of national e-Strategies, many of which lay primary emphasis on the development of ICT as a new growth and export sector. Those that do focus on ICT as an enabler often fail to make the linkage between ICT goals and priorities and those of the other development strategies as though synergies were expected to occur automatically. Similarly, national development strategies in general, and poverty reduction strategies in particular, provide the framework for focus on core development priorities, but the full and necessary integration or mainstreaming of ICT in these strategies is lacking. The OECD estimates that of the twenty nine poverty reduction strategy papers (PRSPs) of Heavily Indebted Poor Countries (HIPC) in 2003 only twelve define or position ICT as a strategic component of poverty reduction and address it as an independent item in their PRSPs.[8]

This problem is a function not only of a lack of full awareness of the potential of ICT and the adoption of mutually exclusive sectoral approaches to development, but also because network access and infrastructure remain an issue. With the trend toward the deregulation and privatization of the global telecommunications industry in the 1990s, development banks and national donor agencies effectively withdrew from public infrastructure finance in lieu of the private sector.[9] In hindsight, this decision may have been premature. Market and regulatory failures, particularly in sub-Saharan Africa, have led to cases of privatised state entities retaining effective monopoly control, limiting competition and reducing network investment. While mobile cellular networks are believed to have now brought some 80 percent of the world's population within reach of a telephone[10], regulatory policy frameworks, licensing conditions and a lack of financial mechanisms to support connectivity have also failed to realize tangible coverage and affordable access, particularly in rural and remote areas. As a result, a broad reappraisal of current policy frameworks, roles, responsibilities and mechanisms to facilitate provision of basic telecommunications infrastructure services is currently the subject of intense debate.

Traditionally, this access gap has been addressed in piecemeal fashion by governments and donors with a limited ability within the ICT for Development community to move beyond mere pilot projects in the scaling-up of investments for mass market deployment. This has partly been due to lack of coordination and duplication among donor agency and government initiatives within countries, where competition for volume has taken precedence over the goal of development impact. Local actors and local content have also often been under-emphasised in initiatives. In other instances, donors and governments have also been slow to recognize the importance of putting in place a supportive enabling environment and fostering the requisite private sector participation at the earliest stage of project

---

[7] See http://measuring-ict.unctad.org
[8] See OECD "Information and Communication Technology (ICT) in Poverty Reduction Strategy Papers (PRSPs) as of August 2003." http://www.oecd.org/dataoecd/4/30/15987925.pdf and "Integrating Information and Communication Technologies in Development Programmes", OECD Policy Brief, OECD, 2003.
[9] For an analysis of trends in financing, see the Report of the Task Force on Financial Mechanisms for ICT for Development: A review of trends and an analysis of gaps and promising practices http://www.itu.int/wsis/tffm/final-report.pdf page 38
[10] See ITU World Telecommunication Indicators Database

implementation essential to ensure buy-in and long term investment. Looking forward, innovative public-private or multi-stakeholder partnerships between government, business, civil society and international organizations while complex are increasingly viewed as essential for large scale ICT for Development projects – for building ownership, ensuring relevance, leveraging core complementary competencies and sharing financial risk.[11] These types of partnerships will often need to be accompanied by scalable approaches for national franchising of public access and the use of (minimum) public subsidy schemes to support provision in under-served areas and uneconomic market conditions.

The focus on the role of the private sector in ICT for Development interventions – including the local private sector - cannot be underestimated: in advocacy for pro-poor growth strategies; in integrating private sector development and poverty reduction strategies; in helping to create enabling legal and regulatory environments; in finance and risk mitigation; in human and social capital and innovation development; in product, commodity markets and trade; in infrastructure investment and deployment; and in interaction with donors and donor organizations. Again, though the role played by the private sector has significantly increased in the digital era, investment shortfall due to the global technology downturn means that careful nurturing of their involvement by donors and governments will be required for some time to come.

Inevitably, perhaps the critical issue concerning mainstreaming ICT for the achievement of the MDGs is that of resource mobilization. The jury is still out on whether enough evidence exists to make the case either for supporting a massive, multi-billion dollar financial infusion toward bridging the digital divide, or for the creation of a dedicated global financial mechanism for its disbursement. And questions remain on many fronts: Should priority be given to the LDC investments? How will funds released by adherence to the Monterrey commitments and HIPC debt relief be channelled? What are the respective roles of the public and private sectors? Can technological transformation be leveraged to provide new and leapfrog business models for affordable provision? What innovative sources of financing for development can be found?

In this context, the United Nations-led Task Force on Financial Mechanisms for ICT for Development that resulted from the first phase of the World Summit on the Information Society has opened the debate by making an in-depth analysis of existing mechanisms and their efficacy.[12] As mentioned earlier, however, for all intents and purposes the science, technology and innovation that need to be invented to meet the unresolved challenges of ICT for Development have by now been invented. But it will be the intersection of ICT and the MDGs that will form the vital nexus for future interventions at the national, regional and international levels. The bottom line in 2005 is whether a global and prioritised policy and programmatic breakthrough in coordination and commitment can be marshalled in time to harness the synergies of ICT and the MDGs over the coming decade toward 2015.

---

[11] e.g., see DFID African ICT Infrastructure Investment Options
http://www.afridigital.net/downloads/DFIDinfrastructurerep.pdf
[12] See "The Report of the Task Force on Financial Mechanisms for ICT for Development – A Review of Trends and an Analysis of Gaps and Promising Practices", United Nations, 2004 http://www.itu.int/wsis/tffm/final-report.pdf

3.   ICT and the MDGs – Work in Progress

In 1985, the landmark "Missing Link" report of the Independent Commission for Worldwide Telecommunications Development recommended that by the year 2000 every village on the planet should have access to a basic telephone.[13] Two decades later, and despite repeated and nuanced efforts by government, business, civil society and international organizations aimed at bridging the digital divide, this simple goal remains elusive. While unexpected market forces in the guise of mobile telephony and the Internet have driven the explosion of worldwide ICT diffusion during this period, the evolving and multi-dimensional nature of the digital divide has stalled moves to adequately express the severity of the problem in ICT for Development policies and programmes.

Nowhere has this been more evident than in the past decade's series of reconstructed global ICT summits that have resulted in a summary failure to deconstruct the global digital divide (Figure 5). Part of the difficulty in framing the debate has been the lack of awareness of the digital divide as effect rather than cause. It has always been largely a reflection of deeper and more ingrained economic and social schisms related to poverty, hunger, illiteracy, healthcare, or geographical location, all of which have justifiably been viewed as of far more pressing concern. Another difficulty has been the flawed perception of the existence of a solitary digital divide between rich and poor nations. In reality, deep divisions and complex cleavages occur both within developed and developing countries themselves, as well as between developing countries.

---

[13] See "The Missing Link: Report of the Independent Commission for Worldwide Telecommunications Development, ITU, 1985.

Fig.5 Scaling the Summits – Situating ICTs and MDGs

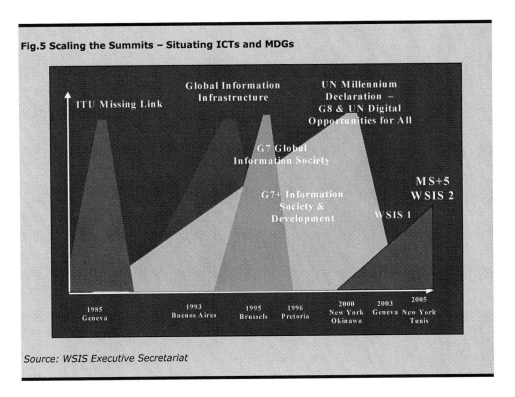

Source: WSIS Executive Secretariat

In common with the MDGs, a shock to the system is required if the necessary breakthrough is to be made in policies, priorities and mobilization of additional financial resources to bridge manifold digital divides. That breakthrough will see a shift from emphasis on universal telecommunications access to the delivery of public and private services in support of the MDGs; from the need for more investment in physical infrastructure to simultaneous investment in an enabling environment, human capacity, innovation and enterprise; from an ICT-based industry focus to a multi-sectoral-based industry focus spanning the breadth of the MDGs; and, from a "one size fits all" approach to detailed differentiation between the policies and priorities most appropriate to individual developing countries whether early or late technology adopters.

For too long the ICT industry has been mired in an internal dialogue on the digital divide. In the process it has lost sight of the endgame of delivering pro-poor products and services matched to the full range of development applications that, with consequent economies of scale, will grow the worldwide market as a whole. As ICT increasingly intersect with the MDGs and overlap with adjacent industries, and as the pace of technological innovation intensifies, the debate is now moving beyond the digital divide. In developed countries, the rush to broadband infrastructure is resulting in multi-billion dollar telecommunication equipment write-offs. In developing countries, those able to embrace knowledge, entrepreneurial skills and competitive business models via broadband networks are now reaping the rewards of the outsourcing and off shoring phenomena. Those unable to do so are falling ever further behind. The playing field is at once levelling and yet becoming more uneven.

That the ICT for Development landscape is remodelling in real time presents key challenges and opportunities to all players. Each must chart a path toward digital inclusion through unknown terrain. For major donor agencies who have been struggling to incorporate ICT into their overseas development assistance (ODA) strategies, the MDGs provide a welcome compass. After years of experimentation on ICTs in often stand-alone, frequently unsustainable pilot projects, attention is now being drawn to the need to leverage ICTs for poverty reduction strategies and the MDGs through a focus on integration, scaling and replication. From experience it is clear that ICT and technology "push" projects have generally been ill-suited to fulfilling the requirements of the MDGs. Rather, "pulling" ICTs into development projects where appropriate and relevant at an early stage – often with a mix of traditional and new media and achieved via multi-stakeholder partnerships – to achieve greater efficiency and service delivery will have far greater poverty impact.

Just how successful the shift from push to pull will be, however, will depend on a combination of full integration in national development plans and PRSPs, again at an early stage, and the prioritization of ICT in sectors with the greatest potential payback, such as income poverty reduction, youth and gender empowerment, and responding to HIV/AIDS. As mentioned earlier, the mainstreaming of ICT in these strategies is currently lacking in a majority of LDCs and needs urgent attention. In addition, many PRSPs suffer from a shortfall of donor support and are rarely ambitious enough to meet the MDG targets. There are often only weak procedural and financial links between the MDGs, the national budgets, and the levels of ODA. And in many cases PRSPs remain too top-down from national governments, with villages and cities yet to be empowered to implement much of the scaled up investment.[14]

Research has shown that in the context of ICT, maximum MDG benefits have accrued in countries that have adopted and implemented bottom-up and holistic e-strategies that are aligned with overall national development strategies, thus bringing ICT to bear on all the diverse components of national development agendas such as governance and institution building, infrastructure and access, health, education and capacity building, local content development and fostering an enabling policy and regulatory environment to stimulate competition, entrepreneurship, commerce, investment, job creation and growth. Thus, when a set of interrelated conditions are pursued in conjunction with one another, the interplay among them becomes catalytic, creating a development or MDG dynamic.[15]

In practice, any blueprint for a national e-development strategy will comprise a number of essential elements: a clear e-strategy vision championed at the highest political level; a multi-stakeholder approach to enhance results; a cross-sectoral holistic strategy; realistic priorities for e-strategy actions and programmes; simplified implementation modalities; national and international cooperation and partnerships for a prioritized and nationally-owned e-strategy; global inclusion of developing countries and ICT in ODA; ICT to facilitate regional integration and regional integration to facilitate ICT deployment; telecommunication and

---

[14] See case for MDG-based PRSPs in Investing in Development: A Practical Plan to Achieve the Millennium Development Goals", Report to the UN Secretary General, UN Millennium Project, 2005. http://www.unmillenniumproject.org
[15] See "Creating a Development Dynamic: Final Report of the Digital Opportunity Initiative", Accenture, Markle, UNDP, 2001. http://www.opt-init.org/

information technology policy cohesion, convergence and low-cost cutting edge solutions; and, an overarching focus on achieving the MDGs themselves (Figure 6).[16]

Fig.6 Mainstreaming ICTs and the MDGs - A Ten Point Bottom-Up Approach

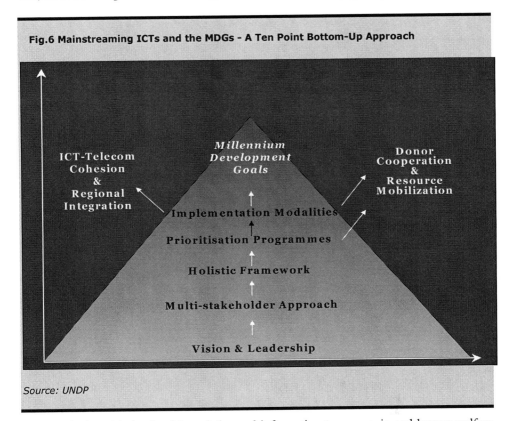

Source: UNDP

So what is the critical role of knowledge and information to economic and human welfare with respect to the MDGs? How can ICT and the MDGs practically contribute to empower stakeholders in the PRSP process, to improve the efficiency of public and private service delivery, and to enhance livelihoods? To what extent should ICT for Development priorities, policies and practices differ with respect to "off-track" versus "on-track" developing countries? While these key questions should have been posed far earlier by the development community, it is in direct response to the MDG challenge of scaling up and replicating that they are now being addressed.

The MDGs provide a robust platform whereby government, business, civil society and international organization initiatives and interventions can coalesce. Yet resistance by government and business to full acceptance of the critical role to be played by ICT in support of the MDGs must quickly be diffused by hard data on development impact and the real potential to scale up and replicate. While significant anecdotal evidence has already been amassed in this direction, major efforts are now underway to produce systematic

---

[16] See "National & Regional E-Development Strategies: A Blueprint for Action", UNDP, in *The Role of ICT in Global Development*, UN ICT Task Force, 2003. http://www.unicttaskforce.org/perl/documents.pl?id=1360 page 29

measurement criteria by the end of 2005.[17] For the moment, mainstreaming ICT for the achievement of the MDGs remains very much work in progress, and the following describes the generic development impact across the first seven MDGs.

3.1 - ICT and Poverty Eradication and Hunger (Goal I)

The multi-dimensional nature of poverty has complex causes. Apart from lack of material wealth and possessions, poor people are often deprived of basic nutritional, educational, and healthcare needs. In addition, they are denied access to knowledge and information, a primary source of economic opportunity and political empowerment, rendering them vulnerable and prey to social exclusion. Though lack of access to ICT is clearly not a primary problem of poverty compared to the basic, urgent needs of the poor like food and shelter, ICT can be seen as both an accelerating and driving force for progress as well as an outcome of human development itself.

Promoting opportunities for the poor is an essential element of poverty reduction. Consensus is building in the development community on the need to focus attention on ICT interventions that match local needs and conditions and concentrate efforts in four principal areas[18]:

i. *stimulating macroeconomic growth*, with the contribution of the ICT sector to the economy and of ICT investments to economic growth and job creation;

ii. *increasing market access, efficiency and competitiveness of the poor*, with micro-level and people-oriented interventions (for example, via the use of village payphones and knowledge centres that improve agricultural practices through access to information on crop selection, irrigation, fertilizers, and fishing and livestock conditions, thereby raising yields and reducing poverty and hunger;

iii. *improving social inclusion of isolated populations*; with the interactivity, permanent availability, reduced cost and global reach of ICT making social inclusion of poor and disadvantage groups more feasible;

iv. *facilitating political empowerment*, with improved planning in the local and PRSP processes through ICT via inclusive, informed priority setting, increasing accountability and good governance. Here, key processes that will inform MDG outcomes include institutional planning, service delivery and efficiency, and direct livelihoods impact, all enhanced by an essential empowerment filter at the local and PRSP levels (Fig 7).

---

[17] See "Youth, Poverty and Gender: ICT for Development Success Stories", GKP, 2003.
http://www.globalknowledge.org/gkps_portal/index.cfm?menuid=201&parentid=179 Forthcoming work on the development impact if ICT and the MDGs is expected from the UN Partnership for Measuring ICT for Development, the UN ICT Task Force and the World Bank Group before the end of 2005. http://measuring-ict.unctad.org
[18] See "ICT & the MDGs – A World Bank Group Perspective", WBG, 2003.

Fig.7 Key Processes and Empowerment Filter that Form MDG Outcomes

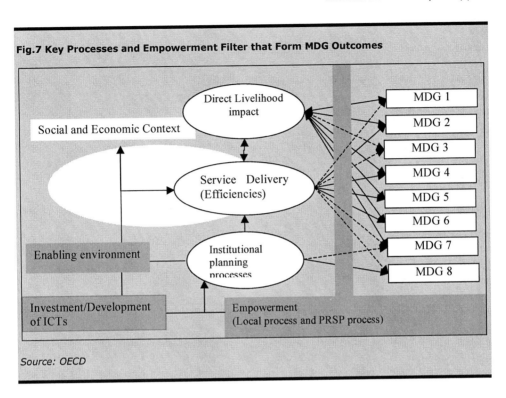

Source: OECD

One of the most compelling examples of the importance of moving from anecdotal to empirical evidence to demonstrate development impact, as well as the necessity of adopting a long term investment and partnership perspective is Bangladesh's village payphone operator, GrameenPhone. At one stage almost a cliché within the ICT for Development community as a stalwart for pro-poor business models, GrameenPhone has recently undergone a surgical re-evaluation by the OECD. While originally held back by local regulatory constraints, over-ambitious growth forecasts, and creative tensions among its multi-stakeholder partners, the venture has since taken off only as a result of openness to innovative and pro-poor business models, and long term investment commitment.[19]

Since 1997, GrameenPhone has provided some 45 000 telephones to 39 000 villages in Bangladesh, bringing access to the telephone to some 70 million people. By 2003 GrameenPhone was the largest source of foreign direct investment ($230 million) and second largest corporate taxpayer ($280 million) in the country. The Village Phone model has now been replicated in Uganda with a like degree of success, while in Bangladesh the company is now leveraging its market power both to lobby government to ease punitive tax rates to boost network investment. With its indispensable role in flood disaster relief the company has also assumed the mantle of a national public good. And with radical

---

[19] See "GrameenPhone Revisited: Investors Reach Out to the Poor", OECD DAC Network on Poverty Reduction, 2004.
http://www.oecd.org/LongAbstract/0,2546,en_2649_37409_33702523_70264_119666_1_37409,00.html

innovations such as 50c prepaid scratch cards (in contrast to conventional $10 cards), it is pioneering the stimulation of pro-poor economies of scale. In practical poverty reduction terms, a 24 percent increase in income of Bangladesh village phone owners (Figure 8, also detailing representative gains across the six other MDGs.

3.2 - ICT and Primary Education (Goal 2)

There are many hurdles to achieving the MDG target of all children receiving primary school education. Of the 680 million children of primary school age in developing countries, 115 million do not attend school, with 60 percent of these children girls and 74 percent living in South Asia and sub-Saharan Africa. ICTs can help overcome the chronic shortage of facilities and teachers in an efficient and economic manner for many countries facing budgetary constraints. UNESCO estimates that an additional 15-35 million educated and trained teachers will be needed over the next decade if all countries are to achieve the MDG of universal primary education by 2015. ICT-based distance training can overcome the shortage of primary school teachers by accelerating instruction. ICT can also supplement primary school teaching thereby helping to overcome shortages. And via the traditional ICTs of radio and television ICT could also be used to emphasise the importance of primary school attendance, particularly in areas with strong social or cultural barriers.

Based on extensive interviews in Bolivia, Ghana, India, Namibia and South Africa, the Global eSchools and Communities Initiative (GeSCI), backed by the United Nations and governments of Canada, Ireland, Sweden and Switzerland has recently identified five education building blocks with respect to key educational challenges and ICT solutions desired by schools:

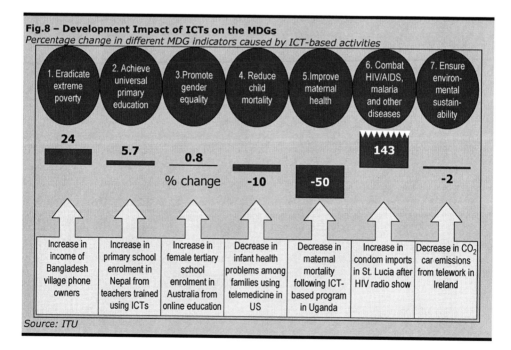

Fig.8 – Development Impact of ICTs on the MDGs
Percentage change in different MDG indicators caused by ICT-based activities

Source: ITU

i.   *teachers*, with inadequate training and ICT-based (TV or computer) teacher training;

ii. *infrastructure*, with long distance to schools in some areas and remote distance learning via ICTs;

iii. *curriculum and content*, with outdated curricula and inclusion of ICT skills in curriculum, and ineffective distribution of content for teachers and ICT-based delivery of traditional and rich content;

iv. *teaching and learning tools*, with under-equipped laboratories and insufficient tools and materials for project work and ICT-based education tools for classroom teaching and for project work by learning;

v.   *administration*, with high volume of manual administration and for teachers and principals with basic ICT applications for administration.

The GeSCI also notes that ICTs in schools also deliver enormous benefits to their local communities in employment, adult education and skills making, health, business services, communication and e-government. It is currently pioneering an end-to-end e-School system with developing country and private sector partners that is claimed to reduce costs by a factor of eight. Based on the 2.5 million schools in the developing world, it is estimated governments spend approximately $250-300 billion on education annually, or about $100 000 per school. ICT spending in developing countries is about $150-200 billion per year, compared to $6-8 billion needed to deliver ICT solutions to all schools.

3.3 - ICT and Gender Equality (Goal 3)

The MDG on gender equality has the specific target to "eliminate gender disparity in primary and secondary education preferably by 2005 and in all levels of education no later than 2015". It is also widely recognized that gender equality is a critical factor for the achievement of all the MDGs. As ICTs represent a global phenomenon with large potential impact on economic and social realities, and if gender equality is central to the achievement of the MDGs, it is then critical to ensure that women and men benefit equally from the opportunities ICTs can provide. Women around the world face a complex web of obstacles in their access and use of ICTs, ranging from literacy and education, to language, time, income and socio-cultural norms. However, ICTs can be used to influence public opinion on gender equality, increase economic opportunities, improve women's education, create opportunities for women as educators and activists, and enhance opportunities for networking and organizing for gender equality, and for participation in political processes. For example, "womenaction.org" was a global initiative connecting hundreds of networks of women's organizations, to strengthen women's participation in the five-year review of the Beijing Platform for Action.

ICTs can promote gender equality by providing online opportunities that are not always available in the "off-line" world, by providing virtual spaces and linkages that favour small-scale entrepreneurship, a sector where women are usually more numerous. ICTs have the potential to assist poor women to improve the economic return of their traditional activities, by providing information and training on methodologies to improve their productivity and their quality of life. Using methods such as the Internet, mobile telephony, satellite based radio, CD-ROMs and distance learning, women can share valuable knowledge, exchange market information and be exposed to new educational opportunities. For example, ICT can help women entrepreneurs, even at grassroots level, to reduce transaction costs, increase market coverage, and even expand across borders. In Guyana, a women weavers' cooperative has used the Internet to market and sell hand-crafted hammocks, resulting in a very high income for local standards. The Self-Employed Women's Association (SEWA) of India, that employs a mix of mobile village phones, Internet, satellites and television ICTs to promote their artisan handicraft network, comprises 5000 women who have used their life savings to access village mobile phones for garnering market information.

ICT can also offer new opportunities for women to be employed in innovative and non-traditional sectors, such as e-commerce and other ICT-enabled businesses, such as marketing of telecommunications and Internet services. For example, in Ghana, a large number of women-owned businesses sell fax, e-mail and telephone services to a largely female clientele, due to the fact that many women in the country are small entrepreneurs and traders.

In education, women's traditional roles as mothers and providers of care, with responsibility for child-care, food and other household tasks, along with context-specific cultural and economic constraints, have hindered girls' access to the formal education system. In some cases, female school enrolment declines after childbearing age. ICT can help overcome some of the social and cultural barriers to girls and women's education through the application of distance learning. Likewise, women have outnumbered men in ICT-based training for teachers via distance learning in many countries. In this context, ensuring that girls and women are properly included and encouraged to participate in formal ICT education programmes has enormous potential for gender equality in the labour market, particularly in a global context where the IT sector has the greatest potential for job creation globally. For example, women are already active as software developers in many emerging markets for software development for export, and many employment opportunities exist in the field of network administration and maintenance, as well as in IT education and training, given the traditionally high representation of women in the education sector in many countries.

The design of gender-sensitive ICT policies and education policies is key to ensure that ICT be a driver for gender equality. In terms if ICT policies, it is widely recognized that the social aspects of ICT should be included in policy-making processes, and important gender implications are embedded in technical policy choices in network architecture and deployment, pricing and tariffs issues. As for education policies, women's globally lower levels of literacy and education are one of the most powerful barriers for women's full access to ICTs. To address this, technology could be integrated into girls' education and women's literacy programmes, and gender balance should be encouraged in science and technology higher education programmes.

3.4 - ICT and Health (Goals 4, 5 and 6)

The influence of ICT on healthcare in developing countries has already been immense. In the field of prevention and treatment for HIV/AIDS and other infectious and communicable diseases, however, it has barely scratched the surface. ICT has enabled healthcare workers to perform remote consultation and diagnosis, access medical information and coordinate research activities more effectively in the past two decades than in the history of medicine. Not only is ICT an essential component in providing remote healthcare services, storing and disseminating healthcare information, and research, training and networking of and for health workers. Through both traditional (radio, TV, video, CD) and new (wireless, Internet) ICT media, ICT can also provide an effective and cost-effective channel for the distribution of healthcare and disease prevention information to the general public.

The role of ICT in achieving health-related MDGs is indispensable. ICT are an invaluable tool for both healthcare workers and the international development community for their combined efforts in the reduction of child mortality (Goal 4), improvement of maternal health (Goal5), and combating HIV/AIDS, malaria and other diseases (Goal 6). Diseases of childhood accounted for nine percent of children not living to see their third birthday. ICT can be used by healthcare workers to establish databases to track vaccination programmes, to coordinate antibiotic shipments and to inform communities of medical services that can reduce child mortality. Maternal death is the leading cause of death for women of reproductive age in the developing world. ICT can critically reduce the incidence of maternal death by facilitating access to information and healthcare services.

In the battle against the HIV/AIDS pandemic, ICT can enhance disease monitoring and management, drug distribution systems (for generic anti-retroviral drugs), training of care givers, patient education and monitoring and facilitation of the development of support networks for people living withy HIV/AIDS and their care givers. Yet the potential to enhance HIV/AIDS response is yet to be fully leveraged in developing countries most affected by the crisis. In many cases, these countries are lacking in both the infrastructure and human capacity (further weakened by the toll taken by brain drain and HIV/AIDS) required to implement comprehensive ICT strategies that could add real value to prevention, treatment and policy support. In addition, the potential of ICT as a cross-cutting tool spanning all the MDGs that can add value in addressing the pandemic is not widely recognised.

A number of ICT initiatives against HIV/AIDS are currently underway, at varying levels of sophistication, scale and range. These initiatives encompass networks aimed at enhancing access to knowledge on HIV/AIDS treatments to the use of geographic information systems (GIS) to map the spread of the disease in relation to socio-economic variables and treatment. In some cases, clinical information infrastructure systems and simpler mechanisms have been used to address the logistics of distribution and monitor the use of essential drugs. Virtual forums and lists have facilitated the discussion of access, treatment and enhanced advocacy and awareness raising. Evaluations of effectiveness, identification of good practices and mechanisms to scale productive intervention and systems is yet to happen. Further, to the extent that HIV/AIDS response needs to be cross-sectoral to address the pandemic's multiple dimensions, a more widespread coordination and strategic deployment of ICT that create new synergies and enhance overall response effectiveness is critically overdue.

3.5 - ICT and Environment (Goal 7)

This MDG proposes integrating the principles of sustainable development into country policies to reverse the loss of environmental resources, halving the proportion of people without access to safe drinking water and achieving a significant improvement in the lives of slum dwellers. Managing and protecting the environment contributes to improving human health conditions, sustaining agriculture and other primary production sectors, as well as reducing risks of natural disasters such as flood, mudslide and wildfire.

The effects of ICT on sustaining the environment are multidimensional. ICT enables greater participation by the population in activities to protect the environment through networking and information exchange. ICT also provides researchers with critical tools for the observation, simulation and analysis of environmental processes. Environmentally friendly work habits are also increasingly the cultural norm in many countries promoted through ICT in areas such as reduction of paper consumption and facilitating telecommuting; raising awareness of the environment through knowledge sharing; facilitating environmental monitoring and associated resource management and risk mitigation; enables greater environmental sustainability in other industries, commercial and agricultural sectors; and improves communications and developing and enforcing policies.

ICT plays a key role in environmental management in activities ranging from optimising clean production methods to decision making. Spatial information is information related to a particular geographical location or area. It allows analysts to view the distribution of income across a country as a grid in order to target areas for action, understand demographic trends, and monitor progress. Spatial information collected by satellite or airborne remote sensing can be used to understand the capability of the land to support economic activity and water use efficiency. This information can help ensure that natural resources are used efficiently and sustainably.

New technologies are being developed that provide more accurate and timely estimation of risk. Spatial information about fire, rainfall, wind, and salinity may help countries identify and estimate risk more accurately.

A great deal of information is currently available to developing countries for use in making policy decisions. Some of this information (such as that obtained from satellites) is not released. Often the systems or skills needed to manage the data are lacking. Capacity building and information donation or exchange would address this issue.

4. ICT and the MDGs – Leadership as Partnership

For champions of ICT for Development, a key objective in recent years has been to elevate networking into the mainstream of development dimensions as agreed by generalists. This has involved articulating the role of networking in the development portfolio, attempting to achieve the right balance of analytical and qualitative argument, and linking into the existing lexicon of development in the areas of poverty, health, education, gender and environment. However, rather than taking the approach to systematically "problematise" ICT in development policy and programmes, there has been a tendency among practitioners to depict ICT almost as a "black-box" solution, and a solution situated within a "win-win" world of common interests between developed and developing countries.

The MDG campaign offers the possibility not only to correct this fallacy but also to contextualise the unresolved challenges and untapped opportunities within the ICT for Development field. Moreover, Goal 8 "Develop a global partnership for development" and Target 18 "In cooperation with the private sector, make available the benefits of new technologies, especially information and communication" suggest a powerful framework to both resolve those challenges and realize those opportunities. This is of critical importance to LDCs because a shift in emphasis away from the unfulfilled and unrealistic expectations of technology leapfrog espoused by ICT proponents throughout the 1980s and 1990s is urgently required if accelerated progress is to be made.

It is important to recall that the great ICT success stories of the Celtic and Asian tiger economies during the above period were built on a long term political vision of market-based incentives backed by strategic investment in infrastructure and human capacity way beyond the reach of any heavily indebted LDC. At the core of the ICT and MDG debate is the question whether or not ICT can contribute to improving efficiency in delivering the MDGs, and hence accelerating the achievement of development targets. This is an essential corrective to the traditional over-emphasis on the creation of a domestic and export-oriented ICT sector, so quickly exposed in the poorest countries to global volatility and competition.

Once ICT for Development policies and programmes are embedded within the PRSP process, even subordinated in the service of the MDGs, many unresolved challenges and untapped opportunities are thrown into relief: policy and regulatory frameworks for ICT investment that achieve the right balance between investment promotion and meeting the needs of low-income customers; profitable business models that engage the private sector in the local delivery of affordable ICTs to rural and urban areas; coordination and cooperation between government, business, civil society and international organization initiatives; and, financing mechanisms that realistically and effectively address the funding deficit in bridging the digital divide. By setting clear development priorities resource allocation to the kind of multi-stakeholder ICT partnerships needed to achieve the MDGs can be pressed far more robustly.

Similarly, the massive scaling up and low-cost delivery of public and private services to the world's poorest citizens inherent in the MDGs also focuses attention on innovative and breakthrough approaches to ICT delivery that exploit the enormous variety of communication technologies. These approaches must allow access to information that is most relevant to people's multi-dimensional livelihoods. It requires forms of ICT transactions that achieve the optimal division of risk between the public and private sectors, and that afford the necessary flexibility for operators to deliver pro-poor services over time. It recognises the importance to livelihood security of social capital, identifying those ICTs that contribute most to building this asset. And it implies knowledge and information delivery critical to sustainable livelihoods that reach the right people at the right time at the right price.

4.1 - Untapped Technologies

Phenomenal growth has been achieved by developing countries in the global ICT sector over the past decade. From 1992 to 2002, the ITU estimates that the developing countries' share of the world's fixed telephones grew from 21% to 45%, mobile phones from 12% to 46%, PC users from 10% to 27% and, most impressively, Internet users from 3% to 34% (Figure 9). Mobile networks have been growing faster in LDCs than elsewhere in the world with an estimated 80% of the planet's population now covered by wireless access. Yet coverage is not usage with still only one telephone per 100 people in LDCs, and 20% of the world's population with no ICT access at all. In this regard, breakthrough technologies are emerging in four key areas to address this deficit that have particular significance for the MDGs:[20]

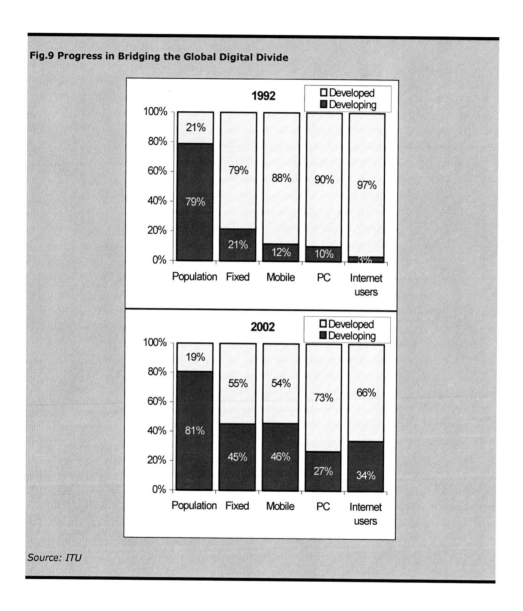

Fig.9 Progress in Bridging the Global Digital Divide

Source: ITU

---

[20] See "The Future of Information and Communication Technologies for Development", Braga, Daly, Sareen, Development Gateway Foundation, 2003.
http://www.developmentgateway.org/download/221030/Future_ICT.pdf

Low-cost devices – These encompass computers, PDAs, terminals, peripherals, routers, communications devices, and embedded software. In theory there is no limit to how cheap computer and communication devices can become. Cellular telephones have already assumed the status of commodity consumer electronic items with pre-paid cards having created a truly mass market and no technical reason today why such cards could not be calibrated in cents rather than dollars for even greater diffusion. Computer costs will also continue to fall precipitously due to the basic laws of physics, while several pioneer projects to deliver the people or volks-computer for developing countries are underway.

As mobile and computing technologies converge progress will accelerate, but the key challenge for low-cost devices will be building profitable business models that work in the emerging rural markets they target. The target market is enormous but unstructured and needs further study along the lines of the GrameenPhone micro-financing partnership model and the use of pre-paid approaches for the creation of robust business plans. Remaining challenges will be to see how cheap devices can become, whether major manufacturers will be willing to produce and sell low-cost devices of shared design, or whether assembly and final checking of these devices could, for example, be converted into a business for NGOs and service-oriented SMEs.

Low-cost software – This encompasses operating systems, utilities, and development platforms. Proprietary operating systems and applications have until now mainly been priced for developed-world market conditions. The advent of "free" and "open source" software has not only captured the imagination of many developing countries, with the promise of low costs and the freedom to modify and adapt software to their local context with linguistic customization, but expanded competition and choice. The potential to adapt intellectual property rights approaches to contribute to the development agenda, as in the case of provisioning for HIV/AIDS anti-retroviral drugs, has had important implications for the MDGs. Yet both open software and nascent social licensing schemes are at a relatively early stage of development and in reality very rarely come entirely free.

Social licensing schemes for cheap or free software programmes for healthcare, education and government offered by vendors can facilitate lock-in, while open source solutions though removing source code IPR, in the spirit of early Internet software pioneers, can often involve significant development costs where capacities are limited. Again the potential market in developing countries is huge. Remaining challenges will include investigating licensing scheme for software targeting the needs and conditions of social entrepreneurs, determining how cheap software could become in such schemes, and evaluating which requirements will have to be satisfied by local governments and NGOs in order to benefit from such schemes.

Wireless solutions – These include satellite-based systems and terrestrial wireless not only for "last mile" but also for back-haul and rural connectivity. The high cost of equipment and licences has traditionally restricted fixed and cellular telecommunication access to densely populated areas in developing countries. The critical factors of affordability, ease of deployment, and appropriate business models in rural areas has increasingly favoured satellite and terrestrial wireless networks in recent years. At the time, the implosion of the low-earth orbit satellite industry at the end of the 1990s was of particular concern to developing countries because of the promised of cheap and universal access from these global systems. In reality, the near-ubiquitous spread of mobile telephones during this period closed the window of opportunity for the small and big LEOs, and expectations for rural satellite provision have since somewhat diminished.

Wireless Fidelity (WiFi) and WiMax technologies are increasingly being seen as the most appropriate solution for rural connectivity due to their maturity, affordability and pervasiveness and the potential to leapfrog.[21] The "de-licensing awareness" among developing country governments of its potential, the backing of major semiconductor manufacturers, and its attractiveness to top telecommunication operators as a less expensive infrastructure alternative may well make it the *de facto* technology of choice as the "first mile" infrastructure for digital inclusion and rural communications for both voice and data in LDCs. More work needs to be done to refine WiFi for ease of deployment while at the same time pursuing business models around WiFi Internet Service Providers in rural areas.

Content and Applications – These include local Internet content, local content in traditional media, local content in analogue form and its digitalization, ICT applications in major areas such as health education and government, and new strategic technologies such as GIS and GPS. The absence of content in local languages is a key limiting factor in the spread of the benefits of ICT to marginalized communities. This can be ameliorated in the use of the Universal Network Language which allows storage on the Internet of domain-specific information in a particular language in its semantic form. Technological advances are now demonstrating access to domain specific information from a different language than that in which it was originally stored. This is enabled by new search technology that allows the querying of information from these semantic representations in different languages.

In many cases, the bandwidth of content must be changed to meet the needs of people in developing countries. In the context of the MDGs and low income markets, inter-modal linkages become much more relevant. Integration of the Internet with community radio and mechanisms to facilitate e-mail dissemination of web content is some of the relevant areas for future research. Overriding questions concern how digital content can become an industry in developing countries, investigation of the requirements for electronic distribution at cost, which technology packages can be offered under social licensing schemes on a commercial basis, which packages can be offered under "copyleft" schemes, which open technology initiatives should be promoted, and how all of these can succeed in developing countries.

None of these breakthrough technologies can exist in a vacuum, and require enlightened if not radical policy and practice adjustment where policy and practice development has

---

[21] See "Birth of Broadband", ITU, 2003.

proven insufficient, or resulted in market failures. A range of programmes may be appropriate here including; support for emerging technologies like WiFi and voice over Internet Protocol (VoIP); support for increased international connectivity; support for low-user programmes such as very cheap cellular handsets; seed-corn finance for application service providers, and other small, niche ventures with low capital needs; programmes that address specific capability gaps such as IP configuration and html creation. In all these cases the potential for multi-stakeholder partnerships to scale up and replicate interventions is compelling.

4.2 - Unique Multi-Stakeholder Partnerships

Extensive research has been undertaken by the Digital Opportunity Initiative and the Overseas Development Institute/Foundation for Development Cooperation/Global Knowledge Partnership in the area of ICT for Development multi-stakeholders partnerships (MSPs).[22] Strategic alliances between government, business, civil society and international organizations are a growing feature of both developed and emerging economies. Such multi-stakeholder partnerships are necessary because it is increasingly clear that no one sector in society can deliver the complexities of sustainable human development alone. MSPs are alliances between parties drawn from government, business, civil society and international organizations that strategically aggregate the resources and competencies of each to resolve the key challenges of ICT as an enabler of development, and which are founded on principles of shared risk, cost and mutual benefit.

Most experts concede that the MDGs can be attained if and only if ambitious yet realistic nationally-determined priorities and initiatives are also promoted and advocated at the global level. And these priorities and initiatives must embed growth models based on sustainability, self-replication and multi-stakeholder partnerships, as evidenced in Internet-based and mobile-based efforts today. In the context of MSPs, the challenge of achieving greater ICT penetration and access in the developing world, and of the subsequent utilisation of this access to reduce poverty and contribute to the MDGs, are manifold. They include: ineffectiveness in the regulatory regime to attract new investment; public-private ICT transactions that fail to deliver affordable ICT solution; unprofitable business models for rural ICT access; ICT strategies that fail to exploit the diversity of technologies on offer; and, content that is irrelevant to the livelihood priorities of poor communities.

Paramount to success is the importance of taking a strategic approach to developing design parameters for a partnership. This will necessarily involve: finding partners able to contribute the necessary 'mix' of resources and competencies, in particular to ensure the long-term sustainability of ICT interventions; the importance of business partners understanding their commercial case for entering the partnership, be that reputation, local knowledge, testing of new products and services, or viable financial rates of return; and, recognition by the public sector that to reach poor communities living in remote locations there may be a need for subsidies for private investors and/or concessional rates for network access (Figure10).

---

[22] See "Creating a Development Dynamic - Final Report of the Digital Opportunity Initiative", Accenture, Markle Foundation, UNDP, 2001, http://www.ot-init.org/ and "Multi-Stakeholder Partnerships", ODI & FDC for GKP, 2003. http://www.globalknowledge.org/gkps_portal/index.cfm?menuid=178&parentid=179

Based on a series of case studies, and drawing from the "development dynamic" model proposed by the Digital Opportunity Initiative, ODI/FDC/GKP have identified several priority areas for further research and experimentation. These comprise: whether GrameenPhone-type partnership business models, for example, are replicable for other businesses interested in tapping into the low-income consumer market in developing countries; whether the engagement of community groups and development NGOs in the design of regulatory frameworks for public-private-partnership-based ICT access in remote rural areas might result in more balance in the competitive bidding of operators between achieving least cost (and/or subsidy) and livelihood-driven performance; and, what the design parameters of partnership projects should be when formulated in part for ICT companies to test the financial viability of marketing or product/service development targeted at low-income consumers.

There is, of course, one business model that already encompasses and exemplifies the unique characteristics of ICT, the MDGs and MSPs – that of the Internet. The deployment of Internet services on a national scale is one of the most challenging tasks imaginable in a developing country. Perhaps nothing today is richer in challenges (and rewards) than the proper planning and implementation of Internet services in a developing nation, because it will require re-thinking about all other infrastructural facilities, from transport to telecommunications. At one level, it requires the combined use of a whole range of communications infrastructure such as satellites, fibre optics, copper cable, and microwave radio links, which in turn strongly depend on the availability of other types of infrastructure, such as power lines, gas pipes, and roads.

At another level, complex partnerships involving governments, large companies and small sized enterprises have to be established in order to make Internet access available everywhere. Similarly, the legal framework which has to be put in place is a moving target changing everyday. Not only can Internet services provide the most compelling model of technological change and organizational learning applicable to other areas through this kind of integration of infrastructures, but the *viral* growth, global governance and citizen empowerment models heralded by the Internet have direct relevance to the achievement of the MDGs and deserve in-depth consideration.

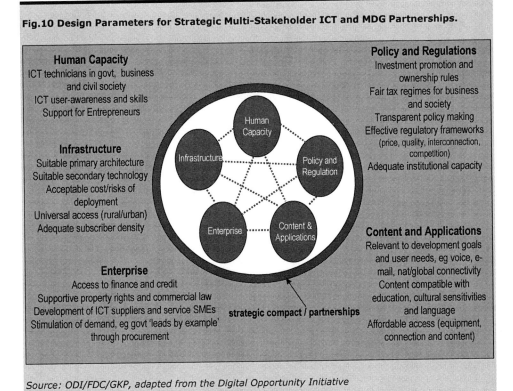

Fig.10 Design Parameters for Strategic Multi-Stakeholder ICT and MDG Partnerships.

Human Capacity
ICT technicians in govt, business and civil society
ICT user-awareness and skills
Support for Entrepreneurs

Infrastructure
Suitable primary architecture
Suitable secondary technology
Acceptable cost/risks of deployment
Universal access (rural/urban)
Adequate subscriber density

Enterprise
Access to finance and credit
Supportive property rights and commercial law
Development of ICT suppliers and service SMEs
Stimulation of demand, eg govt 'leads by example' through procurement

Policy and Regulations
Investment promotion and ownership rules
Fair tax regimes for business and society
Transparent policy making
Effective regulatory frameworks (price, quality, interconnection, competition)
Adequate institutional capacity

Content and Applications
Relevant to development goals and user needs, eg voice, e-mail, nat/global connectivity
Content compatible with education, cultural sensitivities and language
Affordable access (equipment, connection and content)

strategic compact / partnerships

Source: ODI/FDC/GKP, adapted from the Digital Opportunity Initiative

4.3 – Leadership and Partnership Imperatives

The logic of the networked economy and society naturally inclines toward inclusion rather than exclusion. Yet the international system has over the past two decades of the digital network revolution been unable to deliver on promises to or expectations from the developing world on digital inclusion. ICT for Development is a case of unfinished business, and it has become increasingly clear that this endemic failure is derived from the fact that different types of organizations in society view the challenge in different ways. Interestingly, recent research into partnerships in the water and sanitation sector identifies clear comparative advantages between the business, public sector and civil society sectors. Taken with the Digital Opportunity Initiative Development Dynamic framework, this research can help summarise the complementarity of core competencies between the various key stakeholders (Figure 11).[23]

---

[23] See ODI/FDC/GKP above.

Fig.11 Roles, Responsibilities and Core Complementary Competencies for ICT and MDG Partners

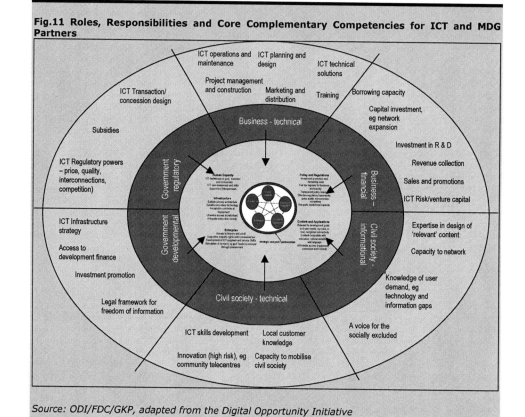

Source: ODI/FDC/GKP, adapted from the Digital Opportunity Initiative

However, to take full advantage of these relative strengths demands vision and leadership in different segments of society, and the need for clear and renewed definition of roles and responsibilities among government, business, civil society, academia and international organizations. For national governments, bridging the digital needs to be part and parcel of every developing country's national agenda. Leaderships is needed in active regulatory support for the deployment of breakthrough wireless solutions and de-licensing of spectrum should be a high priority. Sustained funding for digital divide research and development projects and pilots is a prerequisite. And, leadership by example is essential in areas that can employ ICT reengineer the public sector such as e-government.

For business, leadership is needed in the allocation of investment in financial, human and organizational resources in ICT. It requires bringing ICT technologies that are relevant to the needs of poor countries and poor people to market. It involves increasing corporate social responsibility budgets for technology-based efforts and investment in research and development efforts on technology related to addressing the digital divide. For the technological and academic community, researchers will be needed to step forward and most specifically in developing countries. The community needs leaders to radically improve the response of educational systems in developing countries to the challenge of the information revolution. And the community should lead in the development of content needed in developing countries and the localization of that content.

For civil society, leadership is needed in leveraging the process of transforming ICT technology into tools for transparency, with emphasis on benefits to the poor. It means creating sustainable civil society mechanisms for ICT innovation and development by further engaging grass-roots communities in the delivery of these solutions. It means facilitating the spread of social licensing and open content software solutions and ICT training tailored to the needs of poor communities. And it involves experimenting with innovative mechanisms to magnify the reach of the Internet coupling it with community radio and other conventional media.

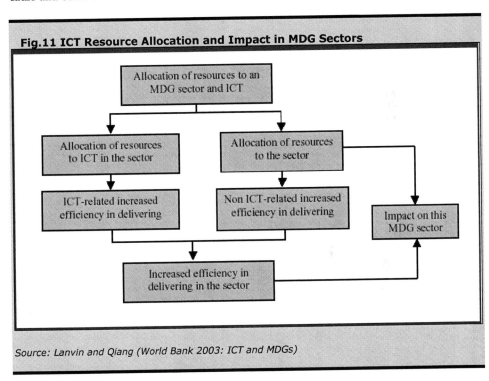

Fig.11 ICT Resource Allocation and Impact in MDG Sectors

Source: Lanvin and Qiang (World Bank 2003: ICT and MDGs)

For multilateral institutions and international agencies, leadership in funding is needed to play a catalytic role in living research projects, pilots to scale deployment, continued and renewed support in mobilizing resources for roll-out of ICT infrastructure, and continued support for applications of ICT in all sectors. The United Nations system, in particular, must as one and for the first time embrace elements of a coherent approach comprising: MDG-focussed e-strategies and their integration in national development strategies; policy and regulatory reform; MSPs; pro-poor business models; connectivity, capacity building and content; participation in ICT policy governance mechanisms; and, financial mechanisms.

Ultimately, in order to reach the targets set by the MDGs, countries can either increase the resources allocated to these objectives, or increase the efficiency with which available resources are used. At the core of the ICT and MDG debate is the question whether or not ICT can contribute to improving the efficiency in delivering the MDGs and hence accelerating the achievement of development targets (Figure 12).[24] With vision and leaderships from all relevant players in the ICT community - whether government, business, civil society, academia or international organizations – the choice is nothing less than to transform the uncertainty of this question into a vibrant and living imperative.

5. ICT and the MDGs – The Way Ahead

One of the definitions of a mature technology is that it becomes invisible to the eye and mind until some catastrophic failure strikes. Today, ICT are some way from exhibiting the simple characteristics of a water, gas or electricity utility or grid. Like ICT, development is in a state of chaotic transition where the environment is ever more challenging and complex. The sheer pace of ICT progress and innovation matches the sheer scale of the task of achieving the MDGs. Similarly, the delicate art and science of multi-stakeholder partnership, so crucial in leveraging ICT in support of the MDGs, is at a very early stage of maturation. For this reason this report has attempted to remain somewhat neutral in its approach both technologically and bureaucratically. It is far too soon to pick winners or losers in the ICT and MDG stakes.

What the report has tried to demonstrate is that the unique characteristics of ICT, the MDGs, and MSPs, taken together and working in tandem, represent a new and powerful dynamic in the promotion of sustainable human development and poverty eradication. The report errs on the side of the potential and the positive aspects of ICT for Development without losing sight of the fact that there is a long way to go. But the emerging consensus is that ICT for Development policies and programmes must be understood as subordinate to, and in the service of, the MDGs. The measurement of success for ICT policies and programmes is not an increase in basic access to ICTs, not mere statistics, but the impact of those ICTs on progress toward the achievement of the MDGs.

The common denominators that bind ICT, the MDGs and MSPs look to the future and not the past. As mentioned earlier, the missing links in the Internet and ICT value chain correspond to the missing links in the value chain of the MDGs and the broader development agenda. The digital divide between rich and poor countries is an effect not a cause. It is largely a reflection of deeper more fundamental divides in economic opportunity, health, education and empowerment. But if ICT, the MDGs and MSPs are on the same trajectory, there is an increasingly urgent need for a high-level, strategic framework for the mainstreaming of ICT for Development for the achievement of the MDGs.

While the MDGs set out goals and targets relating to ICTs, they fail to specify global deadlines and targets, and those laid out in the Plan of Action of the Geneva phase of the WSIS are either too vague, too infrastructure-based or actually close to being achieved.[25] In theory, most of the world's population will soon have access to ICTs. In practice, their ability to use them will depend on knowledge and affordability. The MS+5 and the second phase of the WSIS come at a something of a make or break point in time for ICT for

[24] See WBG above. http://info.worldbank.org/ict/assets/docs/mdg_Complete.pdf
[25] See "ICTs and the Millennium Development Goals", Chapter 4, World Telecommunications Development Report 2003, ITU.

Development and the MDGs, where decisions will have profound long-term impact on whether effective mainstreaming actually occurs or not.

This time, whatever emerges from these Summits must be backed up by concrete and realistic financial commitments that draw from complementary local resources, bilateral donors, multilateral donors and private investment. All parties must take responsibility to make realistic commitments and deliver on them. Given the great challenge of the MDGs and the resource constraints that are likely to continue even under the most optimistic growth scenarios, particularly in ODA, more attention must be paid to maximising synergies among existing resources and using aid strategically as a catalyst for private investment.[26] With evidence of *impact* in place, it will then be possible to *prioritise* in taking the *risk* to *innovate* and *invest* in new *global initiatives and partnerships* for ICT and the MDGs toward 2015.

5.1 - Beyond the Digital Divide

ICT for Development is at a turning point and a shock is needed to the system. Fragmented and piecemeal efforts to mainstream ICT for the achievement of the MDGs must crystallize and coalesce into a common effort with shared objectives. The stakes could not be higher. Failure to urgently and meaningfully exploit the available means to bridge the digital divide may consign many developing countries, particularly LDCs, to harmful and even permanent exclusion from the network revolution. With the strategic, intensive, widespread and innovative use of ICTs in development policies and programmes, the ambitious agenda of the MDGs becomes much more possible to realize. Without this laser-like focus and vision, scaleable implementation of the MDGs in many instances may well be impossible.

The planned MS+5 and the second phase of the in September and November 2005 respectively, mark the convergence of these parallel global MDG and ICT initiatives. A unique and virtuous opportunity therefore exists to galvanise political will and action so that, in harness with ICT, the MDGs can meet the criteria for framing the desired objectives of government, business, civil society and international organizations in the common cause of poverty eradication, sustainable human development and good governance.

The innovative and breakthrough elements of the ICT and Internet value chain not only mirror the missing links in the development value chain, but also impinge on precisely the areas of difficulty and contention faced by the MDGs in meeting the 2015 agenda: namely, intellectual property rights; integration of infrastructure; youth and gender empowerment; and, viral growth models for very large scale projects and initiatives. Most experts concede that the MDGs can be attained if and only if ambitious yet realistic nationally-determined priorities and initiatives are also promoted and advocated at the global level. And these globally supported goals and initiatives must embed growth models based on just the kind of sustainable, self-replicating and multi-stakeholder business models and partnerships as evidenced in Internet-based efforts today.

The fact that unique characteristics of ICT if conceived as means and not ends can, in theory, act as powerful development enable does not mean that it will necessarily do so. Perennial cross-sector complexities and issues must be overcome within existing approaches

---

[26] See OECD above.

to ICT for Development. Specifically: full demonstration of development impact; integration and prioritization within national development and poverty reduction programmes; policy realignment on basic infrastructure deployment; improved government and donor coordination and cooperation; increased private sector engagement; and, enhanced mechanisms for resource mobilization.

Of all the MDG targets it can be said that ICT has made the most rapid progress to date and is "on-track", although progress has been slower as regards application to deliver on the other development goals . Yet Goal 8 also suggests a powerful strategic framework for global partnerships to address the unresolved challenges and untapped opportunities of ICT for Development, a framework to get from here to there that must be exploited in 2005.

5.2 – Scaling Innovation, Scaling Investment

So what are the next steps for scaling up innovation and investment for ICTs and the MDGs? A prerequisite will be the recognition of national and regional differences and needs and to prioritize action and implementation accordingly. In examining the context for ICT deployment in sub-Saharan Africa and low income Asian countries, the most recent study on up-scaling found significant difference. "The governance situation is difficult in a number of African countries, with implications for the enabling environment, including that for ICT. The spread of ICT and capacities to use are somewhat dependent on literacy levels. In Asia over 70% of the countries have a literacy rate of more than 80%, whereas 45% of the countries in Africa have a literacy rate below 80%. The impact and use of ICT is dependent on the extent and affordability of access, Access to ICT, as measured with the digital access index, is lower in Africa, where over 90% of the countries have low access, whereas in Asia over 56% have medium access."[27]

The importance of the establishment of basic innovation systems leading to advanced innovation systems in developing countries must also be recognized and prioritized by donors and countries themselves. Here, platform technologies will be key, infrastructure will be the foundation, investment in science and technology and education needs to increase, and the role of universities change, and governments need to promote business activities in science, technology and innovation.[28] How do innovation systems relate ICTs ands the MDGs? One of ten recommendations of the report of Millennium Project to the UN Secretary General states: "International donors should mobilize support for global scientific research and development to address special needs of the poor in areas of health, agriculture, natural resource and environmental management, energy, and climate. We estimate the total need to rise to approximately $7 billion a year by 2015."

As mentioned previously, establishing an enabling environment for the scaling up of pro-poor ICT policies and practices is also an essential prerequisite. Mainstreaming ICTs in the

---

[27] See "Up-Scaling Pro-Poor ICT-Policies and Practices: A Review of Experience with Emphasis on Low Income Countries in Asia and Africa", Gerster and Zimmermann, SDC/Gerster Consulting, 2005
http://www.gersterconsulting.ch/docs/Upscaling_ProPoor_ICTPolicies_Practices.pdf

[28] See "Innovation: Applying Knowledge in Development", UN Millennium Project Task Force on Science, Technology, and Innovation, 2005

policy and regulatory environment to facilitate pro-poor service deliver and diffusion requires a number of key elements. Competition in ICT infrastructure provision including the last mile must be matched by investment in service development for local content with cost effective and locally adapted software. Critically, mainstreaming ICTs in the PRSPs and related poverty strategies is a central issue if scalability, synergies across sectors and support for more downstream and grassroots, as well as pull rather than push, projects is to be achieved.

Clearly, scaling up of ICT deployment for the achievement of the MDGs will require additional investment and resource mobilization. Here the case will have to be made that mainstreaming ICTs still pays off even when budgets are stagnant or shrinking. But all possible means available must be employed in moving forward. That will include an increase in seed corn ODA financing for technology pull as well as technology push projects, and a similar change in thinking for increased infrastructure financing particularly in landlocked, and small island states and LDCs. Aggregation of resource mobilization must also necessarily be pursued via global coalitions, south-south partnerships and exchanges, and at the local level building on the complementary roles of government, business and civil society through multi-stakeholder arrangements.

Looking ahead, many of the key questions now being discussed on scaling innovation and investment of ICTs for the achievement of the MDGs are the same questions being asked by government, business, and civil society. How to mainstream ICTs in national poverty reduction strategies? How to enhance income generation by the poor through ICTs? How to scale up formal and informal education of the poor by the use of ICTs? What pro-poor ICT regulations and policies, including free or open software, are required for scaling up ICT for poverty reduction? However, the next and vital step will be to candidly pose those questions which have so far been conveniently avoided, namely: 1) how should ICT innovation and investment henceforth be pursued from the policy and practice perspective of a global public good, and 2) for every dollar invested in ICT, under established enabling conditions, what is the actual dollar multiplier return for economic and social development outcomes - one, five dollars, a hundred, more?

5.3 – The Future is Open

In conclusion, the year 2005 will mark an historic milestone as the global population of Internet users reaches 1 billion people, with the majority of those users for the first time residing in developing countries.[29] Along with the now near 2 billion users of mobile telephony, this staggering growth can form the platform for the future scaling up of innovation and investment in ICT for Development. At the same time it is essential to recognize that the network revolution, still barely 20 years old, has entered a radically altered and uncharted landscape in the post-9/11 world. National security will not ultimately be the answer to every question but the significance of networks, and increasingly broadband networks, to national security has profound and inescapable implications for the future direction of domestic and geopolitical policy decision making.

In future, governments will be hard pressed to countenance the chaos of the creative telecommunications market destruction that characterized the 1990s regulatory landscape.

---

[29] See "Worldwide Internet Users will Top 1 Billion in 2005", Computer Industry ALmana, 2004.

This is now happening *de facto* in the United States with market consolidation. The trend is likely to be repeated in Russia, Korea, Japan, and Europe. Likewise, the economic and social import of networks is leading to a shift in standardization philosophy from the marketplace to national self-interest. Meanwhile, a remarkable consensus is building where every nation is becoming to believe that the real priority is maximizing the scope and scale of networks for one hundred percent of the people and one hundred percent of the geography one hundred percent of the time – the debate is quickly shifting from one centered on issues of market liberalization to how best this priority can be achieved through public and private innovation and investment.

That said, many of the fundamental questions facing the future of networking remain open. While it is clear that with the onset of broadband the United States will never again dominate the Internet as is did throughout the 1990s, and that the networked economy and society will be a vital shared interest for every country including developing countries, the future of Internet Governance, for example, is still largely unknown territory. One of the chief architects of the 1990s chaotic destruction believe the only certainty is that the future will be open and "openness" – to content, equipment, network connection, software, volume of throughput, and to everyone in the country at a fair price – will be the fundamental guiding principle for local, national and global policy and regulatory constructs moving forward.[30] For developing countries, the implications of a layered "open access model" in the era of broadband Internet have yet to be fully understood, but the democratization and commoditization of network resources that it implies can only be positive.

Openness is an important concept. For all stakeholders, the scope and scale of information society issues are a daunting prospect. From spam to spyware, privacy to security, Internet governance to intellectual property rights, content to broadband, financing ICTs for development to meeting the international development goals, ICTs at once transcend as they embrace economic and social development. The two dimensions of how the information society can help development and how the information society will be developed remain distinct yet inextricably linked. Like ICTs, the MDGs are not an end in themselves and will remain somewhat controversial in nature. ICTs will not deliver all the MDGs and the MDGs do not cover all development fields. Along with aid, trade and debt relief, both will require a continuing emphasis on, and openness to, economic growth and a transition from market push in the development context to market pull.

ICTs and the MDGs both blur the once obvious borders and boundaries between the technical and political, the social and economic. Moving decisively towards an inclusive information society requires, as an indispensable initial building block, a shared understanding of the nature and scope of challenges and opportunities, and developing broad common approaches to dealing with them. Today, however, the stark reality is that building such consensus is an evolving process at a very early stage of development. The developed and developing countries, governments, the private sector, civil society, international organizations, the development, ICT, trade and foreign policy communities - all have yet to come to a common understanding and prioritization of issues, as well as agreement on the approaches, governance structures and implementation mechanisms for

---

[30] See "Broadband: Will it Really Change Everything?", Reed Hundt, GIIC, 2005

moving forward. The phenomenon of the grand stakeholder collaboration of the mobile and Internet network revolutions show the way ahead. The rest is up to us.

5.4 - Outlook and Options

Against this background, there are five critical areas that must be addressed for the full and effective mainstreaming of ICT in meeting the MDGs:

1. Evidence of Impact

Outlook – The case for mainstreaming ICT to meet the MDGs cannot be made without rigorous analysis and empirical evidence of development impact. Emphasis must shift from simple ICT access to more sophisticated data sets on the improved efficiency of ICT-enabled delivery of public and private services particularly in LDCs.

Option – Develop and promote a common and coherent set of ICT-MDG-based indicators and benchmarks across and within the relevant United Nations agencies via the UNITED NATIONS Partnership on Measuring ICT for Development, to be disseminated among governments, business and civil society and endorsed at MS+5 and WSIS 2 for the purpose of accelerating ICT deployment in service of the MDGs.

2. Policy Development

Outlook – National e-strategies need to be linked far more explicitly to national economic development plans and vice versa. The special case of LDCs demands immediate and full integration of national e-strategies within the poverty reduction strategy process (PRSP), accompanied by enhanced cooperation and coordination among donors.

Option – Promote and Support the prioritisation of ICT for Development in all PRSP and national, regional and global economic development plans as a prerequisite for developing countries in achieving the MDGs, backed by the common voice of academia, government, business, civil society, and international organizations.

3. Resource Mobilization

Outlook – There remains a serious deficit in the current approaches and financing mechanisms for bridging the global digital divide. Flows of adequate funds will fail to materialise until scepticism among donor countries is countered, developing country prioritisation is enacted, and the private sector is persuaded of profitable business models for investment.

Option – Promote and support coordinated activities on the part of national governments, donors, the private sector and international organizations to address bottlenecks and gap and develop innovative mechanisms, with the fulfilment of the Monterrey commitments for 0.7% of GNP contribution to ODA, and comprehensive debt relief for the HIPC nations, with the aim of channelling funds to mainstream ICT in MDG programmes, as well as actively exploring innovative financing mechanisms for pro-poor growth markets.

4. Global Alliance for ICT and Development

Outlook – An open, multi-stakeholder and forward-looking framework for employing ICT and media in accelerating the achievement of the MDGs is urgently required. The MDGs provide a common denominator and common agenda for the creation of a "Global Alliance for ICT and Development" drawn from actors both within and outside the ICT sector.

Option – Develop and support an open, multi-stakeholder platform or Global Alliance for ICT and Development around the MS+5 and WSIS 2 timeframe and follow-up, with the aim of enhancing cooperation, establishing a knowledge network, defining priorities and catalysing ICT Policy and Development Initiatives for achievement of the MDGs.

5. Global Campaign and Initiatives

Outlook - The sheer ambition of the MDG challenge demands an unprecedented response at the global as well as at national level. Scaling and replication of ICT efforts will require aggregation of knowledge and resources across markets, and innovative breakthrough approaches to meet key price points and economies of scope and scale for MDG delivery.

Option – Develop and promote a campaign for a series of fast-tracked and win-win "global" ICT and MDG initiatives, both north-south and south-south in sectors where the aggregated scaling and replication of ICT interventions will prove of most benefit to the achievement of the MDGs, including economic opportunity for poverty eradication, health and HIV/AIDS, education and training, gender and youth empowerment, and public administration.

Selected Reading

"The Geopolitics of Information", Anthony Smith, Oxford, 1980

"Technologies of Freedom", Ithiel de Sola Pool, Belknap Harvard, 1983

"The Missing Link – Report of the Independent Commission for Worldwide Telecommunications Development", ITU, 1985

"Knowledge Societies: Information Technology for Sustainable Development", ed. Mansell & When, Oxford, 1998

"World Development Report: Knowledge for Development", World Bank Group, Oxford, 1998/99

"Toward the Global Internet Infrastructure: the Twilight of Telecommunications", Gilhooly, World Bank Group, in *Masters of the Wired World*, FT Pitman Publishing, ed. Leer, 1999

"The Network Revolution and the Developing World: Final Report for World Bank and *info*Dev", Analysys, 2000

"Report of the High Level Panel on Information and Communication Technology", United Nations, 2000

"Digital Opportunities for All: Meeting the Challenges – Final Report of Digital Opportunity Task Force", G8 Summit 2001

"Creating a Development Dynamic - Final Report of the Digital Opportunity Initiative", Accenture, Markle Foundation, UNDP, 2001

"Human Development Report 2001 – Making New Technologies Work for Human Development", UNDP, Oxford, 2001

"Gender, Information Technology, and Developing Countries: An Analytic Study", Hafkin and Taggart, US AID, 2001.

"The Development Divide in a Digital Age", Hewitt de Alcantara, UNRISD, 2001

"ICT Against HIV/AIDS and other Infectious and Communicable Diseases", Gilhooly & Lal, UNDP Policy Brief, 2001

"The Global Information Technology Report 2002", Harvard University & World Economic Forum, Oxford, 2002

"Louder Voices: Strengthening Developing Country Participation in International ICT Decision Making", CTO/Panos, 2002.

"Human Development Report 2003 – MDGs: A Compact Among Nations to End Human Poverty", UNDP, Oxford, 2003

"Information and Communication Technologies for African Development", United Nations ICT Task Force, 2003

"Integrating Information and Communication Technologies in Development Programmes", OECD Policy Brief, 2003

"The Global Information Technology Report 2003", INSEAD, *info*Dev, World Economic Forum, Oxford, 2003

"National & Regional E-Development Strategies: A Blueprint for Action", Gilhooly & Lal, UNDP, in *The Role of ICT in Global Development*, United Nations ICT Task Force, 2003

"The Role of ICT in Enhancing the Achievement of the Millennium Development Goals", Gilhooly & Lal, UNDP, in *The Role of ICT in Global Development*, United Nations ICT Task Force, 2003

"ICTs and the Millennium Development Goals", Chapter 4, World Telecommunications Development Report 2003, ITU

"Birth of Broadband", ITU, 2003

"The Future of Information and Communication Technologies for Development", Braga, Daly, Sareen, Development Gateway Foundation, 2003

"The Role of ICT in Enhancing the Achievement of the Millennium Development Goals", Lee Yee-Cheong, United Nations Millennium Project Presentation to the World Trade Organization, 2003

"ICT and MDGs, A World Bank Group Perspective", 2003

"Multi-Stakeholder Partnerships", ODI & FDC for GKP, 2003

"Youth, Poverty and Gender: ICT for Development Success Stories", GKP, 2003

"Unleashing Entrepreneurship: Making Business Work for the Poor", Report to the Secretary General of the United Nations, Commission on the Private Sector & Development, 2004

"The Contribution of ICT to Pro-Poor Growth", DAC Network on Poverty Reduction, OECD, 2004

"The Contribution of Information and Communication Technologies (ICTs) to Achieving the Millennium Devolment Goals (MDGs)", DAC Network on Poverty Reduction, OECD, 2004

"ICT4D – Lessons, Innovation and Perspectives on ICT for Development", ed.Weigel& Waldburger", SDC & GKP, 2004

"Grameenphone Revisted: Investors Reach Out to the Poor", DAC Network on Poverty Reduction, OECD, 2004

"Youth and the Millennium Development Goals: Challenges and Opportunities for Implementation: Report of the Ad Hoc Working Group on Youth and the MDGs", 2004

"Innnovative Sources of Financing for Development", Note to the United Nations Secretary General to the Fifty-ninth Session of the United Nations General Assembly, 2004

"The Millennium Development Goals & Information and Communications Technology: Measuring, Monitoring and Analyzing ICT Impacts", United Nations ICT Task Force, 2004

"A More Secure World: Our Shared Responsibility", Report of the Secretary-General's High-level Panel on Threats, Challenges and Change", United Nations, 2004

"The Report of the Task Force on Financial Mechanisms for ICT for Development – A Review of Trends and an Analysis of Gaps and Promising Practices", United Nations, 2004

"Financing ICTs for Development Efforts of DAC Members: Review of Recent Trends of ODA and its Contribution", OECD, 2005

"Innovation: Applying Knowledge in Development", United Nations Millennium Project Task Force on Science, Technology, and Innovation, 2005

"Genomics and Global Health – A Report of the Genomics Working Group of the Science, Technology, and Innovation Task Force", United Nations Millennium Project

"Investing in Development: A Practical Plan to Achieve the Millennium Development Goals", United Nations Millennium Project, 2005

"Up-scaling Pro-poor ICT Policies and Practices: A Review of Experiences, with Emphasis on Low Income Countries in Asia and Africa, Gerster and Zimmeermann, SDC, 2005

"Creating a Global Networked Society: Topics for Tomorrow", GIIC, 2005.

"Broadband: Will it Really Change Everything", Reed Hundt, GIIC, 2005.

Acknowledgments

This paper is based on the recent survey of United Nations ICT Task Force and United Nations Millennium Project members and advisers and draws extensively on their collective work and wisdom on ICT for Development as well as the wealth of emerging literature in the field.

Task Force Members & Advisers

Special thanks in the compilation of this paper to Calestous Juma, Lee Yee-Cheong, Sarbuland Khan, Brendan Tuohy, Richard Simpson, and Richard Bourassa. Generous support was given by members and advisers of the United Nations ICT Task Force and the UN Millennium Project, African Development Bank, Inter-American Development Bank, Development Bank of Southern Africa, The World Bank Group, Organization for Economic Cooperation and Development, International Telecommunication Union, United Nations Conference on Trade & Development, United Nations Development Programme, UNESCO, Regional United Nations Economic Commissions, International Chamber of Commerce, Conference of NGOs, Development Gateway Foundation, Grammen Bank, European Union, Global Knowledge Partnership, Global Information Infrastructure Commission, Global Business Dialogue, World Economic Forum, as well as the governments of Brazil, Canada, Finland, France, Ghana, Germany, India, Ireland, Japan, Latvia, Mozambique, Malaysia, Romania, Russia, Senegal, South Africa, Sweden, Switzerland, Tunisia, United Kingdom.

Individual thanks to Talal Abu-Ghazaleh, Izumi Aizu, K.Y.Amoko, Renate Bloem, Carlos Braga, Lidia Brito, Maria Cattaui, Ilaria Carnevali, Vinton Cerf, Peter Cowhey, Harry De Backer, Amir Dossal, Astrid Dufborg, William Drake, John Dryden, Anriette Esterhuysen, Gary Fazzino, Juan Fernandez, Sakiko Fukuda-Parr, Walter Fust, John Gage, Daniela Giacomelli, Yuri Grin, Ayesha Hassan, Ulla Hauer, Peter Hellmonds, Reed Hundt, K.J.John, Jennifer Johnston, Sergei Kambalov, Serge Kapto, Tim Kelly, Andrei Korotkov, Radika Lal, Bruno Lambourgini, Bruno Lanvin, Julianne Lee, Maria Lehtinen, Karen Lynch, Mark Malloch Brown, James Moody, Kerry McNamara, Richard Manning, Salamao Julia Manhica, Robin Mansell, Tengku Mohammed Azzman Sharifadeen, Jay Naidoo, Eli Noam, Stephen

Nolan, Joseph Okpaku, Maureen O'Neil, Aida Opoku-Mensah, Danilo Piaggesi, Sam Pitroda, Beatrice Pluchon, Nii Quaynor, Rinalia Abdul Rahim, Art Reilly, Tony Rutkowski, Jim Steinberg, Ichiro Tambo, Jeffrey Sachs, Martin Sandelin, Guido Schmidt-Traub, Lyndall Schope-Mafole, Jean-Francois Soupizet, Daniel Stauffacher, Tadao Takahashi, Susan Telsher, Brian Thompson, Paul Verhoef, Bernard Vergnes, Caroline Wagner, Abdul Waheed Khan, Mike Warner, Stewart White, Ernest Wilson, Gerolf Weigel, Mike Yates, Raul Zambrano.

ABOUT THE CONTRIBUTORS

Roberto Bissio is the Director of the Third World Institute in Uruguay, a civil society organization which encourages citizen involvement in global decision-making. He is also the Coordinator of the Social Watch, an international coalition of NGOs advocating for the eradication of poverty and its causes. He is a member of the International Committee of Third World Network and the International Council of the World Social Forum. He serves on the boards of the Forum International de Montreal and the Women's Environment and Development Organization.

Lidia Brito was the Minister of Higher Education, Science and Technology of Mozambique until January 2005. She is a member of several international committees related to higher education and science for development for Africa. She was previously Head of Forestry Department and Coordinator of the Research and Consulting Group at the Faculty of Agriculture and Forestry of Eduardo Mondlane University, where she led a research group on community management of natural resources that aimed at developing an integrated approach for natural resources management. She received her Forestry degree at Eduardo Mondlane University in 1981 and her PhD in Forest Sciences from Colorado State University in 1994.

Thomas Ganswindt is Member of the Corporate Executive Committee at Siemens AG. He was elected member of the Siemens AG Managing Board in 2002. He was formerly Executive Vice President and Member of the Group Executive Management of the Siemens Transportation Systems Group (TS). He started his career in the Automation Group, Division of Numerical Controllers, at Siemens in 1989. Prior to joining Siemens, he spent two years at the Frauenhofer Institute for Production Systems and Design Technology (IPK) in Berlin, where he headed various R&D projects on the development of numeric control systems. In addition to his technical work, he is also a member of the Verein Deutscher Elektroingenieure (VDE), the Verband der Bahnindustrie (VDB), and the Institution of Railway Signal Engineers (IRSE). In 2000, he was named to the Global Leaders for Tomorrow (GLT), a subgroup of the World Economic Forum (WEF). Mr. Ganswindt obtained a Masters degree in Mechanical Engineering from the Ruhr University of Bochum in Germany.

Richard Gerster is a development economist and activist with a PhD in Economics from the University of St Gall (Switzerland). From 1972 to 1981 he was a staff member of Helvetas, Swiss Association for Development and Cooperation, and from 1981 until 1998 he served as the first Coordinator for Development Policy and then Executive Director of the Swiss Coalition of Development Organisations. Since 1998 he has been Director of Gerster Consulting. From 1978 until 1994 he was a Member of the Advisory Committee on Development Cooperation and Humanitarian Aid to the Swiss Government, and since 2000 he has been a member of the Development Cooperation Advisory Council to the Minister of Foreign Affairs of the Republic of Austria. He is the winner of several development policy awards and author of numerous books and articles on development policy issues.

Denis Gilhooly is an Adviser to the United Nations ICT Task Force. He has worked extensively in the public sector as Principal Adviser and Executive Coordinator, World Summit on the Information Society, Principal Adviser and Director, ICT for Development, United Nations Development Programme, and Telecommunications and Information Infrastructure Adviser, World Bank Group. He previously worked in the private sector as Vice President, Business Development, Teledesic, Media and Technology Director, The Wall Street Journal Europe/Dow Jones, and founding Editorial and Publishing Director, CommunicationsWeek International and The Networked Economy Conferences. He was a founding commissioner of the Global Information Infrastructure Commission, and a member of the Irish Government's Advisory Committees on Telecommunications and ICT, the G8 Digital Opportunity Task Force and United Nations ICT Task Force.

David Gross has served as the U.S. Coordinator for International Communications and Information Policy in the Bureau of Economic and Business Affairs since August 2001. He has also been a member of the United Nations Information and Communications Technologies Task Force since 2001. Ambassador Gross has addressed the United Nations General Assembly, led the U.S. delegations to several major international telecommunications conferences, and led the American delegation to the World Summit on the Information Society. He previously worked as a partner in the law firm of Sutherland, Asbill and Brennan where he specialized in communications and telecommunications issues. In 1994, he was named Washington Counsel for AirTouch Communications. He obtained a B.A in Economics from the University of Pennsylvania in 1976 and law degree from Columbia University in 1979.

Susanne Hesselbarth has been working as an independent consultant in development since 1997. She served as senior adviser to the German Federal Ministry for Economic Cooperation and Development for the implementation of the Programme of Action 2015 for poverty reduction, for the OECD/DAC-Infrastructure for Poverty Reduction Task Team as well as for the German Development Cooperation (KfW and GTZ) on operationalising the MDGS for Water Supply and Sanitation and on the strategic orientation of the Geramn Financial Cooperation in the field of governance, decentralisation and post conflict. In 1994, she was a permanent staff member of KfW Entwicklungsbank, the German Development Bank and was in charge of development cooperation with Burkina Faso, Niger and Chad. Her professional experience focuses on the linkages between infrastructure and poverty reduction, including policy-based lending and good governance.

Heike Jensen is a member of the Steering Committee of the WSIS Gender Caucus and a postdoctoral researcher and lecturer at the Department of Gender Studies of Humboldt University in Berlin, Germany. She is also a member of the NRO-Frauenforum, Terre des Femmes, and the Association for Women's Rights in Development (AWID). In the WSIS process, she has worked with the German Civil Society Coordinating Committee for WSIS, the WSIS Gender Caucus and the NGO Gender Strategies Working Group. She also served as a civil society member of the German governmental delegation to the Geneva Summit. Her research, publication and teaching focus is on gender theories and media theories, women's movements and women's organizations, and globalization and global governance. Her volunteer work is dedicated to promoting women's rights. Ms. Jensen received her education at Free University (Berlin, Germany), the University of Minnesota (Minneapolis,

USA), Brown University (Providence, USA), the International Women's University 2000 (Hamburg, Germany) and Humboldt University, where she obtained her doctorate.

Edvin Karnitis is Commissioner of Public Utilities for the Republic of Latvia and a researcher at the University of Latvia. He specializes in researching strategic issues for development for Latvian government. He has specialized expertise in radio engineering and holds a degree in Information Systems from the Latvian Academy of Science.

Motoo Kusakabe is Senior Counseller to the President of the European Bank for Reconstruction and Development and the founder of e-Community Link. Since 1997, he worked for the World Bank for six years as Senior Advisor to the MD and the Vice-President for Resource Mobilization and Co-financing. He led the Bank's initiative to promote global partnership programmes as the Chair of the Council of Development Grant Facility, and has been instrumental in generating support for ICT and development, community telecenters, community-driven initiatives and has promoted partnership with NGOs and foundations. Mr. Kusakabe had a long and distinguished career and held key positions at the Japanese Ministry of Finance including banking sector reform and international finance. He has an M.A. in Mathematics at the University of Tokyo and M.Phil in economics at Yale University.

Bruno Lanvin is an ICT Adviser in the Department of Global ICT at the World Bank. He also serves as Deputy Executive-Secretary of the United Nations International Symposium on Trade Efficiency (UNISTE) and as World Coordinator of the Trade Point Programme. He previously worked in the OECD as rapporteur of the concluding meeting of the 'Technology and the Economy' Programme, where he was responsible for the strategic planning activities of the newly created Special Programme for Trade Efficiency. He had also occupied several posts at the United Nations as the Special Assistant to the Director General in New York and to the Deputy Secretary-General of UNCTAD in Geneva and one of the UNCTAD economists in charge of studies on the services sector in which he specialized in information-intensive services, including telecommunications.

Axel Leblois is Executive Director of CIFAL Atlanta, Senior Special Fellow at UNITAR, and co-founder of the Wireless Internet Institute. He was formerly CEO of ExecuTrain, President and CEO of Bull HN Information Systems, CEO of IDC and President of Computerworld Communications. He also served as a Director of Wang Laboratories, International Data Group, Peritus Software, Executrain and PSI Data Systems.

Peter Orne is Editor of The WorldPaper, World Times, Inc. and Editorial Director of the Wireless Internet Institute. He served as a UN-accredited election observer in East Timor prior to 1999 when he was Managing Editor of The WorldPaper. He holds a B.A. from Wesleyan University and an M.A. from the University of California at Berkeley.

Carlo Emanuele Ottaviani has been, since January 2002, President of STMicroelectronics Foundation, a non-profit organization created by the corporation to disseminate specific aspects of ST corporate culture: deep-rooted commitment to sustainable development, recycling, and research in alternate energies as well as a firm belief in corporate social responsibility. In 1975, he was appointed Head of Corporate Communications of SGS-ATES worldwide, and has maintained this position ever since. He began his career in 1965 in the Advertisement and Public Relations Office of SIT-SIEMENS. Along with the promotion of the audio business of the company, he soon took over responsibility for the activities of the associate semiconductor company ATES Electronic Components. He developed a passion for electronics early on while studying Political Sciences at Universitá di Milano, where he also specialized in electronics and telecommunications.

Danilo Piaggesi has been the Chief of the Information Technology for Development Division (SDS/ICT) at the Inter-American Development Bank since 1999. From 1992 to 1998, he served as a technical staff of TELESPAZIO, Societá per Azioni per le Comunicazioni Spaziali, TELECOM-Italia Group in Rome and was in charge of the Strategic Alliances and International Activities Division. From 1981 to 1991 he worked for the United Nations Food and Agriculture Organization (FAO) at different duty stations in Africa and Latin America. He also served as a consultant to the European Union in Brussels in which he evaluated project proposals for funding in the field of telecommunications and environment. Mr. Piaggesi received professional training in remote sensing, digital image processing and analysis, technical cooperation project formulation and appraisal, and telecommunications and technology transfer. He holds a Masters degree cum laude in Physics with a diploma in geophysics from the University of Rome (1980). He also obstained an Executive International Business Certificate from Georgetown University/John Cabot University in Washington D.C-Rome in 1996.

Gisa Fuatai Purcell is the Secretary and ICT Advisor of the National ICT Committee in Samoa, the committee established to advise the Government on e-strategy to bridge the digital divide in Samoa, and between Samoa and the rest of the world. Mrs. Fuatai Purcell also serves on the recently launched Task Force on Financial Mechanisms and leads the Samoan Delegation at the World Summit on the Information Society (WSIS).

Bernhard Rohleder has been CEO of the German Association for Information Technology, Telecommunications and New Media (BITKOM) since 1999. He was formerly Managing Director of the European Information Technology Observatory (EITO); Director General of the German IT Industry Association; Secretary-General of the German IT Industry Association; and Secretary-General of EUROBIT. He has a degree in Political Science from the University of Saarlandes (1987) and a graduate degree from the Institut d'Etudes Politiques in Paris (1991).

Lucio Stanca is the Minister for Innovation and Technologies of Italy. He coordinates and provides strategic orientation on policies related to domestic use and development of information and communication technologies. He also chairs the Ministers' Committee for the Information Society and is in charge of "E-Government for Development," a programme that helps emerging countries use ICT to modernize their public administration systems. From 1968 to March 2001, he held various positions at IBM in Italy as well as in the United States. He served as Chairman and CEO of IBM Italy, Member of the World Wide Management Committee and Vice-President of the group and Chairman and Director General of IBM in Paris, where he was in charge of operations in Europe, Middle East and Africa. He holds a degree in Economics and Commerce from the Università Commerciale Luigi Bocconi in Milan.

Veli Sundbäck is Senior Vice President of the Corporate Relations and Responsibility at Nokia and a member of the United Nations Information and Communications Technology Task Force. He had a distinguished diplomatic career and held various ministry positions in Helsinki, Brussels and Geneva, including as Under-Secretary of State for External Economic Relations at the Ministry for Foreign Affairs and Secretary of State at the Ministry for Foreign Affairs. He was also chief negotiator for Finland's accession to the European Union. In addition to his technical work, he is Chairman of the Supervisory Board of Nokia (Deutschland) GmbH; Chairman of Huhtamäki; Board member of Finnair; Chairman of the Finland-China Trade Association; Chairman of the Trade Policy Committee of the Confederation of Finnish Industry and Employers (TT). Mr. Sundbäck holds a Licentiate in Law from the University of Helsinki.

Ichiro Tambo is an advisor appointed by the Japan International Cooperation Agency (JICA) to the Secretariat of the Development Assistance Committee (DAC) at the Organization for Economic Cooperation and Development (OECD). He is in charge of matters related to science and technology, including ICTs and biotechnology, and of establishing internal and external cooperative links which includes acting as a liaison between DAC Secretariat and DOT Force, the United Nations ICT Task Force, WSIS, etc. Prior to joining the OECD, he worked as a permanent staff in JICA since 1981, serving at the Headquarters and overseas office in Kenya. He has been seconded to Ministry of Foreign Affairs, to the Embassy of Japan in Côte d'Ivoire and to the Board of Audit of Japan.

Robert A. Vitro is the Programme Development Coordinator for Intersectoral, Regional and Special Programmes, Division of Information Technology for Development, Department of Sustainable Development of the Inter-American Development Bank. His experience in the area of knowledge-based development spans various public, private, civil society and academic organizations at national and international levels. He was as Director of Global Business Development of the Information Industry Association and General Secretary of the Global Alliance of Information Industry Associations (GAIIA). He also served as a Scientific Affairs Officer at the United Nations Centre for Science and Technology. He had worked with the Office of Telecommunications of the US Department of Commerce and at the National Academy of Sciences Committee on Educational Technology. He also served as consultant with the Governments of Brazil and Venezuela as well as the Latin American Economic System (SELA) and the Organization of American States (OAS). Mr. Vitro has been a visiting professor at the Universidad de los Andes (Colombia), Universidad Católica Boliviana (Bolivia) and the College of Information Studies, Universidade Federal da Bahía (Brazil). He was also Adjunct Assistant Professor with the Graduate School of Management and Technology, University of Maryland University College (Maryland, USA). He received a B.S. from Clarkson University and an MBA from Graduate School of Business of Cornell University.

ACRONYMS AND INTERNET REFERENCES

AFD	Agence Française de Développement – www.afd.fr
APC	Association for Progressive Communication – www.apc.org
APEC	Asia-Pacific Economic Cooperation – www.apec.org
ARPU	Average Revenue Per User
BCO	Building Communications Opportunities
BDO	Building Digital Opportunities Programme
CARPE	Central African Regional Programme for the Environment – carpe.umd.edu
CAS	Country Assistance Strategy
CDC	Commonwealth Development Corporation – www.cdcgroup.com
CEDAW	Convention on the Elimination of all Forms of Discrimination against Women – www.un.org/womenwatch/daw/cedaw
CERT	Computer Emergency Response Team
CIDA	Canadian International Development Agency – www.acdi-cida.gc.ca
CIS	Commonwealth of Independent States
DFI	Digital Freedom Initiative – www.dfi.gov
DFID	UK Department for International Development – www.dfid.gov.uk
DGIS	Dutch Directorate-General for International Cooperation
DMFA	Danish Ministry of Foreign Affairs – www.um.dk
DOT-COM	Digital Opportunity through Technology and Communications – www.usaid.gov/info_technology/dotcom
EC	European Commission
EIB	European Investment Bank – www.eib.org
EU	European Union – www.europa.eu.int
FCC	Federal Communications Commission – www.fcc.gov
FDI	Foreign Direct Investment
G8 DOT-FORCE	Group of Eight Digital Opportunity Task Force
GATT	General Agreement on Tariffs and Trade – www.wto.org/english/tratop_e/gatt_e/gatt_e.htm
GDA	Global Development Alliance – www.usaid.gov/our_work/global_partnerships/gda
GDLN	Global Development Learning Network – www.gdln.org
GDP	Gross Domestic Product

GeSCI	Global eSchools and Communities Initiative – www.gesci.org
GIEWS	Global Information and Early Warning Systems on Food and Agriculture – www.fao.org/waicent/faoinfo/ economic/giews/english/giewse.htm
GIS	Geographic Information Systems – www.gis.com
GKP	Global Knowledge Partnership – www.globalknowledge.org
HDI	Human Development Index
HIPC	Heavily Indebted Poor Countries
HP	Hewlett-Packard – www.hp.com
ICB	Informatics and Computer Basics
ICC	International Chamber of Commerce – www.iccwbo.org
ICTD/ICT4D	Information and Communication Technology for Development
ICTs	Information and Communication Technologies
IDB	Inter-American Development Bank – www.iadb.org
IEEE	Institute of Electrical and Electronics Engineers – www.ieee.org
*info*Dev	World Bank's Information for Development Programme – www.infodev.org
IPR	Intellectual Property Regime
ISPs	Internet Service Providers
ITA	International Trademark Association – www.inta.org
ITAA	Information Technology Association of America – www.itaa.org
ITMA	IT Mentors Alliance
ITU	International Telecommunication Union – www.itu.int
JBIC	Japan Bank for International Cooperation – www.jbic.go.jp
JICA	Japanese International Cooperation Agency – www.jica.go.jp
LDCs	Least Developed Countries
MDGs	Millennium Development Goals – www.un.org/millenniumgoals
MENA	Middle East and North Africa
MNCs	Multi-National Companies
MOFA	Japanese Ministry of Foreign Affairs – www.mofa.go.jp
MS+5	Millennium Summit + 5
MSEs	Micro Small Enterprises/Businesses
MSPs	Multi-stakeholders Partnerships
NORFUND	Norwegian Investment Fund for Development Countries – www.norfund.org
NSOs	National Statistical Offices

NTIA	National Telecommunications and Information Administration – www.ntia.doc.gov
NZ	New Zealand
ODA	Official Development Assistance
OECD	Organization for Economic Cooperation and Development – www.oecd.org
OECD/DAC	Organization for Economic Cooperation and Development/Development Assistance Committee – www.oecd.org/dac
OWI	OneWorld International – www.oneworld.net
PCMCIA	Personal Computer Memory Card International Association – www.pcmcia.org
PDA	Personal Digital Assistant
PFI	Private Finance Initiative
PIDG	Private Infrastructure Development Group
PPIAF	Public Private Infrastructure Advisory Facility – www.ppiaf.org
PPPs	Public-Private Partnerships
Proparco	Société de Promotion et de Participation pour la Coopération Economique
PRSP	Poverty Reduction Strategy Paper
PSD	Private-Sector Development
PUC	Public Utilities Commission – www.sprk.gov.lv
ROI	Return on Investment
RTCs	Record of Rights, Tenancy and Crops
RTRP	Regional Telecommunications Restructuring Programme
SDC	Swiss Agency for Development and Cooperation
SECO	State Secretariat for Economic Affairs – www.seco-admin.ch
SEWA	The Self-Employed Women Association – www.sewa.org
Sida	Swedish Development Agency – www.sida.se
SIDS	Small Island Developing States
SMEs	Small- and Medium-sized Enterprises
SOFI	Swiss Organization for Facilitating Investments – www.sofi.ch
STI	Science and Technological Innovation
TFFM	Task Force on Financial Mechanism for ICT for Development – www.itu.int/wsis/tffm
TLP	Telecommunications Leadership Programme
TRASA	Telecommunications Regulators' Association of Southern Africa –

	www.trasa.org.bw
UN DESA	United Nations Department of Economic and Social Affairs – www.un.org/esa/desa
UN ICT TF	United Nations Information and Communication Technologies Task Force – www.unicttaskforce.org
UNCTAD	United Nations Conference on Trade and Development – www.unctad.org
UNDP	United Nations Development Programme – www.undp.org
UNESCO	United Nations Educational, Scientific and Cultural Organization – www.unesco.org
UNITAR	United Nations Institute for Training and Research – www.unitar.org
USAID	United States Agency for International Development – www.usaid.gov
USG	US Government
USTTI	United States Telecommunications Training Institute – www.ustti.org
W2i	The Wireless Internet Institute – www.w2i.org
WIPO	World Intellectual Property Organization – www.wipo.org
WORLD BANK	www.worldbank.org
WRC	World Radiocommunication Conference – www.itu.int/ITU-R/conferences/wrc
WSIS	World Summit on the Information Society – www.itu.int/wsis
WTO	WTO World Trade Organization – www.wto.org

GLOSSARY

ARPU: *Average Revenue Per User.*

Backhauling: (1) In wireless network technology, to transmit voice and data traffic from a cell site to a switch, i.e., from a remote site to a central site; (2) In satellite technology, to transmit data to a point from which it can be uplinked to a satellite; (3) To transmit data to a network backbone.

Beijing+10: A United Nations world conference on women's human rights. Also known as CSW (Commission on the Status of Women) 49. It aims to implement the Beijing Declaration and Platform for Action.

BPfA: *Beijing Declaration and Platform for Action.* BPFA is a set of principles and strategies for action which came out of the first Beijing conference in 1995. It outlines 12 critical areas of concern under the BPFA that are considered as the main obstacles to women's advancement. The BPFA not only provides guidelines for actions on the part of governments, non-governmental organizations and members of civil society, aimed towards eliminating these barriers to achieving gender equality worldwide, but is a powerful statement of the recognition of women's unequal status globally.

Broadband access: High-speed Internet connection technologies. Transmission capacity with sufficient bandwidth to permit combined provision of voice, data and video, with no lower limit.

Broadband-Wireless: Standards and technologies that specify manners by which wireless communication devices transmit signals that carry voice, data and multimedia. Wireless Broadband technology sends multiple channels of data over a single wireless communications medium, typically using radio frequency.

Carrier-grade: A term that implies a system that is designed to have increased performance, availability, security, reliability and timeliness to meet the requirements of a modern communications network element.

Chennai Statement: The "Chennai Statement" presents the insights of development practitioners and policy makers who met from 17-19 November 2004 in Chennai, India, to discuss latest lessons and trends in up-scaling of pro-poor policies and practices. The statement contributes to a multi-dimensional poverty reduction agenda for the implementation of the World Summit on the Information Society (WSIS) Principles and Action Plan to be closely linked to of the Millennium Development Goals (MDGs). The draft of a MSSRF/SDC Study on "Up-scaling Pro-Poor ICT-Policies and Practices" served as background for the Chennai meeting.

Connectivity: The capability to provide to end-users connections to the Internet or other communication networks.

CPE: *Customer Premises Equipment.* Communications equipment that resides on the customer's premises (for example, it is owned or leased by the customer).

Digital Access Index: Measure of the overall ability of citizens to access and use information and communication technologies (ICT). It is based on eight variables, covering five areas, to provide an overall country score. The areas are availability of infrastructure, affordability of access, educational level, quality of ICT services, and Internet usage. (Source: World Telecommunication Development Report 2003, ITU (2004))

Digital divide: Unequal access to and diffusion of ICT both between and within countries. Indicators measure insufficient infrastructure, high cost of access, lack of locally created content, and uneven ability to derive economic and social benefits from information-intensive activities.

Digital Solidarity Fund: The Digital Solidarity Fund is an African initiative within the New Partnership for Development in Africa (NEPAD). Its basic objectives are: transforming the digital divide into digital opportunities to promote peace, sustainable development, democracy, transparency and good governance. The Fund's mode of operation is based on traditional North-South cooperation, in addition to an increased cooperation effort between the emerging South and the least developed countries, an approach which is often better suited to local realities.

Diminishing rate of return: Also known as the law of diminishing returns. A point beyond which the application of additional resources yields less than proportional increases in output.

DSL: *Digital subscriber line.* The two main categories of DSL are ADSL and SDSL. Two other types of DSL technologies are *High-data-rate DSL (HDSL)* and *Very high DSL (VDSL)*. DSL technologies use sophisticated modulation schemes to pack data onto copper wires. They are sometimes referred to as last-mile technologies because they are used only for connections from a telephone switching station to a home or office, not between switching stations.

E-commerce: *Electronic commerce.* Term used to describe transactions that take place online where the buyer and seller are remote from each other.

E-governance: Use of information and communication technologies and the Internet to streamline and improve government processes and enhance the internal and external communications of government.

E-government: Government that applies ICT to transform its internal and external relationships.

E-health: An emerging field in the intersection of medical informatics, public health and business, referring to health services and information delivered or enhanced through the Internet and related technologies.

E-procurement: Purchasing online. E-procurement systems are used to obtain materials and parts via the Internet or using traditional EDI standards either for internal manufacturing (direct procurement) or office supplies and equipment (indirect procurement).

E-readiness: A country's ability or readiness to integrate information technology and e-commerce, etc., in order to provide a baseline that can be used for regional comparisons and planning.

EFTPOS: *Electronic Funds Transfer Point of Sale.* A method of electronic payment which allows money to be transferred from the account of the shopper to the merchant in close to real-time.

Email: *Electronic mail.* The exchange of electronic messages between geographically dispersed locations.

Enabling environment: Regulatory regime conducive to elimination of barriers for competition, encouraging investments and support for the development of comprehensive and sustainable development policies.

Ethernet: A protocol for interconnecting computers and peripheral devices at high speed. Recently Gigabit Ethernet has become available which enables speeds up to 1 Gbit/s. Ethernet can run on several types of wiring including: twisted pair, coaxial, and even fiber optic cable.

Feminization of poverty: A social phenomenon referring to the growth of women in poverty and the widening gap between women and men caught in the cycle of poverty in the last quarter century.

Fixed telecommunications: Electronic communications carried over a hard-wired system, such as the telephone or cable television.

Flash-OFDM: *Flash* (fast low-latency access with seamless hand-off) *OFDM Orthogonal Frequency Division Multiplexing.* OFDM is a cornerstone technology for the next generation of high-speed wireless data products and services for both corporate and consumer use. With the introduction of the IEEE 802.11a, ETSI BRAN, and multimedia applications, the wireless world is ready for products based on OFDM technology.

G2B: Government to Business

G2C: Government to Consumer

G2G: Government to Government

G8: Group of eight major industrial nations (Japan, Russia, U.K., France, Italy, Germany, USA, and Canada).

Global warming: An increase in the average temperature of the earth's atmosphere, especially a sustained increase sufficient to cause climatic change.

GPRS: *General Packet Radio Service.* This is based on GSM technology but enables higher data transmission rates. GPRS is a separate network that piggy-backs the existing GSM networks and is closely linked to it. In the initial stage, maximum data rates of 57,000 bits per second will be possible. At a later stage, the speed will be increased to 115,000 and finally 170,000 bits per second. GPRS devices are permanently online, so you do not need to repeatedly dial into the Internet.

GSM: *Global System for Mobile Communications.* The digital mobile telephony standard GSM is the second mobile telephony generation. This technology is currently the basis for most mobile telephony networks worldwide. GSM uses the frequency range around 900 MHz and 1800 MHz. In the USA, regional GSM networks operate around 1900 MHz. The American 1900 MHz variant has become known as the personal communications system (PCS).

Hotspot: An access point to a wireless local area network (WLAN). Hotspots are areas where wireless data can be sent and received, and Internet access is provided to wireless devices. For example, a laptop computer can be used to access the Internet in a hotspot provided in an airport or hotel.

ICTD/ ICT4D: *Information and Communication Technology for Development.*

Information literacy: The adoption of appropriate information behavior to identify, through whatever channel or medium, information well fitted to information needs, leading to wise and ethical use of information in society

Internet: Interconnected global networks that use the Internet protocol (see *IP*).

Internet backbone: The high-speed, high capacity lines or series of connections that form a major pathway and carry aggregated traffic within the Internet.

Interoperability: The ability of two devices, usually from different vendors, to work together.

IP: *Internet Protocol.* The underlying technology by which all Internet data communication is carried out.

IP convergence: New generation of network solutions ranging from multimedia applications to business services and encompassing the processing of voice, video, image and data information and its transmission over the Internet Protocol.

IPR: *Intellectual Property Rights.* Copyrights, patents and trademarks giving creators the right to prevent others from using their inventions, designs or other creations. The ultimate aim is to act as an incentive to encourage the development of new technology and creations, which will eventually be available to all. The main international agreements are the World Intellectual Property Organization's (WIPO) *Paris Convention for the Protection of Industrial Property* (patents, industrial designs, etc.), the *Berne Convention for the Protection of Literary and Artistic Works* (copyright), and the World Trade Organization's (WTO) *Agreement on Trade-Related Aspects of Intellectual Property Rights* (TRIPS).

IP telephony: *Internet protocol telephony.* IP telephony is used as a generic term for the conveyance of voice, fax and related services, partially or wholly over packet-based, IP-based networks. (See also *VoIP*.)

ISM band: *Instrument, Scientific, and Medical* band. Radio wave bands originally reserved internationally for non-commercial use of radio-frequency electromagnetic fields for industrial, scientific and medical purposes.

ISP: *Internet service provider.* ISPs provide end-users access to the Internet. *Internet Access Providers* (IAPs) may also provide access to other ISPs. ISPs may offer their own proprietary content and access to online services such as email.

Kyoto Protocol: The Kyoto Protocol, an international agreement adopted in December 1997 in Japan, entered into force on February 16, 2005. The Protocol sets binding targets for developed countries to reduce greenhouse gas emissions on average 5.2 percent below 1990 levels, in order to address global warming.

LAN: *Local area network.* A computer network that spans a relatively small area. Most LANs are confined to a single building or group of buildings. However, one LAN can be connected to other LANs over any distance via telephone lines and radio waves. A system of LANs connected in this way is called a wide-area network (WAN). (See also *WLAN.*)

Local loop: The system used to connect the subscriber to the nearest switch. It generally consists of a pair of copper wires, but may also employ fiber-optic or wireless technologies.

MDGs: *United Nations Millennium Development Goals.* The MDGs have been commonly accepted as a framework for measuring development progress. They establish yardsticks for measuring results, not just for developing countries but for rich countries that help to fund development programmes and for the multilateral institutions that help countries implement them. The first seven goals are mutually reinforcing and are directed at reducing poverty in all its forms. The last goal – global partnership for development – is about the means to achieve the first seven. (For more information, see http://www.un.org/millenniumgoals).

Mesh networks: A mesh network is a local area network (LAN) that employs one of two connection arrangements, full mesh topology or partial mesh topology. In the full mesh topology, each node (workstation or other device) is connected directly to each of the others. In the partial mesh topology, some nodes are connected to all the others, but some of the nodes are connected only to those other nodes with which they exchange the most data.

Mobile communications: Electronic communications using portable (mobile) devices, usually through a wireless network.

ODA: *Official Development Assistance.* Official development assistance, or foreign aid, consists of loans, grants, technical assistance and other forms of cooperation extended by governments to developing countries. A significant proportion of official development assistance is aimed at promoting sustainable development in poorer countries, particularly through natural resource conservation, environmental protection and population programmes.

Penetration: A measurement of access to telecommunications, normally calculated by dividing the number of subscribers to a particular service by the population and multiplying by 100. Also referred to as *teledensity* (for fixed-line networks) or *mobile density* (for cellular ones), or *total teledensity* (fixed and mobile combined).

PDA: (*personal digital assistant*) is a term for any small mobile hand-held device that provides computing and information storage and retrieval capabilities for personal or business use, often for keeping schedule calendars and address book information handy. The term *handheld* is a synonym. Many people use the name of one of the popular PDA products as a generic term. Most PDAs have a small keyboard. Some PDAs have an electronically sensitive pad on which handwritng can be received. Typical uses include schedule and address book storage and retrieval and note-entering. However, increasingly, PDAs are combined with telephones and paging systems.

Pro-poor economy growth: It is generally accepted that economic growth is vital for but not sufficient for poverty reduction. Growth is particularly likely to help the poorest, that is useful for poverty reduction if it expands employment, productivity and wages of poor people and when there is a focus on human development and physical infrastructure. Growth tends not to work into that direction if a high proportion of GDP is spent on servicing the public debt etc.

Protocol: A set of formal rules and specifications describing how to transmit data, especially across a network.

PRSP: Poverty Reduction Strategy Papers describe a country's macroeconomic, structural and social policies and programmes to promote growth and reduce poverty, as well as associated external financing needs. PRSPs are prepared by governments through a participatory process involving civil society and development partners, including the World Bank and the International Monetary Fund (IMF).

QoS: *Quality of service.* A measure of network performance that reflects the quality and reliability of a connection. QoS can indicate a data traffic policy that guarantees certain amounts of bandwidth at any given time, or can involve traffic shaping that assigns varying bandwidth to different applications.

RLAN: Network that uses radio waves to transport data between workstations.

SDSL: *Symmetrical DSL.* A proprietary North American DSL standard.

Server: (1) A host computer on a network that sends stored information in response to requests or queries. (2) The term server is also used to refer to the software that makes the process of serving information possible.

SMP: *Significant Market Powers.* Expression used to qualify entities that are deemed to have a dominant position in a given market.

SMS: (Short Message Service) is a service for sending messages of up to 160 characters (224 characters if using a 5-bit mode) to mobile phones that use Global System for Mobile (GSM) communication. SMS is similar to *paging*. However, SMS messages do not require the mobile phone to be active and within range and will be held for a number of days until the phone is active and within range. SMS messages are transmitted within the same cell or to anyone with roaming service capability. They can also be sent to digital phones from a Web site equipped with PC Link or from one digital phone to another.

Spectrum: The radio frequency spectrum of hertzian waves used as a transmission medium for cellular radio, radiopaging, satellite communication, over-the-air broadcasting and other services.

TCP: *Transmission control protocol.* A transport layer protocol that offers connection-oriented reliable stream services between two hosts. This is the primary transport protocol used by TCP/IP applications.

Telecenter: Shared premises where the public has access to training and information and communication technologies (computers, Internet, telephony, ...).

Teledensity: Number of main telephone lines per 100 inhabitants. (See *Penetration*.)

Telekiosk: See *Telecenter*.

Tobin Tax: Excise taxes on cross-border currency transactions. They can be enacted by national legislatures, followed by multilateral cooperation for effective enforcement. The revenue should go to global priorities: basic environmental and human needs. Such taxes will help tame currency market volatility and restore national economic sovereignty. (The name Tobin Tax and the original concept derives from James Tobin, a Ph.D. Nobel-laureate economist at Yale University.)

TRIPS: WTO's Agreement on Trade-Related Aspects of Intellectual Property Rights.

Tsunami catastrophe: On December 26th, 2004 a tsunami disaster killed more than 273 000 people in countries around the Indian Ocean. Hardest hit were Indonesia followed by Sri Lanka.

UMTS: *Universal Mobile Telecommunications System.* The European term for third-generation mobile cellular systems or IMT-2000 based on the W-CDMA standard. UMTS networks are being built in Europe, as of 2002. Thanks to high data transmission rates they will offer new mobile multimedia services such as video telephony, video conferencing and rapid Internet access.

Universal access: Refers to reasonable telecommunication access for all. Includes universal service for those that can afford individual telephone service and widespread provision of public telephones within a reasonable distance of others.

VoIP: *Voice over Internet Protocol.* A generic term used to describe the techniques used to carry voice traffic over the Internet Protocol. (See also *IP telephony*.)

Wi-Fi: *Wireless fidelity.* A mark of interoperability among devices adhering to the 802.11b specification for Wireless LANs from the Institute of Electrical and Electronics Engineers (IEEE). However, the term Wi-Fi is sometimes mistakenly used as a generic term for wireless LAN.

WiMAX: *Worldwide Interoperability for Microwave Access.* Fixed wireless standard that allows for long-range wireless communication at 70 Mbit/s over 50 kilometers. It can be used as a backbone Internet connection to rural areas. WiMAX is the common name associated to the IEEE 802.16a/REVd/e standards. These standards are issued by the IEEE 802.16 subgroup that originally covered the Wireless Local Loop (WLL) technologies with radio spectrum from 10 to 66 GHz. Recently, these specifications were extended below 10 GHz.

Wireless: Generic term for mobile communication services which do not use fixed-line networks for direct access to the subscriber.

Wireless access points/devices: Wireless access points make it possible to set up Internet workstations without having to install cables. A high-powered antenna offers a range of operation within a certain area, providing seamless roaming throughout a wireless LAN infrastructure.

WLAN: *Wireless LAN (Local Area Network).* Also known as Wireless Fidelity. A wireless network whereby a user can connect to a local area network (LAN) through a wireless (radio) connection, as an alternative to a wired local area network. Data transfer is by radio waves in the microwave range. WLAN is especially suited to communication in companies, large conference rooms or at airports where the space is limited but large numbers of people want mobile access to their PC, the Internet or networks.

WLL: *Wireless Local Loop.* (See *Local loop*).

WSIS: (United Nations) *World Summit on the Information Society.* The first phase of WSIS took place in Geneva (hosted by the Government of Switzerland) from December 10-12, 2003. The second phase will take place in Tunis (hosted by the Government of Tunisia), from November 16-18, 2005. For more information see: http://www.itu.int/wsis.